THE HISTORY OF

NORTHAMPTONSHIRE COUNTY CRICKET CLUB

Matthew Engel & Andrew Radd

With a personal view by
FRANK TYSON

CHRISTOPHER HELM

London

© 1993 Matthew Engel, Andrew Radd and Frank Tyson
Christopher Helm (Publishers) Ltd, a subsidiary of
A & C Black (Publishers) Ltd, 35 Bedford Row,
London WC1R 4JH

ISBN 0-7136-8024-5

A CIP catalogue record for this book is available
from the British Library

Typeset by Rowland Phototypesetting Ltd, Bury St Edmunds, Suffolk
Printed and bound in Great Britain by Biddles Ltd, Guildford and
King's Lynn

CONTENTS

AUTHOR'S NOTE

I FIRST WATCHED Northamptonshire play cricket on (I think) August Bank Holiday 1958, when I would have been seven. The mind's eye insists that I saw Frank Tyson bowl in mid-afternoon. The relevant *Wisden* suggests that would have been impossible.

My co-author, Andrew Radd, first went to the County Ground aged nine in 1972. He asked David Steele for his autograph as he went out to bat and was told 'Not now, son.' We have been watching Northamptonshire ever since. For both of us, this is a book written out of lifelong affection, sometimes tempered by exasperation, but very deep affection nonetheless.

By the time Andrew was being refused his autograph, I was starting to report Northamptonshire cricket for the *Chronicle and Echo*. That lasted until 1975. From 1980, I began writing cricket for *The Guardian* and sneaking in Northamptonshire games whenever I could. In 1984 Andrew began reporting their games as a freelance and has not missed a home match since.

Thus we were, in a sense, compiling this book long before we ever thought about it. We gained information first-hand and by talking to men like Nobby Clark, Ben Bellamy, Wilfrid Timms and Fred Speakman, who died long before we began the formal research. When we did start, we were lucky enough to interview William Wilson, who remembered watching cricket at the County Ground before the First World War, and Freddie Brown. Both have since died. So has Ken Turner. We never did get to ask him all the questions we would have wanted but he gave us permission to use material from his unpublished memoirs and for that we were especially grateful. We interviewed many other people, nearly all happily still living, and their help is acknowledged below.

There is only one previous complete work on this subject – 'Northamptonshire Cricket: A History' by J. D. Coldham (Heinemann, 1959). We disagree with Coldham's conclusions in certain areas but otherwise this was obviously a vital source. So were the Northampton papers: the old *Chronicle*, *Echo*, *Mercury*, *Herald* and their later merged incarnations, the *Chronicle and Echo* and *Mercury and Herald* as well as the Kettering-based *Northamptonshire Evening Telegraph*.

The old *Northampton Independent*, once a marvellous weekly paper but now defunct, provided a wonderful vein of material and the name *Independent* in these pages should never be confused with any modern national paper of the same name. The staffs of both the *Chronicle and Echo* and the *Evening Telegraph* were exceptionally generous, both with information and photographs. It was sad for us to discover that there now appear to be no files, in Northampton anyway, of the town's traditional sports paper, the *Green 'Un*.

Steve Coverdale, the Chief Executive of Northamptonshire County Cricket Club, was extremely helpful and supportive, as were the rest of the office staff: Graham Alsop, Jackie Stevens, Frances Allbury and Sue Condon. We would also particularly like to thank John Watson, whose magnificent collection is the basis for the pictures in this book, Laurie Newell, for the statistics, and Dennis Brookes, who showed limitless patience when we needed to tap into his memory. The song on pages 37–8 was collected by David Rayvern Allen for his book *A Song for Cricket*, and is reproduced with the author's kind permission.

Thanks also go to Keith Andrew, Marion Arnold, Peter Arnold, Mike Askham, Des Barrick, Bill Barron, Julian Baskcomb, June Bayliss, Vince Broderick, the family of the late W. C. Brown, Colin Campbell, Jeremy Casey, L. W. Clarke, Geoff Cook, Trevor Cooper, Ian Davidson, Ian Davies, Percy Davis, Max Engel, Jon Fellows-Smith, Alan Ford, David Frith, Stephen Green, Steve Harrison, Mollie Hiam, Derek Hodgson, Derrick Holden, Edward Holland, Jack Jennings, Martin Johnson, Bob Kaufman, Frank Keating, Allan Lamb, John Lamb, Jock Livingston, Lewis McGibbon, Charlie May, Harold Mayes, Mike Newton, Mick Norman, Pat Murphy, Anne Oram, Tony Orbell, Reg Partridge, Brian Reynolds, Andy Roberts, David Steele, Richard Streeton, Alan Swann, Gil Tebbitt, Mike Tebbitt, George Thompson jun, the late Mrs G. A. T. Vials, Rex Walford, Mike Warrington, Jim Watts, Peter Watts, the late Roly White, Roy Wills and Lynn Wilson. Although this is an official history, the opinions expressed are entirely our own.

Our most special thanks go to my wife Hilary and Andrew's mother, Dorothy, who had to live with this book and did so with such tolerance and love. And to Northamptonshire County Cricket Club, for providing what we believe is a rattling good story.

Matthew Engel   October 1992

A PERSONAL VIEW
Frank Tyson

I TOOK MY first step toward Test cricket as a gawky fifteen-year-old playing for Middleton's senior team in the Central Lancashire League. But the road to success did not become a fast motorway until one glorious Sunday afternoon in 1951, in the small Potteries town of Knypersley. I had just turned 21 and was the part-time local professional – and full-time university student – playing in a charity game for the North Staffordshire League against the Commonwealth Eleven: a team of Test and county players just returned from two tours of India, Pakistan and Ceylon. That day at Knypersley I bowled against Test players: Indians Umrigar and Hazare, West Indian Frankie Worrell, the local England hero, Jack Ikin, and – importantly for me – a strong Australian contingent of George Tribe, Jock Livingston, Jack Pettiford, Fred Freer and Des Fitzmaurice.

The previous six years had seen me turn down the chance of playing profession-ally for Lancashire in favour of university studies and then, inexplicably, be rejected as an amateur player by the same Old Trafford authorities on the grounds that I was injury prone! The nagging determination to play county and Test cricket when I had finished my studies lingered on, and on that Sunday afternoon at Knypersley I went out to prove I was good enough. Des Fitzmaurice and Frankie Worrell – who had both experienced my speed in league games – needed no convincing and willingly demoted themselves in the order to give the other blokes a chance to bat! Much of the responsibility for blunting the Tyson assault fell on the shoulders of the left-handed batsman, Jock Livingston, a recent Aussie recruit to the Northamptonshire stable. The 'Doctor', one of whose many cricketing rôles was that of a scout for his adopted county, was so impressed by the experience that he wrote to me the following week asking if I would be interested in a trial for the midland county.

So it was that, at the beginning of the Easter vacation 1952, I travelled south from Durham for my eagerly anticipated trial match. I arrived late at the Well-ingborough ground and the County side were already in the field. My sponsor Jock Livingston was keeping wicket and when I was brought on to bowl, he fell a respectful distance back behind the stumps. Not so the slip fieldsmen, who appraised my short run and judged that I could not be all that fast. My first delivery clipped the edge of the bat, ricocheting towards second slip at the speed of light. The rather rotund fieldsman crouching in that position was still motionless when the ball cracked him on the knee. His fellow slip fieldsmen carried Fred Jakeman off the field, then resumed their positions – three yards deeper. I reinforced my first speedy impression with a few quick wickets and within weeks I had accepted a contract with Northamptonshire. I played my first game for the County against the touring Indian side later that season, taking the wicket of Pankaj Roy in my first over. After twelve months I qualified by residence for my adopted County and was a regular member of the first eleven; two years later I made my Test debut for England.

A world of hopeful cricketers have beaten the same path that I did to Northamptonshire's door. It has long been, and still remains, a common entrance to first-class cricket for many overseas players and the rejects of other English counties. When I first joined Northamptonshire only four players in a professional staff of 19 were native to the County. Even today the 1992 *Wisden* lists only four native Cobblers among the 21 who played in the 1991 Championship.

The minor local representation in the Northants team is understandable. The rural character of Northamptonshire and its comparatively small population has always militated against the wholesale production of native talent. True, the local game has nurtured some gifted sons. George Thompson, the fast-medium bowler who was said to have been largely responsible for the County's elevation to first-class status in 1905, and was Northamptonshire's first — and until 1987 its only indigenous — Test representative, was born in Northampton. So were his team's batting stars, W. H. Kingston and C. J. T. Pool. In the post-Second World War years, the achievements of native players such as Reg Partridge, Brian Reynolds and Micky Norman have often occasioned pride in Northamptonian breasts. But whereas the towns and villages of Northampton have produced their scores of outstanding sportsmen over the years, the industrial cities of larger counties have turned out hundreds of first-class and Test cricketers. Thus demographic statistics dictate that, if Northamptonshire is to survive in county cricket in the same company as the larger counties like Middlesex and Yorkshire, it has to recruit talented mercenaries.

For more than 30 years between 1950 and the mid-1980s, Northamptonshire's chief 'head-hunter' was its secretary, Ken Turner. He began his 'seek and enlist' campaign under the command of that most gentlemanly of club officers, Lt-Col A. St. G. Coldwell. With the support of successive presidents, T. E. Manning, G. A. T. 'Tubby' Vials, Norman Barratt, Brian Schanschieff, Dennis Brookes and latterly the cricket committee chairman, Peter 'Kiwi' Arnold, Turner attracted a galaxy of international talent to the Wantage Road ground. He signed up Aussies George Tribe, Jock Livingston, Jack Manning: Kiwis Peter Arnold and John Guy: Pakistanis Mushtaq Mohammad and Sarfraz Nawaz: Indian skippers Bishen Bedi and Kapil Dev: South Africans Allan Lamb and 'Pom-Pom' Fellows-Smith: and West Indians Winston Davis, Curtly Ambrose and Roger Harper. He sent his scouts — coaches Jack Mercer, Percy Davis — and his players, to all points of the compass looting England of its overlooked players and its promising Minor County and second eleven talents. They channelled a constant stream of top-class men back to the County Ground; Des Barrick, Fred Jakeman, Ken Fiddling, Colin Milburn, Geoff Cook, Malcolm Scott and Peter Willey were pirated from the north-east and Yorkshire. From Lancashire came Syd Starkie, Keith Andrew and myself: from Surrey, Raman Subba Row, Harry Kelleher and Laurie Johnson. And from the Minor Counties he plucked David Larter, Brian Crump, David Steele, Rob Bailey, Micky Allen, Peter and Jimmy Watts and Albert Lightfoot.

I believe Ken Turner, who sadly died in 1991, was one of the major influences in transforming Northamptonshire from a team which was easy meat for the larger counties in the late 1940s into one of the better sides in the County Championship. The former secretary was openly cynical, unashamedly sceptical and audibly sarcastic about the ability – or lack of it – in certain players. But he was a realist. He had a cricketing brain and knew a good – or bad – player when he saw one. He called a spade a bloody shovel. It was the only way, if Northamptonshire were to become a force to be reckoned with in English county cricket. His was the iron foot in the kid boots which kicked the 'Cobblers' upstairs into the trophy winning league.

Turner never had the satisfaction of seeing his midland county win the County Championship – it was second in 1957 and 1965; but he was at the helm when Northants won the Gillette Cup in 1976 and were the bridesmaids in the same competition in 1979 and its replacement, Natwest Trophy in 1981. He also stage-managed Northamptonshire's triumph in the Benson and Hedges' Cup of 1980. Ken Turner's 30-odd years of stewardship won him a reputation for competent professionalism amongst his fellow administrators. For more than two decades his opinions were closely heeded at the deliberations of the Test and County Cricket Board. The standards of integrity and efficiency which he set at Wantage Road suggest that it was perhaps more than coincidence that his small midland bailiwick produced three national administrators in the years following his government: two chairmen of the TCCB in Raman Subba Row and Frank Chamberlain and a leading light in the National Cricket Association, Doug Lucas.

Over the years Northamptonshire CCC have been fortunate in the help they have received from their supporters. After the First World War, for instance, a local business man, Alfred Cockerill, donated the Wantage Road ground to the county club. The Northamptonshire post-Second World War team-building programme would certainly have never got off the ground, but for the industrial paternalism of Sir John Pascoe, the chief executive of the Duston-based roller bearings manufacturer, British Timken. In the 1950s Northamptonshire players were not as well paid as their fellow professionals employed by the more affluent counties such as Middlesex. The Northants ground staff, however, enjoyed one advantage over most of their brothers-in-cricket: they were guaranteed a steady job at British Timken whenever they were not required by the county club.

When I took up residence in Northampton in 1952, people were surprised that I did not go to work for Timken. All but a handful of my fellow professionals were the company's employees. Timken owned its own comfortably appointed cricket ground and employed a former Northants player, Reg Partridge, as groundsman. Each year the company fielded a full county side which usually gave a good account of itself against an invited Cambridge University team in a day of champagne and champagne cricket – eagerly awaited by the Northants pros. The name of the Northamptonshire County Cricket Club was so synonymous with that of British Timken that on the first-class circuit it became known as 'Timkenshire'.

The Northants team has always been a League of Nations. In the 1950s there were seven nationalities in the ranks, and a captain who was born in Peru! The

English players were drawn from ten different counties. In April, when new-comers shiveringly presented themselves at the ancient icy-cold Northampton pavilion for the first frigid training of the season, I wondered when the new signing would be an Eskimo! International diversity within a team can produce charming entertainment on the field; but because individuals brought up in different environ-ments have differing outlooks on life and sport, it is sometimes a divisive influence in the dressing room. Therefore it is not surprising, to me at least, that, over the years, domestic squalls have occasionally disturbed the summers at the Wantage Road Ground.

The absence of the passionate unifying spirit which characterised teams in our native Lancashire puzzled wicket-keeper Keith Andrew and me when we began playing with Northamptonshire in 1953. Keith and I were both products of the Central Lancashire League; he from the Werneth club and I from Middleton. Our common background made us natural and firm friends and our friendship has endured for nearly 40 years during our wanderings through England and Australia. At Northampton we missed the rough-and-tumble camaraderie of the league – so we decided to try to reproduce it at Wantage Road. On reflection, our foundation of the Cosmo Social Club was an adolescent concept. We called the team members

A porter at Northampton's Castle Station gives Frank Tyson a distinctly low-key send-off, as England's fast-bowling hope contemplates the Ashes battle ahead. (Roland Holloway Collection/ The Chronicle and Echo)

together for an hour on one evening of every away game. For 60 minutes we drank beer together and proposed outrageous toasts: 'to wives and sweethearts, may they never meet'. We sang bawdy songs such as 'The Wild West Show'. We fined one another for on-field and extra-curricular excesses and pooled the proceeds to give ourselves and our families a slap-up dinner each September at The Falcon: an 'olde worlde hostelry' hard by the Marquis of Northampton's seat of Castle Ashby. On rest days the team competed in hilarious games of golf; when we were playing at the seaside we sometimes went fishing early in the morning off the local pier – once when it was dark and the tide was miles out. At Worcester the team indulged in a costly golf contest, attempting seven iron chips across the River Severn from the grounds of the Diglis Hotel. We spoofed a fishing contest on the Worcester ground, catching pre-bought kippers out of a pool formed on the New Road Ground when the nearby river flooded it. The funny thing was that the puerile idea of the Cosmo Club worked.

Keith and I played our first big-time game together against the 1953 Australian tourists. Before the game the Northamptonshire and touring teams were presented to the Duke of Gloucester, who lived at Barnwell Manor near Peterborough. The introductions were effected by our skipper, Freddie Brown, then in his forty-third year and his last season in county cricket.

To me Freddie Brown was a latter-day Northamptonshire Alfred Mynn: a manly autocrat fashioned on a grandiose scale. His concept of selection was to hand a list of names to the chairman of the selection committee, together with the comment that these were the players he would like to lead on to the field in the next game. His reputation in English cricket matched his build. Two years earlier in Melbourne, he had inspired England to its first post-war Test victory against the all-conquering Australians. His courage against the Aussie fast bowlers in that 1950–51 series prompted the Sydney coster-mongers to advertise their cabbages as having 'hearts as big as Freddie Brown.' It was a sweet return 'Down Under' for a former Cambridge undergraduate who toured as a supernumerary with England's 'Bodyline' team in 1932–33 and spent so much time playing golf that his skipper, Douglas Jardine, confiscated his clubs!

I admired Freddie Brown immensely; not just because of his hard-hitting batting, his skill at bowling the twiddly leg-spinners or ducking swingers which yielded him 1,221 wickets in his career; not merely because he had the guts to come back into cricket at the age of 39 after spending three years 'in the bag' as a German POW. My respect sprang from the fact that he never ordered his players to do something which he would not do himself. As I watched him wheel down over after over on the moribund Northampton strip, I sometimes feared that he would keel over with a heart attack. His complexion grew ruddier and ruddier; the sweat poured down his face saturating the 'kerchief which he habitually wore around his neck; but he never gave up. Northamptonshire owes much to this man who between 1949 and 1953 turned out 102 times and who, with the aid of his employer, Sir John Pascoe, began the revival which made the County a power in English cricket.

In 1953 Freddie Brown retired and handed over command to his senior professional, Dennis Brookes. Never in the history of English first-class cricket has there been a player more deserving of the meritorious title of 'a loyal servant of a club' than 'Brookie'. The Northamptonshire County Cricket Club has been Dennis's life since he joined the ground staff in 1933. He has served it as a player, a captain, a secretary, a coach, and president for more than 50 years. He and his wife Freda have lived most of that time in a house with a back gate which opens on to the member's car park; they have never seen any reason to move. Dennis joined Northants as a 19-year-old from Kippax in Yorkshire; it was a measure of his loyalty that he stuck by the Club when, between May 1935 and May 1939, his adopted team failed to win a match! As an opening bat, Dennis personified the pride which English craftsmen used to take in their trade. Upright in his stance, calm in his demeanour, he scorned violent movements of the bat, gleaning runs almost imperceptibly with silky drives, subtle deflections and intuitive running between the wickets. He was unlucky to play for England only once. He broke a finger in the West Indies in 1947–48, and had to be sent home when an inexpert medico strapped his injured finger to another causing a dangerous infection.

As captain of Northants, his timing of declarations was uncanny. He seemed to sense the targets which his county opponents would be willing to chase at the risk of losing the game. Dennis made a century against every first-class county, one of his last – against his native Yorkshire – probably giving him most satisfaction. At the end of his career, he was the quintessence of county cricket's senior pro: grey-haired, dignified, accomplished, wise in the ways of first-class cricket and so respected in his local community that he was appointed a JP. It was typical of 'Brookie's' selflessness that, in 1957 – the year he led Northants to second position in the Championship – he agreed to step down from the Northants captaincy so that Raman Subba Row could be appointed the amateur skipper.

Dennis's pre-war colleague at Wantage Road and his next door neighbour on the hard wooden benches of the cheerless Northants dressing-room was Vince Broderick. Brod was a self-made cricketer in every sense of the word. I would not be surprised to learn that he chiselled himself out of the hard rock of the Pennines close by his native Bacup. There was little fluency in his dogged left-handed batting; he evinced only negligible turn when he bowled his left-handed spinners. But in spite of his limitations, Brod held his place on the staff for 18 years. He scored his centuries, turned himself into an opening batsman, did the double in 1948 and ended his career with 7,530 runs and 548 wickets – chiefly the result of the arm ball! The Aussies on the staff could not understand why the selectors persevered with Brod. They believed that success belonged to natural talents. They could not comprehend the virtues of industry and character: qualities which Vince possessed in abundance and which made him one of the most respected coaches Winchester School ever had.

Lancashire were already well represented in the Northants side when Keith Andrew and I joined it in 1953. In addition to Vince Broderick, the red rose county had donated the skills of pace bowler Albert Nutter, opening batsman Norman Oldfield and off-spinner Syd Starkie to the Northants cause.

'Buddy' Oldfield, who joined Northants in 1948, was the most nervous batsman I ever encountered. This small, dapper man with a full-head of black hair always spent the last few minutes before going out to bat sitting next to the window, padded up and fully prepared, smoking cigarette after cigarette and blinking furiously. Apparently during the whole of his cricket career, the hypertensed Buddy never ate breakfast for fear of vomiting before he batted. Norman Oldfield might have been nervous, but he was also one of the finest back-foot players I have ever seen. A fearless puller and hooker even in his forties, he was also a devastating cutter. The scorer of nearly 18,000 runs, Buddy notched 1,000 runs in a season 11 times and 2,000 once. His career suffered greatly through the Second World War. He had appeared only once for England against the West Indies in 1939, averaging nearly fifty in his two innings, when the Great Interruption occurred.

Northamptonshire's most successful poaching foray into Lancashire territory bagged Keith Andrew: a nonpareil keeper and widely acknowledged as one of the best takers of the ball that the game has ever seen. An engineer by profession, Keith applied his powers of scientific observation and appreciation of angles to the art of taking spin. Had he been as interested in keeping to pace as he was to the slower bowlers, he would undoubtedly have been first choice for England in the 1960s; but only an irrational fanatic could become enthusiastic about acting as back-stop to fast bowlers on the dodo-dead Northampton pitch. Keith was, and still is, what the French call un original – a character. Absent-minded to the degree that he often forgot what he was saying in mid-sentence, he frequently wandered off into cloud-cuckoo land, working on theories such as how to 'lap' against the spin of Gloucestershire's slow left-hander, Sam Cook. He once spent an hour practising the shot before going out to face Sam at Gloucester's Wagon Works Ground – breaking many flower pots in front of the mayor's tent in the process. Sam bowled him first ball as he attempted to lap! Keith's popularity with the team and his ability to think made him an effective skipper and, but for a combination of bad luck and tactical manoeuvring by other county teams, he would surely have brought the County Championship to Wantage Road in 1965.

The Northamptonshire of my time was a rare combination in which Lancastrians played happily alongside their supposedly inveterate foes, Yorkshiremen. Our contingent of tykes consisted of Doug Greasley, Ken Fiddling, Fred Jakeman and Des Barrick.

Fred Jakeman was the complex combination of a gifted ball-player and a psychologically insecure individual. At the height of his confident period in 1951 – a year which yielded him 1,989 runs – this super-aggressive left-hander scored 558 runs in four innings before he was dismissed: a record which stood for 39 years. When I played my first match at Grace Road, Leicester, two years after Jakeman's annus mirabilis, the locals were still talking of how the left-hander, in his memorable season, straight drove spinner Vic Munden over the pavilion – and the ball was still rising as it passed over the two-storey building!

One of the most versatile cricketers ever to pass through the C. J. T. Pool gates was Des Barrick. Born in Fitzwilliam and a late developer from the Johnny Lawrence coaching stable in South Yorkshire, this roly-poly all-rounder was a down-market Gary Sobers. A sound enough batting technician to pass the 1,000-run mark in seven seasons, he also bowled tidy medium-pacers, finger and wrist spin and was an outstanding cover fieldsman with a whiplash throwing arm. As a dressing-room humorist and raconteur, he was superb, delivering the punch lines of his jokes with an infectious giggle as he crossed himself with his constant companion, his pipe. He had two pipes: a small one to smoke his own tobacco: and one with an enormous bowl to smoke 'OP' – or 'Other People's'. Des should have worn an England cap – but he enjoyed his cricket too much. Fitness training was an anathema to him. Physiotherapist Jack Jennings once caught Desmond and pace bowler Bob Clarke returning from an early season cross-country run on a Weston Favell bus.

Jack knew exactly how to deal with Des; he was one of the boys and 'knew when the gas was lit.' He was a cheerful but shrewd trainer who had accompanied the England soccer team to the Melbourne Olympics and later went with an MCC side to Australia. He was awake to all of the tricks of the 'lead swingers' in the side: imaginary pulled muscles got little sympathy – just the placebo of an aspirin and the advice to 'run it off!'

In the 1950s, overseas players threw a sometimes long, sometimes short shadow over the Wantage Road Ground. The former Trinidadian batsman Donald Ramsamooj was brilliantly disappointing. New Zealand's elegant left-handed opener, John Guy, failed to produce his international form for the County. 'Pom-Pom' Fellows-Smith gained selection in the 1960 Springbok touring team to England. But in 1957 he scored only one hundred for Northants against Sussex at Hove: an extraordinary knock during which he professed to me his intention of progressing carefully from the late nineties to his century – before striking the next ball for six!

Other foreigners to leave more lasting marks on Northamptonshire cricket were 'Kiwi' Arnold, Jack Manning, Jock Livingston and George Tribe. The red-headed New Zealander Peter Arnold played the juvenile opening role to Dennis Brookes' leading man for most of his 167-match career. His subservient part led to the underestimation of the value of his 8,013 runs. When he was at the crease he gave an innings a hard-working, purposeful tone. Kiwi's minimal backlift was a genuine asset in an era when most counties possessed hostile, English-born, opening bowlers and runs were earned the hard way. When he and Brookie ran between the wickets, they bid for singles with a nod of the head; it was virtually impossible to catch them short of their ground.

The South Australian, Jack Manning, bowled his left-arm orthodox spinners in the manner he lived: with an exuberance and extravagance born of inbred Irish optimism. He did not spin the ball – he ripped it. It hummed like a top as it came down the wicket! He learned his grip from his baseballing days in his native Adelaide and he could make the ball curve into the right-handed batsman like a pitcher in the American game. We called him 'Tanglefoot', because of his dipping, pigeon-toed approach to the wicket. On his day, 'Tangles' was as penetrative as England and Surrey's Tony Lock. Three times Jack took 100 wickets in a season and when Northants finished as runners-up to Surrey in the 1957 championship, he, together with George Tribe and Micky Allen, formed a three-pronged spin attack which accounted for more than 300 opposing batsmen.

We called him 'Doctor' after Doctor Livingstone; we called him 'Jock' because his name had a Scottish ring to it – but whatever else you called him, you had to call Leonard Livingston a great player of spin bowling. The nimble left-handed number three's secret lay in reaching the slow bowlers before they bounced. As an insurance policy he positioned his body behind the line of the ball, so that if the ball eluded his bat he was seldom stumped – the ball rarely got past his pads. An accomplished driver, cutter and hooker, Jock scored almost 14,000 runs in his eight seasons with Northants. A more than useful wicket-keeper – a role he filled for his native New South Wales – he had an astute head for figures and could usually recalculate his current average between the time he was dismissed and regained the pavilion. And, of course, I was living testimony to the fact that he was not a bad judge of a cricketer!

In my experience there have been two outstanding cases of cricketers who should have played Test cricket regularly yet did not. Both were Australians: Cecil George Pepper and my colleague at Northampton, the left-handed wrist-spinner, George Tribe. It was George's misfortune to play at a time when his country placed most of its faith in the fast bowling of Lindwall, Miller and Johnston and the new ball which became available every 65 overs. This combination of circumstances, plus the folly of the Victorian selectors in excluding him from the state side when he returned from his English league commitments in 1947, led to George playing in only three Tests. He never toured with an Australian team. Living in Australia as I do, I know that even today, Aussies do not recognise this criminal neglect of Tribe's superb talents.

After revolutionising bowling standards in the Lancashire and Central Lancashire Leagues in the 1940s, George re-wrote the Northants bowling record books between 1951 and 1959. His baffling medley of three different types of wrong 'uns and chinamen, two top-spinners and flippers bamboozled club, county and Test players alike. A stocky individual with a jutting jaw and matching determination, George hardly missed a match in his 233-game stint with Northants. His batting aggregate of 10,000 runs and his bag of 1,378 victims included seven 'doubles' of 100 wickets and 1,000 runs in eight complete seasons; but these are Mark Twain's 'damned statistics'. A true appreciation of George's bowling could only be gleaned by watching him analyse, out-think and tie opponents in knots. Not infrequently he would bowl mystified batsman behind their legs as they padded up. Yorkshire batsmen, in particular, reared on a regimen of finger-spin, could not 'pick' George. In 1958 at Northampton, George bowled out Yorkshire twice for totals of 67 and 65, returning incredible match figures of 15 for 31. This diminutive Aussie continued bowling in Melbourne social cricket long after he was receiving social security – and still perplexed team-mates and opponents alike with his theories on 'square and top spin!'

From the home counties Northampton recruited the burly Harry Kelleher and Raman Subba Row from Surrey. We called Harry 'Umpety', because of the thudding, bouncy run which prefaced his curving medium-pace. He survived a mauling from Essex's Dicky Dodds in one of his first games, but in the end the benign nature of the Northampton pitch limited him to two seasons, 52 games and 112 wickets.

To the discerning judge of batsmen, 'Rubba Dubba' Row was patently ear-marked for an England cap when he came to Northampton in 1955, fresh from a Surrey side over-endowed with batting talent and Cambridge University. A left-handed batsman of monolithic concentration and unshakable determination, the former blue was an immensely powerful bottom-handed player. The high-water mark of his career with Northants was his 300 against his native Surrey at The Oval in the first year of his captaincy, 1958: an innings which saw him share a record sixth-wicket partnership of 376 with Albert Lightfoot. He gained selection in England's touring teams to Australia in 1958–59 and the West Indies in 1959–60. He was hot stuff with the bat – but not as hot as some of the curries he inflicted on those who were incautious enough to share a meal with him. A lesser well-known facet of Raman's cricket was his ability to bowl leg-spinners, which batsmen underestimated at their peril. A gangling, spidery action produced balls which dropped like Yeats' peace, slow from the heavens, and which E. W. Swanton, the *Daily Telegraph* writer, aptly described as 'seemingly guileless deliveries.' Raman's bag of wickets proved that awkwardness often disguises subtlety.

When poet A. E. Housman wrote that Shropshire had 'many a lightfoot lad', he must have had Albert in mind. Woore was Bert Lightfoot's birthplace and his game oozed a rural upbringing; his left-handed batting was all lethargic grace, his gentle right-handed medium-pacers curled lazily away as they approached the bat. I often wonder if, in the 20 years that Bert Lightfoot was around the County Ground as a player and groundsman, he ever moved up a gear. The only time I ever saw him display any emotion was when one of his deliveries skimmed the outside edge of the bat; this was a signal for him to raise his sizeable proboscis towards heaven and draw in a whistling breath through his pursed lips. I always felt like putting a bomb under Bert; with the get-up-and-go of an Allan Lamb, he could have been a Test player.

Micky Allen was the junior partner in Northampton's match-winning triumvi-rate of left-handed spinners of the 1950s. Unlike George Tribe, his spinning methods were orthodox; unlike Jack Manning, his flight and spin were econom-ical. Indeed, the Bedford-born bowler's accuracy and economy approached nig-gardliness. If there was a modicum of turn in the pitch, he would find and exploit it at the cheapest possible cost. He possessed a good closed action which was expressed in a rasping drag of the rear foot. This necessitated a metal toecap of which I would have been proud. His arm-ball slid on to the batsman like a medium-paced delivery.

In 1956 Northants won only eight games and drew 15 to finish fourth in the County Championship. The following season the left-handed spin quartet of Tribe, Manning, Allen and Broderick dismissed 317 batsmen, and helped to win 15 games and lift the County to second place in the ladder. The explanation of the slow bowlers' new-found successes lay in the changed nature of the Northampton pitch. Previous wickets had been prepared with cow dung and marl puddled into the surface. It was an interesting cocktail – especially when the spin bowlers rubbed their hands in the dust then licked their fingers to enable them to grip the ball better! In 1957, the groundsman abandoned the cow dung treatment and left less grass on the pitch. The result was a surface which spun on the first day of a match and transformed the Northants spinners into match-winners. The role of the faster bowlers at Northampton became that of taking the shine off the ball before handing it to the slow bowlers.

The genuine, home-grown players in the Northamptonshire side of the 1950s were a select bunch: Micky Norman, Brian Reynolds, the two Davis brothers from Brackley – Percy and Eddie – and the inimitable Robert Wakefield Clarke. Percy Davis had completed the last of his 6,363 runs for Northamptonshire the year before I arrived at the Wantage Road Ground. In 1953, he and the former Glamorgan all-rounder, Jack Mercer, were the Northants coaching gurus. Percy loved coaching and found his real niche in life coaching boys, both in South Africa – where he migrated for more than 20 English winters – and later, when he retired from his Northants post, at Harrow School. Nicknamed 'Sparrow', this perky, spare individual was terribly superstitious. When he dressed for cricket, he always insisted on stripping to the buff and donning his Northampton-shire cap first. Small, scraggy and bald, Sparrow was not a pretty sight in the nude.

Percy's brother Ted had the potential, but not the confidence, to be a great batsman. He was an accomplished hooker – if he did not think about the dangers of the stroke. Playing in a second eleven game, I once saw him despatch the bouncers of the Worcestershire express, Jack Flavell – later of England fame – to all corners of the New Road Ground. But Ted never scored runs against Yorkshire and Freddie Trueman. Before the game, 'Ferocious' made a point of coming into the Northants dressing room and cornering Ted. 'That', he used to say, drawing an X on Ted's forehead with his index finger, 'is where I am going to hit you!' It was enough – Ted rarely troubled the scorers.

At the outset of his career with Northamptonshire, I thought that the blond-haired Mick Norman was another Dennis Brookes in the making. The young opener had the style, the talent and the strokes; but he lacked the Yorkshireman's determination. After a period of religious soul-searching, Mick eventually found himself and I was pleased to see him blossom into a fine mature player for Leicestershire.

When I first came to know Brian Reynolds, he seemed to divide his time between his professional football career, national service with the North-amptonshire Regiment at Spencer Barracks, and the County Ground. He was a fitness buff: the first to pre-season training, perpetual motion during the activities and the last to leave. As an opening batsman, he took everything the opening bowlers could fling at him and came back for more. He was a useful keeper in an emergency and an extremely competent trencherman – hence his nickname 'Waddy'.

Fast-medium opening bowler Bob Clarke was living evidence that the early Viking invaders once sailed up the Nene valley as far as Finedon. Flaxen-haired, barrel-chested and built like a bull, he could have been a reincarnation of a Norseman. The left-hander's bowling methods were simple: he bounced up to the wicket from about 15 yards and let the batsman have it. He did not know how or why, but from around the wicket he swung the ball in to the right-hander and could sometimes pitch on leg-stump and hit the off. Whilst he often confessed that he would like to put Ron Johnson, the groundsman who produced the unhelpful Northampton pitches, up against the scorebox and shoot him, he never surrendered to the wicket or the batsman. A short-leg fieldsman who could only catch with his left hand, he brought off some amazing back-handed catches on the right side of his body. On off days, he missed the simplest of chances and would ask keeper Keith Andrew plaintively: 'Were it a catch?'

Fred Speakman and Alan Ford of the Northampton *Chronicle and Echo* were the team's Boswells. We gave Alan a hard time for some of his views, but respected his writing enough to flatter him with the nickname of 'Neville Cardus'. They shared with the scorer a delapidated elevated box with windows on the square leg boundary. For a while, coach Jack Mercer doubled as first-eleven scorer. An accomplished conjurer – and a man who could make himself disappear completely during the winter – Jack was a member of the Magic Circle and could work wonders with cards and figures. When we were bowling, he would come to the dressing room at each interval and intone the bowling analyses, adding a postscript of 'well bowled' after every set of figures, no matter how good or bad they were.

For a time, the scorer was the mild-mannered Bob Muscutt. The scorers communicated their figures by phone to the solitary whitewashed, tumbledown wooden scoreboard on the opposite side of the ground. In the basement of the scoreboard, a clanking hand-press laboriously ground out the up-to-date scorecards which were vended by a white-coated, marooned-capped Northamptonian with a broad accent and a rapier-sharp wit.

I wish I could say that Northamptonshire played on picturesque grounds like Worcester or on grounds with character like Old Trafford. But I always thought that the County headquarters at Wantage Road were drab and featureless. The ground was surrounded on three sides by terraced houses, and bounded on the fourth by the main stand of the Northampton Town Football Club, who, together with the bowling club, shared the ground with the county cricketers. Standing alongside the football stand was the County Hotel, to which the players adjourned for lunch.

The outfield at the football club end was invariably rough, after its winter's ploughing by football studs. The spectator seating on the periphery of the soccer pitch was nothing more than wooden planks supported by boxes. The cavernous two-storey pavilion was early Edwardian red-brick and was flanked by temporary scaffolding accommodation for members and an antique ladies' stand. With the construction of the new administration block, modern dressing rooms and the indoor school, the ground now wears a new look, especially when it is enriched with the addition of sponsors' tents.

Northamptonshire played games outside the county town in Rushden, Peterborough, Kettering and Wellingborough. Wellingborough School was my favourite. Its oval was the ideal setting for an English cricket match: picturesque, ringed by tall trees, and during a county game, by marquees. A rustic pavilion completed the tableau: a pavilion from which one stepped on to the field over W. G. Grace's former doorstep – 'souvenired' by one enterprising Wellingborough master when the Champion's house was demolished.

On the way home from a Wellingborough game, Keith Andrew, Jack Manning, Raman Subba Row, Bert Lightfoot and I would invariably stop half-way for a pint. Now, in distant Australia, I still enjoy fond memories of those evenings after county games: of good companionship, the Northamptonshire countryside, its villages and pubs.

But I do not dwell in the past. I also enjoy seeing contemporary Northamptonshire players do well in the most exalted company. As a commentator, writer and Northants supporter, I have celebrated the triumphs and grieved at the tragedies of Colin Milburn, David Larter, Brian Crump and Peter and Jimmy Watts, all of whom were just beginning their careers as I left Wantage Road. I have rejoiced when the County won a trophy from time to time. I have been sad when domestic disagreements caused rifts between the Club and Bishen Bedi, Mushtaq Mohammad and Peter Willey. I have anticipated even greater successes from such Northants recruits as Sarfraz Nawaz, David Steele, Roger Prideaux, Wayne Larkins and Geoff Cook. I have run into Hylton Ackerman in South Africa and Rob Bailey in Australia and talked about Northamptonshire and Northamptonians. Many to whom and about whom I have spoken and written have undoubtedly been better cricketers than me. They have probably made more money than me out of cricket. But not one player has derived more enjoyment than me out of Northants cricket.

I shall carry to the grave memories of the days I enjoyed in the sun with my Northants playing companions. I shall remember Northamptonshire stalwarts such as Chief Constable 'Bertie' Bolton, Arnold Payne, Norman Barratt, Hugh Wright and Dick Wells. I shall forever taste the tang of Phipps' Ale on the tongue and hear the brogue of farmer Ron Phipps in my ear. There was no purer sound than that of the London Symphony Orchestra in Rothwell Church; no greater theatre than that presented at the Rep. Low comedy at the New Theatre; high jumps at Pytchley. Life in Northampton never was and never will be flat and uninteresting – especially if they change the nature of the wicket at the County Ground!

ONE DAY IN SEPTEMBER

'We fight for lost causes because we know that our defeat and dismay may be the preface to our successors' victory.'

T.S. Eliot

SATURDAY 5 September 1992 turned out surprisingly dry and bright. August had been hopelessly wet. The start of September had been pretty grim. One way and another, there was not much encouragement for people to buy tickets in advance to watch a cricket match.

This, however, was Cup Final Day: the climax at Lord's of the NatWest Trophy, cricket's most important knock-out cup. And it was not just two random teams either. Northamptonshire were playing Leicestershire. These are what the national press usually call 'unfashionable' counties, which is a bizarre concept. How can one county be more fashionable than another? No one can change the place where they were born.

But it is true, in a way. Northamptonshire is a strange county, a place where everyone goes, which nobody knows. Every major route to the north has always crossed the county: from the time the Romans built the Watling Street through the canals and the railways (all four main routes) to the M1. Now motorists drive from Salcey Forest to a cup of tea at the Watford Gap with even less of a sideways glance than the Romans gave when they marched straight through.

It is a place that guards its secrets. It has its own accent (Are yer gooing dane t'N'thampton a-Toosday, m'dook? – Are you going down to Northampton on Tuesday, my duck?), totally distinctive to a Northamptonian, unrecognised by outsiders. The shoe industry has always had an even more private language of its own: of clicking and closing, bottom-stocks and rough-rounders. The county even has its own game: cheese skittles (played in a debased form in Leicestershire, with plastic pins instead of wooden ones), now threatened by pub landlords who prefer games that take more money and less space.

However, it is hard for anyone to grasp the character of the county. In the north-east, Northamptonshire looks like The Fens; in the south-west it looks like the Cotswolds, except that the stone is richer-coloured, more handsome and much less well-known. A researcher once tried to find traditional Northamptonshire folk-songs, and eventually came up with two, only to discover they originated in Hertfordshire. Northamptonshire's best-known poet was John Clare. But his part of the county, the Soke of Peterborough, has been detached and shifted, first into Huntingdonshire and then into Cambridgeshire. If it keeps on going east the next round of local government reform will place it in the North Sea. He came to Northampton itself when he was locked up as a lunatic.

J. L. Carr, the Yorkshire-born writer who moved to Kettering, once claimed that Northamptonshire was famous for six things: 'the Saints forwards in the loose, boots, the Battle of Naseby, V. W. C. Jupp, Earls Barton's church tower and Rushden brass bands.' Of V. W. C. Jupp, there will be much more in the pages ahead; Earls Barton Church stands yet, well into its second milennium; and the rugby team is better than ever. But the boots now have to fight against cheap imports from the Far East, the most famous brass bands come from Yorkshire and the county cares so little for the battle that overthrew King Charles I that people are uncomplainingly letting the Government build a motorway slap through Naseby Field. Anyway, careless historians usually say the village is in Leicestershire.

Leicestershire! In cricket, the battle has raged at least since 1878 when the Northamptonshire club formally began and Leicestershire bowled the team out for 24. Before the First World War, Northamptonshire supporters teasingly referred to their neighbours as 'Woollybacks', which may have been a pun on the 'Steelbacks', the Northamptonshire Regiment, who allegedly earned the nickname because their soldiers were whipped so much by their officers during the Napoleonic Wars. No one knew then how often the county's cricketers were going to be whipped by everyone in the years ahead.

In 1975, the year when Northamptonshire were possibly better equipped to become County Champions than in any year before or since, Leicestershire won the Championship instead. That came in an era of bad blood between the two sets of players which seems to have dated from a game at Grace Road in 1972. Ray Illingworth, who was captaining Leicestershire, felt Jim Watts should have declared. Watts felt he was in no position to declare, that his team was struggling to avoid defeat and that Illy was, as he said later 'trying to have his cake and eat it'. Illingworth put on the wicket-keeper Roger Tolchard to bowl in his pads to make the point. The crowd booed and a few spectators later sent Watts poison-pen letters.

On the same ground four years later, Illingworth had what he thought was his revenge. This was a year when both teams were contending for the title. The game was ruined by rain, there was no prospect of a result but Northamptonshire had Leicestershire at 22 for two in their first innings and were hoping to pick up some bowling bonus points. At that point, Leicestershire declared. This meant they had to follow on but Illingworth had calculated there was no chance of them losing in the short time available and that he could safely infuriate the opposition. This unorthodox ploy succeeded admirably. Eye-witnesses said the Northamptonshire players' reaction ranged from complete bewilderment to cold fury except from one or two irreverent souls who admired the impertinence of it and were as amused as the perpetrators.

In September 1992, we were another 16 years on. Only Nigel Briers, then a new boy and now the Leicestershire captain, survived from that game and he was no grudge-bearer. It was a more peaceful, friendly era. Allan Lamb, the captain of Northamptonshire who was still in South Africa when the 1976 game took place, went out with Briers to toss, and won. In keeping with standard strategy for these September cup finals, he chose to field first. It was a strategy that had proved infallible six years running, usually because there was still enough dew at that time of the morning to make batting exceptionally difficult – Northamptonshire had found this out the hard way against Lancashire in 1990. But this was not a very dewy morning and Northamptonshire thought long and hard about breaking with orthodox thinking. In the end, they played safe.

When Lamb led his team on to the field, they were greeted with something less than a cup final roar. In 1976, when Northamptonshire first reached a final at Lord's, there were empty seats at the start because the crush outside was so bad and many people only heard the shout when John Dye sent Farokh Engineer's stumps clattering. This time there were seats that stayed empty all day. 'Unfashionable counties!' whispered men in the pavilion who knew how to parrot phrases if nothing else.

Northamptonshire had always filled Lord's well enough before. This time there were several reasons why they failed. The first was the continual bad weather: supporters from both counties had lost confidence in the likelihood of much cricket on the day. The second was the price. The authorities had decided to charge spectators £18 for terrible seats, £35 for half-decent ones. With travelling costs and everything else, that made for an expensive day out – especially in a recession when so many people were short of money. And the novelty of these occasions was starting to wear off. Lord's has two Cup Finals every year. This was Northamptonshire's eighth in 17 seasons. Since that first glorious day in 1976 when the County had triumphed and ended 98 years in which the players had won nothing except a set of souvenir ashtrays (of which more later) the fun had gone out of it. They had won again, in the Benson and Hedges Cup Final of 1980, but then the Saturday had been rained off, no one had got any money back and to see any cricket at all they had to come back on the Monday.

Since then, the County had lost four finals in a row, twice without actually losing the game of cricket: the matches had been tied and awarded to the team which lost fewer wickets. Once, against Nottinghamshire in the NatWest final of 1987, they had lost the game from a position that appeared entirely unassailable. Against Lancashire in 1990, they had effectively lost the game inside an hour. Northamptonshire people were starting to think that they would fork out a couple of hundred quid for the day out only to get their hearts broken yet again at the end of it. This is something else outsiders might not appreciate about North-amptonshire people: their fatalistic pessimism.

Every ounce of logic suggested that Northamptonshire had to win this game. Theoretically, the team was much stronger. Leicestershire's most convincing all-rounder Vince Wells had just been admitted to hospital, forcing them to play one man, David Millns, who was palpably not fit and frantically consider the possibility of hauling one of their old boys, Peter Willey or Jonathan Agnew, out of the BBC commentary box. At first, they appeared to come through this crisis rather well. Their score reached 175 for two after a big stand between James Whitaker and Phil Robinson and on the face of it they appeared to be winning.

But Northamptonshire were playing this game very cannily. In the semi-final against Warwickshire they had been fined for bowling their overs too slowly. Now they were zipping through them so fast that the batsmen, used to the 60-over game being a little less pressurised than other versions of one-day cricket, appeared unaware how quickly the overs were disappearing: 40 before lunch, seven in 21 minutes immediately after it. When they did realise, they began to panic. And the innings fell to pieces – from 175 for two to a total of 208 for seven.

This was the 51st cup final at Lord's. As the rest of the game droned on, people would maintain that it was the most boring of them all. No true Northamptonshire supporter could think that. There were so many ways the County have found in the past to lose important games. But Alan Fordham and Robert Bailey

Fordham drives David Millns through the covers during his match-winning innings of 91. Northamptonshire's 12-year wait for a major title was almost over. (Northamptonshire Evening Telegraph)

knocked off most of the runs between them with resourceful, calm and – yes, if you like – boring efficiency. When Fordham skied a catch to wide mid-on nine short of his century, he let in Lamb to accompany Bailey as he made the winning hit. It was only 6.15. Often, these games have hardly warmed up by then.

So 1878 and 1975 were avenged. Leicestershire slunk away and it was the Northamptonshire supporters who were on the out-field cheering as Lamb received the trophy and held it up to them in the approved Wembley manner. In the old days, there might have been dozens of home-made banners. But Lord's have grown very stern and banned them. In keeping with the low-key nature of the day, only a couple – including one reading Wham-Bam Allan Lamb – slipped past the gatemen.

Lamb had himself been wham-bammed in an unexpected manner. That morning he had received a writ for libel from his former Northamptonshire team-mate, Sarfraz Nawaz, whom he had mentioned in connection with the row about alleged Pakistani ball-tampering, which that September was convulsing cricket. When he went out to bat, Lamb was flanked by two Northamptonshire officials, the manager Mike Procter and the coach Bob Carter, to prevent anyone else trying to slip him a writ at that peculiarly vulnerable moment in a cricketer's life. The MCC members must have been absolutely baffled as they all trooped through the Long Room. Those who knew Sarfraz well were inclined to treat this all as a piece of publicity-seeking whimsy. Those who did not were getting in a lather of excitement. This included most of the tabloid press. On the Monday, some of the papers hardly even mentioned that North-amptonshire had won the game. And even Northampton's own sports paper, the *Chronicle and Echo Pink 'Un*, headlined Sarfraz's writ rather than the cricket.

Fortunately, little of this seemed to percolate through to the dressing room. Very few outsiders were in with North-amptonshire as they savoured their triumph. Those who were found themselves unusually impressed. Normally, sporting cele-brations are rather bogus, with the champagne-spraying and mutual back-slapping covering up all kinds of inner tensions and hatreds. This was different. Not that the team did not have its inner tensions – but there was a sense of mellowness, of vindica-tion, of fulfilment, and also a sense that this was not just an end but perhaps the beginning of an era of success. Perhaps the rather improbable, always controversial, figure of Lamb would one day turn out to be Frodo Baggins, completing The Quest on behalf of

Allan Lamb and man-of-the-match Alan Fordham prepare to celebrate victory over Leicestershire in the 1992 NatWest Trophy final. (Northamptonshire Evening Telegraph)

The Shire – in this case by at long last winning the County Championship for Northamptonshire.

For the moment the team were content with the completion of this secondary quest. Five of them survived from the dreadful Nottinghamshire match five years before. Some of the others disliked being tainted with that and hated being described – worse than 'unfashionable' – as 'under-achievers'. All of them took pleasure in each other's success. Nigel Felton sat beaming by his opening partner Fordham, the man of the match. Felton had won the award in the semi-final at Edgbaston and talked happily of the success of his opening partner and pal.

Steve Coverdale, the chief executive, was refusing to let the Trophy out of his sight for a second. 'This bloody thing's not going to go missing tonight,' he said firmly. Procter stopped for a quiet word for everyone; Curtly Ambrose, all six foot plenty of him, wandered round beaming; Kevin Curran was chattering to everyone in sight. Lamb was also chattering to people in sight and out of it, on and off his mobile phone, looking out the window for his mates. 'If you see Sarfraz,' he said, 'tell him to come up for a drink.' Paul Taylor, whose arrival as Ambrose's opening partner had been so vital to the victory, just sat there drinking in the atmosphere as well as the champagne, as were several of the County's gifted crop of second-team players.

Taylor had never even played at Lord's before and had been obliged to ask another left-arm seamer, Mark Ilott of Essex, which end he ought to bowl from. Two days later, Taylor was to be named in the England touring party for India; two years earlier he had been playing Minor Counties cricket. Fordham, the hero of the hour, was to be omitted in favour of palpably less gifted cricketers even from the England A team. These are the breaks of the game. But at this moment cricket was simply a team sport and Northamptonshire were relishing their success as a team. 'The gods,' as one observer put it, 'had at last blown a few puffs of wind their way.'

Cricketers, however, are notoriously bad on history. Hardly anyone in that room can have been aware of how much the Trophy meant, not just to them but to the Club, all its members and everyone with an affection for it. They probably only dimly knew about the years when Northamptonshire strove unsuccessfully to win a game, any game, never mind one that proved their superiority over every other team in the country. They really cannot have been aware of the struggles of their predecessors: of the greatness, and disgrace, of V.W.C. Jupp; of the triumphs and terribly similar traumas of Bakewell and Milburn; of George Thompson and Billy East; of Tyson and Tribe; of Tubby and Nobby; of how, against all odds and even against reason, the club had survived; of how this happy moment was the product of everything that had gone before . . .

IN THE DAYS OF ABRAHAM

'Antiquitas saeculi juventus mundi.'
Ancient times were the youth of the world.

Francis Bacon

MOST CRICKETING record books do not devote much space to Northamptonshire's achievements. They have the lowest score in first-class cricket, something which is likely to remain there forever unless some team is ever daft enough to be bowled out for 11. They have the highest lowest score against them; along with Glamorgan, the County have never bowled anyone out for less than 33.

Until 1990, when the batsmen went mad, the County also had the lowest highest score, never having made more than 557. Northamptonshire have come bottom of the Championship 11 times – more than anyone else – and, along with Somerset, Sussex and, of course, the newcomers Durham, are alone in never having won it. As each season passes, close followers of the County hope that, even if this one is not going to be Northamptonshire's year, at least that their partners in failure will not desert them by winning.

One achievement stands out alone. For some years, *Wisden* has recorded that the Northamptonshire County Cricket Club has existed since 1820, making it, by more than two decades, the senior county. That, at least, is something of which North-amptonshire folk can be proud whenever they apologetically state their origin to aggressive Yorkies or snotty Surrey men. Or it would be, if it were true.

The present cricket club has existed since 1878. Before that, the history of the game in the county depends on fragmentary references in the local press. In one respect, Northamptonshire is better served than most. The *Northampton Mercury* does have a genuine claim to be the oldest continuously published newspaper in Britain, having not missed a week since 1720. Its successor, the *Mercury and Herald*, keeps that record going, rather ingloriously, as a free sheet primarily devoted to estate agents' adverts. But in the 18th century it was a substantial newspaper.

Unfortunately, its 'Sporting Intelligence' columns were more concerned with racing information than cricket. And when cricket did make the paper, 18th-century journalists were more interested in the trimmings than the score. The earliest known reference is in 1741 when teams raised by the Duke of Bedford and the Earl of Halifax contested two games – one at Woburn Abbey, the other on Cow Meadow, Northampton (now known as Becket's Park) – for 'considerable sums'. All we know of the cricket is that Halifax's team won both games. But the *Mercury* noted that there was 'a splendid appearance of Noblemen, Gentlemen and Ladies to see the diversion' at the Northampton match, and all concerned adjourned afterwards for 'an elegant entertainment' at The George, a town centre coaching inn which was to play a far more important role in cricket history many years later.

The following week the Gentlemen of Northamptonshire played those of Buckinghamshire for 20 guineas a side. Wickets were pitched at 10 o'clock and this time refreshments were at the Fleece Inn in Bridge Street but the result remains a mystery. The *Mercury* went back to telling its readers about a robbery in Hackleton 'by a single highwayman mounted on a grey gelding', 'A Melancholy Accident at Wellingborough', King Frederick of Sweden declaring war on the Czar of Russia and winners at the Chipping Norton Races.

Cricket had a good deal in common with racing in the 18th century: it was a betting game. Twenty guineas would have seemed a huge sum to later Northamptonshire players, right up until the mid-20th century. And Northampton Racecourse became, at an early stage, the traditional home of local cricket, a role it still performs, having outlasted the horses by almost a century. But the cricket was a far more private affair and mentions in the newspapers were occasional and tantalising. A Northampton club must have existed in 1775 when its members were reported to have played 'East and West Haddon and Guilsborough' for a £5 silver cup ('the Laws of the game to be strictly observed in playing'); and the following year Northampton met 'The County'. Both games were at Gayton, a village which has remained enthusiastic about cricket to this day. The Laws were those drawn up the previous year at the Star and Garter, Pall Mall, and 1775 is believed to be the year when the third stump came in. At stake on the second occasion were 'eleven hats . . . and a hat each for the umpire and scorer'. From these Town v County games Northamptonshire County Cricket Club appears to have evolved. But it evolved slowly and it is misleading to try and put a date on its foundation other than 1878.

There is evidence that cricket existed in at least a dozen Northamptonshire villages before 1835. What happened in 1820 was that a new Northampton club was founded with around 50 members and a fixture list which rapidly expanded from its initial six games. There were also plenty of contests within the club: Married v Single as early as 1826, an intriguing 'Morning' versus 'Evening' club challenge and, later, Lightweights against Heavy-weights (11 stone being the dividing line). The Heavyweights usually won. By the 1840s the games between 'Town' and 'County' members of the club attracted large crowds to the Racecourse including, the *Mercury* reported in 1849, 'a fair sprinkling of the fairer sex.' On that occasion the paper did report the results: two games were played and the Town won both easily.

In September 1832 a Northampton side went to the village of Sulby for a match against the club founded by the local squire George Payne, an energetic and generous – indeed spendthrift – sportsman in the great tradition of pre-Victorian English eccentrics, who became Master of the Pytchley Hounds three years later. In the post-match dinner at the Swan in Market Harborough he put forward a plan to join forces with Sir Robert Gunning, another local patron, to 'make a ground at Northampton and establish a county club in proper form by next season.' But if the scheme came to anything, the outcome was never recorded. What existed at this stage cannot fairly be called a county cricket club.

The other date offered in the past for the founding of a county club – 'about 1843' – has even less merit than 1820. Perhaps there was confusion because of the references to 'County', as opposed to 'Town'. Also, for matches involving teams outside the area the labels Northampton and Northamptonshire appear to have been switched around casually. What did happen in 1843 was that the Northampton club had fixtures on the Racecourse against Peterborough, Watford and a combined team from Wellingborough and Irthlingborough.

The following year brought the first 'Great Match' to be staged in Northampton between the North and South of England. Alfred Mynn ('The Lion of Kent') and Bartholomew Good ('The Hero of Melton Mowbray') switched sides to play for the North and won the match by 44 runs on a sporting Racecourse pitch. Many deliveries jumped over the batsmen's heads. Modern Town League cricketers will murmur that in one respect at least nothing on the Racecourse has changed.

There were a good many byes and Mynn took 12 wickets. Press reports speak of 'several thousand spectators of all classes' turning up to watch, some of them perhaps catching a glimpse inside the luncheon marquee where the Honourable Captain Spencer – later the 4th Earl – presided over a meal for 100 guests as well as the players, including the only Northamptonshire representative, Henry Osmond Nethercote.

These games became a great deal easier after that because Northampton joined the railway network. The opening of Bridge Street Station in 1845 put the town on the circuit frequented by William Clarke's All-England XI, and such imitators as United All-England. These would take on 15, 18 or 22 locals, maybe loaning them a star player or two. The nearest late 20th century equivalents are the visits to working men's clubs of the leading snooker players, who will happily give the local champions a start, usually win, sometimes lose, do a few trick shots and pocket a fee.

These games stimulated interest in the county and as well as the doings of the Town club, such contests as Daventry v Long Buckby, Towcester v Brackley and Oundle v Peterborough began to be regularly reported. There were county fixtures but there is no evidence of any organisation and it seems that from about 1850 onwards Northamptonshire was simply used colloquially for the Northampton Town club. The county's 22s were selected by the vicar of Tattenhoe, over the border in Buckinghamshire, the Rev John Randolph, and there were always plenty of clergymen in the teams.

But the big games also provided an opportunity for local players to make their name and maybe turn professional themselves. Three would have done credit to the county if its cricket had been more organised at the time. As it was, they had to rove around to make a living and none of them made enough to secure their old age. The first to come to prominence was Jacob 'Jake' Abraham (1833–1914) who came from a cricketing family – three brothers also played – and began with the Albion and Kingsthorpe clubs. He first appeared for the Town club in 1856 and thereafter he coached at Exeter College, Oxford for 12 years and was also engaged as a pro by various clubs in the West Country.

Abraham was mainly a bowler. He was also a sprinter. Once he had to retreat from a match at Naseby when he dismissed the local side for next to nothing and his disgruntled opponents threatened to throw him in the reservoir. He became an umpire before returning to Northampton to work in a shoe factory. He died leaving his fourth wife who was herself being widowed for the fourth time.

One of Abraham's comparatively rare batting successes came in August 1856 when, playing at Newport Pagnell, he went in first and hit 47. In that same match his exact contemporary Tom

Plumb (1833–1905) impressed everyone with an innings of 110 to demonstrate that he was a skilful batsman, as well as one of the best wicket-keepers of the age. His father was captain of the Northampton Tradesmen team and evidently a man of some resourcefulness; a notice in *Bell's Life* in 1841 advertised that Tom, '8 years of age, was ready to play cricket with any boy in the county of his age for from £1 to £5 a side'. The advert was presumably aimed at equally proud parents rather than other eight-year-olds.

Plumb made the All England side in 1860 and appeared in many of the major games over the next few years, including Players v Gentlemen and North v South. As a keeper he was rated alongside the other two great Ps, Ted Pooley and George Pinder, and W.G. Grace described him as 'about the best wicketkeeper of his time against fast bowling'. Plumb eventually returned to Northampton and became landlord of, in turn, the Racehorse Inn in Abington Street and then the Halfway House in Kingsthorpe, where he set up a cricket ground at the back. He brought a strong United Yorkshire XI to play there in 1875, but the weather was poor and the attendance negligible.

He earned himself more money another time by beating 11 other publicans single-handed, and he played for North-amptonshire until he was 51. After that, he fell on hard times, and in 1891 was forced to enter the workhouse. Some of his former colleagues rallied round; the County Club employed him for a time as a gatekeeper and general help, and a benefit match for him in 1892 attracted a good crowd to watch Tom Emmett, Arthur Shrewsbury and Arthur Mold as well as representatives from the Northamptonshire team. But he went back into the workhouse in 1901 and died there.

Another early professional to end his days obscurely was Joe Potter (1839–1906), a Northampton lad who learned his cricket on Cow Meadow. He was a steady medium-paced bowler (and a bit of a boxer on the side) who travelled widely, became a professional with the Royal Engineers at Chatham and played twice for Kent in 1871 before spending seven years with Surrey. He came back to help out Northamptonshire on a regular basis from 1882 to 1888, getting through a lot of overs. Even then his bowling was described as 'still very puzzling' and he was very effective well into his forties. However, he was regarded as difficult, which in the case of Victorian cricket professionals usually meant they wanted paying. He hoped to be the ground manager at the County Ground when he retired but the committee said they could not afford him, or give him a benefit match.

Two years later, in 1890, they did give him a job as a net bowler and coach. Soon Potter was demanding £10 in wages arrears, and threatening legal action. He eventually received a compromise payment of £7 10s, went off to coach at Marlborough School, played for Wiltshire and umpired. He subsequently became landlord, appropriately enough, of The Cricketers Arms in Northampton and lost money in the foundry business.

There were plenty of amateurs too: Canon William 'Deerfoot' Bury, Rector of Harlestone and a marvellous fielder; H. E. Bull, Oxford Blue and first-rate longstop; C. E. – later Sir Courtenay – Boyle, 'a pretty bat' who became Permanent Secretary of the Board of Trade, where prettiness was considered less important; and best of all the Rev Hugh Gillett – hard-hitting bat, medium-paced round-arm bowler, excellent cover point or long-on and, on top of all that, curate of Finedon. But there was still no regular county cricket for them. Gillett's greatest performances, in the 1860s, came for either North Northamptonshire, the Gentlemen of Northamptonshire – or Leicestershire.

Much of the cricket in this era was nothing like the drab game of 20th century professionals. In 1867 the touring club I Zingari came to Althorp House and twice bowled out 18 of Northamptonshire for 77. There was also a *tableau vivant et parlant* of The Seven Ages of Man and the commedietta 'Dearest Mamma'. 'The days . . . were devoted to cricket and the nights to dance, drama, prestidigitation . . . The ball after the theatricals on Friday was not brought to a conclusion until half-past four.' This may explain Northamptonshire's subsequent batting.

In 1870, the hoi-polloi who would not have been invited to the ball or the prestidigitation had their biggest cricketing day so far. The United North of England arrived, complete with W. G. Grace, to take on 22 of Northampton on the Racecourse. The weather was fine, ensuring good business for Mr Higgins in the refreshment tent, and 5,000 gallons of water were used to prepare a green oasis in the centre of an otherwise parched ground. The 22 were no match for the 'oiled thunderers . . . like greased lightning' of George Freeman who took 15 for 127 – in the second innings, not the match as a whole. Grace was bowled off his pads for nine and then caught for one, but he gave the crowd what they wanted during a special contest between himself, Freeman and three others on one side, and eleven Northamptonians on the other: he scored 63 in an hour.

W.G. returned to the Racecourse in 1873, this time with the United South of England team, and the local opposition was cut from 22 to a mere 18. Northampton imported several players from the surrounding districts. With outside help, the locals won magnificently – by 15 wickets, although W.G. scored 45 in the visiting team's first innings and his brother Fred scored an unbeaten 44 out of 86 in the second. Like Bradman after him, W.G. did nothing special on the field in Northampton; unlike Bradman he produced a spectacular display off it.

The incident was hushed up at the time. The *Northampton Herald*, perhaps putting the reputation of the town above a good story, merely said that WG had some business to attend to in connection with the forthcoming tour of Australia and that play resumed late after a long lunch interval. It made an apparently unconnected reference to injuries inflicted on spectators by players practising. Forty-eight years later, a reader sent his recollection of what happened to *The Northampton Independent*:

> W.G. was delaying the game after luncheon by having a few shots at a shooting gallery which stood outside the ground when a very officious and well-known builder of the town reprimanded W.G. and said: 'Why don't you go and play cricket, keeping the crowd waiting like you are doing'.
>
> Other words followed, and the builder struck W.G. on the cheek, cutting it with his ring. Grace did not retaliate then, but his brother Fred, who was also playing, noticing the blood, asked 'Who has done that, Gilbert?' 'Oh, that cad over there against the entrance.' Said Fred: 'If you don't go and give him a good hiding, I shall.' Thereupon W.G. strode across and punished the builder with sledge-hammer blows, and the claret in his eyes darkened, and closed up in no time.
>
> W.G. then led his men into the field as though nothing had happened . . . Grace was applauded for his play without a bat, and the builder received no sympathy. People said: 'Serve him right for interfering.'

In 1990, Vivian Richards received slightly more publicity for being absent threatening to thump a journalist instead of leading his team on to the field in a Test match.

There is no trace of W.G. ever playing in Northampton again. However, he did appear in Wellingborough the following year in a benefit game and frequently returned to Oundle later when his son was an assistant master at the public school.

In 1873 there were also less dramatic but more important moves on the road towards a proper county club. In a preview of the season, the *Mercury* said that 'the question of obtaining a private ground should be immediately considered in earnest. United and properly organised, there is sufficient cricketing power in the county for it to take a much higher position than it at present occupies'. All Northamptonshire needed to make it 'a great cricketing county' was better organisation. That same year, nine greater counties competed in what is traditionally regarded as the first year of the County Championship. No one appears to have suggested that Northamptonshire might join them.

However, the County did get their first-ever match against the MCC. They were beaten by four wickets, despite some good bowling from John Furley, an amateur from Oakham. And the Club made its first really shrewd appointment. An energetic young man called Fred Tebbutt, only 21, was appointed honorary secretary. This history, as much as anything, is the story of a handful of men whose vitality, foresight and devotion enabled this improbable part of the country to become 'a great cricketing county'. Tebbutt was the first.

In 1877 MCC came to the Racecourse and lost by 100 runs. In April 1878 the *Northampton Herald* noted: 'The Northampton County Cricket Club would appear to be throwing off some of the lethargy and endeavouring to make the season of 1878 the start of a new era in its existence, and one more worthy of its name than its course of late years has been. A capital programme of matches has been arranged . . .' That programme included the first-ever match against Leicestershire, who bowled the county out for 24 and 52, beginning the irritation that has afflicted both sides in these matches for more than a century.

The catalyst, though, was a match in Kettering on 3 and 4 July between the Gentlemen of the north of the county and the south. In a closely-fought game the South, captained by the Hon Frederick Henley, edged out the Hon and Rev John Marsham's North team by 20 runs.

Exactly when and where it happened remains confused: one paper said it was 'during a break for refreshments', another said it was after dinner at the George Hotel. But sometime during the game Marsham chaired a meeting called to discuss the reorganisation of the county cricket club. A few years earlier, the gentry had been criticised for not taking enough interest in the Northampton club, which as part of the town may have been thought a little lowly; now the county set were taking the lead.

It was agreed that Northamptonshire had to start choosing properly representative sides, like other counties, and that a private ground was a necessity. Sir Herewald Wake estimated that it would cost £500 to establish one in Northampton. On 31 July the two sides, North and South, began a return match on the Racecourse. Most of the first day was dominated by an innings of

128 by Jim Kingston, a surname that will recur again and again. That night the players went on to The George.

The first, official history of Northamptonshire, meticulously compiled by Jim Coldham, says this was The George in Kettering again. But it hardly seems likely that the players would have gone 14 miles from Northampton Racecourse to Kettering in those horse-drawn and railway days. In any case, the *Herald* reported the meeting in its 'Northampton News' column and referred to the George Hotel without mentioning Kettering. So it seems almost certain that it took place at the hotel where the players of 1741 had gone for their 'elegant entertainment', The George, Northampton.

John Turner, an accomplished batsman who had top-scored for Northamptonshire in their first match at Lord's five years earlier, was voted in as chairman. He said that if support came from outside the borough, Northamptonshire could become a first-class county. This was the right thing to say. It is, however, doubtful that anyone could really have believed him: the handful of counties who began the Championship were all much larger with more vigorous cricketing traditions than this one could ever have. But, amid general enthusiasm, the Hon and Rev Mr Marsham made the momentous proposal that the county club be reorganised or, more accurately, organised. Tebbutt, who had been largely responsible for getting the whole process moving, seconded. There were no dissenters.

Fourteen gents were elected to serve on the first committee, with Earl Spencer as figurehead president, plus Tebbutt as secretary and Thomas Auckland as treasurer. Northampton had seven representatives, Wellingborough three, Kettering and Stamford (presumably covering Peterborough as Stamford was technically in Lincolnshire) two each, plus Frederick Henley to speak for the Daventry area and the headmaster of Oundle School, Rev H. St J. Reade, who had captained Oxford University in 1861.

The presence of the Earl Spencer was important. The Spencers of Althorp have always been a prominent family, down to the present Earl whose sister, Diana, is quite well-known. The 3rd Earl had a punch-up with Byron at Harrow, was important in the passage of the Reform Bill and used to enjoy watching cricket. The 4th Earl, his brother, laid out the ground at Althorp and underwrote several local games. The 1878 Earl was his son, the Red Earl, who had a sumptuous red beard. He became Lord Lieutenant of Ireland and was talked about as a possible Prime Minister. He was also Master of the Pytchley Hunt and, in 1861, President of MCC. 'Nobody should be allowed to escape,' said

Marsham, as he rounded up local gentlemen, and the sight of Spencer's red beard must have cowed any potential escapees.

Next day, the Gentlemen returned to the Racecourse to conclude the North v South match. The North were dismissed for 89 and 83 and went down by an innings and 114 runs. Their minds might have been diverted by the momentousness of their decisions; on the other hand, it was probably a heavy night in The George. The new committee met for the first time on 9 September and began to plan.

The first two years of the Northamptonshire County Cricket Club set a pattern that would become familiar again. They failed to win a game in either 1879 or 1880. In 1879 Sir Herewald Wake made his only appearance for the County and was out for 0 and 1 in an innings defeat against Leicestershire. In sterner times, his most famous ancestor, Hereward the Wake, led the last Saxon resistance against William the Conqueror. Sir Herewald, after one famous victory at Eton over a bully who had thrown a cherry stone at him, devoted most of his life to nature study. He can be forgiven his bad batting; he was a staunch supporter of Northamptonshire cricket.

There was still a hint of shambles. In June 1880, Northampton staged two matches on the same day. While the County team played Hertfordshire on the Racecourse, 18 of Northampton – captained by Tom Plumb and bolstered by Fred Grace, Tom Emmett and Harry Jupp – took on Billy Murdoch's touring Australians two miles away at St James's End. The Australians had advertised for fixtures and 3,000 watched The Demon Spofforth take 17 for 177 in the match to give them an eight-wicket victory. Potter did manage to bowl Murdoch for nought.

It is unclear whether the traditional two humans and one canine were left to watch the official county match. The crowd can hardly have been much greater because the town had other preoccupations as well. That same evening, a 'mass indignation meeting' was held on the Market Square to protest at the expulsion of the local Radical MP, Charles Bradlaugh, from the House of Commons after he had refused, as an atheist, to swear the oath. Bradlaugh's statue now stands in the centre of the town he fought to represent; posterity has treated Potter less grandly.

Twelve months later, two new professional bowlers, Tom Alley and Tom Bowley, were responsible for beating Hertfordshire and giving Northamptonshire their first victory. Alley took 11 wickets in the game and Bowley 10 (the visitors batted 12 men). Alley, born in London in 1857, was another in the rough diamond tradition who bowled fast and drank hard. He was suspended by the Club in 1886 after a late-night rumpus on the new County Ground when he demanded drink from the groundsman, and he was subsequently reported for using 'bad and obscene language' during an athletics meeting. Bowley, born in Nottinghamshire, was a quieter sort who went on to achieve great things with Surrey before taking up a coaching job at Sherborne School and going into the sports outfitters business. He was always welcome at the County Ground and returned in 1905 to watch one of the earliest Championship matches.

Throughout the 1880s and 1890s, there were a number of happy coincidences which enabled the County to reach the point where they would be able to keep players like Bowley. For a start, two schools began to play an important role. The first was Wellingborough, which had only 17 pupils in 1879. Then – like so many of the great public schools – it acquired a muscular Christian head who set about reviving it.

Wellingborough's 'Dr Arnold', Dr H. E. Platt, was known as The Boss and had a particular loathing for motor cars and cigarettes. Cricket he loved and he liked to have cricket men on his staff too. He moved the school to a new 40-acre site outside the town with plenty of space for playing fields and by 1884 the ground was fit enough for Platt to invite the County to play two matches there. Philip Fryer, who was the head for 25 years from 1908, was another enthusiast. Thirty-odd old boys have repres- ented the County in the years since then from Arthur Henfrey, who also played soccer for England, to Jack Timms – five of them as captain. Several more played for other counties, including Dickie Dodds of Essex and Martin Young of Gloucestershire.

The other important school of the era was Abington House, situated in Abington Street right in the centre of Northampton – founder and principal, William Kingston, whose family name was to reverberate through the early years of the cricket club. The Kingstons were the county's sporting dynasty to rank with the Fosters of Worcestershire. They hardly even needed a school to back them up. William Kingston had 12 children, nine of them sons, eight of whom played cricket for the County and most of whom played rugby for the Saints as well. The family picture, taken in 1900, could serve as a motif of the times. They they are, frock-coated and watch-chained; only Billy, the most important as far as this tale is concerned, is even giving the ghost of a smile. There can hardly have been a family in the country which fitted the Victorian ideal quite so neatly. Northampton could safely have changed its name to Kingston-upon-Nene and it makes this story easier to list them all:

1 F.W. (Fred), 1855–1933. Cambridge blue in one of the strongest years ever, 1878; parson, headmaster of Guilsborough Grammar and author. Batsman, wicket-keeper, occasional County captain. He based his keeping style on Plumb's which, it was said, meant 'continually knocking the knees together and pulling on the gloves just as the bowler delivered the ball'.

2 J.P. (Jim), 1857–1929. Solicitor. Batsman, leg-spinner, excellent fielder (reputedly as good a point as E. M. Grace). He was the first captain of the newly organised County team in 1878 and stayed in the job until 1887, before taking over again in 1891 when he became the Club's first paid secretary. Played one first-class match – for Warwickshire in 1894. The sporting papers printed his verses; he wrote Jubilee Odes to both Queen Victoria and W.G. He spent his last 25 years in Italy where he taught English to, among others, the officers on the Royal Yacht.

3 H.J. (Harry), 1862–1944. Brewer. He made 168 against Rutland in 1884, the second century for the County (after another Abington House boy, G. J. Gulliver, had scored the first against MCC)

4 G.H. (Bert), 1864–1959. Parson. Fast bowler and wicket-keeper. Rugby and soccer player and, some said, the best all-round sportsman in the family. His greatest cricketing achievement came as a nine-year-old when he clean bowled W.G. on his 1873 visit on a wicket chalked on the wall of the school playground. He earned himself a shilling. He also claimed to be the first man to use studs in his football boots instead of leather bars.

5 C.A. (Charles), 1865–1917. Schoolmaster. Made a century against the Stoics but was never a regular County player. He did play first-class cricket for British Guiana. Wounded in the Boer War, he lost his memory and was missing for some years.

6 W.P. (Walter), 1867–1937. Another parson and batsman; again not a regular but a top-class rugger player.

7 F.C. (Frank), 1872–1931. The one who never played; we trust the others spoke to him. He was a regular rugby player for the Saints and became a professor of linguistics, eventually following Jim to Italy.

8 W.H. (Billy), 1874–1956. Sports outfitter.

9 H.E. ('Tim'), 1876–1955. Lawyer.

Of both Billy and Tim, there will be much more later.

The Kingston family. The men shown are: Back row, left to right: Charles, Walter, Bert, Billy and Tim. Seated, left to right: Harold, Fred and Jim. On ground – Frank. Of the nine brothers, only Frank did not play for Northamptonshire.

It was said the only time father William prevented them from playing cricket was when some of the boys improvised a game upstairs at Abington House with a hairbrush for a bat and a pair of rolled up socks, to the consternation of those below. This being a modern book, one should mention the sisters M.E., J.K. and A.E. But this was a Victorian family and, one presumes, they knew their place. Their first names are not now known.

Among the other pupils of Abington House School were the brothers Pigg, Herbert and Charles (known as Hot and Cold) who lined up with three Kingstons, Fred, Jim and Harry, against the 1882 Australians on the Racecourse, along with the great Nottinghamshire bowler Alfred Shaw, engaged at a cost of £10 to try and justify the County taking on the tourists on level terms. In the event, Shaw managed just one wicket in 57 four-ball overs and Northamptonshire lost comfortably. Nevertheless, even after paying Shaw and a five-guinea fee to the Freeman of the Borough for the privilege of enclosing the ground, the club made a profit of over £97.

It had been a triumph for the club organisation – sellers of fruit, refreshments and photographs all paid to trade inside the enclosure; the official helpers were issued with distinguishing ribbons to pick them out from the crowd, and a teenager by the name of Albert Joseph Darnell – known from his schooldays as 'Pat' (either after a habit of patting the crease every time he took strike or because he had enough blarney to be Irish) – offered to score for the first day of the match. He would make a marked contribution to Northamptonshire cricket, and to the life of the county town in general, for the next 70 years.

Facilities for the press were forgotten in the excitement, not for the last time.

Progress on the field in the early 1880s was most encouraging, with victories over rival counties and leading club sides becoming commonplace. Between 1881 and 1885, the Club played 35 games, won 18 and lost only eight. Potter, Alley and Bowley shared the bulk of the wickets while the Kingstons kept the runs flowing. The problem now become not whether and how to play but where. There had been disputes with the Freemen of the Borough over the use of the Racecourse for a number of years. In 1876 the secretary of a club side had a summons issued against him alleging four shillings worth of damage to the grass. Local sportsmen were incensed and the case was dropped, but the relationship between County Club and Freemen remained uneasy.

The man on the front line was Alf Stockwin, the groundsman, who had the wretched job of preparing and maintaining pitches on an expanse of grass where the public were free to roam. Stockwin, born in Sheffield, had come to the town as a boy and had been taken on as a ground bowler in 1871. By the time he died, he had completed half a century with the Club in one capacity or other. He was a painstaking groundsman and, in his youth, a successful medium-pace bowler and a man of considerable spirit. In 1879 the Mayor ruled that the ground could not be legally enclosed and at the MCC match that year many people decided to take him at his word and climbed in. But when the numbers were not overwhelming, Stockwin could cope with the situation. Once he was lovingly preparing a wicket when a brewer's dray came straight across it; words followed which ended with Stockwin pulling the driver off his seat and dealing with him the way W.G. dealt with the builder. He told the committee he enjoyed the contest but thought that if this were going to happen regularly, he might want a pay rise.

Meetings of local cricketers and footballers were held to discuss the Racecourse problem and delegations were sent to the Town Council. But the only solution was the one mooted back in 1832 – a private ground. Subsequent history of the County Ground shows that nothing happens unless it has to: witness the continued presence of the football club. But by 1883 something had to be done. After reading the 'cheeriest and rosiest' annual report yet, Tebbutt told the AGM that there was a real possibility of the Club being banned from the Racecourse, despite the money that had been invested in improvements over the years, and by the following summer the search was on for an alternative.

Three sites were considered, all within a mile of one another. One was at Phippsville off the Kettering Road; another was at Gipsy Lane, now Kingsley Road. But on 7 November 1884 a general meeting of members, chaired by Sir Herewald Wake, opted for a 10-acre ploughed field between Abington Lane and Wellingborough Road. It was the property of Sir Robert Loyd Lindsay and was being offered on a 21-year lease for £200 an acre. The money was advanced by Wake and Joseph Hill, the squire of Wollaston. The Northampton County Cricket and Recreation Grounds Company was set up in 1885, aiming to raise £5,000 capital by the sale of 1,000 £5 shares. It would have been considered very fashionable in the 1990s: this was to be what would now be called a multi-sports facility; apart from cricket, there were plans for tennis, bowls, athletics and cycling. There was no mention of football in the original prospectus.

The honour of buying share No 1 fell to Valentine Cary-Elwes of Billing; Wake, Hill and Earl Spencer bought 40 shares each. The former Surrey cricketer, H.H. Stephenson, visited in March 1885 to issue instructions for preparation and commented: 'This would make one of the finest Grounds in England'. The man who listened to Stephenson was one Alfred Cockerill, originally from Leicestershire, who had moved over the border to start up as a farmer, market gardener and greengrocer. Cockerill offered to do the work himself at cost price and accepted payment in shares.

By the end of 1885 James Ingman's plans for the pavilion had been approved. At the Club dinner that year in the Town Hall the Red Earl took the chair in his Knight of the Garter's insignia. Wake proposed the toast 'Success to the New County Ground' and Charles Thorpe sang a special cricket song, written especially for the occasion by Jim Kingston, to the tune of 'Bonnie Dundee'.

> The feast it is over, let wine cups be spread,
> Let mirth and enjoyment run riot instead,
> And ye who love pleasure that's manly and true,
> Raise your glasses to cricket – so fill up anew.

(chorus)
Then fill up your glasses, and drain them again,
And raise high your voices, and sing out like men;
That cricket long flourish, brave hearts to delight,
Is the wish and the toast of all present tonight.

Here's a toast to our County and new County Ground –
May patrons and players in plenty be found,
To pull well together and pull with a will,
And success in the future our hopes will fulfil.

There be clubs in the country more noted in name,
Whom we hope in the future to rival in fame;
Success, like a goddess, in laurel wreaths crown'd,
Has never on courage or energy frown'd.

In fields more important, and works more revered,
Gaunt Failure, the witch, has no cause to be feared,
If hope be man's pilot and wisdom his guide,
As he toils o'er the waves of life's perilous tide.

Stockwin was appointed groundsman, giving him the chance
to work without horses and carts clattering across the middle. He
was offered £1 a week, the use of rooms in Ingman's pavilion as
living quarters, and an assistant. Stockwin took over in March
1886, and within a month the Yorkshire bowler Tom Emmett
was supervising coaching on the ground, while 'several prominent wheelists' were invited to try out the cycle track. The local
press devoted much space to describing the new amenity; the
pavilion was 'red brick, with a roof of blue slates ornamented
with a bell turret . . . and with a splendid well of water at the
rear', while the bowling green, enclosed with holly bushes, lime
trees and poplars was . . . 'a cosy little spot'. 'Without a doubt the
Ground will bear favourable comparison with any in the country,' said *The Sportsman*.

The County Ground has never had such a kindly press since,
but at that time the surroundings as well as the ground itself
would have been pretty rustic. It was to be another four years
before Manfield's shoe factory was built nearby, and with it the
huddle of terraced artisans' houses. St Matthew's Church – on
one of the sites the committee considered – was not there yet and
the County Hotel was not added – at a cost of £1,680 – until 1894.
And there were definitely no ugly football terraces.

T. H. Vials, the solicitor who had replaced Tebbutt as secretary
in 1883, had wanted the Australians for the ground's christening,
but he had to make do with Surrey Club and Ground. A two-day

match was scheduled for Friday and Saturday, 14 and 15 May, and arrangements were made to accommodate spectators and their carriages – members' vehicles would be admitted free with 6d charged for any occupant who was not a member. Other carriages would be admitted at 2s 6d with four occupants, and ex-Colour Sergeant Newling was put in charge of the gate. Mr Roddis of the Black Lion Inn was given the catering rights for the season, and the great day was eagerly anticipated. It rained, solidly.

Play eventually began on the Saturday; it was a bitterly cold morning as Jim Kingston won the toss, and sent brother Fred in to open the innings along with Thomas Beale, later a prominent and very peppery committeeman. Edward Barratt, Surrey's slow left-armer, began with a maiden to Kingston, and Beale played out a maiden from Shacklock. It was the third over of the game before Kingston cut Barratt for the first run on the County Ground. Northamptonshire were all out for 107 just after lunch with 40 from Bert Kingston. The County dropped six catches. Just another Saturday.

Cheaper admission after lunch, and the factory workers' half-day pushed the attendance to around 1,200 by the end of the drawn match, by when Surrey were 114 for four with Monty Bowden (later to captain England in South Africa and die in the Rhodesian bush) scoring a half-century. Bowden had seconded the lunchtime toast to the new ground proposed by Mr Kingston sen.

Marsham's remark about nobody being allowed to escape had unfortunately proved easier to say than achieve. Although membership increased from 230 at the opening of the ground to around 350 by the start of the following season, it was hardly enough. There had long been forces within the Club anxious to reduce the number of professionals, a view that gained support when they behaved like Alley or Joseph Madden, a bowler from Bailiff Street, who also caused 'a considerable disturbance' after Stockwin refused him a drink one Sunday night.

Fred Kingston became the first of umpteen Northamptonshire committee men down the years to suggest retrenchment, proposing that no county matches should be played in 1890 to save money, but that a 'good programme of amateur games' be arranged instead. This drastic step was resisted, and the Club began to attract, principally through the influence of Sir Herewald, some illustrious local figures as vice-presidents. On the playing side, the Club unearthed a rare talent in 1887 when a strong, raw 22-year-old man from the village of Middleton Cheney, on the border with Oxfordshire, arrived at the ground with his kit in a curious black bag, made his first appearance against Staffordshire and took seven for 22 – including a hat-trick – in the first innings.

This was Arthur Mold, who then proceeded to terrify several members when he was fulfilling his duties as net bowler: a Mr Holyoak had two fingers smashed. Mold was soon making a big impression against far more formidable opposition. He took five for 64 against Lancashire at Old Trafford, eight for 25 against Warwickshire a fortnight later and eight for 61 against MCC at Lord's two weeks after that. By the time Lancashire came down for a return game, he was qualifying for them by residence. He was still allowed to play for his native county and took four more first innings wickets, including 'Monkey' Hornby for one and Johnny Briggs for a duck.

Northamptonshire saw nothing of him from 1889 – when he made his Lancashire debut – until 1903 by which time his first-class career, which had included three Tests against Australia in 1893, had finished amidst a storm of controversy surrounding the fairness of his bowling action. Shearing away all old-fashioned delicacy on the subject, he was a chucker. He went back to club cricket and in 1910 – at the age of 45 – took eight wickets without conceding a run for Middleton Cheney against Culworth, including five in five balls.

By the early 1890s, the County Ground must have been a lively enough place with bowls, athletics, archery, bicycle and tricycle racing – the wheelists – and rugby. Lady cricketers were barred by unanimous vote; you can go too far, after all. Mr Gaudern, who replaced Jim Kingston as hon sec, became the first landlord of the County Hotel. Northampton Town Football Club arrived in 1897 after Pat Darnell went to Leicester for a rugby match, watched Leicester Fosse play Notts County as well and conceived the idea of a senior team in the town playing the Association code. Very quickly, the ploughed field had become the centre of Northampton's sporting life.

The problem was that the cricket team were not especially good, certainly not after Mold's departure. There were fixtures against the major counties and there were useful cricketers, not all called Kingston, like the bowler Bill 'Pop' West and the former Oundle schoolboy, Robert Augustus Agincourt Beresford. But once Mold had gone, there was no one outstanding. There was certainly no sign of the Club fulfilling John Turner's prediction at the first meeting about joining the first-class counties. However, close observers of local cricket were already starting to notice two Northampton-born boys. Between them, they would change everything.

THE BOOKIE'S SON, BILLY AND THE BLACKBERRY MAN

'Our only hope lies in grass-roots heroes.'

Yoshida Shoin

GEORGE THOMPSON was born at 42 Louise Road, Northampton on 27 October 1877. The house still exists and a more caring town would have erected a plaque long ago. On his birth certificate, his father was described as a commercial clerk but other sources call him a commission agent, as it was politely termed, or in other words a bookmaker. This presumably accounts for Thompson's unusual social mobility – both as a child, from an ordinary terraced house to Wellingborough School – and as a cricketer, between amateur and professional. The English class system has never been able to sort out the ranking of bookmakers.

In 1884 the family moved to the village of Cogenhoe (then as now pronounced 'Coog-know'). Five years later Thompson's mother died, aged only 36, and a month later he became a boarder at Wellingborough. It was not a happy childhood. His father remarried a woman not much older than George; they did not take to each other. And Wellingborough, George later told his own son, George jun, was a rough school. He recalled The Boss, Dr Platt, as 'a bit of a tartar' and he was initiated early on by being forced to fight a bigger boy in the gym.

But he must have enjoyed the games. In 1893, as a 15-year-old, he was Wellingborough's best bowler and second-best batsman. He told his son later that he would go to any lengths, walk any distance and put up with any inconvenience for a game of cricket and in 1894, the year after he left school, he played for five different teams and did the hat-trick three times. Once he committed himself to playing for two teams simultaneously on the Racecourse; he somehow managed to flit between them.

He might have become a vet; he was apprenticed to one who went bankrupt. But by September 1894 the *Northampton Herald* was already commenting that 'his friends are probably justified in the opinion that he is the coming county bowler', and the following August he travelled down to Wolverton with the Northamptonshire team to play a two-day match against Buckinghamshire. Thompson bowled out the opposition for 93, finishing with nine for 35. The club decided to look after him. That December he was appointed assistant secretary at an annual salary of £75. Two years later he became one of the first public schoolboys to turn professional.

He could easily have gone elsewhere, like Mold, and qualified for one of the first-class counties. There were rumours of him going to Kent. He was courting at the time, walking from where he was living in Northampton back to Cogenhoe with his dog to see his childhood sweetheart Charlotte. Maybe she did not want to leave. One way or the other, their decision determined the destiny of Northamptonshire cricket. One of the clauses in his assistant secretary's contract committed him to 'do his utmost to advance the interest and promote the success of the said club'. Thompson kept his side of the bargain.

George Thompson – brilliant all-rounder and, in effect, the man who batted and bowled Northamptonshire into the County Championship. (John Watson Collection)

Even Thompson could not do it on his own. What transformed Northamptonshire cricket was the emergence of a whole generation of talented players who eventually became too good to be ignored. Northamptonshire did not even compete in the Minor Counties Championship in its first year, 1895. Ten years later they were admitted to the County Championship, not as a calculated piece of ambition (which is how Glamorgan were promoted in 1921 and Durham in 1992), but simply because the team had become too dominant not to be promoted.

The basis of the side was the bowling of Thompson and East. Thompson bowled above medium-pace from a short run with a high, windmilling action and seems to have relied for his success on movement and his command of length. Billy East was not as quick but he was devilishly accurate. He was born in Lower Grafton Street, five years before Thompson and about a quarter of a mile away. He did not have the advantage of public school. Before he died, a *Daily Echo* reporter asked him when he first started playing. 'Blessed if I can remember,' he replied. 'There always seems to have been a bat and ball mixed up in my life. We played on the open road first and I owe now for some of the windows I broke. At one time there was most exciting cricket for a ha'penny a man or we would play for a ball.' He began playing on the rougher Racecourse pitches but in 1892 was persuaded to step up a grade by joining the Star club, thus ensuring that his doings would be fully recorded in the detailed Town League press reports of the day.

Both Thompson and East also joined the MCC ground staff, which meant plenty of journeys to London but left them free to play cricket for the County. By the time Northamptonshire joined the Minor Counties Championship in 1896 there was a fair bit of quality round the side. They started with a victory over Durham at Northampton by an innings and 56. Thompson picked up nine wickets and the County scored 412, thanks to 157 from 20-year-old Charles Pool.

Pool, like Grace and Hobbs, has cricket ground gates named after him: the main gates between the County Ground car park and Wantage Road. Had Northamptonshire been making the decision on their own, they would have named them after Thompson. Pool's brother paid for them. Still, he is worth remembering. As a cricketer, he was never coached – except briefly by his mother and once by Wilfred Rhodes when he came to a Feast match at Rushden and showed him how to back up his defence with his legs. But Pool played with a natural grace that must have borne comparison with the other stylists of the era.

William East was Thompson's cricketing brother-in-arms for nearly 20 years and remained a popular figure at the County Ground right up to his death in 1926. (John Watson Collection)

And, in the old team pictures, he looks stylish too in his cravat and boater. 'He has a natural aptitude for the game,' enthused a profile in the *Independent*, 'for nature has equipped him with a wonderfully supple wrist, an easy elasticity of movement, with a quick eye . . . There is no more delightful sight to our cricket loving crowds here in Northampton than watching the slim athletic form of Mr C. J. T. Pool at the wickets, gathering runs as easy as blackberries.'

The Blackberry Man – elegant Charlie Pool, whose name is commemorated in the entrance gates to the County Ground. (John Watson Collection)

He played briefly for Little Lever in the Bolton League, alongside J. T. Tyldesley, and might have played further up there. Two gentlemen in silk hats came to see him to offer him the sinecure of the secretaryship of the Starr Bowkett Building

45

Society, plus a sovereign from club funds and a collection round the ground for every 50 he made. But he turned them down, went to Australia for three years, and was back to see the County into first-class cricket.

There was also a new captain in 1896, Tom Horton, and he was to remain in charge until 1906, the second year of first-class cricket. None of his successors have lasted as long but then none of them – with the possible exception of Freddie Brown – have been looked on with such uncritical awe. Horton did not miss a game from 1894 until June 1906 (though he had plenty of business to attend to) which differentiates him right from the start from the County's other amateur captains. The contemporary accounts always speak of his popularity and good nature. 'Mr Horton,' said the *Independent*, 'is the least assertive of men, save perhaps when he gets a loose ball.'

He came from Warwickshire, the ninth son of a landed family, and went to Repton where he was one of those breathtaking Victorian schoolboy sportsmen. He high-jumped 4ft 9in when he was 14, which was said to be a record for his age; he played soccer for a school team that would take on Derby County several times a season and never lost by more than one goal; he later gave up soccer and was at the heart of the scrum for Moseley and the Midland Counties. In his later life he was chairman of a brewery and volunteered to become a Birmingham tram driver in the First World War. And of course he played cricket.

Horton's school eleven also included the Palairet brothers and C. B. Fry, so he was slightly outshone. Once he dropped Fry in a crucial house match and lost the game. Fry was of course the ultimate late Victorian all-rounder and, unlike him, Horton was never offered the throne of Albania. On the other hand, he did become president of Northamptonshire after the First World War, at a time when the internal politics were so vituperative that it might have been the harder job of the two.

The Minor Counties were not recognised by MCC until 1901 – when they began to be called, with even less dignity, the Second-Class Counties – but it was the route by which Worcestershire became first-class, in 1899. And Northamptonshire played in the competition while at the same time improving their fixture list all-round. In 1896, they were still fielding 15 against Nottinghamshire; the openers, George Colson from Rushden and F. W. Briggs, alone put on 189 with 13 men to come. The next year the teams met at levels.

Between 1896 and 1904 Northamptonshire played 95 games in the Minor Counties, won 39 and lost seven, four of those in the first two years. In the last three years, they won 22 and lost one. Technically, Northamptonshire won the Championship only in 1903 and 1904, sharing it in 1899 and 1900. The Championship at this stage was based on a particularly ludicrous system of fewest defeats and, on any fair reckoning, Glamorgan would have been declared champions in the years it was shared. But it became clear over this period that gradually Northamptonshire were becoming far stronger than their opponents. This was particularly true in batting. Another Northampton boy, the left-hander Mark Cox, came into the side as a 16-year-old in 1897 and rose to open the innings. The Old Wellingburian Robert Knight played whenever he could. And there was Lancelot Townshend Driffield, a clergyman's son from the village of Old (to this day there is a haulage company called Knight's of Old) who had been an outstanding performer at St John's School in Leatherhead, where he later returned as a master, and went on to win his blue at Cambridge in 1902.

Driffield's finest hour was somewhat overshadowed by news from elsewhere. In 1900, Northamptonshire began the season at Lord's with a fixture against MCC, who included several players attached to first-class counties. After losing Horton and Billy Kingston early on, Driffield joined Thompson and the pair added 190 in just two and a quarter hours. Driffield scored 109, 103 of them before lunch; Thompson carried his bat for 186 and North-amptonshire were all out just before the close for 429.

Next day, MCC were dismissed twice – for 246 and 210 – with Thompson and East sharing 17 wickets. The County won by 10 wickets. Then as now, achievements at Lord's normally got noticed more than those elsewhere. But there were other matters on men's minds; the players may have made it back to North-ampton on the train in time to hear the Mayor announce from the balcony of the Guildhall that Mafeking had been relieved.

Later that season, the County scored 517 for eight against Durham at South Shields with Pool scoring 144. It was all very impressive but as one local paper said at the time 'finance has always been a weak point with the club'. It required two other men to make Northamptonshire a first-class county. John Powys, the 5th Baron Lilford (1863–1945), educated at Harrow and Brasenose, Oxford and a man who inherited 15,600 acres in Northamptonshire and the Scottish Highlands, is as much a local hero in this story as the street urchin Billy East. His cricket career was not very distinguished. Lord Lilford is in the 'Who's Who of Cricketers' because he was invited to play for the County, aged 48, against the Indians in 1911. He scored four but no doubt

47

John Powys, 5th Baron Lilford, in his masonic regalia. He was the club's financial saviour on countless occasions, and was president for 18 years. (Northamptonshire Libraries and Information Services)

everyone was very polite. He used to carry a cricket ball round with him just in case there was the chance of a little catching practice.

His hobbies included shooting, angling, freemasonry (Provincial Grand Master for 24 years), cattle breeding, maintaining the aviaries set up at the Hall by his father and presiding over the annual Peterborough Show. There is, throughout his life, a strain of personal tragedy. He lost his 12-year-old son after a routine adenoids operation in 1909. His wife died just after the outbreak of the Second World War. Lilford Hall was then requisitioned by the military and the contents had to be disposed of in a five-day sale, leaving just a suite of rooms for his own use. He died just before Northamptonshire's cricketers began to repay all his years of investment by starting to win.

Lord Lilford was president of almost everything in the county that an aristocrat could patronise, from the Conservative Association to the Saints rugby club. He became president of the County Cricket Club in 1903, immediately donated £100 and almost every year therafter there would be something, either cash or kind.

His right arm was Pat Darnell (1865–1955), a man we have glimpsed before both as the teenager who volunteered to score against the Australians in 1882 and the young rugby-playing lawyer who was sufficiently attracted by soccer to bring the game to the County Ground. By 1885, he was on the committee and in 1898 he became hon sec, succeeding Gaudern.

Darnell became to the borough what Lilford was in the county. In cricket, he was president of the Town League for the small matter of 63 years. He was president of the Southern League in soccer and the Law Society, a member of the MCC Advisory Council where he was not afraid to stand up to Lords Hawke and Harris, and Northampton Borough Coroner from 1911 to 1951; not only did he outlive his contemporaries, he investigated their deaths. The *Chronicle and Echo* reporter who was assigned to update his obituary in the early 1950s was told by the librarian that he was his fifth man to do the job and the other four were all dead. His letter of application for the post of coroner was said to have comprised one sentence; even in 1911 everyone knew Pat Darnell.

On the night Northamptonshire beat MCC and Mafeking was relieved, Darnell launched fireworks from the Working Men's Conservative Club in Whitworth Road, presumably by way of double celebration. A neighbour, assuming the club was in flames, called the fire brigade. More than half a century later Darnell could still be found in the same club, though by this time

A. J. 'Pat' Darnell, aged 87, presents Northampton Town League's Garnett Cup in 1952. A rare photograph of Darnell without his top hat. (Reg Partridge)

he usually confined himself to bridge or chess. He was president of it for 59 years.

By the 1950s, when he still walked around in his top hat and frock coat (he removed his top hat only for the FA Cup Final when he wore a cloth cap in consideration for the person behind him), he must have been the best-known figure in town by far. He was a tall, thin, angular man who smoked a pipe. Solicitors still practising in Northampton remember both his kindness in court ('You all right there, Sonny Jim? I'm right here if you need any help.') and his eccentricity in age. Once, after what may have been a long lunch, he was teetering a little on the edge of the kerb into the path of the onrushing cars and someone rushed to steady him. 'Thank you,' he said, 'but you needn't have worried. The horses all know me.' He then produced a couple of sugar lumps to prove his point.

Darnell never married and lived right in the centre of town, in Newland, in circumstances that were rumoured to be rather less grand than those of Lord Lilford. But the backstage history of the Cricket Club in the first half of the century might be characterised by Darnell making the journey up to Lilford Hall and putting the financial bite on the President. He never objected to being bitten.

At the same time, another wonderful figure appears. Leo Bullimer (1875–1954) was born in Stoke-on-Trent and came to Northampton in 1899 as the goalkeeper for Northampton Town, the Cobblers; a year later he became the County scorer, a job he took in 1900 – apparently at Thompson's suggestion – and held until 1950. Until 1929, he never missed a game. More importantly, he was also the club's most gifted fund-raiser. Lord Lilford could dip into his own pockets; Bullimer had the knack of getting those whose arms were shorter to dip into theirs. He was also in charge of the away trips; the title baggagemaster diminishes his organisational role. He was a sort of director of operations, a localised equivalent of the Australian 'Fergie', who took Test teams all round the world without losing a bag. Bully could not quite match that record – once Vallance Jupp's portmanteau was stolen from a station – but he was not far behind.

His father was French and he started life as Leon Boullemier. But there was felt to be a limit to what football crowds were prepared to accept. Anyway he was always Bully. His father had been an engraver and painter of miniatures and passed on to his son a flair for penmanship, as shown by the beautifully kept scorebooks. He also had an amazing memory for past cricket and football matches.

Since there was also Alf Stockwin, who prepared every pitch on the County Ground for the first 36 years, Northamptonshire were beginning to acquire a continuity in important areas that would become a characteristic of the club. It was only by finding such people that survival became possible.

All this time, Thompson's reputation was growing, and with it the Club's. His first County century, against Surrey II, came at The Oval in 1897, a year when he also took 90 wickets. It was a damp year, though, and Northamptonshire won only twice, against Northumberland and MCC. In 1898 the increasing strength of the batting became evident but they failed to win until August and there was an embarrassing game when Sydney Santall took eight for 48 to bowl Warwickshire to victory. Santall came from Peterborough and was rejected by Northamptonshire in 1891; he played for Warwickshire for 21 years and took 1,200 wickets, more than anyone in the club's history except Eric Hollies. Enough said. (Except to mention, to get it out of the way, the equally embarrassing figure of C. J. B. Wood, born in Northampton, educated at Wellingborough and a Leicestershire batting stalwart until after the First World War: he carried his bat through a completed innings for his adopted county 17 times.)

It was 1899 when everything started to come together for Northamptonshire. They played 14 games and remained unbeaten though they won only four – all in the Minor Counties Championship which was enough to give the team a share of the title with Buckinghamshire, whom they never played. Thompson and East shared the wickets with Tom Brown, the first of many men from the village of Wollaston to make their mark. In 1900, the year of the great Mafeking-night win at Lord's, the Championship was shared with Glamorgan and Durham which, given the clubs' destinies as the only three to be promoted thereafter, was an appropriate way to start the century. Again, the team was unbeaten but won just three games; the victims included Berkshire, who were bowled out for 47 (Thompson eight for 17) and 34 at the County Ground, and lost in a day.

In 1901, the County did lose, to Durham – Thompson took only 13 wickets, which may explain it – and the touring South Africans. But they bowled out Northumberland for 45 and 29 at Jesmond for a win by an innings and 202. That year, Thompson became the first bowler to take 100 wickets in a Minor Counties season. In 1902 he was chosen to play for 'an England XI' against the Australians at Eastbourne and took eight for 88 in the second innings, the victims including Trumper, Noble and Armstrong. That winter, Lord Hawke chose him for the first full tour of New Zealand, which included a few games in Australia and one in San Francisco. Thompson finished with 76 first-class wickets and 177 in all; he took 10 wickets in an innings twice, but against teams who were batting 18 and 22.

If this part of the County history seems like a monotonous list of successes, then it ought to be taken on board as ballast for the years to come. But Northamptonshire were becoming very big fishes in their small pool. They came third in the Minor Counties in the wet summer of 1902 but in the following two years they were far ahead of everyone else. Some of the victories were absurdly easy. By the time the usual two had bowled unchanged through two innings of a 70-run win at Trowbridge, Northamptonshire were Minor County champions again and the Advisory Committee had recognised that in future the County should be recognised as first-class, provided that they could arrange the minimum number of fixtures.

This was not so easy. 'One of the gratifying features,' commented the magazine *Cricket*, 'to the Northamptonshire executive is that their elevation has not been the result of any direct agitation of their own but rather the spontaneous intiative of the first-class counties themselves . . . For the last few years Northamptonshire cricket has been distinctly of a high order. In Thompson the County has at least one player quite in the front rank as an all-round cricketer, with more than one other, nearly if not quite up to the highest standard of county form. Another thing in its favour is that the leaders of cricket in Northants are particularly keen, and some of them indeed of a high administrative capacity.'

Which was all very well. But organising first-class cricket cost money; the Club only had a membership of 600 and at the start of 1904 was more than £1,000 in the red. Lord Lilford issued an appeal to all the cricketers of the County. Twice the number of members were needed, he said, along with a large and influential list of vice-presidents. He canvassed all those who might possibly be persuaded to subscribe a minimum of three guineas a year if first-class status became a reality: 'I am sure you will agree with me that this proposed promotion is thoroughly deserved, as it is the result of a hard struggle against odds,' he added. As ever, Lilford led by example; he gave £200.

The next step was taken on 6 December 1904 when the secretary's meeting was held at Lord's, with Darnell, Horton and the honorary organising secretary Percy Dale attending on Northamptonshire's behalf. It was decided that, in view of the visit of the Australians in 1905, six home and six away games against existing first-class teams would be the minimum requirement for admission. Hampshire, Sussex, Warwickshire, Leicestershire and Surrey obliged. It was alarmingly late before Derbyshire agreed to complete the programme.

The remaining Minor Counties sent their best wishes, partly out of sheer good fellowship, no doubt; partly because Northamptonshire's success pointed a way forward to themselves (though it was to prove a little-trodden road henceforth); and partly because they were mighty pleased to see the back of Thompson and East. Several, however, were kind enough to leave dates open for games against Northamptonshire in case the plans fell through. The editor of *Wisden*, Sydney Pardon, applauded the County's promotion and hoped that it proved teams could rise on merit and thus ensure 'We shall hear no more of proposals to adopt the system of the Football League'.

With 'Lord Lilford's County Cricket Fund' in full swing, the Club consulted with the County Ground Company in February 1905 on the subject of ground improvements. Pavilion alterations, including separate accommodation for amateurs and professionals (first-class players were fastidious about such matters) plus a new ladies stand were the main priorities. Lower down came a new press and scorers' box: the famous, or infamous, 'signal box' which stands to this day cost the club £72 and hundreds of journalists who worked in it over the next three-quarters of a century would say they were robbed. The directors of the company did not want to build it anyway and the decision to have it at all was only passed by four votes to three.

So the administrators were keen all right, as the magazine said. But were the players up to it? There was Thompson, of course. While all the preparations were being made, Thompson was away in the West Indies with a team put together and led by Lord Brackley, and, as on the New Zealand tour two years before, he was again the top wicket-taker by far: 126 on the tour, averaging just over 10. The Caribbean, Christchurch, Cogenhoe – it did not matter to Thompson where he was.

There was East. And there might have been a Test cricketer, too: in 1903 Mold came back but he was trying to bowl off-spin with a straight arm and by mid-season he had vanished from county cricket. There were two Kingstons. Billy was generally opening or going in first wicket down and scoring steadily. In 1904 he scored 102 out of 162 for seven against a Staffordshire team complete with Sydney Barnes's bowling. And he became the first County player to be chosen for the Gentlemen against the Players, a badge of honour which in that era could be more significant than a Test cap. Tim was an all-rounder, batting down the order and bowling right-arm slows with an idiosyncratic action: William Gunn once likened it to 'someone bending down to tie a boot lace'. Both, of course, were also exceptional rugby players: Tim was close to being picked for England and when he was passed over after a trial in 1900 there was a local outcry.

There were Horton, Cox and Knight. There was Charlie Smith, shoe riveter and wicket-keeper, well-respected but now 45. And there were two further amateurs, both of whom would become County captains. Edmund Mitchell Crosse, a product of Cheltenham College, was a member of the family that put the Crosse in Crosse and Blackwell. His first ever cricket match was at the age of eight against a girls' school; he was out for a pair.

G. A. T. 'Tubby' Vials gave a lifetime's service to Northamptonshire cricket, both on and off the field. (John Watson Collection)

G. A. T. 'Tubby' Vials (1887–1974) was to play an even more significant role. His father, T.H. Vials, had been County secretary. He was yet another spectacular all-rounder: footballer (it was a knee injury received while playing for the Cobblers that forced him to give up the County captaincy), hockey, tennis, chess and billiards player, noted golfer and mean goalkeeper at roller hockey. Like Darnell, he was a prominent Northampton solicitor. By the 1990s their firms – Darnell and Price on one side and Ray and Vials on the other – had been taken over by a firm from Leicester, of all places, and merged. Vials lived on to be the grand old man of Northamptonshire cricket; in 1905 he was the baby of the side and he was certainly not tubby – the name appears to have come from some exploit involving a tub.

The eleven that played in the opening county match also included J.S. Allen, who played only two matches for the County, neither of them with distinction. But in the main the team that took the field for the opening match at Southampton on 18 May 1905 consisted of the men that had earned them the honour. They ranged from 45-year-old Smith to 18-year-old Vials; eight of them were born inside the county, a proportion Northamptonshire would find it hard to achieve again, certainly not if they were ever going to win games. But this was a glad, confident morning.

MOTHER!

'The struggle to reach the top is itself enough to fulfil
the heart of man.'

Albert Camus

AT FIVE MINUTES past twelve (five minutes late, though there is no
obvious explanation) on 18 May 1905, George Thompson settled
over his bat and faced the opening delivery of Northamptonshire's opening first-class match against Hampshire at
Southampton. H.W. Persse, a 19-year-old fast bowler who
would die on a French battlefield in 1918, sent it down; Billy
Kingston was at the non-striker's end, and Thompson placed it
on the legside for two.

It was the culmination of years of striving, but the anonymous
correspondent of *The Times* was quite unmoved: 'At Southampton yesterday, Northamptonshire began their first match as a
first-class county, but their innings provided no feature of interest.' Contrast that with the fanfares greeting Durham's entry into
the Championship in 1992. But in 1905 a new first-class county
was not a major event. In 1890, the first year the Championship
was officially organised, there were only eight teams. By 1899
there were 15. Even if sports reporting had been a little more
advanced and less haphazard, a paper as grand as that one was
unlikely to make a fuss about little Northamptonshire.

And the *Times* man had a point. The County were all out for
221 in little more than four hours, with the left-hander Mark Cox
top-scoring on 36. Hampshire finished the day on 100 for three. It
was the sort of indifferent day that can drive any cricket writer to
distraction even now. Next day, Hampshire secured a first-
innings lead of 50 with Thompson, as was his custom, bowling
unchanged throughout the innings: 37.5 overs, six for 98. Then
he batted for nearly four hours and 94 not out in a score of 403 for
nine declared; East made 83. The men who had sustained Northamptonshire and would continue to do so kept them in that
opening game. Hampshire finished on 291 for five, 65 short of
victory, having extricated themselves, said *The Times*, from a
difficult position.

If it was not a great game of cricket, then the scene must still
have presented one of those happy days of Edwardian summer.
The temperature was in the 70s and there were the beginnings of a
drought. Elsewhere in the world the Labour MP Keir Hardie was

pressing Mr Balfour about the problems of the poor and unemployed. And there was concern about the reckless use of the confounded, new-fangled means of transport: two drivers had been charged with 'furiously driving a motor car' at speeds of up to 40 miles an hour, which the defence contended was impossible; one of them was alleged to have carried a cow for 12 yards. The cow had to be slaughtered; the driver was fined the fearful sum of £20. Poverty and motor cars – in the years to come Northamptonshire cricket would be persistently troubled by them both.

The first win came at the County Ground in the fifth game, five weeks later. Derbyshire were the victims, which given the part they had played in securing the new team's promotion, was a bit ungrateful on Northamptonshire's part. It was a piece of ingratitude the County would keep repeating; Northamptonshire beat Derbyshire at least once, and sometimes twice, in every one of their first 13 seasons of Championship cricket: 18 wins out of the first 25.

Northamptonshire in 1905; the club's first year of County Championship cricket. Back row left to right: Leo Bullimer (scorer), Bob Knight, George Thompson, Charlie Pool, Henry Hawkins. Seated, left to right: Mark Cox, Billy East, Tom Horton (captain), Charlie Smith, Billy Kingston. On ground: Eddie Crosse, Tim Kingston. (John Watson Collection)

NORTHANTS *v* DERBYSHIRE

Played at Northampton, 19, 20 and 21 June 1905

NORTHANTS WON BY 23 RUNS

NORTHANTS

	FIRST INNINGS		SECOND INNINGS	
W. H. Kingston	c Humphries b Warren	2	c Ollivierre b Warren	13
G. J. Thompson	lbw b Bestwick	15	c Lawton b Cupitt	8
C. J. T. Pool	run out	48	c Ollivierre b Morton	23
M. Cox	c Bestwick b Cadman	14	c Wright b Morton	10
W. East	b Bestwick	11	b Warren	12
E. M. Crosse	b Bestwick	12	c Cadman b Morton	28
H. E. Kingston	not out	26	not out	17
G. A. T. Vials	b Bestwick	4	c Storer b Bestwick	8
*T. Horton	run out	5	st Humphries b Bestwick	0
H. Hawkins	c Humphries b Storer	0	b Bestwick	4
†B. C. Smith	c Wright b Storer	9	c Humphries b Cupitt	5
Extras	b 8, lb 4, nb 2	14	b 8, nb 4	12
Total		160		140

1st inns: 1-7, 2-39, 3-88, 4-102, 5-104, 6-115, 7-121, 8-142, 9-142, 10-160
2nd inns: 1-33, 2-45, 3-49, 4-84, 5-89, 6-104, 7-127, 8-127, 9-135, 10-140

BOWLING	O	M	R	W	O	M	R	W
Cadman	10	5	17	1				
Warren	6	1	7	1	9	3	25	2
Cupitt	20	10	34	0	25	15	24	2
Bestwick	22	8	47	4	17	6	38	3
Morton	7	2	24	0	13	3	29	3
Lawton	2	1	8	0				
Storer	3.3	0	9	2	4	0	12	0

DERBYSHIRE

	FIRST INNINGS		SECOND INNINGS	
L. G. Wright	c W. H. Kingston b East	12	c Hawkins b Thompson	25
C. A. Ollivierre	b Thompson	0	c Vials b East	17
A. Morton	c Smith b Hawkins	30	b Thompson	0
G. R. Sparrow	c Vials b Thompson	64	c Vials b East	5
*A. E. Lawton	run out	40	c H. E. Kingston b East	11
W. Storer	c W. H. Kingston b Thompson	10	b East	9
A. R. Warren	c H. E. Kingston b Thompson	8	b Thompson	4
S. W. A. Cadman	b East	5	not out	12
J. Humphries	c Thompson b East	0	lbw b East	0
†J. Cupitt	not out	0	b East	1
W. Bestwick	c Hawkins b Thompson	0	b Thompson	1
Extras	b 6, lb 1, nb 1	8	b 5, lb 4, nb 6	15
Total		177		100

1st inns: 1-1, 2-15, 3-85, 4-149, 5-153, 6-163, 7-175, 8-177, 9-177, 10-177
2nd inns: 1-45, 2-45, 3-51, 4-58, 5-75, 6-83, 7-85, 8-85, 9-95, 10-100

BOWLING	O	M	R	W	O	M	R	W
Thompson	25.2	2	66	5	22.4	8	52	4
East	21	4	47	3	22	9	33	6
Cox	9	2	29	0				
Pool	2	0	9	0				
Hawkins	6	2	18	1				

*Captain; †Wicketkeeper

The first one came after a fluctuating match. Derbyshire led by 17 on the first innings; they were left needing 124 for victory and at lunch on the final day were 58 for four. Veteran, who wrote an eccentric column entitled Sportascrapiana in the *Independent*, was one of those to take the Abington Park tram to the ground in time to see Thompson and East polish off the opposition for exactly 100 by four o'clock.

Veteran was inspired: 'We had succeeded in wooing cricket's goddess, we had crested Derbyshire's peaks.' On he gushed: 'We had put up the number one victory of Northamptonshire in first-class cricket, and to us was the joy, the honour and the glory.' Rather more tangibly, to the professionals, was a share of the £10 donated after the match by Mr Wentworth Vernon, the squire of Stoke Bruerne.

Four years earlier Vernon had obliged with a £100 cheque to pay the pros their wages at a moment when the bank had become more exasperated then usual. And later that season, he gave a silver cigarette box to each member of the side who took part in the only other win: by 231 runs against Hampshire. It was another Thompson match. He took seven for 27 (which 50 years later became Frank Tyson's most famous analysis against Australia) in the first innings, which prompted one lady to suggest that he ought to be made to bowl left-handed, to make it fair.

Northamptonshire give someone else a chance? Whether it penetrated the national press or not, the town and county were still euphoric. Thompson was rewarded with a benefit match against Warwickshire and the grateful punters paid out their sixpences in such numbers that he received over £400. For once, the Club were in funds too. Membership had risen to close on 1,000 and the Australians' match, which Northamptonshire lost by the small matter of an innings and 329 runs (small compared to the 1921 result, anyway), nevertheless attacted more than 3,000 spectators on the last day. It all added up to a profit on the season of £442.

The County lost eight of the 12 games and they finished, under the percentage reckoning used at the time, with the frightening figure of minus 60 per cent in the final table. But the two wins put them 13th, ahead of Derbyshire, Somerset and Hampshire and although there were no fixtures against most of the strongest counties, there were still plenty of names on old Tom Plumb's bat, on which Charlie Smith used to collect the autographs of famous opponents.

Not everyone was convinced. The magazine *Cricket*, so kind the previous year, commented that nearly all the batsmen seemed 'overweighted by their responsibilities', although Pool – who had recorded the County's first Championship century in the big win over Hampshire – was exempted. Thompson was deemed not to have done himself justice with the bat, but no one could argue with his bowling return of 80 wickets in 13 games. East, troubled by injury, was unable to give his long-time partner the necessary support. *Wisden* was also cool about the new boys: 'To put the matter bluntly, they only had two bowlers . . . and only one batsman (Pool) whose performances rose above the commonplace.' But there was some praise, including ready use of the Edwardian cricket writer's favourite word. Thompson had always been 'capital'; Pool played in 'capital' style; and against Hampshire the whole team's form was 'capital'.

The only time the team really did get to the capital in 1905, they got stuffed by Surrey, by an innings and 124.

Only one important figure failed to survive the transition to first-class cricket. Gilbert, the groundsman's horse, was retired after 14 years of loyal service between the shafts of the heavy roller. He was the first horse Alfred Cockerill bred after arriving in Northampton, and Gilbert became, according to one local reporter, 'a symbol of relentless fate as he moved to the roller when the eighth wicket went down'. Now he passed into honourable retirement, replaced by a bay mare from Phipps's Brewery.

There was briefly a danger that Northamptonshire as a first-class county might have a worse fate than Gilbert and end up at the knacker's. The minimum in 1906 was 16 first-class fixtures and again there was a moment of worry that they might not arrange them. Horton was re-appointed captain, having been inadvertently proposed at the AGM as 'captain of the village'. In London, they would have thought this might be a Freudian slip.

In the second season the County began at The Oval and lost by an innings and 214. They were all out for 79 in their second innings. The *Independent* blamed the conditions: the Surrey secretary needed the lights on in his office but the umpires still refused to suspend play; Vials, Horton and Thompson were all out, the paper claimed, because they could not see anything. A London critic had a blunter explanation: 'With Thompson away, Northamptonshire would be fourth class'.

But, overall, the team did not disgrace themselves at all. They bounced straight back to win an extraordinary game at Worcester, winning after following-on, a feat no other county managed between 1890 and 1922 and something this one would not repeat until 1988. The County were 165 behind on first innings, then

Pool scored 166 out of 418; Worcestershire, needing 254, crumbled to Thompson. Pool's innings was not the highest of the season: Dr Harold Pretty, an amateur who had appeared eight times for Surrey and played eight games for Northamptonshire as well, played the innings of his life – 200 in 200 minutes – in the win at Chesterfield. The County beat Derbyshire at home and Leicestershire as well and rose to 11th. *Wisden* was generally dismissive: 'There were days when Northamptonshire played cricket that would have done credit to almost any side in England but there was a sad lack of uniformity and the bad quite outnumbered the good.'

The bad included some desperate fielding and, as everyone was now noting, hopeless reliance on the obvious two in attack. In 1905 Thompson took 75 wickets, East 38; 15 other bowlers were used and took 41 wickets between them. In 1906 their percentage was even more extreme: Thompson got 105 and East 68; 10 other bowlers took 56 between them. It was all very well to praise Thompson and East for bowling unchanged; there was no one else for the captain to bring on. As Horton recalled years later, he 'had Thompson and East to start with, and then changed over to East and Thompson'. So, in a way, the most significant game of the season was a defeat: against the touring West Indians. One of their players took 12 wickets and the County committee liked the look of him.

This is a perfectly normal occurrence at West Indies' tourist matches in modern times. But in those days it was by no means usual for counties to recruit in this fashion – and Sydney Smith was not a black fast bowler. He was a 25-year-old white Trinidadian with a Scottish father and English mother and he bowled slow left-arm. Northamptonshire did not have anyone who bowled slow or left-arm, except for Driffield who was playing very irregularly, so that combination in itself was ideal. And Thompson had seen Smith on the 1904–05 tour and had described him as the equal of Wilfred Rhodes, at least when he was either batting on turf or bowling on matting, not an arrangement that is feasible in the same game.

However, he had proved on the England tour that he could adapt his bowling style. Darnell and Dale contacted him in Trinidad. Since the alternative for Smith was a clerk's desk at the Government Works Department in Port-of-Spain, he appeared at Castle Station the following April. One can only wonder if Smith, turning out for Northamptonshire Club and Ground against Mr Luck's XI and the Kettering Church Institute, still shivering with the combined effects of the bitter weather and

S. G. Smith – Northamptonshire's first overseas signing and an outstanding all-rounder as batsman, left-arm spin bowler and captain. (John Watson Collection)

malaria, ever had his doubts. The County never did.

Smith was no immediate help; he had to spend his first two summers acquiring a residential qualification. The County did have a new captain: Eddie Crosse. Horton had retired and been presented with a pair of silver cups by the Club and a smoking cabinet by the professionals. The committee had actually arranged a more ambitious programme for 1907, adding Kent, Lancashire and Gloucestershire. The season began with some foreboding: 'Unless our batting picks up bowlers will look on Northamptonshire with favourable eyes,' warned the *Independent*.

Too true. In two matches against Kent, at Catford and the County Ground, they were bowled out for double figures four times; in the home game Colin Blythe took 17 wickets for 48, the best single-day analysis in cricket history and, next to Jim Laker's 19 for 90 against Australia, the best match bowling figures in the history of cricket – in quantity if not necessarily in quality. Blythe took 10 for 30 (at one stage his figures were seven for one) in the first innings.

Then, three games later, came the most wretched day of all. It was at the Gloucester Festival, always a week likely to take a battering from the weather. There was rain most of the first day, the Monday, and only just enough time for Gloucestershire to reach 20 for four. On the Tuesday morning they were quickly bowled out by the usual suspects for 60. Northamptonshire went in at a quarter past one.

It is necessary to make a few excuses in advance about what came next. Very low totals in cricket are, in essence, freaks. The greatest batsman can be out at any time for nought; all it requires is a combination of misfortune for ten batsmen to be out for nought. On a quite harmless wicket at Chelmsford in 1983, Surrey, a perfectly competent modern county side, were bowled out for 14 and were lucky to get that. The pitch at Gloucester was not harmless: it was wet and obviously vicious. It could have happened to anyone. But, of course, it happened to Northamptonshire.

Just over three-quarters of an hour later, Jessop dismissed William 'Bumper' Wells for the fifth nought of the innings and Northamptonshire were all out for 12. Twelve? Twelve! The figure needed repeating. Dale sent a telegram from the County Ground: YOUR MESSAGE SAYS 'GLOUCESTER 60; NORTHAMPTONSHIRE ALL OUT 12.' SURELY THIS IS INCORRECT. Indeed, the following year's *Wisden* did get it wrong and, in its summarised scores, kindly misprinted the total as 124. Wentworth Vernon, driving in London, saw a newspaper placard saying NORTHANTS RECORD SCORE, and told his companion 'There you are. I told you they would do it some day.' Then he bought the paper.

Another anonymous cable read: BRING THE BOYS HOME AT ONCE – MOTHER. Twenty-five years later the staff of Westley Bros and Clark, corn merchants of Abington Street, owned up. Fifty years later, in happier times, Vials, then the club president, sent another telegram: HEARTIEST CONGRAT-ULATIONS DEAREST MOTHER ON YOUR JUBILEE ANNIVERSARY SILENT THOUGHTS TRUE AND TENDER WE WHO LOVED YOU WILL ALWAYS RE-MEMBER – PRESIDENT. The art of sending telegrams has unfortunately vanished.

So, it seems, has the art of being bowled out for 12. Every now and again a report reaches the County Ground of a team being hardly-any-for-a-few and the spirits of any Northamptonian with a sense of history start to rise, on the off-chance that the record will finally be expunged. In 1966, Hampshire were four for five at Kettering but recovered to 218. Technically, the record is shared: Oxford University were 12 all out against MCC in 1877 but they were only Oxford, they were batting a man short and somehow it all seems too distant to help. It is Northamptonshire's record. It is part of the County's birthright.

The slow left-armer George Dennett had taken eight of the wickets, for nine runs in 36 balls. His figures included three in four balls and he would have got four in five had East not been dropped next ball; he was out for nought soon enough. When it was over, the crowd came on, waved their hats, as crowds did in those days, and Charlie Pool – of all people – who had scored four, a third of the total, insisted on getting a snapshot of Dennett next to the scoreboard.

Northamptonshire had what might be called the last laugh, though it must have been a pretty joyless one. Gloucestershire amassed 88, with East taking seven for 36 and by the close of a day with 33 wickets had reduced Northamptonshire to 40 for seven. The home captain, Jessop, wanted to finish the match that night, Crosse refused and the players trudged back next morning whereupon it rained all day. Northamptonshire lost 13 matches during the season, but this was not one of them.

They got no credit. Jupiter, a recent replacement for Veteran in the *Independent*, was despondent: 'We have drained the dregs of humiliation to the last drop. Think of it! Eleven able-bodied cricketers, the pick of the County, all out for 12!'

NORTHANTS *v* GLOUCESTERSHIRE

Played at Gloucester, 10, 11 and 12 June 1907

MATCH DRAWN

GLOUCESTERSHIRE	FIRST INNINGS		SECOND INNINGS	
H. Wrathall	b Thompson	4	b Thompson	7
E. P. Barnett	lbw b Thompson	3	b East	0
†J. H. Board	b Thompson	3	lbw b Thompson	5
M. G. Salter	c Buswell b East	3	c and b East	3
★G. L. Jessop	b East	22	c Hawtin b East	24
R. T. H. Mackenzie	b East	0	c King b East	21
T. Langdon	b East	4	lbw b Thompson	4
H. J. Huggins	c Crosse b East	8	c Buswell b East	3
E. J. Spry	lbw b Thompson	6	b East	4
C. W. Parker	not out	2	not out	8
E. G. Dennett	c Pool b Thompson	0	b East	0
Extras	b 2, lb 3	5	b 9	9
Total		60		88

1st inns: 1-5, 2-13, 3-14, 4-20, 5-20, 6-32, 7-45, 8-58, 9-60, 10-60
2nd inns: 1-17, 2-?, 3-?, 4-52, 5-57, 6-57, 7-77, 8-?, 9-?, 10-88

BOWLING	O	M	R	W	O	M	R	W
Thompson	16.5	7	29	5	15	2	43	3
East	16	5	26	5	14.2	4	36	7

NORTHANTS	FIRST INNINGS		SECOND INNINGS	
★E. M. Crosse	c Board b Dennett	4	c and b Dennett	0
M. Cox	lbw b ††Dennett	2	c Barnett b Dennett	12
C. J. T. Pool	c Spry b Dennett	4	st Board b Dennett	9
†W. A. Buswell	st Board b Dennett	1	c Langdon b ★★Dennett	0
L. T. Driffield	b ††Dennett	0		
G. J. Thompson	b ††Dennett	0	not out	5
R. W. R. Hawtin	lbw b Dennett	0	lbw b ★★Dennett	8
W. East	st Board b Dennett	0	lbw b Dennett	2
R. N. Beasley	b Jessop	1	b ★★Dennett	0
S. King	not out	0	not out	1
W. Wells	c Parker b Jessop	0		
Extras		0	b 2, lb 1	3
Total		12	(7 wkts)	40

1st inns: 1-5, 2-10, 3-11, 4-11, 5-11, 6-11, 7-11, 8-12, 9-12, 10-12
2nd inns: 1-17, 2-?, 3-?, 4-52, 5-57, 6-57, 7-77, 8-?, 9-?, 10-88

BOWLING	O	M	R	W	O	M	R	W
Dennett	6	1	9	8	15	8	12	7
Jessop	5.3	4	3	2	10	3	20	0
Parker					5	2	5	0

★Captain; †Wicketkeeper; ††3 in 4 balls; ★★Hat-trick

There were signs that the experience was making the team fractious. During the 33-run win over Hampshire at the County Ground, Thompson suffered some punishment, and took exception to a few cries of 'Take Him Off!' from spectators. Later, when Pool, the acting captain, threw him the ball for another spell, Thompson threw it back and refused to bowl. The *Independent* condemned this 'petulant display'. It was not necessarily out of character: as Sid King, one of his team-mates, said later: 'George bowled till he got tired, and when he got tired he got bloody awkward.'

The *Independent*'s columnist was more complimentary when Thompson contributed 30 shillings to Billy East's benefit fund, in advance of the return game against Gloucestershire. The proceeds from this match would, it was hoped, give East a nice little nest-egg, and a local 'poet' wrote the immortal lines:

> There's a popular bowler named East
> Whose smile will be greatly increased
> If the Gloucestershire match
> Comes up to scratch
> With a win and five hundred pounds at least.

In the event, he got neither. Dennett took 15 wickets – just as he had done at Gloucester – to secure an innings victory for his side. The weather was bad too, preventing any play on the first day until 5.30. This led to a few words being directed from the West Stand towards Jessop for delaying the start. It was duly reported, in the euphemistic way of the times, that Jessop 'went over to explain the position to them'.

It was not a good summer all round. The County won only two games – Hampshire and Derbyshire – and *Wisden* was again unimpressed: 'The men did not seem to have profited by the experience of two seasons and were quite incapable of adapting themselves to the circumstances of the moment. Under conditions adverse to rungetting careful methods were rarely pursued and when the grounds were hard, enterprise was conspicuous by its absence.' No one scored a century and Pool topped the averages with 708 at 22; *Cricket* called the batting 'deplorably weak'. For the first and only time Driffield made a contribution with his left-arm slows, enabling Thompson and East to rest awhile. There were few other redeeming features.

That was the end of Crosse's reign as captain. Lord Brackley – heir to the Earl of Ellesmere and the man who took Thompson to the West Indies – refused the job and the captain for 1908 was T. E. 'Tim' Manning, a Wellingborough School and Cambridge man (though not a blue), only 24, a pleasant young chap in the Horton tradition.

Lord Lilford had given a new scoreboard, which lasted until the 1960s. Its first task was to record Northamptonshire's first-ever contest against Yorkshire, if contest be the word. Pool, Driffield and East were all unable to play; Thompson got lumbago and was unable to bowl properly or bat at all. The effect was horrendous. The County were bowled out by Hirst and Haigh for 27 and 15, next to the 12 all out the previous year still the worst scores in the Club's history. This was probably the darkest hour of the years before 1914. It came remarkably close to the dawn.

The next visitors to the County Ground were Lancashire. A game that had been taut all the way through left Northamptonshire needing 165 to win, 73 of which came in a dazzling opening stand in 55 minutes between Pool, leading the side in Manning's absence, and Billy Kingston. Then came a collapse, and 23 runs were still required when the last man Dave Hardy joined Wells at the wicket. Twenty-one had been scored when Hardy lofted Harry Dean into the outfield, and Harry Makepeace was there for the catch.

He dropped it; the batsmen ran two and Northamptonshire were home by one wicket. Hardy was presented with a stump – 'the wicket that Northamptonshire won by'. A special team photograph was taken to mark the occasion, and art copies offered for sale at 2d each which would make 'a suitable souvenir for framing'. The players did not look particularly triumphant in the picture – the Yorkshire debacle was only three weeks behind them and there was a long, hard season ahead – but Pool's 'clever, not to say cunning, captaincy' was extravagantly praised in the *Independent*. In lengthy quotes he (or at any rate the reporter) talked readers through the closing stages: 'I have never had such a terribly anxious time in all my experience of cricket, and yet somehow I felt certain that Wells and Hardy would prove equal to the ordeal.'

This was the first time Northamptonshire had beaten one of the traditional Big Six counties and Pool hoped it would deepen respect for his team. But he was not over-optimistic. Asked about the team's future prospects, Pool said he thought they ought to win two or three more matches. He was right. They beat Warwickshire and the inevitable Derbyshire. In a fixture list that had expanded yet again, they lost 14 games out of 22. But for the first time the County were now facing all the leading teams; only two counties had never been on the fixture list: Middlesex, who were still 22 years away, and Somerset.

That was a pity: Somerset were the one team who finished below Northamptonshire in 1908. But, looking back, the season can be seen now as the end of the beginning. Once again, the batsmen suffered from the faults that had dogged them throughout the first four years. The men who had set the Second-Class Championship ablaze were often struck strokeless with fear against the major teams – except when they went to the other extreme (as *Wisden* said of Pool: 'he seldom takes pains to play himself in'). And there was no continuity. Most of the amateurs were irregulars and in 1908 the County used 31 different players. Both these faults were on the way to being remedied.

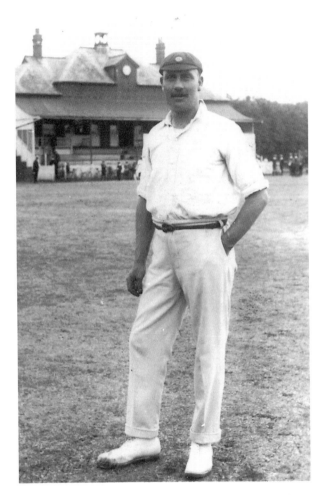

William 'Bumper' Wells – durable fast bowler and hard-hitting batsman from Daventry. (John Watson Collection)

Another problem was already being dealt with: East was overtaken as the second leading wicket-taker by Wells, who was an early example of the County's skill at long-distance scouting. He had been spotted in South Africa by an officer of the North-amptonshire Regiment when he was a private during the Boer War. No one had noticed him back in Daventry, where he came from, 14 miles from the County Ground. Wells was considerably quicker than either Thompson or East and his nickname 'Bumper' was not at all ironic (in contrast to 'Bomber' Wells, who bowled for Nottinghamshire and Gloucestershire off a one-pace run half-a-century later).

Walter Buswell – Northamptonshire's wicket-keeper in the years leading up to the First World War, and immediately after. (John Watson Collection)

There was a new, young wicket-keeper from Welford, Walter Buswell, who had replaced Charlie Smith after 1906 and clung on in the face of much adversity. The following year's *Wisden* was withering in its faint praise of him: 'Buswell kept wicket to the best of his ability and occasionally made runs in his own rather primitive style, but never when his side were really in want of them.' The committee had signed Harold Ellis of Burnley to take over but Buswell saw him off.

There were still an awful lot of occasionals, even among those most closely attached to the Club. A.P.R. – Rawlins – Hawtin (1883–1975) made his County debut in 1902 against Bedfordshire and his first-class debut in the ghastly Yorkshire match. His last game was not until the opening first-class match at Lord's in 1930, when he was 47 and scored 79. In all, kept out by business and sometimes his health, he played only 85 games of first-class cricket; like so many amateurs of the first half of the century no one knows how good he might have been.

Yet he was one of the staunchest supporters of the Club all century: chairman of the general committee for eight years, chairman of selectors for 14, a committeeman for 40. During the Second World War, he more or less kept the Club going single-handed. There was Philip Fryer, who succeeding Platt as head-master of Wellingborough and was a phenomenal scorer in minor cricket as well as a lob bowler of note; but he played for the County just twice. Dave Hardy, who shared the famous last-wicket stand with Wells, was better-known for being a teetotal publican.

Looking back, 1908 can be seen as a harbinger of better times. But it did not look that way in mid-June 1909 after the County had lost seven games out of eight, including the Australian fixture, and had been saved by the bell against Yorkshire at Hull. Manning had tried to resign the captaincy but had been dissuaded. Billy Kingston, the well-known amateur, was hardly playing because he wanted more money. And there was a ferocious dispute involving six of the professionals who were being asked to bowl in the nets for longer hours but at the same rate of pay. The hours had been 4pm to 8pm; the Club now expected them to perform from 10am until dusk. The pros demanded a rise from 30s to 50s. When they refused to sign the attendance book, they were suspended and it was only after prolonged negotiations, with Pool as an intermediary, that the dispute was settled before the opening game. The *Independent* talked about an 'evil spirit . . . brooding over our County Ground this season' – the bowls and tennis clubs failed to win a game early on either.

The evil was exorcised in spectacular fashion. From 17 June onwards, the County won nine games out of eleven, including six in a row, and leapt to seventh place in the final table. There was a sweetly vengeful win over Gloucestershire (all out 98 and 95) and two over Nottinghamshire, Hampshire and, as ever, Derbyshire. Yet there was only one new regular player in the team. Darnell had warned members at the AGM not to expect too much too soon from Smith: he ended up with 833 Championship runs and 94 wickets in an 18-match season. Thompson was delighted with his new companion and responded by taking 118 wickets himself, 46 more than in 1908. Lord Hawke, the chairman of the England selectors, was said to be considering Smith for the Test side, whether he was a colonial or not. In fact, Northamptonshire did have their first Test player that year, not Smith but Thompson, who finally got his chance at Edgbaston in the opening game against Australia.

It was not much of a chance – he batted no 10, was run out for six and was allowed only four overs in a match dominated by the bowling of Hirst and Blythe, who shared all the wickets. He was then promptly dropped for the summer and never played another home Test; men may come and men may go but the minds of England selectors remain ever impenetrable. (Thompson was picked for the tour of South Africa the following winter but the team was nowhere-near full-strength and lost the series; Thompson's own contribution in the five Tests was adequate but unspectacular).

The Club's hold on first-class status was more secure by the end of the season than it had been at the start. Nine thousand watched the three days of the Australian fixture; there were 3,000 to see the first Saturday start at the County Ground, against Warwickshire, and there was a new 14-year lease on the place, which had been eyed lovingly by speculative builders. Cricket's hold on the public's imagination was far less strong in the so-called Golden Age than is sometimes thought: the crowds were nothing like the size of those later on and there were new fads coming along all the time to test cricket's primacy. In 1909, it was roller skating. Most of the town was far more interested in the American Roller Rink Company's new place at Abington Park than anything going on up at the road at the County Ground. By 1910, it was 'motor-mania'.

But there is a limit to the amount of really enjoyable moaning that anyone can do about roller skating. At the 1910 AGM Percy Dale struck back: 'Last year we gave the lie to those carping critics who referred in such scathing terms to our unfortunate failures'.

The Denton twins at the County Ground in 1909: Jack (left) and Billy. Or is it? (John Watson Collection)

He failed to stop them, though, and the carping came from all quarters. The Nottinghamshire captain A. O. Jones condemned the practice of acquiring 'the scourings and cast-offs of other counties'. This was taken largely as a reference to what soon became a beaten path from the Kent nursery in Tonbridge to Northampton. It was first trodden by Bob Haywood from Eltham who calculated that he was unlikely ever to make the Kent team and so spent two summers playing in Peterborough to get qualified for Northamptonshire in 1910. He was soon followed by Claude 'Dick' Woolley, elder brother of the more famous Frank, and John Seymour, whose brother James was also a Kent stalwart.

As it happened, when Nottinghamshire lost by 237 runs at the County Ground, the match-winners were Vials and Pool with the bat and Wells and Thompson with the ball, local men all, so Jones could hardly complain about scourings. And, in fact, the emerging team was becoming more local. In 1909 the Denton twins, J. S. and W. H., Jack and Bill, emerged from Rushden via Wellingborough School.

Most local sports followers could tell their Kingstons apart all right; the Dentons were a different matter – they were as identical as the Bedsers. This caused mayhem in the signal-box one day in 1910 when neither press nor scorers had noticed that Manning had changed the batting order; and it was the source of endless confusion when they opened the innings together. The 1910 season also saw the emergence of perhaps the town's most popular sportsman of all, Fred 'Fanny' Walden from Wellingborough, forceful batsman, brilliant cover, occasional change bowler, inside right for Wellingborough Redwell, Northampton Town (scoring a hat-trick on his debut), Tottenham Hotspur (the Cobblers fans raised £500 to try to stop him going but the fee was a record £1,750) and ultimately, England (once in 1914, again in 1922); first-class and Test match umpire (11 Tests in the 1930s including the famous Hutton game at The Oval); and, for all that, only 5ft 3in tall. Until very recent times, old Northampton men would talk of him with a respect and affection which the years never diminished. Scourings?

The County dropped back two places to ninth in 1910 but they won seven games still, including the first-ever victory against Yorkshire (which is presumably what Halley's Comet had arrived to announce). This came in magnificent fashion at Bramall Lane when Yorkshire collapsed to Wells in the second innings; the County, behind on first innings, won by five wickets. Yorkshire were at full strength – the same eleven had scored a heroic win over Middlesex a few days earlier – but Manning was away and Pool, as happened with the Lancashire match, found himself in charge at the historic moment. Yorkshire were not having one of their great years: they finished only one place ahead of Northamptonshire in the table (it would be 1953 before the County would ever overtake them). Even so, it requires only a modest knowledge of 1910 Sheffield argot and a little imagination to guess the crowd's reaction.

Among the other wins was a very modern one at Chesterfield, where Pool, again deputising for Manning, declared twice and set a target, and another at Portsmouth, based on a stand of 232 between Smith and Thompson, the first occasion two men had hit first-class centuries in an innings for the County.

Manning did give up before 1911 and Vials took over. His captaincy was considered rather shrewd but he had a rotten year with the bat. Pool had also retired to become chief coach and neither Seymour nor Billy Denton quite managed to fill his place as opener. Nonetheless, this was the year the Championship came to the County Ground.

Alas, it only did so in a manner of speaking. An unexpected Midland county were indeed the winners but it was Warwickshire who secured the title with a win at Northampton by an innings and 33. Darnell said it was an honour. It was not an honour the County came close to getting for themselves that year but they finished tenth and won eight games. They beat Yorkshire again, this time at home, where Rhodes took 14 wickets but could not stop his team being bowled out for 140 to lose by 44. There was also the first-ever win against Kent (out for 94 on a sticky wicket at Tonbridge) and the first two against Sussex.

But Warwickshire were not part of the original charmed circle either. If they could be Champions, then couldn't anyone else?

THE UPSTARTS

> 'If a man aspires to the highest place it is no dishonour
> for him to halt at the second.'
>
> Cicero

THE YEAR 1912 is best remembered because in April the *Titanic* went down. The disaster rated a mention in the following year's *Wisden* only because John B Thayer, one of the leading cricketers in Philadelphia, was among those who died. There were many lessons to be learned; for cricket the most relevant was that, in this life, nothing should ever be taken for granted.

The August was one of the wettest of the century and on 7 August bad weather interrupted play up and down the country. It rained at Leicester, leaving Northamptonshire insufficient time to complete what looked like being an easy victory over their local rivals; and of course it rained at Old Trafford, preventing Lancashire completing a win over Yorkshire in the battle between a more illustrious pair of neighbours. If the games had finished as expected, Northamptonshire would have become County Champions in 1912 instead of Yorkshire. In the end, the County finished second with 70.58 per cent of their possible number of points against Yorkshire's 72 per cent. Another two points would have been enough – 10 extra runs in the first innings of the drawn game against Derbyshire at Chesterfield could have provided them. Eighty years have passed since then; everyone who played for the County that year, and almost everyone who watched them, has died. Yet still Northamptonshire have never once been able to call themselves County Champions.

In 1912, the hard luck did not flow only one way. Northamptonshire played only 18 games against Yorkshire's 28 and avoided some of the toughest sides in the country, including Lancashire, Middlesex, Nottinghamshire and Gloucestershire, four of the original Big Six. In both games that Yorkshire played against Northamptonshire they were easily on top and were halted only by the weather. There were nine Test matches that year, six of them involving England, because of the experimental and never-repeated Triangular Tournament with Australia and South Africa. Yorkshire lost their best player, Wilfred Rhodes, for far more of the season than was then the custom. Northamptonshire, in contrast, had a team that was settled to a quite extraordinary degree. Nine players appeared in every one of the

Northampton's County Ground photographed around 1912. Spectator comfort was not a priority. (John Watson Collection)

18 Championship matches – the Dentons, Thompson, East, Haywood, Smith, Seymour, Wells and Buswell; Vials, the captain, missed two; Walden and Woolley effectively shared the other position. Only these 12 men were used in the Championship all season (a 13th, L.E. Holland played against South Africa). As *Wisden* put it: 'The side could not be compared with many less successful rivals but constant association gave the eleven a fighting power that was out of all proportion to the individual talent.'

As was to happen when the County were second again in 1965, the batting statistics were thoroughly unimpressive: no one averaged more than 29 and Smith hit the only two centuries of the season. But the bowling, with Thompson, Smith, East and Wells to the fore, was superb. Haywood never got on to bowl once yet the *Independent* was convinced he would be a principal bowler in many county teams. Above all, the County practised and worked at their game in a thoroughly modern manner. The fielding was also first-rate, with Buswell having turned himself into an excellent wicket-keeper and little Walden moving like lightning. The *Independent* claimed that no county side could have fielded better than Northamptonshire did in their win at Bath.

But there was still a touch of Edwardian insouciance left in their cricket. The most dramatic innings of the summer was perhaps the 82 Vials made in 70 minutes against Surrey at the County Ground to set up the first-ever victory against them and put the County top of the table for the first time. Vials explained years later: 'It was made fairly quickly as I wanted to be out that night to go to the wedding of a great pal the next morning. I had to throw my wicket away in the last over.'

Of the 18 Championship games, Northamptonshire won ten and lost only one, against the reigning champions Warwickshire. They beat Essex, Kent and Somerset twice, Leicestershire at home (for the first time), Derbyshire, Surrey and Sussex. Many of the games were very lopsided, as was to be expected in a wet summer with uncovered wickets. The County bowled the opposition out for under 100 eight times and themselves failed to get 100 four times. Twenty-seven wickets fell for 154 runs on the rain-shortened first day of the game against Derbyshire that ended the home season.

Throughout 1912 it was the opposition who had the worse end of these wet-wicket routs. After beating Essex at home and Kent twice inside a fortnight before Midsummer's Day, the County were well clear at the top. They then went to Bradford to play Yorkshire, with Rhodes at the Test and George Hirst injured. For once, Northamptonshire dropped catches and Yorkshire got to 241 for nine. Then it rained and there was some trepidation about what Schofield Haigh might do on a damp wicket.

Fortunately, it rained hard enough to prevent any play until after lunch on the third day when Haigh and J.T. Newstead reduced the County to 74 and 24 for seven before the batsmen crawled away with a draw. Nonetheless, this was not regarded as a bad performance in impossible batting conditions. Four second innings wickets went down for one run and Jack Denton was hit and forced to retire hurt. Thompson then batted 50 minutes for one and Vials 45 minutes for six. A Bradford man felt moved to write to the *Northampton Chronicle*, praising the team's fighting qualities. Northamptonshire were still top of the table. 'Cock of The Walk', the papers called them.

Surrey briefly took over after that. Then they came to the County Ground and collapsed from 86 for one to 95 all out in 39 minutes, Thompson taking five for nought. For once, a wet wicket was not to blame. Vials played his remarkable innings, went to his wedding and came back to hit the winning four in a nine-wicket win. The County were top again and stayed there after winning their first-ever match against Somerset by ten wickets. Next they went to Edgbaston.

No one could say a controversial declaration cost the County the title in 1912, as was to happen in 1965, or the loss of a crucial toss, as in 1987. They were bowled out on a hard, true pitch for 53 and lost by 303 runs in the first over of the third morning. Defeat, said the *Chronicle*, was due wholly to 'indifferent batting', which sounds like a temperate description. Any team is entitled to one bad match a season and Northamptonshire had several more excellent performances later on. But they never led the table again, not then nor indeed for many years. Even after the last game, there was still a vague mathematical hope that Yorkshire might lose their remaining matches and throw the title to Northampton. That was never likely. The team had to settle for the disappointed applause of their supporters and the rather patronising praise of everyone else.

The season had a surprisingly bitter aftertaste. The bowlers had been so successful that there were a lot of early finishes. This affected the gate receipts, along with the bad weather, and the Club actually lost £466 on the year. They were forced to resort to various gimmicks, including a competition offering a new car, to try to get the money back.

The committee, however, thought it had the answer to its financial difficulties, and everyone else's. Darnell went to Lord's in the spring of 1913 and put a new scheme to try and improve cricketing finances to the MCC's Advisory Committee, which ran county cricket. This involved playing two-day fixtures with seven-hour days, every county playing everyone else and the bottom two to be forced to apply for re-election, as in football.

Now county cricket has been full of crack-brained schemes to reform the game ever since it started. Some of them even get enacted. What is mysterious at this distance is why this plan should have aroused the fury that it did. Lancashire responded by calling a secret meeting of what were described as 'the 11 leading counties', which did not include the previous season's runners-up. They proposed that the other five counties who failed to produce the attendances they did (Northamptonshire, Derbyshire, Essex, Somerset and Worcestershire) should simply be turfed out of the Championship; they reckoned that was a far better way of safeguarding the game's revenue.

This cabal, which might have been the working model for the clubs who broke up the Football League eight decades later, was defended the following year by Sydney Pardon of *Wisden* in his Editor's Notes with what seems like a PR man's blandness: 'The leading counties had no desire to act in an arbitrary or ungenerous spirit. Their proposal meant no more than that they were determined to be masters in their own house.'

A deal was done. Northamptonshire dropped their plan and Darnell was forced to apologise for putting it in a manner that 'had unintentionally aroused antipathy'. Lancashire then dropped theirs. It was agreed that the structure of the game would remain fundamentally unchanged until after 1917. Two-day cricket was eventually introduced for just one season, in 1919. At the time the idea seemed less ridiculous than it would in the late 20th century because so many games were finishing in two days anyway. But the 1919 system completely exhausted everyone. And it is extremely fortunate that no one ever took up the re-election idea because it is certain as anything that Northamptonshire would have been kicked out in the 1930s and never voted back.

Why was everyone so upset? Had Darnell's manner really 'aroused antipathy'? It seems improbable; he was an experienced sporting administrator. Did the other counties simply resent Northamptonshire, on the strength of one successful season, getting ideas above their station and thinking they could take over the game? This is certainly what upset Lord Hawke, who complained that Northamptonshire 'were taking too much of a lead'. Did they also resent the thought of being forced to take on fixtures they did not want? We shall never know. Anyway, it all blew over and Pardon looked forward to the game carrying on in the old way through 1915, 1916 and 1917 – which shows that he had not absorbed the lesson of the *Titanic*. Something entirely unexpected was to blow the comfortable old world apart.

A few days after Darnell was forced to apologise, Northamptonshire beat Yorkshire by 20 runs in a thrilling match at Headingley, with Thompson and Smith sharing 18 wickets. Very satisfying, it must have been.

This was one of 12 wins out of 22 in 1913. The bowling was again magnificent although East hardly played through injury. The batting was also much improved, in a more favourable summer, with Haywood, Smith and the Dentons all making runs. The successes included 230 for Billy Denton at Leyton and a total of 516, the County's highest yet, against Gloucestershire at Bristol, which was a distinct improvement on 12 all out. Vials, however, was forced to retire with a knee injury after only three games. Smith took over the captaincy. The team lost the continuity of 1912 and never pestered Kent for the Championship. They finished fourth, though, and two more points would have put them ahead of Surrey in third. These could easily have come at Dover in late August, against the eventual champions, after a century by Smith. But John Seymour's brother James batted supremely well on a worn wicket to win the game for Kent by five wickets.

At the County Ground, the committee offered a £10 reward for the conviction of those responsible for 'a series of outrages'.

Someone had cut a piece out of the square and a pipe leading from the covers was slashed in an apparent attempt to flood the wicket. No one was found; the committee saved its precious tenner. Lord Hawke was not suspected; the suffragettes were. Perhaps the ladies' toilets were in their usual upsetting condition.

Contrary to the myth of the Golden Age, it was a struggle to make sport pay in the last years before the First World War. 'Is Sport Declining?' the *Independent* asked on 9 May 1914 noting that the Cobblers had lost £1,000 and the cricket team £131. The football club did not have the easy access to cash that Lord Lilford offered the cricketers; he sent the County a cheque for £500 which was needed to ensure that they fulfilled their fixture list. Even then Wells had to demand his benefit money from the committee and Seymour was sacked because he wanted a pay rise. The team started 1914 magnificently, beating Gloucestershire and Lancashire by an innings, then faded; *Wisden* thought they had practised too hard and peaked too soon. Overall, they won seven games, lost six and finished ninth. Smith did the double for the third time and made 177 against Sussex at Hove in a score of 557 for six, which was to remain a County record for 76 years.

The Northamptonshire side which amassed 557 for six declared against Sussex at Hove in 1914, shortly before the lights went out all over Europe. Back row, left to right: Billy East, Bumper Wells, Dick Woolley, George Thompson, Walter Buswell, Leo Bullimer (scorer), Fanny Walden. Front row, left to right: Don Denton, Billy Denton, Sydney Smith (captain), Jack Denton, Bob Haywood. The Dentons all wear their Wellingborough School blazers. (John Watson Collection)

NORTHANTS *v* SUSSEX

Played at Hove, 30 and 31 July and 1 August 1914

MATCH DRAWN

NORTHANTS	FIRST INNINGS	
W. H. Denton	c Street b Vincett	71
J. S. Denton	c Jupp b E. H. Relf	74
R. A. Haywood	b Bowley	57
★S. G. Smith	c Wilson b Roberts	177
G. J. Thompson	c Chaplin b Roberts	73
C. N. Woolley	c Street b Roberts	4
A. D. Denton	not out	51
W. East	not out	22
W. Wells		
F. I. Walden		
†W. A. Buswell		
Extras	b 13, lb 12, nb 2, w 1	28
Total	(6 wkts, dec)	557

1st inns: 1-145, 2-155, 3-255, 4-475, 5-?, 6-490

BOWLING	O	M	R	W
Roberts	25	4	90	3
A. E. Relf	22	7	53	0
Vincett	26	7	64	1
Cox	16	2	72	0
Vine	11	0	38	0
Jupp	11	2	44	0
E. H. Relf	21	5	64	1
Wilson	9	0	42	0
Bowley	10	4	27	1
Chaplin	10	0	35	0

SUSSEX	FIRST INNINGS		SECOND INNINGS	
E. H. Bowley	b Thompson	12	c Walden b Smith	27
V. W. C. Jupp	c Buswell b Smith	50	c East b Smith	56
A. E. Relf	c Thompson b Smith	12	b East	44
★H. P. Chaplin	c Buswell b Wells	13	b Thompson	4
J. Vine	c Thompson b Smith	17	lbw b Thompson	1
A. K. Wilson	not out	78	c East b Smith	12
J. H. Vincett	c J. S. Denton b Smith	7	lbw b East	3
G. R. Cox	b Smith	25	c Wells b East	5
E. H. Relf	c Woolley b Smith	36	not out	22
†G. Street	c Smith b Thompson	0	b Thompson	26
H. E. Roberts	b Thompson	10	not out	0
Extras	lb 7, nb 1, w 1	9	b 1, lb 3, nb 6, w 1	11
Total		269	(for 9 wkts)	211

BOWLING	O	M	R	W	O	M	R	W
Wells	20	4	75	1	7	0	21	0
Thompson	31.1	3	85	3	18	8	43	3
Smith	41	15	66	6	31	10	87	3
East	16	8	18	0	17	4	39	3
J. S. Denton	2	0	6	0				
Woolley	5	0	10	0	4	1	10	0

★Captain; †Wicketkeeper

One of the wins was against Leicestershire over August Bank Holiday. Meanwhile, German troops were marching into Belgium. William Wilson of Billing Road was one of the last people left alive who were at the match. Nearly 80 years on, he recalled the County Ground scene of the time: how Thompson's arm used to go over twice before he actually bowled; how there was no food on the ground except from a wooden hut near the bowling green and an old man selling 'George Hirst' toffee; and, how whenever Leicestershire played there would be a special atmosphere of leg-pulling and banter. He reckoned the Northamptonshire supporters called them 'Woollybacks' because they made vests in Leicester.

Wells and Thompson bowled well in that game which Northamptonshire won by just four runs. Leicestershire batted one man short in the second innings; Captain Aubrey Sharp, one of their amateurs, had to leave the ground because he had been summoned to his regiment. The crowd thought this was ridiculous. 'You'll be back in a fortnight,' they shouted.

But he wasn't. And there were many more who never came back at all.

PEACE WITHOUT GRATITUDE

> '. . . and bugles calling for them from sad shires'
> Wilfred Owen

SYDNEY THOMAS ASKHAM did not return. He was 17 years old during that match against Leicestershire, still at Wellingborough School and making his County debut.

Oh! To be 17 and playing county cricket! Could there have been a schoolboy in England who did not envy him? 'Tommy' Askham played for the rest of that strange season. He shared an unbroken ninth wicket stand of 62 with East which saved the game with Essex at Leyton. And in the final game at Old Trafford he took two wickets, including that of one of the Tyldesley brothers, William, who was caught by Askham's Wellingborough schoolchum Don Denton for 92. Tyldesley was killed in Belgium in 1918; Denton lost part of a leg in 1917. Both lasted longer than Askham.

He was still at school in the summer of 1915. He scored three centuries and took 62 wickets. In 1916, he was due to go up to Cambridge. Instead he found himself in uniform with one pip on his shoulder: 2nd Lt S. T. Askham of the Suffolk Regiment, aged 19. On 21 August Askham, described in *Wisden* as 'an exceptional boy cricketer', was killed in action on the Somme. And so another telegram went out and another photograph appeared in the local paper's roll of honour. Tommy Askham's name survives on the team-boards in the Tea Pavilion that acted as a press box whenever the County played at Wellingborough School.

Thousands upon thousands of Europe's young men suffered the same fate. Two other Northamptonshire cricketers were killed: John Ryan, an occasional amateur who, like David Capel many years later, came from Roade, died at Loos in 1915; Charles Tomblin, a professional from Brixworth, was killed in France in June 1918. The other men survived their seemingly endless night but when they came back the best of them were no longer able to resume where they had left off. Another, even longer, war would have to pass before Northamptonshire cricket would be in a position to do anything more than the young men had done and just try to survive. It would be Cock of the Walk no more. When cricket resumed, the Club's very existence was in jeopardy and was to stay that way. The miracle is that it did survive.

Don Denton's brothers, the twins, Jack and Billy, were both prisoners of war. George Thompson served with the Royal Garrison Artillery but fell seriously ill in 1918 and spent a long period of convalescence at Netley Hospital in Hampshire. He was left with osteomyelitis in his right ankle and when cricket re-started was still unable to walk without sticks. It was 1921 before he could play again and his effective bowling days were over. For many years, he had recurrent influenza.

Billy East had been ill and injured for much of the 1913 and 1914 seasons and by 1919 there was no question of him being able to play. The club, sentimentally, found the cash to slip him £1 a week in the winter of 1919–20 and managed to employ him round the ground as coach, subscriptions collector (on commission), scoreboard operator and general help. He loved the band concerts in Abington Park, took photographs, grew roses and enjoyed talking about old times with his cronies in front of the pavilion at the end of a day's play. During the summer of 1926 he was seen collecting autographs – including those of the Australian tourists – on a bat, in aid of charity. Everyone loved Billy East. But he died that year, on the Sunday before Christmas, leaving a widow and a £36 mortgage on his house. He was 54. A fund was set up for the widow, which quickly raised more than £500. Thompson was one of the pall-bearers at his funeral, and Lord Lilford's wreath was inscribed simply: 'He played the game.'

Then there was Sydney Smith. The Club paid him a salary during the winter months for secretarial work, but early in 1915 agreed to release him to enable him to take a job with a bank. By November of that year Smith had gone to New Zealand 'without communicating his intentions', as a hurt minute put it. His Northamptonshire days were over. Smith continued playing first-class cricket in New Zealand until 1926, when he was 45, club cricket until he was well past 50 and he died, aged 82, in Auckland in 1963.

Thus, in 1919, the team's three greatest players were all gone. And the Club were broke. The enthusiastic and generous Went-worth Vernon also died in 1916 and once wartime reality had finally set in – in the winter of 1914–15 the committee was still discussing the 1915 fixture list – its meetings began to be domi-nated by financial troubles with occasional mournful footnotes when there was bad news from France or Flanders. The military had occupied the County Ground buildings (though it is not clear what they did with them) and much of the Club's time was spent trying to extract some rent – without success, though they did get £82 compensation for a fire the soldiers caused. The committee was also trying to get cash from an even more recalcitrant tenant, Mr Marriott of the County Hotel, who decided not to pay his rent for the duration. Fortunately, there was good old Lord Lilford, who subscribed £100 in 1917; one of the Rothschilds, the Hon Charles, gave 20 guineas, and Eddie Crosse remembered his old Club with £10. There was nothing from Marriott. There was evidently some Town League cricket on the ground at least in the early part of the war. Twice, however, the committee decided to try and raise funds by letting sheep graze on the ground; this was considered most urgently in February 1918 when the authorities refused to let the Club have any allocation of petrol for the mowers.

The first committee meeting after the Armistice was far from triumphal and there was much moaning over money. However, there was one positive influence: W.H. Holloway, editor of the *Independent*, launched a personal fund-raising crusade with £3,000 as his target. He set about the task with such energy, assisted by the new organising secretary, Charles Brown, that more than two-thirds had been raised by June 1919. It was going to be a struggle but Northamptonshire were at least there when county cricket resumed; Worcestershire were not.

The main problem then became who was going to captain the makeshift side. There were still hopes, rapidly fading, that Smith would return from New Zealand. Tom Horton, 48 that May, was approached but declined. Tim Manning and Robert Knight both said no but in the end Manning, ever loyal, agreed to fill in for the first match against Lancashire; and then Joseph Beasley, a good rugger player who had played a few games for the County before the war, was officially appointed for the rest of the season. He began the inter-war tradition of Northamptonshire captains who deflected any criticism by self-deprecation: he called himself 'a third-class cricketer who played first-class cricket'.

This was the season when Darnell's plan was tried. Matches were played over only two days, with stumps drawn at half-past seven. The County had also proposed a scheme restricting the number of professionals to four per team (rejected) and no winter pay for the pros (accepted, with alacrity no doubt) and they resumed with a game against Lancashire at the County Ground. Their final game five years earlier had been up at Old Trafford. Before this one, they wrote asking Lancashire if they could employ a runner for the crippled Don Denton who, despite his artificial leg, was keen to play. A reply came back (though it is unclear whether it was from the club captain Myles Kenyon or his deputy R. A. Boddington): 'If any fellow has been to the war and has had his leg off and wants to play,' it said, 'he is good enough for me and can have twenty runners.'

Denton's brave comeback did not, in fact, materialise until the following match against Leicestershire when, although in obvious discomfort, he scored an unbeaten 29 in just short of two hours. For the Lancashire match, Manning led out four other local amateurs and six professionals – Woolley, Haywood, Wells, Walden, Buswell and – making a brief reappearance – Seymour. J. T. Tyldesley, who had made 144 for Lancashire in the previous match, returned with 91; Walden made a century in reply. The game, like most that year, was drawn.

There were counties in 1919 which were actually in worse shape. Northamptonshire finished ahead of Middlesex, Essex and Warwickshire, winning two of the 12 matches – the home games with Sussex and Derbyshire. Sussex included for the first time a 24-year-old war veteran called Jack Mercer; he batted no 11 and was not given a bowl, which was a mistake. Rawlins Hawtin, playing his first game since the war, made a century and Wells took 11 wickets.

The Derbyshire game was the highlight of the season. Derbyshire declared 228 ahead with two hours 25 minutes left for the County to get the runs; they did it with 10 minutes to spare. Haywood scored 88 not out in 90 minutes and was carried shoulder-high to the pavilion by the spectators. Holloway the editor should have had the same treatment. By October he was able to announce that for the first time ever, the long-standing debts had been written off.

With Darnell and Brown scurrying round the county selling raffle tickets, there seems to have been air of enthusiasm before the 1920 season and Lilford described the fixture list as 'the best we have ever had'. There was no captain, though. Knight and Beasley both refused. Eventually 'Punch' Raven, an Old Wellingburian and local licensee, did the job in both 1920 and 1921. He was not a huge success. As with Beasley, cricket was not his sport; Raven was more of a hockey player. He was popular all right but could not make himself available regularly enough; he missed the first six matches of 1920 and a variety of amateurs had to fill in. He missed more in 1921.

The Club were less pleased with the fixture list by the end of the season. They played 20 matches and lost 16. 'A sad experience' said *Wisden*; 'A deplorable display,' said a local headline after five defeats in six games at the start of the season. Fortunately, there were again worse teams: Worcestershire, newly returned to the Championship, and Derbyshire, who managed the barely credible feat of losing all their 18 matches except for one that was entirely washed-out. Derbyshire were on the 'best-ever' fixture list twice. Northamptonshire also beat Leicestershire. Haywood's forthright batting paid occasional dividends, and Wells pounded in as optimistically as of old. But Northamptonshire were nearly always outclassed and the only bright spot was the regular introduction of Albert 'Taffy' Thomas, a medium-paced bowler from Denbighshire. Thomas had been billeted in Northampton during the war, and had been noticed bowling in the nets by Stockwin the groundsman. He played against the Australian forces side in 1919 without achieving much, but the Northampton Grammar School took him on as coach and groundsman and proximity gave him another chance.

He cemented his place with a remarkable spell against Yorkshire at Bradford when he took nine for 30 – the last seven for six runs – getting pace and lift. One ball lifted enough to hit Buswell the wicket-keeper smack in the eye and put him out of the match. Yorkshire were bowled out for only 166. It is an unfortunate extra detail that Northamptonshire were bowled out for 67 and 51. Thomas was an important member of the team for the next 12 years.

The last game of the season was one of the most astonishing in all Championship history. It will be remembered forever for Percy Fender's century, still the fastest ever in first-class cricket against bowlers who were trying. This game has been exhaustively researched both by Laurie Newell and Richard Streeton ('P. G. H. Fender: A Biography', Faber & Faber 1981). The figure of 35 minutes for Fender's hundred has since been sanctified, and Streeton is convinced it was approximately correct though Fender himself – who lived to be almost 93 – confused the issue and told one of the present authors that he was sure he did it in 33 minutes.

The century came either side of tea on the second day as the climax to a Surrey innings of 619 for five. It was a warm Thursday in late August; 666 runs were scored in the day, watched by a crowd of between three and five thousand; it is hard to know which of these figures, when one considers modern Championship Thursdays at the County Ground, now seems the more extraordinary. With no pressure, Fender went out to have a little hit and, against tiring bowling, succeeded brilliantly; he should have been caught at cover point for one.

Amid the confusion, even Bullimer's copperplate scoring wavered a little. And Newell and Streeton found it impossible to be certain even how many balls Fender faced: somewhere between 40 and 46. One can imagine what it must have been like up in the signal box: the scorers getting understandably flustered, with the reporters in the cubicles either side of them opening and closing the little communication hatches and demanding information as the final edition deadlines approached. The business of keeping cricket records was far less sophisticated then and at the time only one newspaper, the *Daily Sketch*, even mentioned that it was the fastest hundred ever scored.

The figure was equalled by Steve O'Shaughnessy of Lancashire in 1983 and passed by Tom Moody of Warwickshire in 1990, both times with the help of joke bowlers trying to get a declaration. The editor of *Wisden* has subsequently put these in a separate category to restore Fender to his rightful place. Northamptonshire bowlers were not a joke but to batsmen like Fender, Ducat, who made 149, and Peach, who made 200 not out, they cannot have been all that serious.

Wells, Murdin, Thomas and Woolley must all have been wearied both by the game – the County themselves scored 430 in the second innings and Stockwin's pitch yielded 1,475 runs in all – and the trying season. Poor Vernon Murdin, the fast bowler from Wollaston, had started the innings by having Hobbs caught behind by Ben Bellamy from Wollaston – playing his first match as wicket-keeper – for three; he finished with figures of one for 162 at almost eight an over.

Something had to be done. That December, the committee responded in the only way it really knew; Brown was instructed to write to George Thompson and ask what terms he would require to return as player and coach. The great man, 43 by now, was living in Leamington at the time, having got over the worst of his illness. Thompson knew his own worth, and had received a tempting offer of £300 from Haileybury School, but the County were so anxious to get him back that they raised their own bid for 1921 to £400, to be reviewed at the end of the season.

Brown negotiated long and hard, supported by Raven, and the bargain was struck. Thompson still had commitments as a member of the MCC bowling staff at Lord's, which would account for nine days during the summer, but the remainder of the time he would be back where he belonged. He was also to be consulted on selection, and his first task was to take charge of pre-season practice, in which he placed great store on catching. Haywood was called in to knock up plenty of high ones, and the reassuring presence of the local legend encouraged many in the Club to talk publicly of a revival. 'There is every reason to hope that we shall enter upon a new era of success,' Brown told the AGM.

It was a dispiriting season for English cricket as a whole. England used 30 players in five Tests against Warwick Armstrong's Australians, a figure not approached until the equally confused days of the late 1980s. It was even more dispiriting for Northamptonshire. While Brown was talking about success at the AGM, members were murmuring about his £400 expense allowance which had been attacked in an anonymous letter to the local press. He told them he had 'neither sought nor desired the position', that £300 had gone in clerks' wages and other costs. 'This leaves a balance in my favour of less than £100 for two years hard work, or less than £1 per week for out of pocket expenses. . .I am not grumbling at the amount of money this has cost me out of my own pocket. I am merely hurt by the ingratitude of it all.' Ingratitude! The word was to recur. Less than a month later, Brown resigned.

Before the end of May the County had played five and lost five, all by big margins. The team were lucky to be playing at all. Most of the players travelled to the Old Trafford match by charabanc. Just short of Derby, at midnight, the coach ran off the road, just missing a telegraph pole, and landed in a ditch eight feet below with its windows smashed. For once, a car crash played a less-than-fateful role in the Club's history. The team were shaken but not hurt.

Murdin bowled them to an innings win over Worcestershire before they went to The Oval and lost by an innings and 341. Fender got nought this time. But he was able to declare at 616 for five after Sandham, dropped on 22, made 292 not out. There followed two matches at the County Ground, both of which must rank among the most amazing ever played there. The first produced a new local hero: Wilfrid Timms, an 18-year-old boy from Northampton Grammar School whose home in Clarke Road overlooked the County Ground. Timms had made his debut against Kent in May and done nothing. But he continued to make runs at school, and a century for the Club and Ground earned him another chance. He had to wait in the field a while: Essex declared on the second morning, at 604 for seven. Northamptonshire were all out for 223, despite 69 from Thompson, the competitive edge still as sharp as ever even if the movements were not as free. At the close they were 63 for one, following on, with Haywood and Timms at the crease.

Only a handful of spectators turned up next day to witness what looked like being another humiliation, but the second wicket pair settled in. Timms was content to let the senior partner take charge: Haywood reached a hundred well before Timms got

Dick Woolley and Wilfrid Timms go out to open the Northamptonshire innings against Kent at Tunbridge Wells in 1922. (John Watson Collection)

his fifty, just after lunch. Then Haywood was out for 132. Woolley, who had retired hurt the previous evening, came back to add another 57, and then came Thompson with Thomas as a runner. The afternoon wore on; Timms's schoolmates left their classes and strolled up the road to watch and cheer as he edged nearer to three figures. A push into the legside, Thomas responding, and Timms was there after four-and-a-quarter hours. He was unbeaten on 154 when the match was left drawn at six o'clock, and his friends carried him off the field to a rapturous reception. One committee man presented Timms with a new cricket bag,

Darnell gave him a bat and Raven made sure he had the match ball. Timms was to captain the County twice later in the season on a couple of occasions, by virtue of being the 'senior' amateur present in terms of appearances. Thompson was there to nurse him through the experience.

Timms failed to win his blue at Cambridge but played on-and-off for Northamptonshire until 1932 when he settled into a life of teaching modern languages. Years later, he recalled Thompson's 'genial and amusing' presence, and was grateful for his loyal support. The next match was against the Australians, but it clashed with his Cambridge entrance exams, and Timms had to miss it. For the sake of his enthusiasm, it was just as well he did.

The 1921 Australians, under Warwick Amstrong, had already cut a swathe through the country. This was believed to be mainly connected to the strength of their team as opposed to the general disarray in war-weakened England. The players affected to believe it was more to do with the lucky horseshoe tied with ribbons in the team colours, which they carried everywhere (one Northamptonshire official turned it upside down in the dressing room to drain the luck out of it), along with the team mascot: a rubber kangaroo. Stockwin produced Northamptonshire's equivalent, which was at least alive: a black billy goat he had bought for a shilling. It earned its keep by helping to keep the grass down; it was just not as lucky as the kangaroo.

The press photographers lined up the gargantuan Armstrong alongside little Fanny Walden (until he died, Walden kept one of the pictures at his post behind the bar of the Peacock Hotel). Then Murdin ran in to deliver the first ball to Edgar Mayne, who missed it and was bowled. The second part of the game then began.

At lunch the Australians were 158 for one. Macartney reached his century the second ball after lunch and finished with 193. At the close they were 538 for six. The County did bowl them out before lunch next day – for 621, the third match running they had conceded more than 600. In three and a half hours therafter, Northamptonshire were bowled out for 69 and 68 and lost by an innings and 484 – which remains the fifth-biggest margin of defeat in a first-class match in England.

Four days later the Australians beat Nottinghamshire by an innings and 521, which must have made the boys feel a bit better. But the Club lost the third day's takings, which would have been enormous – the crowds were so large that play was held up when they encroached on the pitch – and the older members must have been forced to think back 41 years to the time when 18 men had

NORTHANTS *v* AUSTRALIANS

Played at Northampton, 22 and 23 June 1921

AUSTRALIA WON BY INNINGS AND 484 RUNS

AUSTRALIA	FIRST INNINGS	
E. R. Mayne	b Murdin	0
T. J. E. Andrews	b Thomas	58
C. G. Macartney	c Buswell b Haywood	193
C. E. Pellew	lbw b Murdin	13
J. M. Taylor	c Knight b Murdin	63
J. M. Gregory	c Woolley b Murdin	107
*W. W. Armstrong	b Falding	43
J. S. Ryder	c Ball b Woolley	93
H. L. Hendry	b Woolley	16
†W. A. Oldfield	not out	15
A. A. Mailey	b Murdin	0
Extras	b 12, lb 6, nb 1, w 1	20
Total		621

1st inns: 1-0, 2-185, 3-214, 4-318, 5-349, 6-438, 7-539, 8-589, 9-619, 10-621

BOWLING	O	M	R	W
Murdin	32.2	1	157	5
Falding	20	2	119	1
Thomas	35	4	119	1
Knight	3	0	27	0
Woolley	29	0	117	2
Haywood	9	0	62	1

NORTHANTS	FIRST INNINGS		SECOND INNINGS	
W. Adams	b Gregory	12	c Gregory b Mailey	0
C. N. Woolley	c Oldfield b Gregory	19	run out	2
R. A. Haywood	c Oldfield b Gregory	7	b Mailey	15
R. F. Knight	c Andrews b Armstrong	2	c Armstrong b Mailey	9
G. J. Thompson	c Gregory b Armstrong	4	c Taylor b Mailey	7
K. J. Ball	b Hendry	10	b Gregory	13
S. W. Falding	c Oldfield b Armstrong	0	b Gregory	8
*R. O. Raven	c Oldfield b Armstrong	6	c Pellew b Mailey	6
†W. A. Buswell	st Oldfield b Armstrong	5	not out	4
J. V. Murdin	not out	4	b Gregory	0
A. E. Thomas	c Taylor b Armstrong	0	c Gregory b Mailey	2
Extras		0	b 2	2
Total		69		68

1st inns: 1-30, 2-31, 3-38, 4-40, 5-45, 6-45, 7-59, 8-61, 9-67, 10-69
2nd inns: 1-2, 2-2, 3-21, 4-28, 5-47, 6-51, 7-62, 8-63, 9-65, 10-68

BOWLING	O	M	R	W	O	M	R	W
Gregory	9	2	30	3	3	1	4	3
Armstrong	20	8	21	6				
Ryder	7	2	10	0				
Hendry	3	0	8	1	14	7	16	0
Mailey					16.2	2	46	6

*Captain; †Wicketkeeper

lost to Billy Murdoch's team. Sixty men would not have been enough on this evidence. It may all have been to do with the fact, which the local papers noted, that most of the visiting Australians had exemplary temperance habits and the beer most in demand was ginger. This was not true of every Australian team that passed this way.

Wisden thought it was 'ludicrous' that Northamptonshire should play the Australians on level terms. And for the first time a sense of the futility of it all was starting to creep in. There were still worse teams; the County won five games and came 13th out of 17. That year, they ceased to be the cadet members of the Championship; Glamorgan, the last team to be admitted for 71 years, had come in, though unlike Northamptonshire, they had done nothing on the field to deserve promotion. There was a widening gap between the best teams and the worst and there was a proposal to split the Championship into two divisions. North-amptonshire supported it though there could be no doubt now which division they would be in; the following year they gave up the unequal struggle of playing Surrey.

Life itself was becoming a struggle. The County Ground company wanted more rent; Mr Hawtin, in the splendid amateur tradition, wanted £10 to play each game, more than the profes-sionals received; and by July the Club had total debts of £2,000. Only £700 of that was guaranteed by Lord Lilford. The first consequence concerned the star batsman, Haywood, who made 1,909 runs in 1921 and scored eight centuries, still the County record. He was 34 but this was by far his best season and the Club assumed he had plenty more left in him. However, before the season was out the Scottish public school Fettes offered him a coaching job at £400 plus the takings from the shop. Haywood went to the committee who were dismayed but phlegmatic. He asked for a matching salary to be guaranteed for ten years, with a benefit of at least £500 in 1930.

There was a succession of committee meetings. Haywood cabled the Club from Edgbaston, where he scored 128 against Warwickshire in the last match of the season, to say he had not yet accepted the Fettes offer. But the Club simply did not have the money and had to let him go. Haywood played occasionally in the holidays in 1923 and 1924 (the committee grumpily refused to pick him in 1922, though he was willing) but the Club had effectively lost the one batsman who had been capable of wresting the initiative from the opposition over the previous two seasons.

It is hard to know whether the Haywood affair had any bearing on what was happening in the pavilion in 1921. But by August a

Bob Haywood – imported from Kent, his forthright batting style gave Northamptonshire the capability to counter-attack, particularly in the difficult years following the 1914–18 war. (Northamptonshire CCC)

new figure moved to centre stage. Stephen Schilizzi, a wealthy Old Harrovian and former High Sheriff of Northamptonshire who had succeeded Wentworth Vernon as one of the club's trustees, told his fellow committee men that the time had come for drastic action: 'The Club must now be run along business lines and the hour for reconstruction . . . has struck'. He proposed the appointment of a paid secretary. This prompted an angry response from Darnell who objected to such a 'revolutionary proposal' being sprung at such short notice, and returned to the theme of ingratitude. He felt such matters could not properly be discussed in the absence of Lilford, who was away in Scotland, so it was agreed to call a special General Meeting of members on 10 October. In the meantime various committee men, including Darnell, Holloway and the outgoing Brown, offered money from their own pockets to see the Club through.

The meeting, held at the Town Hall on a Monday afternoon, heard eight members of the committee calling for a paid secretary and a reduction in the number of professionals. Darnell and Brown talked of ingratitude again; Schilizzi, however, had something new to say. He announced that 'one of the finest amateur players in the country, a man who has played Test matches' had offered to be secretary. He would not say who he was but the announcement was theatrical enough to turn the meeting.

The committee and all the officials – Darnell, after 23 years as hon sec and Holloway, the hon financial sec, followed Brown into resignation and, despite pleas to the contrary, Lilford decided he had to step down too: 'No gentleman in the room could expect me to do otherwise.' Lilford devoted his attention to his own XI's matches at Lilford Hall, where until the Second World War there was wonderful country house cricket. His Lordship's XI usually had at least half a dozen first-class players; there was luncheon (it was definitely luncheon rather than lunch) of cold roast beef, whole hams, steak and kidney pie and rosy-red apples served by retainers in yellow and black uniform while Lady Lilford's pet macaws flitted through the trees. During the war, the Americans took over the hall and baseball was played on the square. After that, the Hall became a refugee hostel and it was covered with Nissen huts. It was not the memorial such a whole-hearted cricket lover deserved. *Wisden* never gave him an obituary either.

There was a little gratitude. Lilford was made a life member of the committee, Darnell was given life membership of the Club and Holloway was granted a complimentary ticket. Brown departed still arguing over his money.

There was a danger that the members might have unseated the committee in 1977. The 1921 business, however, was the first and last successful 'coup de cricket club' at Northampton. But what seemed at the time to be a subsidiary matter turned out to have far greater long-term significance. Alfred Cockerill, chairman of the County Ground company, offered his shares as a free gift and announced that he had persuaded several other shareholders either to do the same or sell theirs to him. He had been promised 500 of the 646 shares and was anxiously trying to trace the others before the Club's lease expired in 1923. No single act of generosity did as much to ensure that Northamptonshire County Cricket Club still exists.

But who was Schilizzi's mystery man? After that mad summer, when the selectors had picked almost everyone, there were dozens of people who had played for England. The answer was Mr V. W. C. Jupp of Sussex, who was taken on at £400 a year, although under the stern qualification rules of the time it would be 1924 before he could be any help as a player. Holloway, in the *Independent*, wondered how he could ever combine both jobs. Jupp was already 30, having started as a professional in pre-war days before switching to the not necessarily less lucrative status of amateur. He had also switched his bowling method from fast to off-spin and was selected – without conspicuous success – for the Tests at Trent Bridge and Headingley. By December, he was in office.

Tom Horton was the new president and he explained the new set-up to the local press, which failed to discover how close the Club had been to losing Dick Woolley as well as Haywood. Woolley was on the verge of heading south to join his more famous brother Frank at Kent, but he was talked into staying. There was a further unsuccessful attempt to get Smith back from New Zealand, and there were also hopes that Vials might be able to spare a little time to play again. He did spare a little time: he turned out once.

The Club needed a captain for 1922 as well. And the reformed committee came up with a beauty: Captain S. H. Beattie, adjutant of the Northampton depot of the Northamptonshire Regiment was appointed to take charge for the opening fixture with Yorkshire. He may well have been a brilliant choice – a marvellous sportsman and inspiring leader. We shall never know. He never played.

He did play a social game that April for Schilizzi's XI against Captain R. C. Fowler's XI on Schilizzi's own newly laid-out ground at Guilsborough. He was out for four which, perhaps, left plenty of time for Schilizzi to broach the subject. Captain Beattie appeared again four days later for the Club and Ground side against the Kettering and District League. He was out for nought. That night the selection committee met to discuss the captaincy and split 6–6 between Captain Beattie and the rather better-known Billy Denton. Unfortunately, there was a small drawback to Denton as captain: he could only play during Whit Week. So Beattie it was.

For the opening match against Yorkshire, the County had to field three amateurs who had never played before plus Cyril Baker, who had last appeared in 1906. But there was no Beattie. He 'stood down through, it was understood, a domestic affliction,' murmured the *Chronicle* discreetly. Manning had to step in, presided over a more than normally wretched start – all out 81 and 42, Macaulay six for eight in the first innings, Rhodes four for six in the second. Soon Bert Tyler, another occasional pre-war player (and son of the 1892 captain Fred) took over as captain. Thirty-three different players appeared for Northamptonshire that season – almost everyone, it seems, except Captain Beattie.

The County were now starting to attract a little sympathy; there was a special fund-raising show at the New Theatre early in 1922. But the season might have been worse. There was an excellent win in June over powerful Kent (Dick outplayed Frank) and two over both Worcestershire and Glamorgan. Woolley and Walden had passable batting seasons; so did Bellamy, who made 168 at Worcester. Despite his traumatic start in Fender's match two years earlier, Bellamy now took over from Buswell as the regular keeper, a position he held for almost all of the next 13 years through thin and thinner. He was no great stylist, in appearance or anything else, but he was a battler and a local hero. In the 1930s he became the team's father figure, then spent 22 years as coach at Bedford School and when he died, in 1985, he was 94 and the oldest surviving Championship cricketer. Even then, he referred to all the amateurs as Mister and talked generously about all of them.

Murdin took 91 wickets and there were encouraging performances from two youngsters, one of whom proved of great significance. The less significant one was Hamer Bagnall, born at Field Burcote near Towcester, and a Harrow schoolboy who became, at 18 years and 188 days, the youngest Northamptonshire batsman to score a first-class century when he took 103 off Sussex in August. He was a few weeks younger than Timms had been the previous year. This innings failed to save the team from defeat. He reputedly had a wonderful off-drive but little skill against spin. He played patchily through most of the decade.

The newcomer who mattered was a 19-year-old left-arm fast bowler, Edward Winchester 'Nobby' Clark from the village of Elton, just over the county border in Huntingdonshire. Despite his local connections, Clark first came to prominence as a bowler in league cricket in Yorkshire, where he was an engineering apprentice. The former Warwickshire bowler Frank Field recommended him to Northamptonshire and Clark took 20 wickets in 1922 at 17 each. It was just a beginning.

Clark's action was considered immaculate and his picture, with his arm high, was used in an poster for Worthington E – for which he received a crate of beer. And indeed he remained as upright as a guardsman until he died. He also had a genuine fast bowler's sense of grievance, as we shall see. Years later, Dennis Brookes would say that only Douglas Jardine could handle him properly. Certainly, the Northamptonshire committee never could. One committee man popped in to the dressing room brightly one morning and asked what he thought the team's chances were in a particular game. '£1,000 to a pinch of shit,' replied Clark.

Oh, he was moody all right. But he could be magnificent too, and Northamptonshire players soon learned to work out which it was going to be. When, at the end of his run, he started picking the mud out of his spikes, the men in the slips would take half a step backwards; Nobby meant business.

Even more than the war itself, 1922 marked the end of the old era. On the second day of the Derbyshire game at the County Ground in May, Alf Stockwin said to his son Tom: 'We'll roll the pitch earlier this morning. Anything might happen.' That evening, Stockwin complained of chest pains, went into the secretary's office, collapsed and died. Darnell, as coroner, ruled that no inquest was necessary. Tom took over. A month later Thompson played his last match; three-day matches were now physically trying for him. After a winter in South Africa he took a coaching job at Clifton College and, except for a brief return to Northampton when he retired in 1940, lived contentedly in Bristol until he died, aged 66, in 1943. Friends used to pop by, especially Walter Buswell, who became a first-class umpire, and he loved to chat about the old days. In 1946 a plaque was unveiled in his memory at the County Ground; it now stands in the George Thompson Suite in the New Pavilion. It says: 'To him largely belonged the credit of raising Northamptonshire to the first class in 1905, and he was recognised as the greatest player the County has ever produced.' And no one has ever argued.

There was a third piece of symbolism. The George Hotel, where it all started in 1878, was demolished to be replaced by a bank.

But the club's home was safe. Cockerill chased up the remaining shares, paid off the mortgage to Lord Overstone's estate, wound up the County Ground company and handed the property to the trustees – Lilford, Horton, George Drummond and Schilizzi – on a 1,000-year lease. There may be problems in the year 2923. In the meantime, the land can only be used 'as a recreation ground where cricket, football, bowls, lawn tennis and other sports and pastimes' are played by and for the people of Northampton. The Cockerill Trust has to ensure that is what happens; and if Northampton Town Football Club ever does leave the County Ground it will be obliged to do its duty and make sure the land is used correctly.

At the AGM Thomas Beale said the town itself deserved congratulating for having a citizen 'so noble-minded', and the Club passed a unanimous vote of thanks. Cockerill, alas, was ill at the time. But he lived on in his villa opposite the Grammar School until his death in 1927 aged 85. If the headmaster ever happened to mention a deserving case then the pupil concerned would mysteriously find his scholarship fees paid with no mention of where the money had come from. Cockerill's obituary in the *Independent* spoke of him as 'a fine old English gentleman'.

A fine young English gentleman was found to be captain in 1923: Arthur Bull from Wellingborough via Mill Hill school. He was a very good bowls player but a more modest cricketer. Clark was developing but Murdin was injured and the batting was again dependent on Woolley. The County beat only Glamorgan and Derbyshire and lost 16 matches out of 22. This time they did finish bottom, for the first time. But not the last, definitely not the last.

A bill arrived in January 1923 demanding £369 to cover three years' entertainment tax. But Northamptonshire's luck held again. Sir Thomas Beecham took the trouble to contact the Club and offered to conduct a concert at the New Theatre, the proceeds to be divided between the Club and the YMCA. It raised £645 (minus the entertainment tax), which meant the County's share was almost enough to pay the first tax bill.

The next year, 1924, was wet. Once again, the County's only victims were Derbyshire, who did not win at all and somehow slithered underneath Northamptonshire in the final table, and Glamorgan. Jupp was able to play at last, which helped a little but his own form was unspectacular and he was not a happy man; he counted 55 catches dropped off his own bowling.

The Club's debit balance began to approach £5,000. There was the usual philanthropy: Major Rennie offered to pay for the 250 meals at the Club's annual ball, but the professionals were left wondering whether they would have jobs in the spring of 1925. Walden and Woolley both had requests for benefits deferred, and the pros only agreed terms for the following season on the understanding that they would be compensated if the Club was

Alfred Cockerill – a 'fine old English gentleman' and donor of the County Ground to the club in 1923. (Northamptonshire CCC)

wound up. George Drummond, the new president, and Cockerill both made public appeals for donations: £1,300 was needed immediately. 'My sole object in giving the County Ground,' said Cockerill, 'was to help the club and provide permanent facilities for sport and recreation . . . It should be the birthright of every boy in the town and county, whatever his social position, to aspire to qualify for representing his county in first class cricket. It is inconceivable that, for the sake of £1,300, cricket lovers should allow the Club to be wound up.' An issue of debentures produced only a slow response, and in July 1925 Drummond issued a 'final warning' about the club's finances, appealing for money by the end of the following week. That hint of urgency worked.

And, suddenly, the sun shone for a while, literally and otherwise. The country generally seemed to be prosperous again. It was the summer of the Charleston. And even Northamptonshire's cricket team caught something of the mood. The 1925 season was Northamptonshire's most successful – at any rate least unsuccessful – of the inter-war period. The County finished 11th and won nine matches, beating Kent, Essex and Hampshire as well as the usual victims. The credit belonged partly to the best captain of this era: Maurice Fitzroy, an ex-Navy man and son of an MP for Daventry who later became Mr Speaker.

Fitzroy was not a great player but he was a cheery sort and he may have brought the best out of Jupp; he was certainly given the credit for the team's improved fielding. Jupp did the double of 1,000 runs and 100 wickets, which he achieved 10 times in all –

Maurice Fitzroy led this Northamptonshire side to an exciting one-wicket victory over Worcestershire at Kidderminster in 1925. Back row, left to right: Fanny Walden, Leo Bullimer (scorer), Vernon Murdin, Nobby Clark, Dick Woolley, Ben Bellamy, Jack Timms. Front row, left to right: Dick Wright, Bill Wright, Maurice Fitzroy (captain), Vallance Jupp, Wilfrid Timms.

more than anyone in cricket history except Rhodes and Hirst. Clark became a true front-line bowler. And the find of the year was a Cambridge blue from Wellingborough: P. A. 'Bill' Wright (not to be confused with eight other Wrights, related and otherwise, who played for the County in these years), who took 100 wickets when he came in to replace the aging and injured Wells. His cousin Dick Wright scored two centuries.

The performance of the season was a win over Worcestershire at Kidderminster. Needing 301 to win, the County were 92 for five when 18-year-old Jack Timms joined Wilfrid Timms in a stand of 140. Jack made 72, Wilfrid made a century and Northamptonshire won by one wicket with Fitzroy too tense to watch. At least one national newspaper raved about the Timms brothers. They were unrelated.

Jack Timms had left Wellingborough School the previous year and was now beginning a career with Northamptonshire which was to stretch until the next good year: 1949. Through all the bad ones, he was a cheerful presence, usually taking his portable gramophone on away trips. He was born in Silverstone into a cricket family; his grandfather had been a prominent local player in the 1860s, and his father was on the committee. Timms developed into an enterprising, quick-footed batsman and an outstanding fielder deemed by *Wisden* to have been 'a not unworthy successor to the great Fanny Walden' in the covers. In 1927 he followed in the footsteps of the other Old Wellingburian George Thompson by turning professional, and five years later he played in a North v South Test trial. He was later cricket coach at Bloxham School and professional and greenkeeper at Buckingham Golf Club.

By June 1926 the club was actually in credit at the bank though not, alas, on the field. Northamptonshire lost six of their first eight matches and finished ahead only of Worcestershire. Bill Wright hardly played; Thomas was now struggling against illness and injury and Wells was finally forced into retirement. At 45 the spirit was still willing. The flesh, however, was not so much weak as too plentiful. He asked for a benefit in view of his long service and was turned down. He died in March 1939, shortly after receiving a £10 grant from the MCC Benevolent Fund. He had been ill for some time.

Wells's departure severed the last link with the pre-first-class era. All kinds of unknown people popped up at the County Ground around this time. There was Sidney Adams, a council clerk and leg-spinner who took wickets with his first two balls in first-class cricket in what was then an annual fixture against

Dublin University. Adams did not play for the county again until 1932. His first victim was one S. Beckett, subsequently slightly better-known for writing the odd play and winning the Nobel Prize for Literature. Anyone who played cricket at Northampton between the wars needed a well-developed sense of the absurd.

In the middle of 1927 – when Northamptonshire again finished second-bottom – Fitzroy retired through injury and Jupp took over as a 'caretaker'. The committee were clearly reluctant to let him have too much authority within the Club but he lasted for four years, a reign unsurpassed until Freddie Brown's era. A promising fast bowler, Austin Matthews from Penarth, began to qualify – a natural successor to Taffy Thomas in more ways than one – and the *Independent* reported in June 1927 that 'North-amptonshire is very well off for young players of promise, including the Tiffield boy Blakewell.' It was not to be long before Alfred Harry Bakewell had his name in far grander papers, usually with it spelt correctly.

Rawlins Hawtin and Fanny Walden in 1927. Hawtin's involvement with the club, as player and administrator, spanned nearly seventy years. (John Watson Collection)

There are shadows over Bakewell's name in cricket history, of which much more later. It is worth noting that the side was starting to be dominated by characters who had, shall we say, sunny intervals rather than remorselessly cheerful souls like Billy East. Clark was already acquiring the reputation which was to dog his career. The committee withheld his match money for one fixture in 1926 because of his 'disobedience and bad conduct'. Jupp's character is harder to unravel. At least two young professionals of the inter-war period – Dennis Brookes and Reg Partridge – recall Jupp as a kind man towards newcomers, but he was not one to adopt a conciliatory approach towards wayward individuals like Clark, and he seemed to enjoy the confrontation. Probably they had too much in common: both were incensed by dropped catches, which meant they were angry a lot.

Jupp began to feud with the committee too, even in his first full season as captain in 1928. He insisted at once that a masseur should travel with the team, which was not appreciated by the committee: the accounts were back in the red. Soon afterwards he was reprimanded for absenting himself from a match without giving adequate reason. Relations between captain and committee were to remain frosty until Jupp was deposed.

But the team improved in 1928 and 1929, finishing 13th both years with the hint of better to come. Jack Timms's innings against Worcestershire at the County ground was interrupted by an appearance at the magistrates' court to answer a charge of dangerous driving – yet another of the County players' unhappy incidents with the infernal combustion engine. He was fined £2 and stumped for 61.

In one of his occasional appearances Wilfrid Timms scored 74 not out at Trent Bridge against Harold Larwood at his fiercest.

Giving himself room to play the rising ball through the offside, Timms was anticipating the methods of other, greater, batsmen. Jupp was unimpressed. He called Timms 'a bloody coward'. Jupp later defended Douglas Jardine's use of Larwood's bodyline against Australia and said Bradman had been frightened. In that sort of scrap, Jupp would have been in his element. The Northamptonshire committee was feeble opposition.

Jupp was re-appointed for 1929 only after he had been reminded of the need for close co-operation between team and committee 'almost totally lacking during the 1928 season'. Clark was moody again and wanted to leave. But he left his notice too late and was obliged to stay. It was lucky he did: he took 141 wickets, six of them for 41 against the touring South Africans. In The Oval Test he became Northamptonshire's third Test cricketer after Thompson and Jupp, who had been recalled briefly in 1928.

The 1929 season was Bakewell's first full one and he passed 1500 runs. The team won four games out of five in June, including a victory over Surrey – who had not even played them for most of the decade. It was a relatively cheerful summer. In the late 1920s the team was not significantly worse than half-a-dozen others. By then, the County Championship consisted of some good teams and some who had a few good players, but had to fill out the sides either with class amateurs who genuinely could not spare the time to play regularly or no-hopers who were making up the numbers. Years later, Jack Mercer used to tell the story of the chap picked by Glamorgan who played one game, made no runs, dropped a catch and for the rest of his life was known as 'the former county cricketer'.

On the other hand, there was Mr Victor Rothschild, who was chosen by Northamptonshire to play against Somerset in 1929, hit his first ball in county cricket for four and made 36 against Nottinghamshire with Larwood in full cry. He was still at Harrow at the time. He played ten games over the next three years but attended to other matters in his subsequent career as a banker, scientist, war hero, improbable Labour peer, government advisor and, so rumour sometimes had it, Russian spy. When the committee were bitching about Jupp's captaincy, someone moaned 'the club should secure some County gentleman to do it.' But most County gentlemen of calibre had other ways of spending summer days, whether or not they were spying for Russia.

Everything was still awfully amateurish in the worst sense of the word too. Reg Partridge, another youngster from Wollaston, was persuaded by Ben Bellamy to take a day off from the boot factory to have a trial at the County Ground in front of some committee members. Partridge turned up but no one else did. Fortunately, Partridge was keen enough to fix up another date and was taken on to the County staff the same day. A few weeks later he made his debut against Yorkshire at Bradford, nipping one back to bowl Herbert Sutcliffe for his first wicket, and he remained a hard-working member of the attack until 1948.

'Glamorgan, Worcestershire, Northants – they were all weak, undoubtedly, but not so weak that they might not push a strong side hard with a little luck.' That sentence sums up the situation as well as anything. It appeared in *The Boys' Realm* in August 1923 in an account of a victory by 'Cardenshire' at the County Ground. The story is mostly concerned with the hero Ken Carden's attempts to marry Sylvia Prideaux (of all names) and to put one over the caddish Hon Alistair Burgeon. But it includes a – persumably fictional – conversation with Jupp which seems pretty perceptive.

'Our fellows aren't such a bad crowd as the results make them out to be,' said Jupp. 'We miss Haywood, naturally. It would make a lot of difference to have someone else besides Woolley to depend upon for runs. But he's gone and it's no use to worry about that. It's the future we're looking to, and I don't see that as so terribly gloomy. We shall always have the handicap of a shifting team, I suppose; but there are more than eleven good cricketers in the county, and other sides are in the same boat.' Cardenshire won by seven runs; even in fiction our lads were the losers.

Back in the real world of 1929 Schilizzi became president after unsuccessful soundings of Lilford and 'Ingratitude' Darnell. It was a tough year for the Club. In the way a canary keels over at the first whiff of gas, Northamptonshire's financial position began to weaken even before Wall Street crashed in October and everyone went broke. Schilizzi appears to have had a fondness for the grand gesture and in November an EGM was called at the Gas Board rooms to answer the question 'Is county cricket wanted locally?' It was agreed unanimously that it was. But only 65 people had attended the meeting. And had they known what the next decade would bring, they would probably have voted differently.

THE DEVILISH DECADE

'What a glorious thing must be a victory, Sir.'
said to the Duke of Wellington

BETWEEN 1930 and 1939, when the trivial torment of Northamptonshire County Cricket Club was halted by an infinitely
greater one, Northamptonshire played 250 matches in the
County Championship. They lost 138 and won just 18. Nine of
those wins came in two seasons, 1930 and 1933. They came 17th
and bottom in the table seven years out of ten, 16th in two of the
others (1932 and 1939) and 13th in the comparative year of
miracles, 1933.

Add in the three years after the war, when Northamptonshire
finished 16th, 17th and 17th and the record reads: Played 328,
won 25, lost 174. Between 14 May 1935 and 29 May 1939, the
County famously failed to win a solitary match. Four years!
Britain had three kings and three Prime Ministers. European
history lurched forward at a terrifying rate. Meanwhile, Northamptonshire played 99 Championship cricket matches and failed
to win one of them. Never in cricket history can anyone have
been so relieved at missing a hundred.

It is a period of failure that can stand comparison with anything
in the history of sport. It is often possible to read stories in the
papers of jokey Sunday soccer and cricket teams that get beaten
every week for years; for the players the hopelessness obviously
becomes part of the fun. But Northamptonshire's players – some
of them – were professionals. They were participating in the
premier competition in the land.

There are comparable experiences in rugby league, including a
very modern one. The Second Division team Runcorn Highfield
managed to go from October 1988 until March 1991 without
winning – 76 games, and they lost 61 of them in a row. Back in
1906–07, Liverpool City lost all 30 matches; Doncaster lost 40
successive games between 1975 and 1977. In soccer, Vale of Leven
went through an entire Scottish season without a point, but that
was in 1891–92; and there is nothing in the history of the English
Football League to match it – the system of promotion and
relegation provides a built-in defence mechanism to save really
bad teams from utter disaster.

In rugby union Cheltenham went 19 months without a win in
the 1970s and lost every game in the 1976–77 season. And the

Welsh club Penarth have traditionally maintained the fixture list of a top club without, unfortunately, having the players (Old joke: When do Penarth kick off? About every two minutes.) But it is hard to match Northamptonshire cricket of this period for sustained failure.

Take out the years 1930 to 1948 and this book would be a record of something approaching success. Northamptonshire came bottom in only two other summers (1923 and 1978). The story would then be far less interesting. For the point of this book is that county cricket in Northampton came through this wretched period. It survived and it flourished. In itself, that makes the gloomy years a sort of triumph. A well-run sport would have booted Northamptonshire out. A logical club would have packed it in. This one kept going. For heaven's sake, why?

The richly talented Fred Bakewell in action for Northamptonshire against Middlesex in 1932. (David Frith)

The County were never without players of quality. When Bakewell disappeared, Dennis Brookes emerged. But such planning as Northamptonshire were able to do hung round the presence of three international cricketers: Jupp, Clark and Bakewell. All were flawed. Two had their careers blighted by the curse of this cricket club, the automobile; Bakewell's was destroyed. It was 1936. He was 27 years old, exactly the same as Colin Milburn when the same thing happened 33 years later. Those of us who saw Milburn find it difficult to explain to anyone else the excitement he brought to a cricket field and the emptiness we felt when the privilege of watching him was removed from us. For the pre-war generation Bakewell had the same effect.

He played only six Test matches (to Milburn's nine), none of them against Australia. He was a cricketer of extraordinary gifts. He was a great short-leg fielder in a team full of non-benders. And he was a batsman of sufficient style and individualism to make even Northamptonshire worth the admission ticket. At times in the early 1930s he was talked of as Jack Hobbs's natural successor. Cardus said that anyone who had not seen Victor Trumper could get some idea of his methods by watching Bakewell's strokeplay and footwork. But.

'He was his own worst enemy,' one reference book sums up, rather glibly. R. C. Robertson-Glasgow put it more eloquently:

> He feared neither tradition nor bowlers, and he hated convention as a boy hates tight collars and polite talk. Therein lay his strength and his weakness. He did not bother to hide his love of freedom and company, and he remained the boy who just wouldn't touch his cap to the important visitor . . . he needed a leader-manager, not merely a captain, and it was not all his own fault that he never found one. The artistry was always there, waiting to be uncovered, but among the bright colours there lurked a dull thread of negligence, even apathy. Neither his own temperament nor external comment could always make him care . . . When his mind and his fortunes were warm, he could have batted with Bradman on not uneven terms.

Taffy Thomas would spend hours on Bakewell's bed on away trips trying, he said, to 'talk some sense into him'. If he had more sense, Northamptonshire might never have discovered him. He was sent to the approved school, St John's, Tiffield, and was encouraged there in his cricket by the headmaster, Trevor McColl.

It is something of a paradox that such a genius was lurking in the Northamptonshire team of the early 1930s. Peter Dawson, the Australian baritone, gave a benefit concert for the County in April 1930. The crisis meeting of 1929 had thrown up various ideas, some of them rather desperate: 'a vigorous attack on hunting people keen on cricket'; others were more imaginative like the plan to make the August games against Hampshire and the Australians a Northampton cricket week.

The committee was still not without ambition. In one respect the County joined the Championship fully for the first time. There were two fixtures against Middlesex. In 21 seasons of first-class cricket Middlesex had never made the short journey north and Northamptonshire had never played at Lord's. They made a very respectable debut there too, getting first innings lead in a draw. The Club also decided to do something about the deteriorating pitch, by ending the Stockwin dynasty, sacking young Tom and hiring Ron Johnson from Wisbech instead. And there were grand plans for a new pavilion.

The Cobblers' supporters' club had organised the Dawson concert but now the County began to discuss having a supporters' club of their own. The team was young – the average age of the professionals was 23. Bakewell had the first of his vintage years. On the surface, things did not look at all bad.

Unfortunately, in 1930 Jupp's skirmishes with Clark finally reached the point of open warfare. Clark wanted to fit in a Lancashire League game for Rochdale on a Saturday when the County had no match; it was worth a very useful £20 to him. Jupp phoned the committee from Worcester to ask permission on his behalf, which was granted. However, Jupp deemed Clark guilty of 'insubordination' during that game and that, together with what the committee described as his 'general attitude of late', led to the permission being withdrawn. Clark played for Rochdale anyway. Northamptonshire decided to sack him. He then joined Todmorden to earn the sort of money the County could never have afforded. And that, for the time being, was that. Northamptonshire won only one further match all season.

Clark's departure left the bowling dependent on Jupp, Matthews and Thomas, who had such a good year that Percy Fender talked of him as a Test player, though he was 37 by now. The committee tried a left-arm seam bowler off the Racecourse, Jim Kendall, whose greatest achievement was to score five consecutive ducks. Very often, the batting consisted of Bakewell alone. The second-most successful batsman was Rawlins Hawtin who returned to the team, aged 47, for the last time and played nine matches, 22 years after his first appearance.

The Northampton Cricket Week never materialised as such;

the Northamptonshire regiment said they were unable to supply the band. It was to be 62 years before this idea was to be revived. This was perhaps a good thing: it is hard to imagine that it could ever have become a major event in the 1930s social calendar. The

The hostile Nobby Clark – Northamptonshire's leading wicket-taker in first-class cricket, dismissed 1,097 batsmen between 1922 and 1947. (Northampton Chronicle and Echo)

ground hardly looked like Canterbury even then, when the football stands were a little less ancient and decrepit. But the two games earmarked for the festival did provide some of the greatest moments of the entire era. First, Jupp beat Hampshire almost single-handed, making the two highest scores of a low-scoring match and taking 11 wickets. Then the Australians arrived.

Remember 1921 and *Wisden*'s word 'ludicrous'? The weaker Australians of 1926 had won by an innings and 147. In 1930 they arrived with the prodigy Bradman. His appearance at Northampton attracted interest comparable to the occasional visits of Royalty or (1964) the Beatles. He visited sick children in Manfield Hospital and attracted huge crowds at the New Theatre. There was the customary social round for the other players too: visits to shoe factories, golf at Church Brampton and entertainment at the Schilizzi home, Loddington Hall.

It must have worn them out. And for once in this history Northamptonshire got lucky. Bakewell and Jack Timms helped the team to 249 on the Saturday; on the Sunday it rained on the

Northamptonshire v Australians in 1930. Club president Stephen Schilizzi, seated in the centre of the front row, kept Northamptonshire afloat in the 1930s when oblivion beckoned. Back row: Arthur Cox, Fred Bakewell, Jack Timms. Middle row, left to right: Allan Liddell, Ted a'Becket, Alexander Hurwood, Albert Thomas, Austin Matthews, Alan Kippax, Dick Woolley, Archie Jackson, Vic Richardson. Front row, left to right: Tim Wall, Charlie Walker, Don Bradman, Edgar Towell, Bill Woodfull (Australian captain), Stephen Schilizzi, Vallance Jupp (Northamptonshire captain), Alan Fairfax, Rawlins Hawtin, Percy Hornibrook, Ben Bellamy. (Northamptonshire CCC)

uncovered pitch; on Monday the sun came back out and Jupp and Thomas were unplayable. The Australians were bowled out for 93, their lowest score of the entire tour, and had to follow on. They drew the game safely enough but Northamptonshire had created a real impression. Thomas received £2 from the Mayor and Jupp was pictured in the papers looking mighty pleased with himself. The reports included descriptions of the assistant secretary, Mr Bradley, carrying 'bags of money . . . manna from heaven'.

But the bags were nowhere near big enough. There was very little manna when the Australians were not the visitors, and 1931 was the worst year yet. The team were losing and no one wanted to watch them. The pavilion alterations, when they were unveiled, were far less grand than the original conception (not for the last time). The bank was becoming fractious and Schilizzi was getting disheartened again. 'Personally, I am not prepared to ask for a single shilling in the borough or county,' he said.

The question of 1929 was posed again more urgently: could first-class cricket in Northampton continue? Two former captains, Manning and Vials, argued on opposite sides. Manning felt it would not be a disaster to drop back into the Minor Counties competition as more amateurs could be put into the side, meaning less expense. Vials, however, was convinced it would be a mistake to pull out as it would then be extremely difficult to get back in. His only argument was Micawberism: something, surely, would turn up. It failed to convince the committee, which called a special meeting of members for 16 September, recommending Schilizzi's view that the County should retreat.

The idea seems so ghastly now that one can guess how dispirited Schilizzi must have felt. Vials was surely right – why on earth would the first-class counties ever agree to take Northamptonshire back?

Schilizzi took the chair and insisted the committee was not bluffing: £7,500 per year was needed to maintain first-class cricket in the county. The club had £62 in the bank with £500 worth of unpaid bills already and the winter wages to come.

But in the manner that has always attended arguments about Northamptonshire cricket, the members could not bear to discuss such matters for long; they wanted a good old moan. And very soon their attention had focused on Jupp, who was away playing in the then traditional end-of-season match, for The Rest against the County Champions. Norman Andrews, who had played half-a-dozen matches as an amateur in the early 1920s, talked about the absence of discipline in the side. There was no 'ginger', he said. Others complained that players did not know until just before the start who was actually playing; Jupp, said a Mr Hodge, should make a 'sporting gesture' and resign at once as captain and secretary. By now, the members were well away from the general and deep into the particular: someone said the slip-catching cradle was not being used enough.

How could Northamptonshire possibly resign from the Championship? What on earth would anyone have to grumble about?

After two hours, an amendment that the County should carry on was passed unanimously. Schilizzi (who had told Leo Bullimer: 'I can only say that I have been a ghastly failure') was given three cheers, a vote of confidence and a rendering of 'For He's a Jolly Good Fellow'. This was all very well, but it did leave open the question of exactly how the County would carry on. Bullimer was put in charge of a special sub-committee to solve this tiny problem.

Bullimer's special emergency committee had no magic formula. It considered ground advertising which the committee of management, more fastidious than later bodies, rejected as 'an eyesore'. Soon its attitude became more personal, against Jupp and in favour of getting Clark back. Throughout this winter there were two committees, not working in harmony. In the spring, they even had to hold peace talks.

By then, however, Jupp had agreed to resign as both captain and secretary while Clark wrote an apologetic letter to the committee, asking to be allowed to play in midweek when Todmorden did not need him. Jupp had enough authority left to put a stop to that. He wrote and told the committee that Clark was too temperamental and probably not the bowler he had been. The one casualty of all this was the Club's most prolific run-getter: Dick Woolley, then 45, was released. He joined the umpires list until 1949, emulated Walden in reaching Test level, and then returned to work on the County Ground until shortly before his death in 1962.

The club were hardly looking to the future, though. The committee first asked Fitzroy to be captain and enquired about the health of the 42-year-old Denton twins. Eventually, the mantle fell on W.C. 'Beau' Brown. He might have been yet another in the dim line of amateur captains but he had a sense of application that sustained him as a player – he had been nowhere near the XI at either Charterhouse or Cambridge – and an enthusiasm for the cricket club which was to serve Northamptonshire well for many years. He later moved to Sussex and became secretary of the local

RSPCA, a job for which running Northamptonshire cricket must have been useful preparation.

Luckily, Northamptonshire still had Jupp as a player. Relieved of responsibility, he had, at the age of 42, a wonderful season in 1932. At Tunbridge Wells, he took all ten Kent wickets, the only time a Northamptonshire player has done this. He conceded 127 runs in the process; and though he made the two highest scores for Northamptonshire (34 and 32), could not prevent Freeman taking 16 wickets or Kent winning by an innings and 188. Like Thompson, even Jupp could bat or bowl from only one end at a time.

By now, there was a new chairman, W. C. C. Cooke, and neither he nor Brown had quite the same bitter memories of Clark. By the end of May, the prodigal was back playing part-time. He helped the County off the bottom, just. In October 1932, Jupp's successor as secretary started work. He was Eric Coley, a 29-year-old rugby wing forward for Northampton and England, who was chosen out of 200 applicants to work at £250 a year. His first job was to move the office out of Abington Street in the town centre and into the pavilion – 'economically', instructed the committee, just in case he was unaware what kind of organisation he was joining.

Actually, the County were having one of their bright intervals. Bullimer's committee had raised £1,464, which Schilizzi described as 'a miracle' given the depression of the early 1930s. There was a small profit to report. The emergency committee had been so successful that it could itself be wound up, rather than the Club. With Larwood absent hurt, both physically and mentally, after his efforts and the controversy on the Bodyline tour, Clark was the fastest bowler in the country in 1933. He led Northamptonshire to an innings victory over the touring West Indians in May and by the end of the summer he was in the England team, playing together in The Oval Test with Bakewell, who made 107.

Bakewell also became the first Northamptonshire player to score 2,000 runs in a season and *Wisden* thought that, by being more careful at the start of his innings, he was at last fulfilling the highest expectations. Both men were chosen for the tour of India, which was not merely an honour but saved the Club two sets of winter wages. On 18 July Northamptonshire were seventh in the Championship table. They slipped to finish 13th and on occasion, they were still overwhelmed: 27 all out against Yorkshire on a sticky at Kettering when Sutcliffe made a century, pulling Jupp for eight sixes to the short boundary; 46 all out at Dover and defeat by 429 runs.

But it was the best year of this decade by a long way. In 1934, Northamptonshire contrived to lose seven matches before the end of May – six in the Championship and the Cambridge match – and 18 in all. Jupp missed the whole season with rheumatism. Clark and, to a lesser extent, Bakewell were both affected by the arduous tour of India. Clark did become the first County player to play in an Ashes Test since Thompson in 1909 and took five for 98 at The Oval. But he missed half the county season one way and another, including the Australians' match at the County Ground.

In that game an improbable team once again distinguished itself. Matthews, with some help from Partridge, bowled the Australians out for 284 and 234, better than any other county had done. And a 20-year-old amateur from Peterborough, Alex Snowden, scored the first-ever century for Northamptonshire against the Australians. Who better to tell this remarkable story than Snowden himself? Forty years later, in *The Cricketer*, he recalled the scene after he had taken his score to 97:

> Reg Partridge deflected a ball to leg for a single and I was facing Fleetwood-Smith again. Tall, dark and handsome, he prepared to move in, over the wicket, to three men close and three men out on the leg side. My tension had built up, for these were the mighty Australians, and I was only 20 years old.
>
> I was in for a shock. Fleetwood-Smith bowled me a high full-toss! It was head-high and flighted to drop on to the leg stump. I went for my shot, aiming a really vicious tennis smash at the ball, downwards and towards square leg. I felt the ball bang in the middle of the bat. It was hit as hard as any ball in my life and it flew 20 yards then scorched its way across the grassy outfield, scudding over the boundary line with deep square leg and mid-wicket lengths away. I had made it!
>
> The County Ground had about 7,000 spectators on parade that day, for it was the plum match of the season and also half-day in Northampton. They gave me a great hand – firstly a shout of triumph, as if a Cup goal had been scored, and then the trumpeting of the car horns – every one in Northamptonshire, it seemed. Don Bradman and 'Tiger' O'Reilly came over and congratulated me, but I was in a complete dream. Surely all this wasn't true? But it was. For 'tis written: Every dog has his day. This was mine.

The County scraped an honourable draw with the last pair at the crease.

By then, Snowden, in the quaint way of the time, had already captained the side: at Bristol in 1932, when he was still 18, and in

1934 at Bradford in a game which happened to be Dennis Brookes's debut. It was also the game when the County borrowed an improbable substitute from Yorkshire: an unknown youngster who scurried round the outfield and declined the traditional payment, saying he had enjoyed himself. Len Hutton was the name. Snowden also took part in a curiosity when he shared two century opening stands with Bakewell on the same day at Edgbaston. In between the whole team had collapsed to Hollies and Paine. Only Northamptonshire could manage this sort of thing. Bakewell whispered the explanation to an interviewer many years later: 'We hadn't got a very good side.'

They didn't have a very good side in 1935 either and once again there was no Jupp. This time it was not the rheumatism. The explanation never appeared in the Club minutes nor in Jim Coldham's original club history. It was in the local evening paper, the *Chronicle and Echo*, though, on 14 January 1935: NORTHANTS COUNTY CRICKETER IN FATAL ROAD CRASH. But it was not the cricketer who was killed, not this time: 'A Northampton young man received fatal injuries and his companion is in Northampton General Hospital as a result of a collision between the motor-cycle they were riding and a car being driven by Mr V. W. C. Jupp . . .'

It happened near the Pitsford turn, very close to Jupp's home at Brixworth, just before midnight on the Saturday night. It was the pillion passenger who died, a 19-year-old clicker in a shoe factory, Wilfred Denis Moisey. Jupp himself was badly cut and was still in bed later that week when an officer arrived to charge him with manslaughter. At the police court hearing, the motor cyclist, Charles Barrett, gave his evidence from a stretcher and said he saw two cars coming up the hill. One overtook the other and then continued on the wrong side of the road travelling very fast. The other motorist corroborated this story. Jupp reserved his defence.

Justice worked swiftly in those days. Only a fortnight later, Jupp was at Northampton Assizes before Mr Justice Humphreys with his solicitor Vials and the cricket-loving KC, Norman (later Lord) Birkett. Jupp told the court that he was driving the car, a 12-horsepower, six-cylinder Vauxhall, for the first time. He said he skidded twice and was dazzled. 'I had the wall and the ditch to contend with and I hoped the motor-cyclist would realise my plight, but unfortunately he did not.' Police Constable Rainbow said there were no skid marks on the road.

Even the great Birkett could not save Jupp. The jury was out for 35 minutes. 'Vallance William Crisp Jupp,' said the judge, 'for

Alex Snowden – occasional Northamptonshire captain and centurion in the county's match against the 1934 Australians. (Northamptonshire CCC)

the rest of your life you will have it upon your conscience that a jury of your own countrymen found it necessary to say that you have unlawfully killed, by your negligence, a human being . . . The least sentence I can pass upon you for this serious offence is that you be imprisoned in the second division for nine months.'

The second division in this context represented a middle-ranking form of punishment in which prisoners were allowed monthly letters and visits. It did not allow any opportunities for cricket or for running the sports shop which Jupp had opened at the top of Hazelwood Road two years earlier with smart adverts in the local press proclaiming 'V. W. C. Jupp at Your Service'. It is hard to imagine that a proud man like him found either service or servitude particularly satisfying. A seven-year-old went into the shop once and demanded: 'Who is the best wicket-keeper in

England?' 'Ben Bellamy,' came the reply. 'What about Les Ames?' Jupp had had enough: 'Bugger off and don't waste my time.'

But he was a convivial man. Alex Snowden described an evening with Jupp driving down to a game at Hove in Jupp's Overland Whippet, a car that was ancient even in the 1930s, while the professionals went by train. 'I was the baby of the side, on tour for the first time and was unprepared for a journey as long as ours was to be.' This included a number of stops, the last in a pub at Guildford. 'Soon he (Jupp) was in earnest conversation with the locals on the intricacies of off-spin bowling and showing them his pet trick of plunging a pin through the spinning finger of his right hand just to prove it was all hard skin. Having proved his point he sank a few large whiskies. He could not bother with singles; he always thought big.'

Snowden travelled back with Jupp after that game too, for a game at Peterborough, his home town:

It was a perfectly plain and straightforward journey of 150 miles from Brighton to London and up the Great North Road. But Juppy's sense of timing was seldom in tune with Greenwich. It was, strangely, mid-evening before we set out and we had Bill Reeves, the Clown Prince of umpires, as our passenger as far as London. What a scream he was: one comic tale after another . . . then Juppy set out for St Albans, where he knocked up the irate proprietor of the Pea Hen Hotel in the wee small hours.

Juppy reported for breakfast at ten, and after feeding well we drove up the Great North Road as far as Biggleswade, where refuelling was necessary. It was now 11.30, and I tentatively pointed out that the match was about to start and we were still 40 miles short of the ground. He brushed this off, saying that Bellamy, the senior pro, would toss up and that it was unlikely we should lose many wickets before lunch. If the toss were lost, only two substitutes were needed.

We reached Peterborough shortly before the lunch interval and proceeded right across the ground towards the pavilion. To my horror Jupp marched happily along inside the boundary for all the assembled crowd to view. I, a mere boy of 17, was conscious only that I was an hour and a half late for a match in my home city. Juppy was conscious only of the fact that that silly old fool Bellamy had lost the toss.

Almost needless to say, we took another beating from Warwickshire, and Juppy was just about our only successful player in the match.

It is said that when Jupp left the George Row club on the night of the fatal crash he was so drunk that his companions tried but failed to stop him driving home.

Before the 1935 season had started the County had lost the present captain as well: Brown was injured at the nets and Snowden had to take over. He began in extraordinary fashion, with a win from an improbable position at Taunton when Clark and Matthews bowled out Somerset, who needed only 124 to win, for 75. It is worth savouring that victory for a moment; it was 1,476 days before they would beat a county again and by then only three of the Taunton team, Jack Timms, Brookes and Partridge, were still playing.

There were the usual sort of occurrences that attend ill-starred teams: Clark missed the Nottinghamshire match because he tripped over a cricket bag. On one level, Snowden could not say he was unlucky: he won the toss ten times running. But his own form went to pieces and in July he damaged a hand fielding against Essex and did not play again that season. There is a hint of a diplomatic headache about this injury; all that is known for sure is that Schilizzi took the trouble to visit Snowden's father to 'resolve the unpleasant situation' – and that Clark and Bakewell were disciplined and the committee yet again recommended that Clark should be sacked.

The Club were not far away from having no bowlers at all; there was only one other who was remotely successful, Cyril Perkins, who enjoyed bowling to his fellow Wollaston man behind the stumps, Ben Bellamy. Perkins was talked of as the natural successor to Sydney Smith, a comparison that old-timers at the County Ground would fondly make at the first opportunity. The major difference was that Perkins played 56 games and never once appeared in a winning team.

The new captain was Gerry Cuthbertson. He was a hard-hitting batsman and, by all accounts, an optimist and a genial man ('a helluva nice chap, Gerry,' as Bakewell put it), who had appeared briefly for Sussex, Middlesex and Free Foresters, though he too had failed to get his blue at Cambridge. He had an impossible job. In July and August Northamptonshire lost 13 consecutive matches. Still, Cuthbertson was appointed for the season – on Beau Brown's recommendation – in 1936 and even when he said he was going to the United States in the spring and merely 'hoped' to be back at the end of July, the committee stuck by him and just asked two other amateurs to fill in.

Northamptonshire had five different captains in 1936 (a record not quite surpassed even in The Month of the Four Captains in

Three Northamptonshire cricketers from the village of Wollaston. Cyril Perkins, Ben Bellamy and Reg Partridge. (John Watson Collection)

1975). There was Cuthbertson, when he came back. There was Tony Allen of Evenley Hall near Brackley, a brilliant batsman at Eton who impressed George Hirst on his debut and was chosen by Bullimer, in 1937, in his all-time County side. He only ever played eight games. There was Jupp, back in business and showing in flashes something of his old ability with the ball if not the bat. There was Beau Brown. The fifth was John Lamb, a 24-year-old Cambridge graduate and articled clerk in his father's solicitors' firm at Kettering.

Lamb was never in the XI at Winchester nor in the running for his blue but he had played for the County Club and Ground and Lord Lilford's XI. He had answered an SOS to play in the Kettering match against Warwickshire two years earlier when Partridge, bowling his off-breaks, had taken nine for 66 and won the game. Back in the happy days of 1934, Northamptonshire did win the occasional match. 'It was a dangerous precedent,' Lamb said many years later. Perhaps the committee thought he was something of a lucky mascot. He had scored 32 in pleasant fashion and doubtless made an impression as a decent sort.

In 1936 he was called out of his father's office to be county captain; the Law Society then were a little more relaxed about how articled clerks could spend their time. But above all cricket clubs had a very different idea of what was required from a captain. Interviewed in 1989, Lamb admitted that he did not have much expertise in captaincy but said the players 'were jolly good about it' and the other captains helped: 'All these people were so frightfully kind. They made no attempt to take advantage.' In the modern era, it seems extraordinary that such a youth with so little experience of cricket or life could be chosen to direct a county cricket team. But this was a society not unused to military ways, in which spotty subalterns would work with grizzled sergeant-majors. The problem with Lamb's army was that there were too few people who could fire the bullets.

Ben Bellamy had retired by now, though he briefly re-appeared in 1937 as a batsman. His replacement as wicket-keeper was the New Zealander Ken James, who had arrived to coach the previous year and was now qualified. He was in a sense a harbinger of the days to come when Northamptonshire would look to Wellington more often than Wollaston to find players. He had kept in Test matches and acquired a little celebrity for the catch he took to dismiss Eddie Paynter in the Old Trafford Test of 1931. He was another cheery soul, which was lucky, but on his arrival he tried to change Cyril Perkins's bowling style and make him bowl more on off-stump. Perkins's form never recovered.

Looking for comfort, Coldham points out in his history that the County lost fewer matches in 1936 (nine) than at any time since 1924 and not once did they did lose by an innings. A less charitable chronicler might have mentioned that it was a very wet summer. Reggie Northway, the former Somerset amateur, had some limited success but even Bakewell struggled until the very last game, when he scored 241 not out at Chesterfield, an innings that almost brought the team victory and was by every account a masterpiece.

And then, for the team that believed that at least things could not get worse, it happened. The best one can do is to quote Bakewell's own poignant account, given to David Frith of *Wisden Cricket Monthly* 45 years later:

Of course, everybody thought: last match of the season and we'd been on the booze. But they were wrong. Reggie Northway was driving. He was practically a teetotaller. The Sunday before we'd driven all round the Derbyshire hills. Absolutely marvellous driver.

I should never have been in that car to start with. I normally went with Jack Timms. Called in at the Trip to Jerusalem in Nottingham, and we had one drink. Reg only had a half-pint. And he only drank half of it.

I don't think anyone really knows what happened. A friend of mine came to fetch me out of the hospital six or seven weeks later, and he took me up and down the hill where we had the accident. Six or seven times at varying speeds, and the only thing that we can ever think of is just a slight bend – nothing to worry about – you know, they have a lot of these little round stones. And maybe we hit one of those.

It was a little sports car, with no roof at all. It was kind of a windy night, and you could hardly hear one another to talk to, you know. That's how I kind of got down, and probably dozed off. Whether Reggie dozed off or not nobody will ever know.

The accident happened on the A50 in Leicestershire. Once again it was just around midnight. Northway's body was found in the ditch.

It was a harrowing night for many people. Eric Coley, the secretary, initially understood that Timms, not Northway, had died; Bakewell, in delirium, was asking for 'Timmy'. Coley drove out to Timms's parents at Whitfield near Brackley to tell them to prepare for bad news. They went round to Timms's house to see his wife and found him safe in bed.

Bakewell was right about his first point: to this day Northampton folklore has it that he survived because he had so much to drink that his body was relaxed. He told Frith that he knew the truth all along about the question everyone was asking. Once it was clear he would survive – and that was by no means certain for a day or so – people wanted to know when he would play again. 'I used to say "I'll be playing very shortly." Knowing very well that I wouldn't.' His arm had been very badly broken and never felt right again. Three years later, he was picked for a Second XI match against Leicestershire. But he did not turn up.

Eventually, Bakewell gave all his cricket gear away. He kept a couple of pubs in East Anglia but his later life was full of troubles. His first wife died; there was a spell of probation involving the theft of a bottle of ginger wine and biscuits; and to add to the almost unbearable parallels with Milburn, he was involved in another car accident, in 1965, in which he lost an eye. Before he died, he returned to the County Ground just once and sat among the crowd: 'I didn't want anyone to know I was there.'

There was a further loss. Austin Matthews, on being told he could not have a testimonial in 1937, announced his intention to leave the Club and, once term had finished at Stowe School where he was coaching, threw in his lot with Glamorgan. A disgruntled message went out from the County Ground that Matthews could play for Glamorgan 'without comment from this committee but also without our approval'. The move transformed Matthews and he did so well in his first season there that he was picked for the 1937 Oval Test against New Zealand. It also helped transform Glamorgan, who jumped into the top half of the table and ceased to be Northamptonshire's companions in adversity.

The boys he left behind had an awful season. They actually got first innings lead in the first two games, against Middlesex and Leicestershire. But no one was fooled and it only happened twice more all season: at Leicester and Trent Bridge, against a Nottinghamshire team which had been travelling all night back from Taunton and dropped a load of slip catches.

There was a hopeful medical prognosis to the effect that Bakewell might play in 1938 and that provided some optimism for the future, as did the form of Brookes who made his maiden century against the New Zealanders, an innings, as a local paper put it 'he will not excel for a long time'. In fact Brookes's excellence was to be a steadying feature of the Club for a very long time indeed.

It is difficult to discuss Dennis Brookes except in old-fashioned terms since he has always been very old-fashioned, in the best possible way, both as a cricketer and as a man. There was a simple elegance about his game, which is obvious even from the old pictures. 'His many big and patterned innings,' wrote Tubby Vials in Brookes's benefit brochure 20 years later, 'have been based on the first principles of batsmanship, correct footwork and eternal watchfulness, and if a scratch appeared it was instantly eliminated.'

The cricketer sprang from the man. Of his batting and captaincy, there will be much more in the pages ahead. But there was something else about Brookes. 'Some of us who have watched first-class and Test cricket for 30 years or so,' wrote E. W. Swanton, who enjoyed playing the old buffer even in 1958, 'are uneasily conscious that the good manners of the game are in some danger . . . Suffice to say that in point of chivalry and courtesy, the younger players could not have a better example than Dennis.'

He only ever played one Test match, on the unhappy tour to the West Indies of 1947–48; he would undoubtedly have played more had he not been an opener, competing with the likes of Hutton and Washbrook, or if he had never left Yorkshire. But his

Dennis Brookes scored more runs for Northamptonshire – 28,980 – than anyone else; his contribution to the Club in the years since his retirement in 1959 has been just as impressive. (David Frith)

most characteristic virtue was staunchness and North-amptonshire, in their dark hours, have been lucky to have such men. Brookes was to be associated with the Club, as player, captain, Second XI captain (until he was 53), coach, assistant secretary and president for the next half-century. No one did more over such a long period to keep the wagon on the road. And it was never quite as bumpy as in 1937. On the day of his maiden century, the gate receipts were £4.

Five thousand people did go to the County Ground to watch the opening day of one international three-day game: this was the first-ever women's Test in England against Australia. Such a crowd must have made life more galling than ever for the County players. It did, however, expunge the insult done to women cricketers when they were banned from the ground in the 1890s.

The other good news that year also stemmed from that second innings against the New Zealanders. The County, set to make 430, finished on 308 for four and 69 of them came from Robert Prynne Nelson, a Cambridge blue who had played nine times for Middlesex in the early 1930s, who was now teaching at Maidwell Hall School and would be qualified the following year. He accepted the captaincy for 1938 with James as senior professional and coach.

There was not much to coach. Clark and Perkins had gone now, leaving Reg Partridge and Jack Buswell to form the seam attack with very little support. There was more experience in the committee room where no one forgot the past at all. When it was proposed that Darnell should accompany Schilizzi to the Advisory Cricket Committee meeting at Lord's, Schilizzi promptly said he would resign from the committee. He was mollified more slowly.

The gloom continued in the first home match of the season, against Nottinghamshire, when it was announced that Mr Clifford, the scorecard printer, had died. The gatemen clubbed together for a wreath only to be informed that he was still alive, having suffered merely 'a slight seizure'. The 1938 Australians, unlike their two predecessors, took no nonsense from North-amptonshire. Bill Brown's 194 not out equalled the County's entire first innings and was the prelude to a victory by an innings and 77.

It rained throughout the first day and the tourists were initiated into the game of darts by a local journalist. Bradman, as one would expect, threw a double 16 to beat Arthur Chipperfield. Next day, however, he was caught behind off Partridge for two, an event which attained enough national publicity for the Western

Brothers (famous for such songs as 'Play the game, you cads' and 'The old school tie') to pen one of their popular topical songs in honour of Partridge, 'such a cocky young bird'. For a team that had not won a game in three years, this match was not a disaster at all. The County Council nipped quickly through its agenda so councillors could get to the match. There were a lot of other people there on the final two days and Nelson hit defiantly for 74.

The Australians then turned their attentions to their routine of retaining the Ashes, and Northamptonshire slipped back into their routine of losing County Championship matches. In terms of results, the 1938 campaign was no more successful than its immediate predecessors, yet there was a gut feeling – expressed by players and press alike – that the corner had been turned. Nelson was able to lead by example, exceeding 1,000 runs along with Brookes and James as well as picking up the odd useful wicket with his left-arm slows, and he did his best to make the most of his limited resources by making the players believe in themselves.

Nelson was a stylish left-hander and a cricketer of substance in his own right; that in itself marked him off from his predecessors. When the side lost to Yorkshire at Scarborough, Nelson and Maurice Dunkley, a handy cricketer and outstanding footballer – carried the fight to Hedley Verity in an eighth wicket stand of 102 and a lady spectator felt moved to send £1 to Northamptonshire club funds.

The final match of the season, at Worcester, saw Northamptonshire on top with the home team, chasing 237 for victory, on the ropes at 91 for six. The opportunity slipped away and Worcestershire battled their way through by two wickets, but it was something just to think about winning a game. In his captain's report Nelson talked of his 'genuine confidence in the side's ability to show a much improved record next summer'. Bill Merritt, the New Zealand leg-spinner who had been a colleague of James's on the 1927 and 1931 tours of England, would be qualified in 1939 and there was talk of finding the money to employ a full-time coach.

Having gained some experience on the Stock Exchange during the close season – which confirmed him in his belief that his future lay in teaching – Nelson led the team in their opening match of 1939, against Cambridge University at Fenner's. Brookes and Timms made centuries and Merritt took seven for 69 in the first innings. Nelson was able to set his old university 323 to win in five hours. They were still in with a chance at tea with another 130 required and six wickets standing. But Merritt took five more

Robert Nelson – captain of Northamptonshire in 1938 and 1939, killed by enemy action in 1940. Under his leadership, the tide began to turn. (John Watson Collection)

wickets, for 92, and the County won by 78 runs. It was not yet the moment for dancing down Abington Street but the winless run, including non-Championship matches, had by then stretched to 101; and a victory over Cambridge was far more significant then than it was to become half a century later (two years earlier, Northamptonshire had been well beaten, bowled out twice by a sprog of the Norfolk cricketing family, the Rought-Roughts). And it was a start. It was a win.

The next four games were as hopeless as ever, though. The County just evaded an innings defeat against Hampshire and lost heavily to Middlesex, Derbyshire and Glamorgan. Next came the Whit Bank Holiday game against Leicestershire on the County Ground. Years later, Dennis Brookes remembered hearing the visiting pros talking about their Australian leg-spinner Jack Walsh bowling them to victory in two days. They were right in one respect: the game WAS over in two days.

Indeed, the scene was set inside the first 35 minutes: Leicestershire won the toss, batted and Partridge and Buswell suddenly had them eight for five. A local teenager, Len Clarke, turned up a little late, looked at the scorecard and instantly assumed that Northamptonshire were batting. There was a recovery but only to 134 all out. At the close, the County were 280 for two, after runs from Timms and young Percy Davis from Brackley, and with Brookes 120 not out.

A crowd of 5,000 turned up on a beautiful (in more ways than one) Bank Holiday Monday. Brookes reached 187 after little more than four hours and at 3.20 Nelson declared at 510 for eight. At tea, Leicestershire were 53 for nought. Then Merritt made things happen and when Gerry Lester was caught at 6.40 pm, ten minutes into the extra half-hour, Northamptonshire had not just won but done so by an innings and 193.

'There is not a name strong enough for such a scene,' as Nelson said, though that was Horatio not Robert. The young Club and Ground player Vince Broderick remembered a blonde woman rushing across to try and grab the stumps and Ron Johnson just beating her to the finishing line. After the crowd had swarmed across towards the pavilion and demanded a speech, this leader gave a speech that had something of the Nelson touch: 'I want to pay tribute to the team who have struggled through a trying period without losing heart, and who have kept cheerful in all circumstances. I feel we have welded ourselves into a good side and I do not think this should be our last victory.' But in fact, for very different reasons, the next win was seven years away. And Nelson would not live to see it.

The *Chronicle and Echo*, not a newspaper in those days which indulged in wild hyperbole, reported: NORTHANTS BREAK A BAD SPELL.

In other circumstances, June, July and August would have counted as a bad spell too and one win in 24 games was not much of a show even in a very wet summer. The County lost 12 matches, two of them – against Middlesex and Sussex (who made 428 for five to win) – after Nelson had declared. He was one of the first county captains, after Fender of Surrey and Bev Lyon of Gloucestershire, to pursue the strategy of challenging declarations – not that he was able to do it often, given Northamptonshire's frailties. Partridge took seven for 49 in a rain-ruined match at Blackpool to impress Cardus and in the next

NORTHANTS *v* LEICESTERSHIRE

Played at Northampton, 27 and 29 May 1939

NORTHANTS WON BY INNINGS AND 193 RUNS

LEICESTERSHIRE	**FIRST INNINGS**		**SECOND INNINGS**	
L. G. Berry	b Buswell	3	b Buswell	31
G. S. Watson	b Partridge	1	st James b Merritt	36
N. F. Armstrong	b Partridge	1	lbw b Buswell	20
F. T. Prentice	lbw b Partridge	1	lbw b Buswell	1
★†C. S. Dempster	b Buswell	0	b Partridge	10
M. Tompkin	run out	32	st James b Merritt	13
G. O. Dawkes	b Timms	16	c James b Merritt	1
G. Lester	not out	44	c Greenwood b Merritt	29
J. E. Walsh	b Buswell	14	c Partridge b Merritt	4
H. A. Smith	b Nelson	13	st James b Merritt	8
W. H. Flamson	b Nelson	0	not out	10
Extras	b 6, lb 3	9	b 7, lb 10, nb 3	20
Total		134		183

1st inns: 1-2, 2-6, 3-6, 4-6, 5-8, 6-34, 7-71, 8-97, 9-134
2nd inns: 1-60, 2-100, 3-100, 4-103, 5-120, 6-121, 7-136, 8-152, 9-164

BOWLING	**O**	**M**	**R**	**W**	**O**	**M**	**R**	**W**
Buswell	14	2	43	3	12	2	47	3
Partridge	13	2	38	3	12	3	45	1
Merritt	6	0	21	0	10.7	0	56	6
Timms	5	0	22	1	6	2	15	0
Nelson	1.6	0	1	2	1	1	0	0

NORTHANTS	**FIRST INNINGS**	
H. W. Greenwood	c Smith b Flamson	8
P. C. Davis	st Dempster b Walsh	84
D. Brookes	c Armstrong b Lester	187
J. E. Timms	c Tompkin b Flamson	55
★R. P. Nelson	run out	44
F. P. O'Brien	b Walsh	10
†K. C. James	not out	42
M. E. F. Dunkley	c Smith b Flamson	12
W. E. Merritt	lbw b Flamson	7
R. J. Partridge	not out	20
J. E. Buswell		
Extras	b 30, lb 11	41
Total	(8 wkts, dec)	510

1st inns: 1-18, 2-194, 3-295, 4-387, 5-418, 6-421, 7-467, 8-477

BOWLING	**O**	**M**	**R**	**W**
Flamson	27	2	125	4
Smith	31	1	99	0
Walsh	33	1	157	2
Lester	13	0	60	1
Armstrong	3	0	7	0
Prentice	4	0	21	0

★Captain; †Wicketkeeper

match Eric Dixon, the young Yorkshireman who had captained Oxford to a varsity match victory earlier in the season, scored an admirable 123 against Somerset. But mostly the news from the County Ground was not much less grim than it was from everywhere else in Europe. The cash flow began to dry up again and on 25 August the committee realised that the Club had no money to pay the pros' wages for the following week or the match money for the last two games.

The bank provided an overdraft to cover these expenses, but as soon as war broke out the following week, the contracts already drawn up for 1940 were cancelled, the staff given a month's notice and the telephone disconnected. In a way, 1939 was the most optimistic season the County had had for several years. It might be argued, however, that only the war saved the Club. Without the breathing space of the six-year hiatus and then the stimulus of the national sporting revival of the late 1940s, it is hard to imagine that this time Northamptonshire cricket could have kept going.

That fateful weekend, 2 and 3 September, before Chamberlain went on the wireless to announce that Britain was at war with Germany and the air-raid sirens sounded for the first time, actually saw one of Northampton's greatest sporting humiliations. But for once it was nothing to do with the cricket club. On the Saturday, the Cobblers were at Bournemouth for a fixture in the Third Division (South). They lost 10–0, to this day their worst Football League defeat. There is a wonderful edition of the *Chronicle and Echo* in which the Stop Press column intersperses the news of Chamberlain's ultimatum and general mobilisation with news of Bournemouth's fifth, sixth, seventh, eighth, ninth and tenth goals. It was said the Northampton players had assumed the game would be cancelled and got blind drunk.

Nelson had been invited to join the MCC touring party to India in the winter of 1939–40, but when the trip was cancelled he returned as a master to his old school in Harpenden. Although exempt from military service because of his job, Nelson was not the kind of man to be content to spend such a time at the blackboard. In July 1940 he answered an Admiralty advertisement in *The Times* inviting applications for commissions in the Royal Marines. On being accepted he began his training at Portsmouth but managed to fit in a match for Northamptonshire against Leicestershire, played at the Spinney Hill ground in Northampton in early August. He scored a defensive 60 but the opposition gained revenge of a sort for the events of Whitsun 1939, winning by 68 runs.

Nelson's last appearance of the season was for the British

Empire XI against the Buccaneers at Lord's on 1 September, a match eventually abandoned after the second interruption caused by the air raid sirens. In the play that was possible the Buccaneers' skipper, a Lt F. R. Brown, made 77 and took six for 59, his victims including Nelson for 45.

On 29 October 1940, 2nd Lt Nelson was in the officers mess at the Royal Marine barracks in Deal – playing cards, so it was said – when it received a direct hit from an enemy bomb. Thirteen Marines were killed, including Nelson. He was 28. Eric Dixon, another of the 1939 successes, died on active service with the RNVR six months later. The first Nelson Memorial Match between the Empire XI and Northamptonshire was played at Spinney Hill in July 1941. Messages from Sir Pelham Warner and R. C. Robertson-Glasgow were read out, and Cooke, as club chairman, told the crowd that 'Northamptonshire has had many gallant captains, but never a more gallant one than R.P.'

Nelson's death prompted at least two poems – one written by the father of a schoolfriend which was read at the Memorial match, and another penned by S.I. Phillips, who had played half a dozen games for Northamptonshire under Nelson's captaincy. It was reprinted in the Club's 1947 Year Book and is as good an indication as any of the affection engendered by Nelson in those who played alongside him:

> But he did more than hit a six or two
> In that brief happy knock, to help his side;
> His jaw was set, his bat was straight and true
> When patient strength was all could stem the tide.
>
> He taught us how to play the game we love
> And when the umpire's finger said him nay,
> A lesson of importance far above
> All else he taught – he smiled and came away.

Percy Davis, one of the youngsters in the pre-war team, talked later about how he had hero-worshipped Nelson so much that he used to try and stay near him. Beau Brown wrote to Desmond Donnelly, organiser of the British Empire Eleven: 'Having known him, you will appreciate what his loss means to this County. His own prowess allied to his patience with, and encouragement to, those under him worked wonders. At the end of 1937 the Northamptonshire side was a disorganised rabble. In two seasons he quietly and imperceptibly moulded them into a team which it was impossible to recognise as the same lot who had done duty before he took over the captaincy. His promise to carry

Brackley-born Percy Davis. Like Dennis Brookes, he followed a long playing career with sterling work on the coaching side. (Northamptonshire CCC)

on for at least one season after the war had been the mainspring of the committee's exertions to keep the Club together since county cricket lapsed. His loss has left a great gap.' In reply, Donnelly praised his fund-raising efforts for the Red Cross and added: 'From his quiet, unassuming manner it was impossible to gather that he was a personality in the cricket world. We who played with him admired him immensely.'

Maybe Plato put it best of all: 'This was the end. . .of our friend, a man of whom we may say that of all whom we met at that time he was the wisest and justest and best.'

THE DOUBLE-BARRELLED YEARS

'Pray heaven we shall not let them down
And leave disgrace upon our town . . .'
Verse on Northants cricket (1946) by G.H. Winterbottom

IN 1949, FOUR years after the war, Northamptonshire were due to play their fixture against Sussex at Worthing, which in those days still had an annual Cricket Week. As soon as the fixture list was published, the Town Clerk of Worthing began complaining about being fobbed off with such awful opposition. W.C. Brown, the former Northamptonshire secretary had by now moved to Brighton. 'Many rude things were said,' he reported to his successor, Colonel Coldwell.

Sussex finally wrote back to the Town Clerk: 'With regard to Northants, somebody must have them. This year (1948) they were at Horsham, in 1947 there was no home fixture, in 1946 they were at Eastbourne, in 1939 at Hove and in 1938 at Hastings. So far you have had not them at Worthing.' 'It did not seem in the best of taste,' wrote Brown sadly, 'for one county club to refer to another in much the same way as a smallpox epidemic.'

This story has a satisfying ending. Northamptonshire won the match very easily; and 15 years later Worthing lost its cricket week. But Worthing was just part of that story; 1949 is the pivotal year of this whole history, the year town clerks, rival secretaries and everyone else had to stop describing Northamptonshire in terms of contempt, patronage or even sympathy and take them seriously as one of the country's leading cricket clubs.

When Nelson – the best hope the club had had – was killed, this was nine years away. The return of organised cricket itself was still 5½ years off and there were some bleak times to come after that. But Northamptonshire, in an area that was not a prime target of enemy action, came out of the war better than many of their rivals and did more than most while it was on to keep the cricketing fires burning. The Club maintained some kind of programme every year of the war, which few others did, and this won them some credit in official circles. It was a situation made for the determined optimists who have always run the Club and at this time the most active was Rawlins Hawtin, he of the lengthy if disjointed playing career.

The committee had been elected for the duration of hostilities and continued to meet in the darkest hours. The County Ground's committee of management was holding its AGM on the day Winston Churchill became prime minister. The ground, however, was unavailable even for meetings. The pavilion was at one time considered as a possible billet for conscientious objectors (traditionally given the most uncomfortable quarters imaginable) and was eventually requisitioned by the National Fire Service. Sheep grazed on the field for a while, but a few local club games and even a baseball match were played there in 1943. Ron Johnson loyally acted as caretaker and kept the bowling green in shape.

Most of the County's games were staged a mile from the County Ground at Spinney Hill. In May 1940, a crowd of 3,500 – paying nothing except into a collection – watched play on a Sunday between a not unrecognisable Northamptonshire team, including Clark again, and a strong London Counties side. It was a festival sort of match and, almost three decades before Sunday cricket became the norm in peacetime, far-sighted administrators might have noted the turn-out.

Hawtin was instrumental in getting official matches restarted in 1943. The captain for these games was Peter Murray-Willis, two years older than Nelson, from the same school, St George's, Harpenden, and a man with at least the same quality of enthusiasm. He had played under Nelson a few times in 1938. Then, while fielding in a club match at Liverpool, he had collided with a team-mate, been knocked unconscious and left, for a time, completely paralysed.

They were obviously strong on sense of duty at St George's. Murray-Willis got into the RAF, which had no business to admit such a sick man, but he was soon found out and discharged on medical grounds. By 1944 he was leading a team with a lively fixture list of 14 games, some up to 100 miles away. They even won four of them – though perhaps the sight of Clark, aged 41, bowling out the Oxford Authentics, did not impress even the most biased Northampton man as an omen for the future.

Four days after VE Day Northamptonshire played the RAF, for whom Bob Wyatt made 92. No fewer than 14 players turned up at Spinney Hill to play for the County and Murray-Willis unselfishly stood down himself. When the County Ground was returned to civilian use, Northamptonshire played the strong Australian Services team in a one-day game and beat them – a feat matched only by one other county, Surrey. Since the County then beat Surrey at Hastings – arranged as part of an impromptu festival by Murray-Willis, who lived there – the club had every reason to be proud of itself. They were even £1,000 in credit at the bank.

Peacetime cricket brought a sense of normality, and a pretty cold sort of thing normality was for this cricket club. But Northamptonshire were alive, and, by their standards, kicking. Sixty-six people applied for the post of secretary and the position went to Lt-Col Alleyne St George Coldwell, late of the Northamptonshire Regiment and devoted to the British Legion, the restoration of the church spire at Greens Norton and the occasional day's shooting – for which, in the years to come, he would regularly take a member of the ground staff to act as beater.

He was always to be known as 'The Colonel' (though heaven knows there were plenty about) and always appeared in either the regimental tie or the purple and green of the Stragglers of Asia.

Alleyne St George Coldwell, the colonel who loved to shoot and who was Northamptonshire secretary, 1945–58. (Northamptonshire CCC)

He was the epitome of the old school of tight-ship but long-lunch secretaries of the days before sponsorship; outside Northampton they lingered into the late 1970s. Alan Ford, later the *Chronicle and Echo* reporter, recalled that the Colonel would begin informal letters to him 'Dear Ford'. And his announcements over the Tannoy were rather more clipped than might be acceptable today: 'Attention please'.

But he had considerably more charm or, as it might now be called, public relations sense, than many of his counterparts. 'After the war, when the ground was in a terribly bad state,' recalls one old player, 'he was able to convince ladies who complained that they really ought to go to the lavatory before they got here.' He was a good choice.

Before Christmas 1945 nine players had agreed terms for the 1946 season: a scare that Yorkshire might try and sign Brookes blew over. And when the first post-war team took the field at Lord's in May 1946 it included four men (Brookes, Percy Davis, Jack Timms and Partridge) who had played at Taunton in the final match before the war and was good enough to come within one wicket of beating Middlesex, with Denis Compton in full flow. There were a few small problems – for instance, in that time of shortage it was a while before a reliable supplier of caps could be found – and one major one: the captaincy.

The list of county captains for 1946 is a very curious one, mixing has-beens and never-wases. The war, if anything, had increased the perception that men needed to be led by the officer class and the idea of appointing a professional remained, if not unthinkable, then barely credible. Surrey wanted a chap called Bennett but asked the wrong one and were far too polite to amend their mistake. Northamptonshire would have wanted Robert Nelson. With this tragically impossible, they went for what they believed was a reasonable facsimile.

Peter Murray-Willis was 'enthusiastic', according to *Wisden*. His worst critics praised his sportsmanship. Players remember him as kindly, if a touch naive. When Bill Barron scored a century at The Oval, instead of buying him a pint, he asked him if he would like a basket of fruit. This was, in that time of rationing, a very kindly gesture; however, since the best-known story about Bill Barron concerns the time he deliberately dropped his false teeth in the communal jug of beer and shouted 'That's mine', it was a considerable misreading of his man. Murray-Willis was not a county-standard batsman and, after his accident, no fielder. The most famous tale about him is so enshrined in the club's folklore that one had the feeling it had to be untrue. But W.C. Brown, in

Jack Timms – one of Northamptonshire's most loyal yeomen. His career spanned the quarter-of-a-century from Maurice Fitzroy to Freddie Brown. Part of a series of caricatures of Northamptonshire players drawn for The Chronicle and Echo *by Pat Adams. (Ian Davies)*

the letter to Coldwell mentioned earlier, provides the evidence:

> I ran into Harry Lee, who stood umpire in the Surrey match at
> Kettering in 1946, the other day. He immediately plunged into
> recalling the incident in that match when Peter M-W in a flurry
> of arms and legs set off to pursue the ball and having lost his cap
> abandoned the chase to reclaim his headgear. As Lee said
> though, he didn't give away any runs as the Surrey batsmen
> were laughing so, they couldn't move.

By then, Murray-Willis's leadership was already coming under
very close scrutiny. Captain R.H.D. Bolton, who had played
briefly for Hampshire himself, was in charge of the appeal fund
and – incidentally – chief constable of the county. He had been
opposed in committee to Murray-Willis's appointment in the first
place. By mid-June he was referring to 'public dissatisfaction'.
The *Independent* was making it very public: 'Murray-Willis could
be criticised for his handling of the game,' it said after the
Kettering match. Two weeks later, on 21 June, the headline read:
'Are Tactics At Fault?' and attacked both the batting order and the
use of bowlers. Two weeks after that, it had made up its mind:
'Strange County Tactics'. The players had made up their mind
too, and Jack Timms conveyed their dissatisfaction to the committee.

It was known that Jack Webster, a Harrow School master and
Cambridge blue who had first appeared for the County in 1941,
would be available in the holidays and that gave the committee
their get-out. Murray-Willis was said to have resigned for 'business reasons' but the truth was that there was an embarrassing
meeting of the selection committee on 30 July in which Murray-
Willis more than once asked, with a plaintiveness that breaks
through even Colonel Coldwell's dry minutes: 'Where have I let
you down?' He does not appear to have been given a straight
answer, which might have been difficult to convey. The trouble
was simply that he was not Robert Nelson.

Whatever Murray-Willis's failings, it is possible to discern the
first faint rustlings of a new and improved Northamptonshire in
1946. Despite a very wet summer, Dennis Brookes became the
first Northamptonshire player to score 2,000 runs for the County
(Bakewell's 1933 total included other games) and Percy Davis and
Timms both passed 1,000 in the Championship, as did Barron, a
left-hander from Philadephia, County Durham who had come
down before the war to marry a Northampton girl and play left-
back for the Cobblers. Davis was to become almost as much part
of the County Ground scene as Brookes. He was in the grand

local tradition, dating back to Fanny Walden and ahead to Brian
Crump and Richard Williams, of jockey-sized Northamptonshire players. More than the others, he looked like a jockey –
indeed, his dad was a stud groom and Percy had wanted to be a
huntsman; he had arrived for his trial in 1933 wearing breeches
and leggings.

In those pre-war days, ground staff boys, on 30s a week, were
expected to bowl to members from 10.30 to 12.30, 2 to 4 and then
again from 6 to 8. Quite often, after Brookes made the first team,
Percy Davis WAS the ground staff. Either that or he was the 12th
man and was expected to get the bags to the station. 'I did a lot of
12th man,' he later recalled sorrowfully. In 1946, he finally came
into his own as Brookes's opening partner. There was still the
occasional horror: from 90 for nought to 106 all out at Brentwood
and 39 all out to Tom Goddard and Sam Cook of Gloucestershire
at Peterborough. But with Timms and Barron at four and five,
the batting had some stability even though the ex-Surrey player
Ted Whitfield had an early bang on the nose and never established
himself at no 3.

The other departments were less stable. The lost years and age
had perhaps mellowed Clark. Coldham claimed that, even at 43,
he was the fastest in the country but only for his first four or five
overs. Often, the support consisted primarily of Partridge, and
Bill Nevell, a medium-pacer who had drifted from Lord's to The
Oval to the County Ground. The variety was provided by two
overseas leg-spinners: the West Indian doctor C.B. 'Bertie'
Clarke and the New Zealander Merritt, who topped the averages.
But neither was a regular: Merritt was playing League cricket and
Clarke had his medical career to consider. But Clarke played a
major role in the only home win, against Glamorgan, and Merritt
(along with Nevell) in the only away win, against Derbyshire.
The fielding throughout was patchy and the wicket-keeping a
particular problem. Only Sussex finished lower and even they
won four games.

In that wet summer of rationing and diminished expectations –
so long in the anticipation, so disappointing in reality – the
County Ground must have seemed a bleaker place than ever. At
the first home match, against Worcestershire, spectators could
not even get a cup of tea or sandwich owing to a cock-up
involving post-war catering regulations. The crowd took it out
on the visiting team. 'We were barracked continuously,' complained their captain, A.P. Singleton. 'Anything done by the
home side was greeted by thunderous applause, anything done by
us with stony silence.' This does not quite sound like the County

Ground we all know and love, where everything is greeted with non-partisan moaning and groaning, but six years of deprivation and the absence of tea must have had strange effects.

The captaincy for 1947 was advertised in the papers. The local amateur Frank Chamberlain was suggested but he was unavailable (it was to be another four decades before Chamberlain was to find much time for cricket and then he would be elected in quick succession chairman of both Northamptonshire and the Test and County Cricket Board). Among those interviewed were Reg Simpson, just establishing himself with Nottinghamshire, and Jack Davies, the Cambridge blue. Davies suggested Freddie Brown but Brown said simply that he was 'not interested'. The choice fell on the rather less distinguished figure of Arthur Childs-Clarke, who had played a few games for Middlesex, the last of them 13 years earlier, and only cost £400 instead of the £600 the club feared it might have to pay. From this distance, it is tempting to wonder whether double-barrelled names in themselves appealed to the committee.

There was good news, though. After the war an appeal committee had been set up. The original aim was to raise £2,000 but Captain Bolton grandly insisted on aiming for £10,000 and it was presented to the population that unless the money was raised, county cricket might disappear etc, etc. When the fund closed at £3,284 Bolton apologised for having failed; in fact he had done rather well. There was now also a supporters' club under Leo Bullimer's organisation and Bolton's committee was directed to resurrect an idea from 1938 and try and raise money for an indoor school. Supporters were invited to pledge £1 for every game the County won during the year which, predictably, turned out to be an example of the maxim about it being better to give than to receive – in 1947, as in 1946, Northamptonshire only won twice.

But it also happened that there arrived at this club which was so sorely in need of optimism one of the most endearing – and certainly the most enduring – optimists cricket has ever produced. Jack Mercer had served in both wars. He spent the years before the first one in Czarist Russia and the years between the two taking wicket after wicket for Sussex and Glamorgan with fastish medium-pace, seam, swerve, swing, slant and sheer relentless enthusiasm. He might have played for England countless times had he not been a contemporary of Maurice Tate. He loved the game and loved imparting his knowledge to youngsters and, whenever that palled, loved showing card tricks instead. He was also deaf even then, an affliction that worsened with age, which meant that he was not always aware of what was going on around

The ever-optimistic Jack Mercer coaching the Northamptonshire players of the future at the County Ground in the 1950s. (Matthew Engel)

him. This often meant, at the County Ground, that Jack was an island of sunshine amidst a sea of depressed humanity. 'He couldn't hear except when he was on the phone,' recalled one of his proteges, 'and unless it was the name of a horse or a player.' He coached for almost two decades and was first-team scorer from 1963 until 1981, when he was close to 90. Even after that, he spent two years scoring for the Second XI. It was not quite clear how close to 90 he was because his age, like his scoring, had by that time lost a little mathematical accuracy. As he would cheerily observe: 'Everything's approximate'. There was no one else in cricket for whom the county scorers would cover up as readily as they would for Jack.

He was, officially, 52 in 1947 but he still had to turn out to open the bowling at a time of particularly bad injuries at Southampton. Seven bowlers were used in the only innings possible in that game and Mercer (26–4–100–2) bowled more overs than anyone else. Some of his time was devoted to making Vince Broderick's flighted left-armers an integral part of the attack. In his first season of regular first-team cricket Broderick had 860 runs and 87 wickets (including eight for 16 against Derbyshire at Rushden) and was talked about as a possible for the tour to the West Indies. Broderick had been on the staff before the war and it had taken him a long time to become an overnight sensation. The other triumph of 1947 was the arrival of Yorkshire's reserve wicket-keeper, Ken Fiddling, who was to plug that crucial gap for seven years. Herbert Strudwick, scoring for Surrey at Peterborough, called him the best keeper in England. But when one door opens for Northamptonshire, another one usually slams shut, and the Nobby Clark years finally reached a conclusion when his knee gave way; his last departure was achieved with no acrimony and a decent collection.

The batting fell away too: Brookes took an unusually long time to find his form though Percy Davis scored his first double-century and his brother Eddie began to establish himself in the middle-order. But apart from a tie with Essex at Ilford, there was nothing for the team to celebrate until August. In that summer of sun and Compton, the two wins were matched by 16 defeats and the County were back to rock bottom.

Childs-Clarke escaped much of the blame. He seems to have looked the part more than Murray-Willis, though one of his players remembered him later mainly for 'changing his bowlers by the clock'. In his official report, the captain himself blamed an unreliable middle-order, a shortage of guts and, as usual, the fielding. The committee were unimpressed by the discipline but they re-appointed Childs-Clarke for 1948, offering him £10 for every place the team finished off bottom. They probably guessed this would not cost them anything.

On the face of it, 1948 seems like yet another of the bad old years. This was the season when Glamorgan, the junior members of the Championship, won the title, proving that anything was possible; Northamptonshire, yet again, finished easily bottom. But, for what it was worth, the three wins were very good ones: the first over Nottinghamshire, Gloucestershire and Kent since 1910, 1926 and 1929 respectively. The victory over Kent, by an innings and 200, was the first at the County Ground since the famous one of Whitsun 1939. There was more than normal ill luck with rain, which came regularly when the County seemed to

Arthur Childs-Clarke – captain of Northamptonshire in 1947 and 1948. He was unable to lift the side off the bottom of the Championship table. (Ian Davies)

have a chance. And there were increased signs of what now would be called a more professional attitude at the Club. For a start, it was decided the selection committee should be reduced to people with experience of first-class cricket.

145

Secondly, there was a little money in the bank (gate receipts for all the counties, even this one, had been magnificent in 1947), and the committee decided to spend it on improving the team. In this, they found an ally who was to play as important a role as anyone in the years to come.

Whenever a Northamptonshire player had a benefit in the 1950s the key advert on the back page on the brochure was always taken by the same firm, bearing a message like this: 'No matter whether the vehicle is a sports car, a stately saloon, a heavy 'bus or a lorry; bearing problems that in the past were a threat to safety and reliability have for many years been solved by the use of TIMKEN tapered-roller bearings.'

British Timken, based at Duston on the edge of town, was under the very firm control of John Pascoe (later Sir John), a small man with what even Freddie Brown, who knew about such matters, described as a ruthless business sense. But all this ruthlessness turned to jelly when faced with Northamptonshire County Cricket Club, which any true hard-head would never have countenanced. He joined the committee in 1948 and for more than a decade all kinds of problems that were a threat to safety and reliability were solved by the use of Timken – specifically Pascoe's willingness to offer cricketers winter jobs with flexible hours, and duties that were sometimes a little vague.

It is always hard to disentangle the motives of such a man. Philanthropy? Sentimentality? Civic duty? Did he, like so many modern sponsors, get a kick from having well-known men on his payroll whom he could command and parade? Or was it a sound business-like decision to associate Timken with the Cricket Club thus improving the company's standing in the town. Whatever the reason, and it seems to have been a combination of all five, it was a wonderful relationship for Northamptonshire.

At the same time, the cricket authorities had begun the process of relaxing the once stone-faced rules of county qualification, by allowing 'Special Registrations'. Players would now be allowed to move counties without spending a year idling. It might have been specially designed for Northamptonshire and in 1948, they signed three ex-Lancashire players. Before the war, Norman 'Buddy' Oldfield had ranked with Cyril Washbrook as the most stylish of the county's young batsmen. 'No better young bats-man,' wrote Cardus in 1935, 'none so rich in natural gifts, has been found by Lancashire since the year which saw the blossoming of the Tyldesleys.' In August 1939 he made the England team and played what was, by Cardus's and every other account, a lovely innings of 80. It was not a good time to begin an England career.

Bert Nutter, in 1938, his first full season, had nearly performed the double. After the war, both he and Oldfield refused Lancashire's terms: Oldfield had a pub and Nutter had a good job as welfare officer with a cotton firm. They glided to Northampton with the help of Timken bearings, along with Gordon Garlick, who had played for Lancashire after the war but had struggled to find a place in a team well-supplied with off-spinners. These people had another advantage: they could field.

At the 1948 AGM Arnold Payne, the deputy chairman, explained that the recruitment policy was intended to be short-term and they hoped to implement a longer-term plan of finding local players. This proved to be so long-term that it stretched into the infinite future. But one local player had started to come through: Bob Clarke from Finedon, who like Broderick both batted and bowled left-handed, but did the bowling rather quicker. Clarke had spent the war on the cruiser HMS *Glasgow* and won seven medals, having been involved in Russian convoys, the Denmark Straits Patrol, the Battle of Biscay and D-Day. It was a record that appealed to Colonel Coldwell.

However, there was less of a sense of military discipline about the Club in 1948 than ever. Percy Davis was suspended for two matches and Clarke reprimanded, both for rudeness. By July, Hawtin was grumbling in committee about the captaincy. It was becoming increasingly clear that Childs-Clarke would not be reappointed and he was not surprised when he was told in August. He was 43, after all. As with Murray-Willis, it was agreed that the Club would present it as if he had decided to retire.

Most of the speculation about the succession had centered on Leo Bennett, an eminence in London club cricket and the man who should have had the Surrey captaincy in 1946. He had been playing irregularly, in the old amateur way, for Northamptonshire since then when not required by the BBC, and there were the old, familiar, 1930s-style discussions with the committee when he said he might be free in August and he might not. He was then told that negotiations had opened with Freddie Brown. By November, with the help of Pascoe, the negotiations were concluded.

Down in Worthing, they were moaning about how wretched it was to have to watch a terrible team like Northamptonshire. Back in Northampton, a revolution was under way.

RIGHT, SAID FRED

'I love the lovely bully.'

Pistol in 'Henry V' (Shakespeare)

THE BEST STORY about Freddie Brown at Northampton is so deeply ingrained in local folklore that, like the tale of Peter Murray-Willis and his cap, one thinks it cannot possibly be true.

The legend is that at his first selection meeting, Brown sat, saying nothing, while the selectors went through the time-honoured rigmarole about which amateur might be on holiday and who might be able to pinch a couple of days from the merchant bank and so on. Then he rose to his feet, pulled a paper out of his inside pocket, said 'There's my team' and strode out.

Once again the odd thing about this is that, in essence, it is perfectly true. 'The selection of this side has not been unanimously approved by the selection committee,' says the relevant minute, ponderously, 'but the captain's view has been accepted.' Brown's version of the story was that Tubby Vials, who was chairing the meeting, began to read out a list of names at which point he interrupted and said: 'I'm sorry. I'm the only one, with Dennis Brookes and Jack Mercer, who has attended all the net practices and this is the team I want.'

'Tubby could see I meant business and said "I think you're right."' Brown recalled when he was interviewed shortly before his death: 'Mind you, it's lucky I won the first match.' Anyway, for the next five years there was never any further doubt about who was in charge of selection.

Brown was different from the captains of the double-barrelled era, different from the captains of the 1930s, different from Nelson and even Jupp, because he came with the reputation as one of the most brilliant cricketers in England. It was, however, a rather elderly reputation. After coming down from Cambridge, he did the double in his first season with Surrey and was picked for Jardine's tour of Australia in 1932–33, where there was not a lot of work for young leg-spinners to do, except to learn how not to captain.

After that, like so many amateurs of his time, he played cricket only intermittently. In the war, as a lieutenant in the Signals Corps, he was awarded the MBE for his welfare work and then taken prisoner at Tobruk. He spent three years in various camps; his weight fell from 14½ to 10 stone. In the three years after that he returned to his old physical self but hardly played any cricket, except for a colliery team in Yorkshire, where he was working, and just once for Surrey. That was only at the request of the England selectors who were desperate to find someone, anyone, to put up against the mighty 1948 Australians. Brown tore an achilles tendon and that was the end of that idea.

He had told the Surrey secretary after the war that he would be available if they could find him a job. But he had heard nothing and simply wandered away. After the Yorkshire coal mine, he had gone to work for a plastics firm in Birmingham, a place he and his wife both detested. Coldwell rang him up and suggested a five-year contract and a job at Timken. He leapt at it.

Freddie Brown was a particular sort of Englishman: gruff, brusque, never suffering anyone much gladly and fools never at all. He knew exactly what he thought and, by happy chance, what he thought about cricket made excellent sense. He had played under Percy Fender, whom he admired, and Douglas Jardine, whom he did not. He adapted as much as he could of the Fender philosophy – when in doubt, try and make something happen – and discovered, probably to his great surprise, that he inherited a team capable of making things happen.

Above all, Brown could make them happen himself. In that opening match at Taunton, he took six wickets and when the team, needing only 64 runs for victory, wobbled, he came in at 27 for six and was there at the end. He had opened in the first innings but Brookes persuaded him to stay down the order. He made plenty of important runs there too. Vince Broderick remains convinced that it was Brown's playing ability that made the difference to the team, not his captaincy. Others, like Brian Reynolds, say the important thing is that he would never expect anything of a player he would not or could not do himself. The team's fielding improved through his example. He was stern and, if he suspected someone of slacking – especially in the field – he could veer towards bullying. The evidence is that Northamptonshire were starting to construct a good team in the years before Brown arrived. But he was the cement.

It was an extraordinary season, 1949. The County won ten games and climbed to sixth place. By the end of May, they had beaten Kent twice, their first double over anyone since Worcestershire in 1929. They beat Sussex twice as well (at Worthing and Rushden – it is unclear whether anyone at Rushden complained about the quality of the opposition). Many of the wins were very easy indeed: three in succession by an innings at the County Ground in August. For the first two of these, Brown was actually absent and Webster was captain again. By then, Brown had other responsibilities: three months after his return to cricket England appointed him captain against New Zealand in place of George Mann. Word was out about his achievements at Northampton. The catchphrase of the year was New Look, the fashion for longer, less austere skirts; Northamptonshire, obviously, became the New Look county.

Brown was soon fighting the committee – and winning, as usual – to get Brookes instead of the amateur Webster as vice-captain. 'I was lucky to have Dennis Brookes as senior pro and he kept it going. We spoke the same language and were honest with each other.' The County began the 1950s with boundless hope. But, though Brown was to be captain for four more seasons, Northamptonshire never went quite as high again: they finished 10th, 13th, 8th and 11th, positions they would have died for in almost any of the preceding three decades, but below the expectations that were building up.

The team was growing stronger all the time. There were two important signings before 1949, both Yorkshiremen. Jack Mercer waited all evening outside a cinema in Nelson in Lancashire to have a word with the left-hander Fred Jakeman who was to be an important addition to the middle-order for the next six years, though he was always nervous – especially against the Kent leg-spinner Doug Wright. Once he went out to face him without

'The New Look County' – Northamptonshire in 1949. Back row, left to right: Fred Jakeman, Bob Clarke, Eddie Davis, Gordon Garlick, Buddy Oldfield, Bill Barron, Ken Fiddling, Percy Davis. Front row, left to right: Vince Broderick, Jack Timms, Freddie Brown (captain), Dennis Brookes, Albert Nutter.

NORTHANTS _v_ SOMERSET

Played at Taunton, 4, 5 and 6 May 1949

NORTHANTS WON BY 2 WKTS

NORTHANTS

	FIRST INNINGS		SECOND INNINGS	
D. Brookes	b Tremlett	32	b Wellard	10
*F. R. Brown	c Luckes b Wellard	11	not out	22
N. Oldfield	st Luckes b Lawrence	63	b Buse	1
J. E. Timms	c Gimblett b Tremlett	57	c Lawrence b Buse	4
F. Jakeman	c Luckes b Tremlett	48	c Wellard b Buse	8
P. C. Davis	c Lawrence b Tremlett	0	lbw b Buse	1
V. Broderick	c Woodhouse b Wellard	100	b Buse	8
A. E. Nutter	st Luckes b Hazell	41	b Buse	0
R. W. Clarke	c Mit-Innes b Wellard	26	st Luckes b Buse	1
R. G. Garlick	not out	10	not out	7
†K. Fiddling	b Wellard	1		
Extras	b 4, lb 4, w 3	11	lb 2	2
Total		400	(8 wkts)	64

1st inns: 1-19, 2-78, 3-138, 4-210, 5-213, 6-220, 7-310, 8-389, 9-392, 10-400
2nd inns: 1-2, 2-14, 3-14, 4-24, 5-27, 6-27, 7-48, 8-52

BOWLING	O	M	R	W	O	M	R	W
Wellard	25.2	6	57	4	10	0	36	1
Buse	15	2	43	0	9	1	26	7
Tremlett	32	7	80	4				
Hazell	22	7	52	1				
Lawrence	35	2	140	1				
Gimblett	6	0	17	0				

SOMERSET

	FIRST INNINGS		SECOND INNINGS	
H. Gimblett	c Nutter b Broderick	51	lbw b Nutter	42
E. Hill	lbw b Nutter	4	c Brown b Garlick	37
H. T. F. Buse	c Oldfield b Brown	42	c Clarke b Broderick	9
N. S. Mitchell-Innes	run out	24	c Fiddling b Garlick	42
M. Coope	run out	3	c Timms b Brown	26
*G. E. S. Woodhouse	b Brown	5	c Oldfield b Brown	17
M. F. Tremlett	b Garlick	40	c Clarke b Brown	17
J. Lawrence	c Nutter b Garlick	9	c Oldfield b Brown	2
†W. T. Luckes	not out	9	not out	30
A. W. Wellard	b Garlick	8	c Garlick b Clarke	14
H. L. Hazell	c Clarke b Garlick	7	b Clarke	0
Extras	b 10, nb 2	12	b 11, lb 1, nb 1	13
Total		214		249

1st inns: 1-17, 2-78, 3-126, 4-130, 5-130, 6-137, 7-179, 8-184, 9-200, 10-214
2nd inns: 1-60, 2-75, 3-110, 4-147, 5-166, 6-184, 7-200, 8-215, 9-247, 10-249

BOWLING	O	M	R	W	O	M	R	W
Clarke	9	2	26	0	9.4	1	37	2
Nutter	16	5	33	1	14	2	52	1
Brown	29	13	60	2	24	12	51	4
Broderick	26	9	64	1	23	9	50	1
Garlick	9.3	4	19	4	18	6	46	2

*Captain; †Wicketkeeper

putting his fag out, and came back to finish it. Another time he was in such a dither that he forgot his bat.

The other was Des Barrick, a former Bevin boy who came into the side against the touring New Zealanders and made 147 not out (it was not quite his debut as he had played in one first-class friendly). Barrick was another in the great County tradition of pocket dynamos. He came from Fitzwilliam, the mining village that later produced a player named Geoffrey Boycott, another man who, in an entirely different way, was a strange mixture of shrewdness and naivete. What made Barrick very different from Boycott was his humour. He had never played cricket until he was 19 when his father suggested that he go along to the cricket school run by Johnny Lawrence at Rothwell – the one in Yorkshire. He spent an entire winter there, developed into a legspinner of some promise and was recommended to Northampton for a trial. This ultimately required a little deception on his part.

Fred Jakeman repaid Jack Mercer's patience with some sparkling innings. (Northamptonshire CCC)

Even Northamptonshire, who were by now practised at acquiring players from everywhere, had to notify a player's home county if they wanted him. Yorkshire insisted that he come in for a trial first. Barrick did and took seven for 32 with his leg-breaks. This is Barrick's account, given many years later, of what happened next:

> They said 'That's it, you can't go to Northampton.' I said I think I can get into first-class cricket more easily with Northampton but I'll stay if you can give me a contract. John Nash, the secretary, said: 'Even the great Leonard (Hutton) doesn't have a contract.' I said 'Excuse me, Mr Nash, the great Leonard doesn't need a contract.'
>
> Then he said 'Why do you want to go to Northampton?' I said 'I'm engaged to a Northampton girl.' It was on that premise alone that I got my release from Yorkshire. She actually came from Knottingley, near Pontefract, and we still live there. No way was I a Yorkshire cast-off, I cast them off.

Barrick's shrewdness about his prospects was far removed from his innocence about the game. While he was batting against New Zealand, Gordon Brice came on with the drinks and a message from the Colonel to make sure that they avoided the follow-on in order to preserve the third day's takings. 'Right,' said Barrick. Then he called Brice back. 'Gordon, what's the follow-on?' This is how he described an early event:

Yorkshireman Des Barrick collects more runs against his native county, watched by Jimmy Binks and Fred Trueman. (Northamptonshire CCC)

When I started I knew so little I didn't know there was such a thing as a senior pro. There were three or four showers and one bath in the dressing room and I got in the bath. It was meant for the captain. After 20 minutes I'm still soaking. F.R.B. was standing there with a towel wrapped round him, smoking his pipe. He said 'No hurry', so I stayed in another 20 minutes. When I went back to the dressing room there was a deathly hush. Brookey said 'Young man, come here, I want a word with you.' He went through the whole team and explained the order of seniority. Then he said: 'If at the end of the day there's enough hot water left to wash your big toe, you'll be bloody lucky.'

Whether the incident of the bath had anything to do with it or not, it took Barrick another three years to establish himself in the team. He was kept out because the batting kept improving. The signing in 1950 was particularly spectacular. Jack Mercer was on one of his trips round the Lancashire League and had gone to watch a quick bowler appearing for Heywood in the local derby with Royton. The bowler, anxious to impress, kept bowling bouncers, forgetting that the ground had a short boundary on one side and that the batsmen, a small but nimble Australian left-hander, happened to be a rather useful hooker. The bowler has been forgotten; the batsman was Jock Livingston.

There are plenty of people who will still contend that Livingston was a more gifted player than Neil Harvey. But Harvey won selection for the 1948 tour and Livingston went off to try and make a living. In 1950 he scored 1,886 runs and set a standard from which he hardly wavered. He had an extraordinary range of attacking strokes and a defence based on getting in line and staying there. One bowler said bowling to him was like trying to prise out a winkle. Livingston's peculiarly Australian mixture of chippiness and chirpiness seems to have appealed to the Club's benefactor, John Pascoe. It appealed less to the more reticent Dennis Brookes and their mutual coolness was a factor in the dressing room for years to come. Fortunately, it was tempered by respect.

With Livingston around, Northamptonshire began the new season brilliantly. They won five games in May and June, including the first-ever win against Middlesex, the last of the set, by an innings and 105 at the County Ground. The off-spinner Garlick destroyed the batting, taking three for one to finish off the first innings and ending the second innings with figures of 10–9–1–4. But Garlick was on the way out: though he was the leading

Jock Livingston. Australia's loss was undoubtedly Northamptonshire's gain. (Northamptonshire CCC)

wicket-taker in 1950, he was struggling to stay fit and decided to return to the Leagues. He departed accompanied by a poetic but bitter epigram from Hawtin: 'He leaves the limelight for the shadow and the cricketing public will know him no more.'

One suspects that, though the team grew ever stronger, the initial flush of enthusiasm that Brown brought to the job was beginning to fade. But Northamptonshire's tigerish fielding against the West Indies had been favourably compared to England's, and by the last Test of summer Brown had become England captain again, a job he kept for the 1950–51 tour of Australia. In 1951 when, handicapped by a shoulder injury as well, he played only 12 Championship matches out of 28.

Brown was still trying to impose his methods. The occasional bad fielder stood out in this team of terriers. This was Eddie Davis, younger brother of Percy, and a man who was in many

Bob Clarke enjoyed life both on and off the cricket field. (Ian Davies)

ways more suited to previous Northamptonshire generations. He had played soccer for Newport County and was in the team that had lost 13–0 to Newcastle United in the Second Division in 1946–47, equalling the heaviest defeat in the history of the Football League. Once at an empty, echoing County Ground on a murky day, a Warwickshire batsman aimed a skier in Davis's direction and Brown's despairing cry, when he realised who was underneath it, of 'Oh Christ, Eddie' was heard by every one of the handful of spectators.

He also attempted to control Bob Clarke, the Finedon fast bowler who was the best exponent at the time of the boys-will-be-boys school of cricketers. Once Brown is alleged to have hidden under Clarke's bed in a hotel to catch him bringing a girl back after curfew. Clarke got wind of this and locked him in. For some years Brown played Tom to Clarke's Jerry; he never could quite catch him.

Inevitably, though, Brown became less of a visible presence. In 1951, there were a succession of injuries to other players too, and the attack often looked very threadbare. Jakeman, who had a magnificent year, Oldfield, Livingston and Brookes produced a cascade of runs but only Nutter and the new off-spinner Syd Starkie, who never did as well again, took more than 50 Championship wickets.

Help, however, was at hand. The committee asked Jock Livingston if he knew of a spinner. Livingston later recalled: 'I said there were two spinners in the Leagues streets ahead of anyone playing first-class cricket: Cec Pepper and George Tribe.'

Freddie Brown and friendly rival captain Eric Rowan before Northamptonshire's game against the touring South Africans in 1951. (Northamptonshire CCC)

Both were Australians and it happened that Tribe had been best man at Livingston's wedding and was living near him on the outskirts of Rochdale. They were very different men: Tribe was quiet and diffident. However, like Livingston, he gave up any hopes of Test cricket for Australia (though unlike Livingston, Tribe had actually played – three times in 1946–47) and settled for the lesser though more predictable glory of life at Northampton. And like Livingston, he was an immediate, rip-roaring success.

Indeed, his success could not have been more immediate. His first ball in Championship cricket took the wicket of Clay of Nottinghamshire. He finished that game with 11 for 119. In his first four games he took 40 wickets. His rate of success fell off a little, because if conditions were against him he did not increase the wear and tear on his fingers by trying too hard. But he spent the rest of the decade perplexing batsmen. He had small fingers but a wide palm and was an extraordinary bowler who could deliver from the back, front or side of the hand and spin the ball at banana-like angles. Yet he managed to maintain quite extraordinary control and accuracy. He was also a charming mixture of enthusiasm and cunning: 'He would run under a bus to take a catch,' said Richie Benaud before pausing . . . 'off his own bowling.'

But he would also stop his car and get out to correct the grip of a schoolboy playing by the roadside. Many county cricketers never learned to read him, including some very distinguished ones, and some particularly distinguished Yorkshire ones (above all, Brian Close). He could fool wicket-keepers too and there is a theory that Tribe would have had a far longer Test career if Don Tallon, then the Australian wicket-keeper, had been able to read his bowling. At Northampton, he was to be far luckier. He did the double in 1952 and every year except 1958 throughout his stay. His left-handers' googly, leaving the right-handed batsman, could be completely unplayable, especially on a hard pitch.

Unfortunately, Northampton in the early 1950s rarely provided hard pitches. 'What is the point,' asked a local paper, 'of engaging men like Tribe if he and the bowlers of all sides have to keep labouring away on unresponsive pitches?' The game against Essex produced three double centuries (Brookes, Barrick and A. V. Avery) but never the hope of a result. The captains, Brown and Doug Insole, called the pitch 'quite useless'.

The problem of Northampton pitches was about to become far more urgent. At the end of July 1952 the Indian touring team came to the County Ground and, for this game, the County were able to include a young fast bowler born in Todmorden, blithely

Preparing for the new season. George Tribe loosens up in the County Ground nets, watched by (left to right) Fred Jakeman, Syd Starkie, Des Barrick, Vince Broderick (at back), Dennis Brookes. (John Watson Collection)

released by Lancashire, and then studying at Durham while qualifying for Northamptonshire. A spell of bowling that concludes with the analysis 21–4–47–1 does not normally become famous. What made this one famous was the opening over: the first ball swung so much it was taken by first slip and the slips had to move back five yards. The next four were all blindingly fast. The sixth had Pankaj Roy caught behind. These days we have had our fill of 'new Larwoods' and 'fastest-white-men', judged on very slender evidence. This young man was authentic.

Frank Tyson was a grammar school boy from Middleton, outside Manchester. He learned to play on the grey shale wasteland at the back of his council house with an old drum as stumps. At first his brother, eight years older, would not let him play so Frank's mum had to play with him. It was not long before his friend Geoff was complaining that Frank had bowled before he was ready.

He played League cricket for Middleton and then for the Royal Signals, the Army and – once – for Lancashire Second XI. He arrived late because of a rail strike, was given a rollicking by George Duckworth the coach, pulled a muscle after five overs and was never asked again. He was playing at Knypersley at

Staffordshire in an exhibition match when Livingston sidled up to him: 'We're not supposed to poach for players but if you want to play county cricket there's a place for you at Northampton.'

It was a year later before he reappeared against the next touring team. The game against the Australians in 1953 must have been one of the most remarkable occasions ever seen at the County Ground. On the Saturday, something like 14,000 people were inside, packing the three sides of the football ground where they had only distant views of the wicket. One latecomer recalls taking a bus up the Wellingborough Road and passing Bullimer's news-agents where the scores would be chalked up on a board in the window. It said something like 10 for three, which would have been quite predictable were it not that Australia had been put in to bat.

The latecomers had missed all the excitement. With his second ball Tyson had Colin McDonald not merely lbw but limping off after being hit on the inside of the knee. Graeme Hole still had his bat up in the air when his middle stump was down. 'We thought we knew that Tyson was good,' recalled Brown. 'In fact he'd never let himself go. This was the first time I'd seen him do this.'

For the rest of his life, Brown would recall this thrilling moment with relish. It did not set a pattern for the game – Australia recovered and won in two days – and it was to be a long time before Tyson acquired any stamina to go with these amazing opening bursts. And for the captain, it was a last hurrah. By now Brown was beginning to get impatient not just with the commit-tee and his less responsive fielders but with Northampton specta-tors – more numerous and more vocal in those post-war years than at any time before or since. The crowd would be especially large in the evenings when the 5.30 whistle blew at the four nearby shoe factories and the workers would pour in at half-price for the last hour and a half.

Brown, hating criticism of any kind and, Northampton-fashion, getting plenty of it, called the crowd 'the worst in the country'. He was still a magnificent cricketer: he was one wicket away from the double himself in 1952, having been robbed by rain on the final day of the MCC v Gentlemen of Ireland match. But by now disenchantment was piling up.

Before the 1953 season Brown told the committee it would be his last. He also told them that he would be chairman of the Test selectors for the summer series against Australia and that MCC wanted him to attend all five Tests, the Test trial, MCC v Australia and Gents v Players, which would mean missing 11 Northamptonshire games. The committee men knew the outline of this already: they had read it in the papers, which did not improve their reaction one bit. 'Discourtesy,' said Captain Bolton. Perhaps Brown's terms would have to be reviewed, said Vials. Brown apologised but said England had to come first. He offered, rather touchingly, to take over the captaincy of the second team in 1954.

Dennis Brookes was in charge for Northamptonshire's two great moments of 1953: their first-ever win at Old Trafford (achieved by one wicket with a team so weakened by injury that the Cobblers goalkeeper Peter Pickering had to be sent for to play his only first-class match) and, much more convincingly, the first win against Yorkshire in 40 years.

The County missed Brown as a player as much as anything. Livingston had a wonderful year; so did Clarke who just missed 100 wickets but that extra spark that might have made them Championship contenders was still missing. Before his death Brown said that he might have carried on another year if anyone had asked him. 'Once Frank Tyson was qualified I thought we could win the Championship. If someone had said do it another year, I'd have given it a lot of thought. But no one did.'

It is unclear how seriously he meant this. 'It was agreed that I would do five years and I was delighted to finish. I'd had enough, I was 43 and doing batting, bowling and fielding I was starting to feel it.' But Brown was not the only name people failed to consider when they talked about the captaincy.

Before the 1953 season the *Independent* examined the likely candidates and failed to mention the man who eventually got the job. The committee floundered as though the Brown years had never happened, and nice-chapmanship was the only criterion. It advertised in *The Cricketer* and got precisely two replies (the early 1950s was a time of unusually full employment), neither of them worth considering.

At least their sights were aimed a little higher than in the 1930s. One committee man said he knew Peter May, at that time much nearer the captaincy of England than of Surrey, who had Stuart Surridge in charge and winning the Championship regularly. Captain Bolton was keen on H. B. Birrell, a South African rugby and cricket blue at Oxford, who eventually wrecked his plans by returning to South Africa. There were protracted negotiations with Robin Marlar of Sussex. With hindsight, all this discussion seems quite ridiculous. The players appear to have thought so at the time. But it was March 1954 before Dennis Brookes was appointed as the County's first professional captain. Even then Vials said it would be 'an enormous mistake' to appoint a professional vice-captain as well, so the post was left vacant.

It was the end of more than one era. Despite the massive crowd for the Australian match (21,000 paid over the two days), attendances were generally down. There was a particularly small turnout for the Saturday of the Middlesex match at Peterborough. No one was to know it would end in a tie; they did know they could cluster round one of the growing number of TV sets and watch Stanley Matthews play for Blackpool in the Cup Final.

Never again would people turn up unquestioningly to watch professional sport just because it was there. For a few short years Northamptonshire cricket had been a naturally profitable enterprise. Those days were never to come again. Fortunately, Northamptonshire adapted quicker than most. In 1954 they began running a local football pool competition under the control of Coldwell's young assistant, Ken Turner, who spent every afternoon down at the competition office to the disgust of some members of the committee. They felt there were more important jobs for him to do.

THE PROFESSIONAL TOUCH

'This happy breed of men . . .'
      John of Gaunt in 'Richard II' (Shakespeare)

BETWEEN 1954 and 1957 Northamptonshire were as well run and successful as a cricketing county of such a size could reasonably expect. The team finished seventh, seventh, fourth and second. In all these years Surrey were the County Champions and achieved a dominance of the County Championship that was unique in cricket history. But by the end of the period people were making comparisons, matching the bowlers man for man, reckoning that Surrey's fielding was superior but that the batting might not be.

The captain of Northamptonshire was one of the most respected men in cricket, within the game and, with a rare unanimity, within his own dressing room. Part of that derived from his batting: by now there was probably no one who mastered spin bowling with such assurance and there was a certainty about all his strokes, based on eliminating the risky ones and playing the rest superbly. As far as Brookes's captaincy went, players of that generation regarded him with an awestruck affection which Brown somehow never quite commanded. It was unthinkable that anyone else should have succeeded Brown. But the committee thought it.

As late as June 1954 feelers were put out to another county captain about the suitability of one A. C. Burnett, who had played for Cambridge in 1949 and 1950. The message came back that he had been 'rather pompous' at university and was 'rather portly' now. The issue remained a scab for the rest of Brookes's tenure and every now and again the committee insisted on returning to pick at it. Professional captains were not a novelty by 1954: they were becoming quite voguish. England had replaced Brown with a professional, Len Hutton, two years earlier. Jack Crapp was captain of Gloucestershire, Doug Wright at Kent, Cyril Washbrook at Lancashire and Tom Dollery at Warwickshire. But the old habits died hard.

The team of the Brookes years – and the nucleus remained the same throughout – was almost certainly the strongest ever to represent Northamptonshire. In 1954 Tyson became qualified and the County also acquired its best-ever wicket-keeper. This had become a problem in the later Brown years. Ken Fiddling had done a very adequate job over seven seasons but had become prone to injury and ill-health; he had been temporarily replaced by Brian Reynolds whose real forte was batsmanship. Fiddling had been particularly useful in the years after the war because he was one of these people with the gift for obtaining, perfectly legitimately, goods that were hard to come by. Keith Andrew was, quite simply, a beautiful wicket-keeper. He was another success for Livingston, who had spotted him playing for Werneth in the Central Lancashire League. At first, Lancashire were reluctant to let him go but in those days of National Service, when young men were sent unpredictably round the country at bureaucratic whim, it was not always easy for counties to keep tabs on people and Northamptonshire, smarter than most, picked him up when he left the army.

Never had the Tudor Rose, marking the symbolic merger between the red and white of Lancashire and Yorkshire after the Wars of the Roses, been such an appropriate emblem for the County. Northamptonshire's recruitment policies were working brilliantly, so well that Lord's began to re-tighten the laws concerning special registration. In 1954 the committee voted Livingston an extra £50 a year 'special service grant'. The downside of this was that some committee members thought Mercer, whose recruiting skills were needed less, was now redundant and his job was saved only by Hawtin's argument that he 'breathed, talked and lived cricket' and by Vials's casting vote.

The crowds at cricket were falling fast in the 1950s but the afternoons young Ken Turner was spending away from the ground were proving mighty fruitful. The Club's football pool soon had 80,000 members paying a shilling a week and building up a surplus that was to provide the basis of the Club's future survival. Football pools of this type escaped gaming tax through a loophole in the law. Given the Club's uneasy relations with their cohabitees over on the soccer side, dependence on the ruffians' winter game was a little undignified. Ronnie Aird, secretary of MCC, sternly told the county secretaries: 'These receipts seem to come under the heading of "easy money", which I believe is a dangerous thing.' But as Turner put it later: 'It was like old age, better than the alternative.'

The Timken connection was at its peak. Pascoe, soon to be knighted, provided work for pretty well any player who needed it. This was not always easy as there was considerable jealousy within the company about the pampered players. Happily, some of them were worthy of their hire aside from their names: Tribe and Livingston were good salesmen (Jock could have sold snow to eskimos); Andrew was a skilled draughtsman. But the policy was dependent entirely on the Boss's whim, which meant it could not last forever.

Northamptonshire now had a terrific team. At full strength it had five past or future Test cricketers – Brookes, Tyson, Andrew, Tribe and Oldfield (and after Oldfield's retirement, Subba Row). This was a figure surpassed in the 1980s but by then Test caps had, in England anyway, become altogether cheaper. There was also Livingston, who had he not left Australia might have played in dozens of Tests. In 1954, more than any other year, he proved the point. He passed 2,000 for the first time; he scored double centuries at Trent Bridge and Maidstone and finished behind only Denis Compton and Tom Graveney in the national batting averages. And Tribe, as well as doing his traditional double, took 149 wickets, many of them achieved on wickets at Northampton that were blander than ever. Now that Tyson was free to wreak havoc on county teams as well as tourists, Northamptonshire had the fastest bowler in the country. But he produced only one match-winning performance all season at the County Ground. In July Brookes and Tribe went to a special committee meeting to consider the lack of pace in the pitch.

Fortunately, Tyson did enough elsewhere to let people know what he could do. His reputation was growing fastest among the fellow-pros who had to face him. There is a wonderful story about George Lambert of Gloucestershire, who had to face him as a night-watchman and came back quivering. He was met by his team-mate Sam Cook: 'Here's your pint. And there's a double scotch chaser. The bugger will be fresher in the morning.'

By August Tyson was in the Test team and he was chosen along with Andrew for the 1954–55 Ashes tour. The two men were lifted shoulder-high by their team-mates in front of the pavilion when the news came through, though the committee concluded that a civic reception would be 'unbalanced and unnecessary'. Both played in the First Test at Brisbane, which turned into a disaster. Hutton won the toss and put Australia in; they made 601 for eight with Arthur Morris scoring 153, having been dropped by Andrew on nought. Tyson had figures of one for 160. Australia won by an innings.

The aftermath for the two men was very different. Tyson shortened his run and produced a succession of devastating bowling performances. Andrew, who had only come in because Evans was ill, was made a convenient scapegoat. He only ever played one more Test, nearly nine years later. Even a Northamptonshire player probably gets forgiven for one aberration made at what must have been a moment of quite exceptional

Frank Tyson and Keith Andrew congratulate each other on their selection for the MCC tour to Australia in 1954–55. Tyson's impact on the series was to be immense. (John Watson Collection)

nervousness. But, like George Duckworth before him and Jack Russell afterwards, Andrew became a victim of the England selectors' continual temptation to go for the quantifiable virtue of an ordinary keeper who could make a lot of runs rather than a better keeper who could not: hence Jim Parks's 46 Tests to Andrew's two.

These were good times, though. In 1955 the Club treasurer, Brian Schanschieff, was still muttering, the way all treasurers do and those of this Club in particular. He said that without the £1,600 from the Board of Control the Club might have had to consider withdrawing from the Championship in 1956. Chancellors of the Exchequer always talk the same way, except at elections. Compared to the old days, the Club's position was magnificent. The 1955 season was marked by a Jubilee Year Book, thick with advertising (it even had job adverts: 'If you want a good job with good pay and conditions, call in to the Crown foundry') and containing the most bare-faced editorial imaginable, celebrating the achievements of 1912 and recent years, and then noting blandly: 'Space prevents reference to the years 1919–39'. By March 1955 the committee were meeting to consider the first-ever modern improvement, an indoor school.

There were characters in those days, off the field as well as on it. There was Stan Rowell, known to everyone as The Linnet, a supporter from The Fens who began by making annual appearances in the beer tent at Peterborough where he barracked everyone loudly and graduated to appearing with a bowler hat and black suit in the pavilion at Northampton. The hat and suit were not so much a sign of upward mobility as a result of the job he got as night watchman of a heating firm's show house that toured the Midlands. He would still barrack very loudly even after he graduated to the pavilion, but less often. 'He was like a street-corner Communist who ended as a Socialist life peer,' noted one observer, 'red-faced, plump, with a cross eye, a typical old-time village beer drinker.'

The observer was Fred Speakman, himself one of the County Ground's most durable and remarkable characters. Speakman was a journalist who arrived at the County Ground from Wrexham after the war, firstly as the *Chronicle and Echo* correspondent before he succeeded Jim Purvis as the local freelance. This meant serving every newspaper who could not afford or be bothered to have their own man at the game, from the *Northamptonshire Evening Telegraph* to the *Daily Mirror*.

Speakman was a bachelor who lived in digs near Abington Park and would wander up every morning, summer and winter, to say hello to his contacts at the County Ground on both the soccer and cricket side who provided both his living and his life. He was an old-fashioned journalist, with no literary pretensions but a perfect shorthand note. A combination of natural amiability, professional assiduousness and the fact that he was undiverted by a family meant that in his heyday, the 1950s and 1960s, when he covered the news as well as the sport, not a dog barked in Northampton without Fred knowing and, if necessary, reporting it to every national paper. For more than 30 years from 1946 he never missed a day's cricket that Northamptonshire played at home. Even then, he might not be aware whether the leg-spinner was getting turn from the Pavilion End, which was understandable given the absurd angle of the press box, but he always knew if he was sleeping with a committee man's daughter. He was a lovely man but he had the freelance's natural insecurity and was terrified of spending money, particularly on himself. He was never ruffled but generally rumpled and, as his successor on the *Chronicle and Echo* put it: 'his pockets usually contained a piece of toast, a bundle of cheques and fourpence for the telephone.'

Then there was Bill Smith, a small sharp-faced man with glasses, popularly known as 'Irish', who sold scorecards with a geniality and sharp wit that has probably never been matched in his profession. 'Up-to-date cards,' he would shout. Then, if a wicket fell, he would add the word 'Almost'. He would pull a card out of his satchel and shout 'I've just got one left.' Someone would then rush up and buy it and he would reach into his satchel for another: 'I've just got one left.'

When he died in 1961 the *Chronicle and Echo* provided a plaque for the scoreboard with a quote from John Arlott describing him as 'the world's greatest scorecard seller'. It vanished when the old board was knocked down, and never re-appeared. It was said some committee men objected to a mere scorecard seller being honoured in this way. Anyway, the 1960s were an unsentimental decade.

Ah, happy days. When Tyson and Andrew came back from Australia they organised the Cosmopolitan Club, a nice piece of self-deprecation in itself since everyone was referring to Northamptonshire as either the League of Nations or the British Commonwealth. In those carefree days, with no cricket on Sundays, teams on away trips could relax – i.e. get roaring drunk – on a Saturday night and play golf on the Sunday. The Cosmopolitan Club took charge of all this, collecting fines for the end-of-season binge; they invented the 'Rams' tie, awarded for the amorous adventure of the week, and had their own obscure rules: on Saturdays, players had to dress and undress wearing their caps, on pain of a fine.

On the whole, it seems to have been a very happy team. It was also a team that knew it need be frightened of no one. Tyson saw to that. He was becoming less diffident than in the early days out of university when the press were characterising him as the fast bowling swot; Bob Clarke had made it clear to him that fast bowlers were not expected to drink halves. Once a reporter arrived early at an Essex ground and found Trevor Bailey helping the ground staff move the sight screens so the game could be played on a slower pitch: they had just established that Tyson would be playing. Keith Andrew would threaten to 'tell my friend Frank' if anyone dropped one short at him.

Still the committee were restless about the captaincy. At the end of 1954 Surrey gave permission for Northamptonshire to approach Raman Subba Row. A local firm of accountants offered him a job and a salary of £525 a year was agreed. This of course was to be paid as 'expenses' in order to maintain the fiction, which had another seven years to run, that there was such a thing as amateurism. Perhaps only a Northamptonshire committee man could still believe in this nonsense. It was clear from the moment he arrived that Subba Row was the captain-in-waiting though Captain Bolton was still looking hard: he was indignant that none of the selectors had gone down to Timken to watch the Cambridge Crusaders and Oxford Authentics play. Why, there might have been another Murray-Willis or Childs-Clarke there.

Even those most determined to get an amateur captain again no longer had any need to look. Subba Row hardly came from a conventional background: his father was a Bengali businessman married to an Englishwoman. But he was a public school and Varsity man who played in the strong Cambridge teams of the early 1950s with both Peter May and Robin Marlar; Cambridge at that period was as thick with candidates for the North-amptonshire captaincy as it had been with Russian spies in the 1930s. He was a tall left-hander, strongest on the leg-side, and was never an elegant cricketer; but he was a run-getter of unusual determination, good enough to get a place in the Surrey team in early 1954 ahead of his contemporaries Ken Barrington and Micky Stewart. Some said he had only three shots – the leg-glance, cut and off-drive. But if you play them well enough, who needs more?

His path to the Surrey captaincy, however, was entirely blocked and Northamptonshire accepted him gracefully. Within weeks he was in the County record books. The highest score for Northamptonshire had been attacked several times over the past few seasons. Bakewell's 257 at Swansea in 1933 had been equalled by Brookes at Bristol in 1949; two years later Jakeman had improved that by one against Essex at Wellingborough; in July 1955 Subba Row scored 260 at the County Ground against Lancashire, sharing a large stand with Tribe and a County ninth-wicket record with Syd Starkie. All four of these perfor-mances had something in common: none of them gave North-amptonshire victory. But the Lancashire match marked a turning point in 1955. The team had struggled for almost three months but they won the next six games, equalling the sequence of 1909:

Barrick played a match-winning innings at Chesterfield; Tribe bowled them to victory at Leicester; Tyson returned to his best form against Somerset; Livingston played a blinder (172 not out in 160 minutes) to win a run-chase against Essex at Wellingborough; Broderick and Tribe bowled out Worcestershire twice at Stourbridge; and the team returned exuberantly to the County Ground to beat Surrey there for the first time since 1912.

This was the fourth of Surrey's seven consecutive Championship seasons and they finished it with a quite astonishing record: won 23, lost five, drawn none. This is generally put down to a dry summer and Stuart Surridge's positive captaincy; at Northampton they were simply outplayed by a combination of Tyson, Tribe and the New Zealand opener Peter Arnold, newest of the Cosmopolitans, who had slipped easily into the role of Brookes's opening partner. Northamptonshire still finished only seventh in the final table.

In 1956, yet another Cosmopolitan arrived: Jack Manning, a South Australian slow left-armer – faster and more accurate than Tribe. He was already rising 32 and with no hope of international cricket had spent the two previous years at Colne in the Central Lancashire League. At Northampton he was an immediate success: the foil to Tribe's rapier. And another left-armer, Mick Allen from Bedford, also appeared and finished ahead of everyone in the Championship averages, in spite – or maybe because – of the fact that he rarely got on before third change. It was a wet summer and with the County Ground pitches seemingly getting even milder, the County drew 15 of their 28 games. But they won eight, two of them against Surrey, both times on non-Test match days when the champions were at full-strength: in the two games Manning took 12 wickets, Tribe 11 and Jim Laker – in his year of years – only seven. At Northampton, with Livingston leading the charge to victory, Laker took nought for 73 in 22 overs. He found it much easier bowling against the official Australians.

Reynolds, relieved of the wicket-keeper's job, came through as a batsman in 1956, getting his chance because Subba Row was in the RAF. Subba Row played only two matches for the County but he was at the centre of the committee's thinking: in June it decided to offer him the captaincy for 1958, when his national service finished, provided a job could be found for him. In August, the committee was told that Brookes had agreed to play under Subba Row. The absurdity of appointing a captain two years in advance was to return and haunt the committee later. There was considerable turbulence behind the scenes in 1956. At

Another of Northamptonshire's Commonwealth contingent: Australian left-arm spinner Jack Manning. (Northamptonshire CCC)

various times, Tribe and Manning both asked to be released: Manning because he was worried about his knee; Tribe because he was upset at rumours that he planned to take a testimonial and leave. There were also complaints about bird droppings in the Ladies' Stand.

Tyson was injured for much of the summer and played only once in the Test series: the Australians, who had suffered so much 18 months earlier, had to face him for only 14 overs. When they came to the County Ground, Colin McDonald may have been particularly relieved to discover that there was no Tyson pawing the ground just in front of the sightscreen. The County still had the better of the game. Brookes emulated Snowden by scoring a century against the Australians, batting all through the first day for 144 not out. In the end, the Australians were struggling to avoid defeat: Livingston, Tribe and Manning – sons of Sydney, Melbourne and Adelaide – had naturally all played important roles for Northamptonshire.

Fourth place in 1956 was the County's highest since 1913 and there was better to come. This was a team good enough to win the County Championship and in any other decade of the century they might have reasonably expected to do so. They reached their highest plateau in 1957, finishing second. But Surrey were on a peak far ahead of anyone else: the gap was 94 points and Surrey were assured of the Championship by 16 August. Surridge, the team's captain and mentor had retired, but the formula he established was continued by May and (during his long absences with England) Alec Bedser.

Nonetheless, the games between the teams had an intensity that would have been unthinkable in the old days. One match coincided with the Edgbaston Test. This made no difference to Northamptonshire because England had now turned to Trueman rather than Tyson. But at The Oval in late May Tyson found his best form since his wonderful tour more than two years earlier: eight for 60 and five for 52; Brookes scored a hundred, far more than anyone else, to complete his set against the first-class counties and give the County their fourth successive win over Surrey. Then a week later, after May had returned from an epic performance at Edgbaston, Surrey won at the County Ground with Stewart taking a world record seven catches in the second innings: six at backward short leg and one in the gully.

Even when almost half the team were playing in Tests, Surrey's batting was strong, the bowling superb and the fielding of an athletic excellence that no one else – and certainly not Northamptonshire – could match. They had another advantage: they prepared The Oval pitches to match their bowling strengths. In this department, however, Northamptonshire were now at least trying to match them.

Ron Johnson, groundsman since 1930, had had another heart attack in 1956. He died the following July aged 62. He had taken the ground from the era of the Stockwins and for more than a quarter of a century had been as much a fixture at the ground as old Alf and his horse had been. In 1950, he turned down the chance to be head groundsman at Edgbaston, then expanding and flourishing, to stay at his post. His two assistants, Jack Mason and Dick Woolley – both in their way great County Ground characters – were both getting on. Mason had been on the staff since 1932 and even after he retired in 1965, stayed on to tend the

NORTHANTS *v* SURREY

Played at The Oval, 29, 30 and 31 May 1957

NORTHANTS WON BY 72 RUNS

NORTHANTS	FIRST INNINGS		SECOND INNINGS	
*D. Brookes	c Stewart b A. V. Bedser	9	c Fletcher b Loader	100
P. Arnold	lbw b Loader	8	c Willett b Loader	26
L. Livingston	lbw b Loader	22	c Stewart b A. V. Bedser	12
D. W. Barrick	c Cox b Loader	4	c A. V. Bedser b Barrington	57
B. L. Reynolds	c Barrington b A. V. Bedser	7	c and b Barrington	0
G. E. Tribe	c Constable b Cox	38	c McIntyre b A. V. Bedser	2
J. S. Manning	c Barrington b A. V. Bedser	1	c sub b A. V. Bedser	11
F. H. Tyson	c Barrington b A. V. Bedser	2	b A. V. Bedser	2
M. H. J. Allen	b A. V. Bedser	1	c Cox b Loader	1
†K. V. Andrew	b E. A. Bedser	16	c Barrington b A. V. Bedser	5
H. R. A. Kelleher	not out	0	not out	0
Extras	lb 3, nb 2	5	b 8, lb 4, nb 4	16
Total		113		232

1st inns: 1-11, 2-24, 3-38, 4-48, 5-66, 6-67, 7-73, 8-75, 9-111, 10-113
2nd inns: 1-64, 2-94, 3-186, 4-186, 5-191, 6-219, 7-224, 8-225, 9-228, 10-232

BOWLING	O	M	R	W	O	M	R	W
Loader	26	5	51	3	22	2	68	3
A. V. Bedser	24	7	28	5	25.5	6	51	5
Cox	12.1	2	27	1	11	1	38	0
E. A. Bedser	3	1	2	1	11	3	25	0
Barrington					11	1	34	2

SURREY	FIRST INNINGS		SECOND INNINGS	
T. H. Clark	c Andrew b Tyson	3	lbw b Tripe	10
M. J. Stewart	b Manning	24	c Allen b Tyson	0
B. Constable	c Allen b Tyson	11	b Manning	29
K. F. Barrington	b Tyson	4	c Arnold b Tribe	5
D. G. W. Fletcher	c sub b Tyson	29	c Kelleher b Tyson	12
M. D. Willett	b Tyson	4	c Reynolds b Manning	26
D. F. Cox	c Tribe b Tyson	5	b Tribe	54
E. A. Bedser	b Kelleher	17	c Andrew b Tyson	1
†A. J. McIntyre	c Andrew b Tyson	7	b Tyson	0
P. J. Loader	c and b Tyson	7	b Tyson	4
*A. V. Bedser	not out	3	not out	12
Extras	nb 2	2	b 4	4
Total		116		157

1st inns: 1-20, 2-32, 3-56, 4-63, 5-71, 6-92, 7-102, 8-106, 9-107, 10-116
2nd inns: 1-0, 2-54, 3-77, 4-102, 5-102, 6-103, 7-103, 8-130, 9-135, 10-157

BOWLING	O	M	R	W	O	M	R	W
Tyson	20.5	2	60	8	22	7	52	5
Kelleher	23	6	46	1	8	3	19	0
Manning	7	2	8	1	12.3	9	12	2
Tribe					25	6	64	3
Allen					2	1	6	0

*Captain; †Wicketkeeper

bowling green until he died in 1980. Perhaps a younger man was required for the slightly cynical task that was now in order. The job went to Bert Brailsford, a Wellingborough man who had been down in Wales. The technique he employed was described later as shaving the top and then rolling it hard. That made the surface nice and receptive for the work of the three spinners but even then it was not fast enough to help Tyson. Did that make the 94-point difference?

Northamptonshire won 15 of their 28 games, five more than in 1912 when they only played 18. They lost two, both at home, against Surrey and Glamorgan when the batting caved in during a run chase. Of the 11 draws, seven were disrupted by rain. The bowlers were unable to despatch Kent at Rushden; Essex held out against a tail-up Tyson at Westcliff and the games at Harrogate and Trent Bridge were played on hopelessly lifeless pitches.

There is very little more the team could have done, certainly not at the County Ground. But if Tyson felt frustrated that was understandable. In the first home win against Lancashire since 1914 (part of the first-ever double against them), he was required to bowl only ten overs; Harry Kelleher, his opening partner, bowled five. Manning, Tribe and Allen took 19 wickets between them. Tyson missed only four Championship games, three of them at the County Ground. In the seven he played there, he took 15 wickets compared to 71 in the 17 games he played elsewhere. Tribe took 124 Championship wickets in all (55 at the County Ground), Manning 104 (51) and Allen 77 (35). Groundsmen away from The Oval and Northampton were not daft either and Tyson rarely had Australian-type wickets to bowl on; he developed instead as a purveyor of swing and cut.

Such an attack was perfectly designed for the County Championship, a competition usually won by the most powerful bowling side. The leading batsmen, Brookes and Livingston, were 48th and 49th in the national averages, each averaging barely 30, which in the context of the season was not especially important. What mattered was that five bowlers (including Broderick, then 37, who intervened tellingly to finish off Lancashire at Blackpool) averaged under 22. Unfortunately, Surrey had five bowlers averaging under 17.

John Arlott had predicted that Northamptonshire would be their closest challengers. In the 'County Year Book' the following season he issued praise all round, as was his nature, and went further: 'Let us grant Surrey as great an advantage in fielding as Northamptonshire have in batting – even the excellence of Reynolds and Allen does not close the gap. The decisive factor may still be the wicket – the true dictator of all cricket. For all that has been done to the Northampton pitch, it still, as yet, lacks the pace that really inspires bowlers. Some have said that Surrey have the stronger attack – but would it seem so if they played all their home games at Northampton and Northamptonshire played at The Oval?'

In the 1958 *Wisden*, Jim Coldham, then engaged on the County's first official history, wrote an article on 'The Ups and Downs of Northamptonshire Cricket', defending the football pool ('Whatever else one may think of it, it makes football serve the needs of cricket') and the policy of importation: 'Heading for the title of Champion County, Northamptonshire consider they are doing a real service to English cricket by making so many excellent craftsmen available for our delectation.'

But they were not heading for the title of Champion County. The descent was about to begin again.

THE LONG, THE SHORT AND THE BIG LAD

'You might be any shape, almost.'
Through the Looking Glass (Lewis Carroll)

KEN TURNER had arrived for a two-month trial as assistant secretary of Northamptonshire on 24 October 1949. He took over as secretary in April 1958 when Colonel Coldwell was forced to retire through ill-health. Turner himself retired exactly 27 years later. When the Club held a presentation to mark his 25 years on the staff he quoted the French cleric Abbé de Sieyes who, when asked what he had done during the Revolution, replied 'I survived'.

When Turner was first appointed, he discovered that he was to share the Colonel's office, lit by one tiny gasfire, but retreat into an even colder dressing room if anything confidential was to be discussed. He was told that his predecessor, a spinster lady, had collapsed and died of overwork.

He had no background as a player and had only recently come out of the Army. No one could have predicted that he would not merely be with the Club for almost three decades but come to dominate its decision-making. For years, when two or three Northamptonshire players or members would gather together, the subject of Ken Turner would come up. He was never loved and only the more astute of the County's followers and employees realised that he ranked high among the small group of men who kept the County in first-class cricket. More than that, he was, with Brown, one of the two men who made them a modern, successful cricket club.

The colonel probably took him on because he seemed a decent chap and had a good service record. In fact, Turner was a visionary who pioneered methods of fund-raising and acquiring players which took the other counties years to cotton on to. Coldwell was a particularly fine example of the old-style county secretary; he could have run a small African colony just as efficiently. Turner was the pioneer of a new breed: resourceful and commercially minded. It was 1991 before his successor, Steve Coverdale, adopted the fashionable title 'chief executive'. But Turner was fulfilling the role soon after he took over as secretary, leading the committee rather than following its dictates. Two years later, Mike Turner was to take over as secretary at

Leicestershire and was to prove even more durable. The two Turners became firm friends as well as rivals (their players were sometimes less friendly) and dealt with similar problems in similar ways.

Ken Turner's ways included a strong streak of cynicism and a brusqueness of manner that was to play an important role in the build-up to the confrontation which convulsed the club in 1977. No more would the secretary charm lady members into going to the toilet before leaving home. But it was clear that the club needed a strong figure to control its affairs rather than smooth out its rough edges. The committee had one major decision to take before 1958: name a captain. It could hardly have botched the job more spectacularly had it tried.

In September 1957, Turner asked the chairman, Arnold Payne, who would be captain in 1958. 'Brookes, of course,' he was told. Indeed, who would dream of sacking such a successful captain? There was already speculation that 1958 might be the year when Brookes would lead Northamptonshire one place higher. But the promise had been made to Subba Row, two years earlier before he went into the RAF, and he expected the committee to stick to it. At a meeting with Payne and Hawtin, the chairman of selectors, Subba Row was – as the minutes said: 'obviously surprised and disappointed that the offer of the captaincy for 1958 might possibly be withdrawn. Should the committee wish to appoint Brookes, Subba Row felt he would be serving his own best interests if he were to devote his time to his employment rather than cricket.' The message was unequivocal. Yet it seems that Brookes had also been offered the job himself.

Freddie Brown, along with Hawtin, was all for Subba Row; Tubby Vials was vehemently opposed, saying 'it was not only a mistake for the Club not to appoint Brookes, but also a blunder for Subba Row to accept the offer, thus depriving Brookes of the opportunity of leading the side to more success.'

However, Brookes was 42; Subba Row was 26. At the end of 1957 Livingston had announced his retirement with what was then generally known as 'Compton's knee'. Without Subba Row's runs the medium-term prospect would have been very bleak. It was the sort of decision a committee could convince itself was harsh but necessary, looking to the future and all that. In fact, it may well be that the disruption caused to the dressing room cost the Club its impetus and perhaps the Championship. This, however, is speculation. What seems certain is that Subba Row would have left had he been denied the captaincy. The Player proved the Gentleman: the professional Brookes accepted his demotion; Subba Row was given a five-year contract with a clause that gave him the right to opt out if he was not offered the captaincy.

Brookes's reward came in another form. The money Turner's football pool had been pulling in produced the first significant modernisation of the County Ground. The tennis courts on the south side of the ground disappeared and were replaced by a new indoor school that converted into a bar and cafe in the summer with seats above. It was – and is – a hideous building, like almost everything built in the late 1950s, particularly by institutions. The School was out of scale with its surroundings and ensured that the County Ground's reputation as the ugliest venue in cricket would continue into the next generation. But it was a very useful facility, which a few years later would have musical uses the Club could never have imagined in 1958. And the seats under the state-of-the-art cantilever roof provided perhaps the best view down the wicket in first-class cricket, matching the top tier of the Lord's pavilion, at least for anyone with no feeling in their backside.

Above all, it was an investment in the Club's future. A County that had spent half a century believing that tomorrow would never dawn had spent £37,000, a significant sum in 1958, on a building primarily designed to produce players not just for tomorrow but for the distant future. It was a magnificent step forward. Brown, who had done so much to get his ally Brookes out of the captaincy, headed a sub-committee which proposed him as the school's professional coach, on a five-year contract after his retirement.

Subba Row never saw out his five-year contract. He was captain for four seasons in which time the County declined from second to second-bottom in 1961, via fourth, eleventh and ninth. This was not Subba Row's fault. A whole generation retired in this period and, with MCC becoming tougher on overseas signings, the County had to work harder to find players. Subba Row's captaincy is defended by, for instance, Mick Norman: 'He was a very good psychologist. Once he said to me "You average 30 but you save 15 in the field each innings because they don't dare run to you. So I want you to go out and think you're 15 not out each time you bat." It did wonders for my confidence and I went out and made a sequence of big scores.' But it is impossible to avoid the thought that another year of Brookes might have at least put off the disruption.

Northamptonshire had their chance in 1958. On 28 July, after Tribe, with nine for 43, had bowled the team to victory over Worcestershire in two days (an outcome not to everyone's taste, since this was Brookes's second benefit match), the County, as in 1955, had won six in a row and they were second in the table. But they won only one more game, the last of the season. There was a lot of rain and somehow Northamptonshire always seemed to be batting when Tribe might have been making the most of a rain-affected pitch. They finished only 52 points behind Surrey this time but also behind Hampshire and Somerset.

It was symptomatic of the season that the most famous performance should have been of no direct use in the Championship. Replying to Surrey's 378 for five declared, Northamptonshire were 18 for three and then 95 for five when Albert Lightfoot joined Subba Row. They put on 376, then a record for any Northamptonshire wicket, and Subba Row broke his own county record, giving his wicket away on exactly 300 after 9 hours 26 minutes and 42 fours. It was Lightfoot's maiden century. Having been signed as a medium-pacer, he now began to be talked of as a potential England batsman. Like Barrick who won similar praise before him, this was never Albert's destiny: he had county yeoman stamped through him, as through rock.

Tyson and Subba Row were in a different class. Both were picked for the 1958–59 tour of Australia. When they returned, after one of England's worst-ever tours, there was no mention of a civic reception. Tyson had played two Tests and taken three wickets; Subba Row had not played a Test at all.

Meanwhile, the Northamptonshire committee was about to surpass itself with the incident known at the time as 'the jumble sale'. In July 1959 Brookes and Subba Row were on opposite sides of the Gents v Players match at Lord's. Tribe was captaining Northamptonshire at Trent Bridge, and taking eight for 53 in the process. (This is incidental to the story. Tribe and Thompson are the only bowlers in Northamptonshire history for whom eight for 53 could ever be incidental).

Tribe was asked to nominate two players to be dropped for the return of the two stars. He refused; that was Subba Row's responsibility, not his. The selection committee then ordered that Brookes should be dropped, or at any rate rested. But the captain had not been at the meeting and by the time the team reached Taunton for the next game nobody knew what was happening. Subba Row decided that Arnold should be left out. Arnold then went home and was attending to business at the start of the next game when he was ordered to report at once to open the batting. He was suspended for three games by the committee for being absent; his defence, that he had been told by the captain he was not playing in that game either, was given short shrift.

*Raman Subba Row, record-breaking batsman and captain of
Northamptonshire 1958–61. (Northamptonshire CCC)*

Shortly afterwards, Subba Row went to see the selection
committee and said that morale was very low. By now, an
alliance appeared to have developed between Subba Row and
Turner to reform the selection system again to enhance the
captain's authority.

If the wickets were too wet in 1958, they were too dry in 1959.
Tribe, who had scored only 737 runs in 1958 and so missed the
double for the only time, made sure enough the next year. But he
was well down the County averages, which were topped by
Tyson who took 84 Championship wickets, just 15 of them at the
County Ground. Hawtin admitted to the committee after the

season ended that all efforts to put more pace in the wickets had failed. This was not a revelation. At the end of the season, Brookes and Tribe both retired: Brookes replaced Broderick – who became coach at Winchester College and stayed there for 28 years – as second XI captain and became, as promised, chief coach; Tribe was given a farewell cocktail party and a tea set.

There was a transitional season in 1960. At the end of June Northamptonshire were bottom of the table, and the only wins had been against Cambridge and the South Africans (the first victory over a touring team since 1933, achieved with four balls to spare against the bowling of the adopted Northamptonian Jon Fellows-Smith). In July they began to fight back in the Championship, starting with a victory over the Champions – still a speciality of the house – Yorkshire and continuing with another over Worcestershire on a relaid pitch which was exploited by both Tyson and his new young oppo, all 6ft 7in of him: David Larter.

This was not enough to keep Tyson in cricket. He retired, along with Peter Arnold. Manning went too. And Barrick, who had become increasingly injury-prone, drifted out of the game halfway through the following season, after being passed over in favour of Andrew as Subba Row's vice-captain. Ninth place was considered something of an achievement in all the circumstances. But by the start of 1961 the team Brookes had led into second place had broken up beyond recognition and recall. Of the regular players of 1957 only Reynolds, Andrew and Allen were left.

It must have been the youngest team Northamptonshire have ever fielded. All season, only one player appeared who had passed his 30th birthday and that was Andrew, who was just 30. There was only one foreigner, the Trinidadian middle-order bat Donald Ramsamooj, who had spent three years qualifying and then scored a century on his Championship debut in 1960. His contributions in 1961 were negligible. There were more local players than at any time in the modern era including the two regular openers, the fair-haired Mick Norman from Northampton, who looked like a monk and indeed almost did take holy orders, and Reynolds from Kettering, who was starting to settle into Brookes's role as lynchpin of the batting and dressing room.

There was also John Wild of Northampton, not merely a County player but the father of one, and Mike 'Tex' Dilley, the fast bowler whose county career was brief but who would later become a local club cricketing legend. In 1961 he got only 38 first-class wickets but took six of them in hat-tricks. The Wellingborough amateur John Minney also popped in briefly. Three other players – Allen and the two Watts brothers, of whom much more anon – were from next-door in Bedfordshire. Years later Dilley would maintain that the team was never happier than in this period when it was closer than it ever would be again to being a local team. Maybe it was happy, but also disastrously unsuccessful, in a manner forgotten since Brown's arrival. If the team had not won the last two matches, at Dover and Swansea, they would have been bottom.

Subba Row was a Test match regular and missed half the season, disappearing completely after the Wellingborough match in mid-August. This was adieu not au revoir. For some time, Lord's had been sniffing around enquiring into Subba Row's amateur status, which had been maintained for 1961 by a private donation to cover his loss of earnings. The Club was becoming resigned to losing him though it was shaken by the manner of it: in July he said he could not play in 1962, adding sideswipes about the club's discipline, groundsmen, nets, medical facilities and even the catering.

Some of his points were taken. Bert Brailsford had resigned and Norman Hever from Peterborough was appointed as the new head groundsman. And the County Ground salads WERE particularly grim around this period. But, as was true in 1948, just before Brown's arrival, the Club's position was not nearly as bad as the results made it look.

The best evidence came from the Second XI Championship. This had started in 1959 in an attempt to give players experience in a less formal atmosphere than was possible in the Minor Counties Championship, which had to have strict qualification regulations for the benefit of those counties obliged to take it seriously. From the start of the new competition, Northamptonshire organised more games than anyone else. In 1959, they came second; and in 1960 they won it with players who by 1961 were regular first-teamers.

The second-team averages provide a flash-forward to Northamptonshire's future and a succession of players whose adaptability was to be crucial to the team's next wave of successes. There were the Wattses: Peter, a leg-spinner who batted and Jim, a batsman who bowled seamers. There was little Brian Crump, at that stage primarily a batsman, who was to do more or less everything for the County in the years ahead, except grow. And there was the man with no need to grow, the player whose triumph and ultimate tragedy is the most heart-breaking of all the heart-breaking stories in this book: Colin Milburn.

Now that it had become much harder to sign overseas players,

Turner's approach was to scour the Minor Counties energetically. Perhaps his first major contribution to the Club was to turn its scouting activities in that direction and to pursue them with a vigour and professionalism that hardly any other county could match. His first signing, while still acting on behalf of the Colonel, was the Geordie Malcolm Scott, slow left-armer and Newcastle United centre-half. And from then the Club developed a connection with the North-East that would last until Durham were promoted to first-class status and the drain was to turn in the other direction.

It seems to have started almost by accident. Bill Coverdale from Gateshead, who had played for the County in the early 1930s, recommended four Durham lads to Northamptonshire and they came for a trial in 1959. It was the day of the Club's annual dinner and Turner was too busy to watch a routine trial. 'Have you seen much?' he asked Jack Mercer. 'Not really but the big lad can hit the ball.' As Mercer confessed later, he was such a big lad that his first reaction had been to want to send him home.

Turner thought the same and did nothing further until he was lying on a Welsh beach at the end of the 1959 season and heard on the radio that this 17-year-old, 'a well-built lad', as the next *Wisden* referred to him, had scored a century for Durham against the Indian touring team. He rang Coverdale at once. 'You'll have to hurry,' he was told. 'I think he's going to Warwickshire.'

Coverdale found the lad, of all things, teaching a Sunday school class; Colin's mother was desperate for him to become a teacher. On behalf of Turner, Coverdale offered £10 a week. Nothing happened for six months. Then Turner rang up and upped the offer by another ten shillings. Colin Milburn said yes. 'The best ten bob I ever spent,' he would say later. Turner thought that Warwickshire's decision probably hinged on the outcome of a committee meeting which is why, slow though he was, he was still quicker than they were. It convinced him, more than anything, that cricket clubs should not waste too much time waiting for committees to decide anything.

The 1961 season also produced one match that warmed everyone's hearts. It had nothing to do with anything: Northamptonshire were bottom of the Championship; Australia were on the way to their famous win in the Old Trafford Test. But having bowled out Australia twice, the County were left with 198 to win in 145 minutes to beat them. The last over began with four wanted and six wickets left. The last ball arrived with one wanted. Alan Davidson bowled to Malcolm Scott. He missed and the ball went behind to the substitute wicket-keeper Bob

Simpson. By now, the non-striking batsman Lightfoot should have been hurtling down the pitch. But he remained motionless at the other end.

A few years later, every county player would know how to react instinctively; one-day cricket would see to that. That era was dawning fast. At the start of 1962 Northamptonshire took part in an experimental four-team 65-over tournament called the Midland Knock-Out Competition. They beat Leicestershire in the final at Grace Road by five wickets and the players were each rewarded with a souvenir ashtray as county cricket's first one-day champions. It was not the most resonant victory of all time but it was the first time since Minor Counties days that the first team had ever won anything. Years later, one of the players said it was the only prize he had in his trophy cabinet.

It was also an auspicious start to the new captain's reign. Once again Northamptonshire were back in the hands of an old pro and team man. Like Brookes, Keith Andrew was widely considered to have been shabbily treated by the England selectors. His craftsmanship as a wicket-keeper was universally respected within the game and he did not have to spend time worrying about impressing anyone: in his first season as captain he broke the County record with 90 dismissals.

His popularity was never in question. 'If Keith fell out with anyone,' said the long-serving physiotherapist Jack Jennings, 'he must have been driven to it.' He was a captain whose thoughtfulness could go to extreme lengths: Turner once found him reading *Wisden* on the toilet in an attempt to discover how the team's current opponents usually got out and he would argue endlessly over probabilities of winning the toss. This may have been very prudent since Brian Reynolds would note admiringly that he would usually win the toss when it really mattered; during the Championship run-in of 1965 he won 12 out of 13. His flaw as a captain was sometimes reckoned to be indecisiveness but there may have been a certain method even in this. Crump, for instance, was an aches-and-pains player who needed to complain about his long list of troubles. ('The only person I know,' said one contemporary, 'who could bowl 50 overs on Saturday, see a quack doctor in Staffordshire on Sunday and bowl 40 overs on Monday.') Andrew would listen with the utmost sympathy and then take not the blindest bit of notice.

It was an approach that had an immediate effect. By mid-July 1962 Northamptonshire were fifth in the table and though they faded to eighth, everyone was delighted and a membership campaign brought in 600 new recruits. There were only seven

Championship wins but three of them were against the top three in the table – Yorkshire, Worcestershire and Warwickshire – and two were against the 1961 Champions Hampshire. Andrew had two pieces of good fortune. One was the arrival of the Cambridge blue Roger Prideaux as, in effect, replacement for Subba Row.

Brian Crump, 'The Atomic Pill' who blossomed as an all-rounder. (David Frith)

Prideaux was granted special registration despite the objections of his former county Kent and, in that last year of the absurdities of amateur status, given the job of assistant secretary at £1,000 a year, though it was hard to imagine him running Turner's errands. More relevantly, Prideaux was made vice-captain with Reynolds as senior professional. Naturally, there were committee men still obsessed with nobbery and snobbery who would plot to replace Andrew with Prideaux. But this troika was to remain in place for the next five years with very happy results.

The other useful accident concerned Crump. He was already established as a very handy all-rounder who could bowl seamers and cutters. Then at Kettering, during a sluggish, purposeless match against Gloucestershire, Larter went off injured, not for the first or last time. Andrew gave Crump the new ball and he started bowling zippy inswingers. He at once began taking important wickets and when Andrew managed to put the 6ft 7in Larter and the 5ft 4in Crump on together the variations in bounce caused batsmen no end of trouble. Crump was soon christened 'the Atomic Pill' by the Essex players. Since Milburn would often come on as first-change seamer, there was something of the freak show about Northamptonshire's attack. But it worked and the team again began to give the impression that it enjoyed playing cricket.

David Larter, 6ft 7in fast bowler with a gentle nature. (David Frith)

Though he needed nursing, Larter took 101 wickets in 1962, nine of them on his Test debut against Pakistan; and for the fourth time in a row Northamptonshire were represented in the touring team to Australia. Larter was what would now be called a 'laid back' character. Indeed, some say he was usually laid-back when he was off the field, fast asleep in the dressing room. He was a gentle man who had to manufacture the fast bowler's aggression. He might have lasted longer if there had been less pressure on him to be the new Tyson and he had concentrated on bowling slower, shifting the ball and conserving his fitness.

Though he failed to make the Test team on tour, the Aussies were impressed by what they called 'Sky balls' and he did his reputation no harm. The next summer he took 110 wickets in the Championship alone. Tyson had never taken 100 for the County; nor had any other fast bowler since Clark in 1929. What was entirely unexpected was that Crump also took 100. And for the

Team-mates, opponents and spectators look on as Roger Prideaux receives his 'man-of-the-match' award from Frank Woolley after Northamptonshire's first-ever match in the new Gillette Cup competition. The County beat Warwickshire by six wickets, Prideaux contributing an unbeaten 52. (Northamptonshire CCC)

first time the big lad began to show what he could do. Against this most powerful of West Indian touring teams, Milburn scored 100 and 88. It must have been on this occasion that he walked into the pavilion to be capped by Linnet with his bowler hat. The official cap came in a more formal ceremony.

At the end of July Northamptonshire were third in the table, having beaten Derbyshire in two days in Andrew's benefit match. They reached the semi-final of the new 'Knock-out Competition', the national extension of the previous year's Midland competition and shortly to be known as the Gillette Cup. They lost to Sussex at 8pm on a July evening, in front of what was probably the biggest County Ground crowd since 1953. In August they fell away, beaten out of sight in game after game on pitches where Tribe and Manning would have been unplayable. Livingston was despatched, as of old, on a trek round the Leagues to find a spinner but he came back in October and reported no success.

The County did eventually find two men who could spin the ball, though none of them could exactly be called the new George Tribe. One was already on the staff: Crump's cousin and soul-mate, David Steele. Both had been coached by Brian's father Stan, who should have been a county player himself, in the back garden of the Crump house in Stoke-on-Trent, sweeping the snow away when necessary. All the Crumps and Steeles were cricket-daft and every one of them an all-rounder too. Soon after they could walk, their grandfather carved a little bat for them and kept it behind his outside toilet. Whenever the lads went round there Granddad would say at once: 'Go and get your bat out. We'll have a go in the yard.'

Though he was of normal height and weight which was in itself was quite unusual in the Northamptonshire team of the early 1960s, Steele actually looked even odder than his cousin since he had turned grey when he was 16 ('It was fine if I wanted to get into a pub under age, but dodgy when I tried to get into the boys' entrance at Stoke City') and he wore a thoroughly unfashionable pair of specs. It required an effort of will to imagine that a man in his early 20s who was already a dead ringer for the Ancient Mariner would make a career for himself in cricket; the idea that he would become an England player, the BBC Sports Personality of the Year and for a brief, bizarre but happy period a sort of national icon would have been entirely beyond belief.

The other new spinners included a cricketer of even greater quality: on the principle that if you can't beat 'em, sign 'em, the County took a shine to the young scion of the Pakistani family

Mohammad, Mushtaq, who had made a century against them for the Pakistan Eaglets at Peterborough in 1963 and could also bowl leg-breaks as a sideline. Unfortunately, he would not be qualified until 1966. For the short term, they picked up Haydn Sully, an off-spinner who was kept out of the Somerset side by Brian Langford.

One spin bowler left: Mick Allen went to Derbyshire. Another responded by having the season of his life: the left-armer Scott took 113 wickets in 1964. Larter and Crump were not far behind. Prideaux and Reynolds scored regularly; Milburn occasionally, but thrillingly. Milburn also took 43 catches, a County record, mostly at short-leg. The most memorable individual performance of the summer was achieved by Norman, who was out to Ossie Wheatley first ball twice in a day at Swansea – 'a super king pair' it was called at the time; an emperor pair might be better.

But despite a bleak period in mid-season when they managed only two points in seven games, Northamptonshire surged through the summer of 1964 and finished third. 'They began as if convinced of victory over their mediocre opponents,' said *Wisden* of the late-August innings-win over Leicestershire, which is the sort of remark its correspondents used to pass when other teams were playing Northamptonshire. 'The cricket played by Northants in 1964,' said the almanack's review of the season, 'suggested that the county are now equipped to reap full reward for their extensive rebuilding.'

The financial position was not too bad either. The optimists were slowly poking their heads above the parapet again.

THE SPARTA OF THE MIDLANDS

'. . . the selfish hope of a season's fame.'

Sir Henry Newbolt

IN THE SUMMER of 1965 *The Sun* newspaper, then not in the hands of Rupert Murdoch and thus less inclined to exaggerate, ran a paragraph in its sports diary nominating the most successful sporting town in Britain. There was no argument. The football team had just won promotion to the First Division; the rugby team had finished the 1964–65 season with the best record of any club in England; it had supplied other sportsmen like Billy Knight the tennis player; and the cricket team was apparently on the brink of becoming Champion County.

For one brief, shining moment Northampton was a sort of sporting Camelot. Then everyone woke up. The rugby club was to go through many far leaner years in the decades to come. The football club, having climbed out of the Fourth Division four years earlier, was back there four years later. However, Northampton Town FC – bizarre though it seemed at the time looking at the squalid football side of the County Ground – did play a season in the First Division, and did not disgrace themselves either, not on the field anyway, being relegated with more points than any other team before them. They were left with memories, which is all a club so over-promoted could expect.

For the Cricket Club, the legacy of 1965 was far more bitter. Sisyphus was the mythical king condemned to spend eternity rolling a boulder almost to the top of the hill then watch it escape his grasp and roll back to the bottom again. Northamptonshire County Cricket Club seem to be doomed to spend eternity doing precisely the same thing.

Northamptonshire came second in 1965, four points behind the eventual champions Worcestershire. In 1912 the gap was only two points but the whole experience had been a surprise, a delight and an adventure; no one really expected the team to be Champions and it would have set an absurd standard for the future if they had been. In 1957, when they were also second, the gap was 94 points and the winning post never came in sight. The County finished 1965 convinced they wuz robbed.

They began the season very badly and failed to get a single

point until the very end of May. They then climbed the table, even though at first they were without Andrew, who missed four games with an injured finger and was replaced by Prideaux as captain and by Laurie Johnson as wicket-keeper. Johnson was an extraordinary man who had moved from being no 3 keeper at The Oval (behind Arthur McIntyre and Roy Swetman) for the even less rewarding task of being Andrew's deputy: he took ten dismissals in the match against Warwickshire at Edgbaston and was immediately dropped.

In the third week of June Larter bowled out Somerset at the County Ground and Yorkshire at Headingley, taking four for 28, eight for 28, five for 43 and seven for 37 in successive innings – 24 wickets, average 5.66: even Test selectors noticed that. By now Northamptonshire were second in the table. On 29 June Crump and Larter bowled out Leicestershire for 113 and North-amptonshire were top equal with Middlesex. With Larter back in the Test team, his deputy Mike Kettle took five for 53 at Trent Bridge and Northamptonshire won in time to come back home and see the Queen's visit to Northampton. On 16 July they beat Somerset and went clear at the top, where they stayed until 31 August, the day the Championship was won by Worcestershire, who had never led the table at any other time.

There were several remarkable features in all this. Individually, the County's players achieved very little. The most successful batsman was Jim Watts, 37th in the national averages at 30.57 and without a century. Indeed, only four centuries were hit for the County all season. In a sense, this just emphasises the point that successful teams in the Championship do not waste their time piling up runs, they go out and take wickets. But only Crump took 100 wickets. The essence of Northamptonshire's year was a one-for-allness that was very appealing. The team was full of what would later become known, disparagingly, as bits-and-pieces men.

There is an argument that the team just lacked that little extra bit of adventurousness that might have made them Champions. In late July, Middlesex, also Championship contenders, came to the County Ground and in a low-scoring match typical of the season neither captain would take a risk. Andrew delayed his declaration and then set Middlesex a completely theoretical 158 in 80 minutes. One County supporter has maintained, almost alone, ever since that it was Andrew's conservatism that cost North-amptonshire the title.

At the time, this game was soon forgotten. The County won the next five, including a thriller at Cardiff against the team who

Waiting to toast Northamptonshire's first Championship title? Brian Reynolds inspects his special benefit year tankards in 1965. (The Chronicle and Echo)

appeared to be their main rivals, Glamorgan. Amid enormous tension Crump and Lightfoot (who otherwise hardly bowled all season) stopped Glamorgan getting 139 to win and secured victory by 18 runs. Crump had bowled more than 76 overs in the match and taken eight for 142. He was carried into the pavilion, in exhaustion as much as in triumph.

Then came a two-day win at Old Trafford, in which Sully took 11 for 87. To Worcester: two games to go, 28 points clear. Back at the County Ground, the executive committee met to discuss how the Club might celebrate the Championship: the Borough

NORTHANTS *v* GLAMORGAN

Played at Cardiff, 4 and 6 August 1965

NORTHANTS WON BY 18 RUNS

NORTHANTS	FIRST INNINGS		SECOND INNINGS	
M. E. J. C. Norman	lbw b Wheatley	4	b Miller	3
B. L. Reynolds	c and b Wheatley	9	c Miller b Shepherd	14
C. Milburn	c E. J. Lewis b Shepherd	16	c Pressdee b Miller	0
R. M. Prideaux	c Walker b Shepherd	40	b Miller	2
D. S. Steele	lbw b E. J. Lewis	55	b Shepherd	0
P. J. Watts	b Shepherd	26	c Walker b Shepherd	51
B. S. Crump	c Hedges b Shepherd	5	lbw b Pressdee	31
P. D. Watts	c and b Wheatley	25	c Evans b Shepherd	10
A. Lightfoot	c E. J. Lewis b Shepherd	0	c Walker b Shepherd	17
M. E. Scott	c Walker b Shepherd	1	c Walker b Pressdee	3
*†K. V. Andrew	not out	0	not out	0
Extras	lb 3, nb 2	5	b 4, lb 6	10
Total		186		141

1st inns: 1-8, 2-15, 3-29, 4-115, 5-139, 6-144, 7-164, 8-166, 9-186, 10-186
2nd inns: 1-13, 2-13, 3-19, 4-19, 5-19, 6-32, 7-78, 8-131, 9-139, 10-141

BOWLING	O	M	R	W	O	M	R	W
Wheatley	16.3	9	16	3	9	6	23	0
Miller	15	5	45	0	12	4	21	3
Shepherd	34	20	32	6	31	15	51	5
Pressdee	10	3	20	0	11.3	5	14	2
E. J. Lewis	24	8	68	1	8	3	22	0

GLAMORGAN	FIRST INNINGS		SECOND INNINGS	
B. Hedges	lbw b Steele	47	c P. D. Watts b Crump	12
A. Jones	st Andrew b Scott	21	c Andrew b P. J. Watts	13
P. M. Walker	c and b P. J. Watts	55	lbw b Lightfoot	10
H. D. S. Miller	c Steele b Crump	1	c Steele b Lightfoot	1
A. R. Lewis	c Reynolds b P. J. Watts	20	c Milburn b Lightfoot	15
J. S. Pressdee	c Steele b P. J. Watts	0	c Steele b Crump	2
A. Rees	c P. D. Watts b Crump	2	lbw b Crump	37
E. J. Lewis	c Steele b P. J. Watts	0	run out	2
†D. L. Evans	lbw b Crump	3	lbw b Crump	9
D. J. Shepherd	not out	22	c Prideaux b Scott	9
*O. S. Wheatley	b Crump	10	not out	0
Extras	lb 6, nb 2	8	b 4, lb 6	10
Total		189		120

1st inns: 1-27, 2-83, 3-84, 4-129, 5-133, 6-138, 7-143, 8-150, 9-158, 10-189
2nd inns: 1-22, 2-26, 3-36, 4-54, 5-57, 6-77, 7-79, 8-86, 9-115, 10-120

BOWLING	O	M	R	W	O	M	R	W
Crump	41.2	15	77	4	35.1	11	65	4
P. J. Watts	28	9	43	4	15	4	17	1
Scott	13	5	43	1	1	0	4	1
Steele	10	4	18	1				
Lightfoot					20	8	24	3

*Captain; †Wicketkeeper

193

Council planned a civic reception and the Supporters' Association wanted a special presentation. At Worcester, the triumphant Sully was left out so Larter could return. An obvious if harsh decision, on the face of it – except that Larter broke down, the pitch started to turn sharply and Northamptonshire collapsed to the slow left-armer Doug Slade without means of redress.

It seemed like a lost opportunity more than anything else. Victory in the last game, at home to Gloucestershire would make it almost a certainty. What a weekend it was for local sport. On the Saturday, the Cobblers were starting their First Division career at Goodison Park; on the Wednesday they were at home for the first time, to Arsenal. Everyone was thrilled except the poor wretched ground staff who were expected to turn a cricket ground, which might have been filled with fans celebrating the first Championship, into a First Division football stadium fit for the Arsenal in the space of 24 hours. Sporting Camelot? National laughing stock, more like.

Fortunately for the ground staff the turnaround was much less rapid than expected. On the opening day, as the Cobblers were going down 5–2 at Everton, the cricketers sat in the pavilion watching the rain. Then Milburn tried to make up for lost time, hitting his first century of the season: 152 not out in 3½ hours with seven sixes, denuding the press box stock of adjectives. But it was hopeless. It rained again on the Tuesday and the crowd drifted away early enabling the sightscreen to be shifted from the centre circle long before Arsenal took the field.

Meanwhile, Worcestershire were winning again, for the seventh time in eight games. But they still had to win both their remaining matches, at Bournemouth and Hove, to overtake Northamptonshire. It is easy to guess the rest now but at the time it caused consternation. There was rain, as there often was that season, and at Bournemouth, Hampshire declared as soon as they had avoided the follow-on; Worcestershire reciprocated by going out, facing one delivery and declaring at 0 for 0, setting Hampshire 147 to win. Now any Northampton person who goes to Bournemouth for his holidays knows that the sun never shines to order. But at that moment, it did. The sun wreaked havoc with the wet pitch and Flavell and Coldwell wreaked havoc with the batsmen. Hampshire were bowled out for 31.

A modern cricket follower might be surprised by the idea of the sun drying the pitch, which was considered part of the luck of the game in the days of uncovered wickets, but not by the mutual declarations, which subsequently became normal practice in county cricket. But the regulations governing first-class matches in 1965 specifically forbade such deals between the captains and instructed umpires to report any suspicions in this matter to MCC: 'If the MCC Committee is satisfied that agreement is proved, any points shall not be counted in the Championship table.'

The Bournemouth game certainly looked very fishy. Indeed, conspiracy theorists were convinced the 31 all out was a fix – though if Worcestershire had bribed Hampshire to hand them the

The first three captains to lead Northamptonshire to second place in the County Championship, pictured in May 1966. Left to right: Keith Andrew (1965), 'Tubby' Vials (1912) and Dennis Brookes (1957). (Northamptonshire CCC)

Championship, they might have slipped them a bit extra to do it more subtly. Don Kenyon and Colin Ingleby-Mackenzie were experienced captains; they could have got each other's message without even a nod or a wink and we have to presume that they did. Ingleby-Mackenzie certainly made his intentions clear: he bowled the one delivery Worcestershire faced in their second innings, the only one he bowled all season. And there was something slightly artificial about Northamptonshire's indignation. Four weeks earlier, Andrew had made precisely the same kind of reciprocal declaration with Essex at Clacton with precisely the same effect: Northamptonshire 0 for 0 declared then Essex 88 all out.

The end, though, was inevitable now. Who can trust British seaside weather? Flavell rolled over Sussex before lunch on the first morning at Hove and on the Tuesday Worcestershire were Champions. As that other Albert, Camus not Lightfoot, put it in the quote at the top of Chapter Four: 'The struggle to reach the top is itself enough to fulfil the heart of man. One must believe that Sisyphus is happy.' In 1966 Northamptonshire came fifth in the Championship and the chairman Arnold Payne pointed out that the County had now finished in every position in the table. Except one.

A SHOOTING STAR

'We never know the sweets o'joy
Until it goes away.'

John Clare

THERE WAS ONE compensation. Actually, there were a lot of compensations because Northamptonshire in the mid-1960s were an attractive cricket team in an era when they were in short supply. But there was one compensation in particular.

In the modern era, only Ian Botham in his pomp has ever offered a similar thrill to the one that coursed round a cricket ground when Colin Milburn went out to bat. What followed was usually brief, often painfully so, and he would go back to the pavilion, red-faced, as fast as he had emerged. But if he stayed, the cricket could not fail to be enthralling. He blocked good balls and thumped bad ones, or even indifferent ones. He emptied bars as certainly as he filled them when he was off-duty. At a time when cricket was losing popularity rapidly he did more than anyone else to stop it.

Milburn's batting was based fundamentally on a sound technique. Allied to that, he had the enormous power from a body that weighed about 19 stone at peak, stunningly quick reflexes (the 43 catches in 1964 did not happen by accident) and, most bitterly ironic of all, a magnificent eye.

Like most geniuses, he had a conspiracy of dunces against him. England captains would despatch him to the deep and make him look idiotic running round the outfield while they spurned the brilliance of his close fielding. England selectors had no patience with him. A fair proportion of the dunces were at the County Ground. In a sense this was understandable. Like Tyson before him, but with less discernible reason, his greatest performances did seem to come far from home. Hence the grumblier sort of supporter in the West Stand cared for him less than, say, David Steele. In 1966, Milburn scored 1861 runs but only 299 of them came at Northampton. But whatever anyone said in the West Stand, this was the season his star began to shoot across the world cricketing sky. It blazed for just three short years and when anyone considers the tragedy of Colin Milburn, the bright light still shines beautifully through the murk of memory.

Milburn was picked for the first four Tests in 1966; in the second, at Lord's, he scored 126 not out in 2½ hours – to save the game, mark you. It was a brilliant, daring, wonderful innings. When he reached his century, four men ran on from in front of the Tavern and tried but failed to lift him off his feet. Milburn beamed his way through it. 'In more than 200 Tests,' wrote Crawford White of the *Daily Express*, 'I don't recall a richer moment of sheer fun than this.'

A few weeks later he was dropped with a Test average of 52. Too fat, they said. He went to Clacton instead of The Oval and took out his frustrations on the Essex attack. No one (not even Allan Lamb 20 years later) has ever executed this traditional act of cricketing vindictiveness quite so savagely. He scored a double century before tea and shared an opening stand of 293 with Prideaux that smashed the County's Championship record of 243, set more placidly by Brookes and Percy Davis in 1946. Prideaux made 153. In the second innings, both were out for nought. *Sic transit gloria mundi*, or in this case, Wednesday.

In complete contrast to 1965, the individual successes were needed to divert attention from the collective disappointment: fifth place, after the previous three seasons, was nothing to cheer about. The County did what rain prevented them doing three years earlier and beat the West Indies; Milburn was the one player on either side, Gary Sobers not excluded, to master a green wicket. The best non-Milburn moment came at Cambridge when Roy Wills, the Northampton boy whose intermittent first-class career preceded long involvement with the Club, surpassed himself by scoring 151 not out, sharing an opening partnership of 155 with Peter Willey, who scored 78. Willey was five months past his 16th birthday.

He had been recommended to Turner in a letter out of the blue from the Durham Schoolboys coach, Doug Ferguson, whose scouting instinct was to prove mighty influential in North-amptonshire's subsequent history. Turner never did find out why Ferguson chose Northamptonshire. Subsequently, he suggested George Sharp who became Northamptonshire's regular wicket-keeper and Chris Old, who unfortunately turned out to have been born just inside the Yorkshire border and had other plans. Dennis Brookes knew at once that Willey was an exceptional cricketer and he advocated that he should be promoted to the first team on a regular basis as fast as possible.

Generally, however, the season was gloomy. Mushtaq was not an immediate success with the bat though his leg-breaks were more handy than might have been expected – the County needed all the wickets they could get. Larter's season ended with an ankle injury after just 56 overs. The following April, he broke down

Colin Milburn in typically belligerent action for Northamptonshire against the 1968 Australians. (Northamptonshire CCC)

again in the opening Gillette Cup match against Bedfordshire and promptly announced his retirement. For the next five years Northamptonshire were to be a powerful batting side but without the bowling to make them really competitive. Across the County Ground, meanwhile, the Cobblers were beginning to hurtle back down the divisions, not so much Sisyphus as Icarus.

Andrew retired after the season. He was presented with a watch plus the pair of cups that had been given to Tom Horton 60 years earlier. There was no immediate problem: the extraordinarily patient Johnson was a ready-made replacement as keeper and Prideaux had been destined for the captaincy for years. Anyway, with the football pool in steep decline and cricket itself unfashionable, the Club were spiralling back into one of their traditional financial crises. Any savings on the wage bill were gratefully received. The Watts brothers both departed. Peter wanted to stay in the game but was keen to find a county more interested in leg-spin; as it turned out his reincarnation at Trent Bridge was to be a brief one. Jim Watts, worried about a groin injury affecting his bowling and the hot competition for batting places if he could not bowl, went to work for a building firm. Percy Davis left the coaching staff to join Jack Webster at Harrow School but he was another one who found himself being drawn back to the County Ground and he continued to coach in the school holidays.

In 1967, the Club decided to reduce the number of second team games and the Colts team pulled out of the County League. It was a gloomy season. Cecil Penn, the organising secretary of the Supporters' Association, killed himself. There was the Larter news. Then Prideaux fell ill with shingles and missed a chunk of the summer. Milburn's return to the England team was less than triumphant. When Northamptonshire bowled out Hampshire for 99 on a wearing pitch at the County Ground, the wicket was reported as unfit and the inspector, Bert Lock, was summoned. Reynolds was told he was no longer considered an automatic choice and the following year was replaced as senior pro by Crump. And Malcolm Scott was banned for the last two matches because his action was considered suspicious. He was hardly taking any wickets anyway.

There was one significant new player on the horizon, the South African Hylton Ackerman. But he broke his residential qualification by playing for Northern Transvaal in the winter. This meant that when the counties voted to allow immediate registration of overseas players in 1968, Ackerman became the County's one signing and they were prevented from getting anyone else at once. Northamptonshire actually voted against this reform which, from the Cosmopolitan County was considered a curiosity if not a downright cheek. Turner said there was a world of difference between players qualifying and fully integrating into a county side and merely turning up as a mercenary.

Ackerman made his debut the following April. Whatever Turner said about mercenaries, Ackerman would have been turfed out in favour of Gary Sobers if it had been possible. Percy Davis spent two days scouring London to find the great man; Turner went to see him at a League match with £1,000 in the glove compartment of his car just in case Sobers was interested. He was not; he signed for Nottinghamshire.

Ackerman had much in common with Milburn, since he hit the ball almost as hard and lived his life off the field just about as frantically. They did not meet the approval of the sterner senior players and some of the youngsters would have done better not to try and match them pint for pint. But they gave North-amptonshire – even without Sobers – the basis of one of the most exciting batting line-ups ever seen in county cricket. Prideaux was often overshadowed but he was an impressive strokemaker himself and a consistent one, which was useful in this team. Mushtaq was now beginning to settle. There was Steele to add ballast and the young Willey, making progress. In reality, and history was to repeat itself in the 1980s, most of the players seemed to be out-of-form simultaneously when most needed. In mid-season Lightfoot had to be recalled from the second team and had his best run for six years.

The bowling, meanwhile, leaned heavily on dear old Crumpy. The main spearhead was Tony Durose, a bowler who was magnificent in very occasional spasms. On the committee, the old guard was changing: Vials, now past 80, retired as president to be replaced by Arnold Payne; Hawtin, at 85, retired from the selection committee after 41 years. But there was a sniff of the old days about the place: the players were complaining about their toilets and the lack of hot water. As a special concession, they were graciously allowed to use the upstairs loo 'in an emergency'. The team finished 13th.

In two different ways, this declining team almost supplied the England captain again in 1969. Cowdrey, who was in possession, broke his achilles tendon and missed almost the whole season. Prideaux, by now an experienced county captain, had started his England career in 1968 and was an obvious contender. Before the first Test, he was named to captain a strong MCC team at Lord's against the touring West Indians. He failed with the bat, there was a lack of inspiration about his team and the job went to Ray Illingworth, released by Yorkshire and the new captain of Leicestershire.

Illingworth himself could have been a Northamptonshire player. Turner thought he had his man but when he failed to keep an appointment, he soon realised that his quarry, driving down from Yorkshire, had stopped off at Leicester first. Mike Turner was able to offer him the captaincy, which was decisive. In the long-running, friendly contest between the namesakes, this was one, very clear success for the Leicester Turner. Six years later Illingworth led Leicestershire to their first Championship.

If Turner could have made Illingworth captain, he would almost certainly have done so. Prideaux's five years in charge are not remembered kindly. The team's deficiencies were not his fault; the Archangel Michael Brearley could not have won the Championship with an attack so reliant on Crump. But he often seemed preoccupied by personal problems; he was inclined to be quick-tempered and the players sometimes found him less than sympathetic. He might not have been one of the great England captains.

The event that dominated and destroyed Northamptonshire's season was nothing to do with Prideaux. Thirty-three years after Bakewell, the curse of the motor car struck the club again. As mysteriously as Basil D'Oliveira (but less consequentially) Colin Milburn had originally been left out of the winter tour that was meant to go to South Africa and ended up in Pakistan. He went instead to play for Western Australia and on a roasting tropic day in Brisbane he scored 243, 181 of them between lunch and tea. He was called from a beach in Perth to reinforce the England team which was then less comfortably placed in Dacca. He arrived to be greeted by a team joke to the effect that there was no room at the Intercontinental Hotel and he was to be billeted in a nearby rathole. It had been a wretched tour. Before he arrived, no one was thinking of jokes.

'The sight of him walking down the steps of the airplane,' wrote Clive Taylor of *The Sun*, 'his great brown face split by a grin, removed the desperation and brought back the cheerfulness which is a normal part of a cricket tour. Milburn raised by 100 per cent the morale of a party which had talked increasingly in terms of mutiny.'

He was included in the team for the Karachi Test in place of Prideaux. On a pitch where, as Taylor said, a dwarf would have hesitated before hooking in case the ball passed underneath, Milburn hooked, cut and drove to 139. It was an innings of the utmost precision as well as his usual attributes. The Pakistani spectators were not interested; they were too busy rioting. But Milburn came home with everyone now accepting that he was a Test cricketer and likely to remain so.

He returned to the first season of the Sunday League, a competition that might have been invented for him. He played two games. He also played one Championship match, hitting 158 against Leicestershire with five sixes, a masterly innings even by his standards. He played his part, though less of a dominant one than usual, in the County's second successive win over the West Indians (it might have been three in a row but for the rain in 1963).

His selection for the Test team was no longer even a subject for discussion. He was a certainty. And then it happened, late at night after the West Indies match. It was ten to midnight in The Avenue, Moulton. He had been at a party at the Sywell Motel and was driving home with Dennis Breakwell and George Sharp. On the narrow lane, his Austin 1800 collided with a lorry. Sharp was not hurt at all, Breakwell had a few cuts. Milburn's face went smack into the windscreen. The surgeons removed the slivers of

Milburn recovering in hospital from the car accident which ended his effective playing career. On the right is Sister Janet Lowe who greatly admired Ollie's courage in adversity. (The Chronicle and Echo)

glass from his forehead. But his left eye had to be removed and the right eye was severely damaged.

He never moaned, not once. Through the next week, he staggered his nurses and doctors by his refusal to complain or give way to even the slightest hint of depression. 'Colin Milburn is one patient I will never forget,' said Sister Janet Lowe. 'He was an affable character, contented and with a smile for everybody.' The hospital management committee's annual report for the year reported: 'Colin endeared himself to all those who looked after him and somehow his infectious good humour and indomitable spirit raised morale throughout the hospital.'

Amid the publicity he picked up some work in broadcasting and journalism. 'Not once during that summer of spending night and day with Milburn,' said Peter Smith, the reporter assigned as his ghost-writer, 'driving him thousands of miles round England, did I hear him bemoaning his luck.' When he should have been playing in the Old Trafford Test, he had to go to the Manchester Eye Hospital for treatment every morning. The nurse said she would try to find him a false eye to match his brown right one. 'Better find two,' said Milburn. 'One to match it now and a bloodshot one to match it in the mornings.'

He was a naturally gifted commentator too: perceptive, funny and fair-minded. But the truth was that the damage to his right eye made cricket-watching difficult. Unlike Bakewell, he did attempt a comeback. Four years after the accident he returned to the Northamptonshire team. It almost worked. His reflexes were such that, with a bit of his medium-paced bowling, he could still do an adequate job. But the glory had departed, and he knew it. Like Bakewell, the rest of his life was spent in shadow.

There were still good times, and roistering, and wonderful humour. But as the years went by, and he failed to find a regular job, it became possible to glimpse just a little of the bleakness that must have lain beneath the joviality. He left Northampton and went back to his family in the north-east. On 28 February 1990 he had a heart attack in a pub car park and died. He was 48. A friend said afterwards that had he survived to see Durham in first-class cricket it might have given him the impetus to go on living. This is not a book with many happy endings.

When the accident happened, he was 27. It is no offence to the other 200 professional cricketers in England at the time to say that the game could have spared any one, two or a dozen of them more easily than it could have spared Colin. For the game at large, he was a jewel that sparkled briefly and then was stolen. For Northamptonshire both the gain and the pain, were far, far greater.

IT'S ONLY ROCK AND ROLL

'We had joy, we had fun, we had seasons in the sun. . .'

No 1 hit by Terry Jacks (1974)

COLIN MILBURN was to have one more momentous effect on Northamptonshire cricket. For years his batting had done more than anything else to draw young people into the County Ground but the effect, it has to be said, was marginal. In 1970 he said to Turner: 'Why don't you run a disco?' It was like the moment Wilbur said to Orville that man might fly.

By 1970 Northamptonshire's finances were back to normal. The football pool was ten years past its heyday and by this time had become almost moribund. When it began, betting shops were still illegal; now there were dozens of competing forms of gambling on which people could chuck their money away. Championship cricket was increasingly ill-attended and the Sunday League was just getting started. And that year cricket's economy in general had been blown to smithereens by the cancellation of the planned tour by South Africa.

Turner claimed later that he was the only county secretary to resist the bizarre notion that, 18 months after refusing to accept an England player, Basil D'Oliveira, the South Africans ought to tour this country, even if they had to be protected from demonstrators by barbed wire and guard dogs. Finally, the Home Secretary, James Callaghan, leaned on Lord's and the tour was cancelled. A replacement quasi-Test series against the Rest of the World was hastily organised, but was a financial flop. In 1969, Northamptonshire had lost money for the first time since the Supporters Association had begun in 1952. In 1970, they were staring at an £11,000 deficit.

Turner's knowledge of popular music stopped some time around Al Bowlly but he knew a money-making idea when he heard one. He approached Bob Kaufman, a Northampton disco operator who was (and is) a fanatical County supporter. Kaufman was enthusiastic. Another local cricket follower was not. 'Ken,' said Chief Superintendent Tom Nicholson, 'there will be trouble.'

The indoor school was always intended to be what would now be called a multi-purpose facility. But discos had not been invented in 1958. It was not an intimate venue and the ambience was

Ken Turner, Northamptonshire's energetic, pioneering and often controversial secretary from 1958 to 1985. (Northamptonshire CCC)

never classy. The County Ground disco began with a show hosted by the Radio One disc jockey Emperor Rosko, of whom Turner had never heard. He was stunned when he was obliged to pay him £300, a month's wages for a half-decent fast bowler. He was even more stunned when 400 kids turned up and the Club made a good profit. The show was on the road. The attendance reached 900 for a DJ called Mike Raven a few months later with queues out of the car park and past the main gate.

Eventually Turner, who ran the Cricket Club rather like an impresario, began to run the discos himself. He started reading *New Musical Express* and *Melody Maker* more enthusiastically than

The Cricketer. He applied his flair for spotting up-and-coming talent to signing acts like Leo Sayer, Suzi Quatro and Elkie Brooks. He booked the Sex Pistols, who failed to appear, which might have shocked him more if he had not by that stage acquired some experience in dealing with Pakistani fast bowlers. Otherwise, the money rolled in, especially after Turner applied for a bar licence himself so the Club could take the profits instead of handing them over to the County Hotel.

He took no more nonsense from the musical artistes than he did from his cricketing ones. When a group called Cado Belle presented a contract demanding that their dressing room be stocked with 'orange juice, fresh fruit, one bottle Lambrusco, one bottle Blue Nun and a tin of Pedigree Chum' he just crossed it all out and wrote instead 'Reasonable refreshments provided'.

Chief Superintendent Nicholson was right, though. There was trouble. One of the most important figures on the staff in the early 1970s became one Derek Law, a man who briefly achieved national celebrity as the owner of Tartan Khan, the winner of the 1975 Greyhound Derby. Law was not a small man and Northamptonshire now needed bouncers of a non-cricketing nature.

The Club began to get very unpopular with the local residents. After the split with Kaufman, Turner decided to appeal to a younger and sometimes rowdier crowd. He used to pray for a south-westerly wind to carry the music away from most of the houses and towards the park, and then for a downpour at chucking-out time to clear the streets quickly. Every session of the licensing magistrates, whose chairman Dennis Brookes was unable to sit because of the conflict of interest, used to be as tense as a close one-day finish. Once Turner saw off 18 objectors. Another time, the Club was raided by police, who found three under-age girls drinking alcohol. Turner was fined £100. As with the football pool, he knew it could not last forever. Fortunately, Ronnie Aird was no longer secretary of MCC to add his disapproval.

On the field, meanwhile, the Club endured three dismal years. The 1969 season was played in the shadow of the Milburn tragedy and, though the County had a late surge with three consecutive wins at the end of August, they could finish only ninth. Steele had his arm broken by Mike Procter at the end of June and Mushtaq found himself top of both the batting and bowling averages. Larter made a comeback, but it lasted only three games. There was, however, a new, Milburnesque figure opening the batting with Ackerman towards the end of summer; the Rhodesian Oxford blue, Fred Goldstein. But in the Sunday League, an event ideal for a team with hard-hitting batsmen and indifferent bowling, the County finished fourth-bottom. Prideaux's captaincy was questioned in committee. But there was no obvious replacement. At the AGM members complained about 'slovenly' fielding and 'dull and dreary' cricket. The chairman Norman Barratt's defence was less than combative.

The following season was even bleaker. This time the team began well and then failed to win after 23 June, falling to 14th in the Championship and finishing only one place higher on Sun-

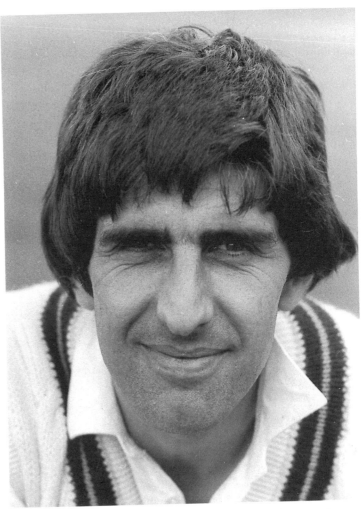

Jim Watts came on the Northamptonshire scene as a talented teenager in 1959, and then captained the County – on-and-off – for most of the 1970s. (Northamptonshire CCC)

days. The one unexpected success was the appositely named slow left-armer Dennis Breakwell. Brian Reynolds was not retained; Lightfoot chose to go voluntarily, severing the last links with Brookes's team. Fortunately, Jim Watts had left his job and come out of his premature retirement. In October Prideaux announced that for 'personal and business reasons' he would not be available for the captaincy in 1971. Watts was on hand. He was appointed unanimously.

The two Watts brothers were never committed county cricketers in the way that, say, Reynolds was. They were both far too wide-ranging in their interests. Peter, the elder brother, was a particular individualist and even the placid Keith Andrew once sent him home from an away game because of his attitude. Jim was an easier man. He was never a great cricketer but he could do a little of everything and as he passed 30 there was something of the natural leader about him. He was to captain Northamptonshire in three separate spells. One of these lasted a matter of days. The other two lifted the team out of different crises and back towards the heights.

He was hardly an immediate success. Prideaux had decided to play for Sussex and his runs, whatever anyone thought of his captaincy, were irreplaceable. Perhaps Northamptonshire's greatest success of the season was in manipulating the system so that Mushtaq played on the Pakistan tour only in the Test matches and was available for the County the rest of the time. Watts himself, by application and commitment, was the most successful batsman. Peter Willey, who was improving year by year, came top of the bowling with his medium-pacers. But he then acquired the cartilage injury that was to force him to switch to bowling off-breaks. The opening attack comprised Alan Hodgson who, as happened throughout his career, was dogged by injury and the only Northamptonshire-born player left on the staff, Peter Lee from Arthingworth near the Leicestershire border, who had, unusually, been picked up playing village cricket. There was another fast bowler, an amiable young Pakistani called Sarfraz Nawaz, but he had injuries that seemed to be beyond any diagnostician.

This could not go on. Fortunately the club had not lost its ability to seek out the disgruntled and displaced – or the plain ambitious – and persuade them to step through the unprepossessing portals of the County Ground pavilion. The first triumph came in August. Bishen Bedi was in London about to play a supporting role in India's first-ever Test match victory in England. Also in London were Ken Turner and Percy Davis. They thought they were meeting Bedi at the Indian team hotel at 7.30; Bedi turned up shortly before midnight.

There is not much doubt who the supplicants were in this job interview. Bedi was already regarded as the world's most effective, most interesting – and with his multi-coloured range of Sikh headwear – most distinctive spin bowler in the world. And when Northamptonshire found the Bedi family a house in Duston, on the outskirts of town, the Club secretary, regarded by most newcomers to the Club as a thoroughly forbidding figure, found himself acting as a sort of dogsbody-wallah. He began this role very badly by switching on the central heating when there was no water in the system and almost burned the house down. Thereafter he went shopping for the Bedis, bought a supply of Oriental pots and pans, went to their hotel to collect their luggage and then loaded and unloaded it while Bedi, who was merely obeying the custom of the Indian middle class, stood and watched. For five

The weaver of spells, Bishen Bedi, took wickets for Northamptonshire for six seasons. (David Frith)

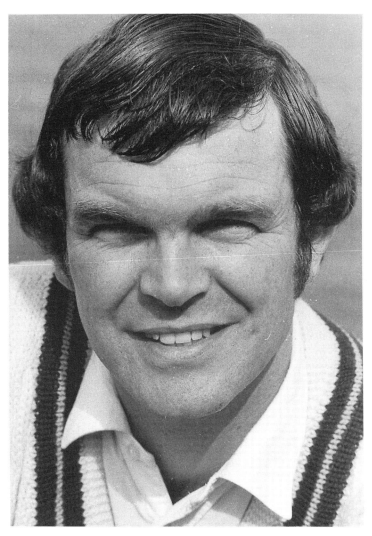

Bob Cottam left Hampshire to spearhead Northamptonshire's attack from 1972 to 1976. (Northamptonshire CCC)

seasons, anyway, Turner never doubted that it was all worthwhile.

Then in December Turner struck twice more. John Dye was a left-arm quick bowler from Kent who could not get on with his captain, Mike Denness. He was rising 30 but the sort of player who just needed sympathetic surroundings to give his career second wind. And there was Bob Cottam of Hampshire, a forceful, intelligent man and a good enough fast bowler to have been picked for England, who was convinced he needed to move if he was ever to get another chance. It was a brilliant treble.

There were a few loose ends. One was Ackerman's position. Some talented young batsmen were starting to come up through the system now – Geoff Cook, Wayne Larkins, Alan Tait – and there was no question that Bedi was more important to the Club than Ackerman. The County were allowed only one immediate overseas registration. Ackerman, having been sacked once, was told he would be kept on if he would re-qualify by residence; faced with a winter in Northampton or a job in South Africa, he departed.

Another problem was the position of Peter Lee, who with his career prospects now dramatically reduced, was allowed to leave for Lancashire. This was disappointing to sentimentalists; until Jim Griffiths emerged in 1974 the County were entirely without a local-born player. By 1973, even Turner, who would have preferred a Martian to an Arthingworth lad if he believed he would get one more wicket, might have been having second thoughts: that year only two bowlers in the country took 100 wickets, Bedi and Lee.

A third loose end concerned Cottam. Hampshire fought his move and Cottam was barred from cricket, initially for the whole season. Then, as the legal phrase 'restraint of trade' first began to echo through the corridors at Lord's, he was allowed to play in mid-June. By that time Northamptonshire were already on their way. In 1972, they leapt ten places up the table and came fourth. Their 77 bowling bonus points was, equal with Gloucestershire, the most of all the counties; their 38 batting points among the least. Not surprisingly, the team failed completely in the one-day competitions, now increased to three by the invention of the Benson and Hedges Cup. This was won by Leicestershire: Northamptonshire's oldest enemy (bankruptcy aside) had beaten them to a trophy.

But in the first-class game it was different. Dye finished sixth in the national averages, Cottam seventh, Mushtaq twelfth and Bedi seventeenth – and it was a cold old summer for a man from the Punjab to be starting in county cricket. His triumphs included taking nine wickets for 110 against Ian Chappell's Australians. They were bowled out for 191 and 143. The County knocked off the runs just before lunch on the third day. It was said that Milburn played his part in this victory too; his hospitality for the touring team was magnificent.

The Australians, it has to be said, were not at their best. It is quite usual for modern touring teams to go into low gear between Tests but this time they did not seem to bother getting out of neutral. The *Sydney Sun* called the closing stages 'a circus' and attacked Dennis Lillee for bowling leg-breaks, Dave Colley for bowling lollipops and Ian Chappell for exchanging golf strokes with Brian Taber. 'Losing to one of England's poorer county sides is a pity,' said the paper, 'but to show we didn't really care about it is enough to make even the most ardent cricket hater squirm.' It was not seen quite that way in Northampton – 'the greatest moment since I became captain,' said Jim Watts. And, by heaven, after the near-misses in 1930 and 1961, Northamptonshire deserved this win.

The runs in that match, after an extremely promising innings from Cook, came mainly from Steele and Mushtaq. The pattern of the summer was that the County would be very-few-runs-for-two-wickets and success or failure would depend on the ability of Nos 3 and 4 to dig them out. In 1971 and 1972 there were 11 different opening combinations tried in the Championship. Wayne Osman from Hertfordshire was given a run then discarded; he became a policeman instead. Crump, who had almost given up bowling by now, had a turn. There was the left-hander Alan Tait, highly gifted and a favourite of Turner but personally disorganised and doomed never to succeed in county cricket. Geoff Cook, a steadier sort of chap, had to be dropped down the order when he failed.

One of the emergency openers was George Sharp, who was soon afterwards to find a more plausible role as wicket-keeper. But Sharp could bat, which in the circumstances of 1972 inevitably made a difference: Laurie Johnson's habit of batting as though he were practising nine-irons to the green was perhaps less amusing than it once had been. John Dye, magnificently though he bowled, was no help at all with the batting problems. This was not for any want of seriousness on the subject. One summer evening, his car drew up behind that of the *Chronicle and Echo* reporter at the Abington Park traffic lights. 'Oy,' he yelled, 'you've got my average wrong in the paper. It's 3.09 not 2.93.'

But the accent of this era came mostly from much further north. In 1973 seven players from the north-east of England played Championship cricket for Northamptonshire: Cook, Milburn, who was making his short-lived comeback, Willey, Sharp, Tait, Hodgson and the straw-haired all-rounder Norman Maltby. An eighth, Paul Romaines, was just coming on to the staff. There was not one Northamptonshire-born player on the books. Cook was from Middlesbrough and Maltby from nearby

NORTHANTS *v* AUSTRALIANS

Played at Northampton, 5, 7 and 8 August 1972

NORTHANTS WON BY SEVEN WICKETS

AUSTRALIANS	FIRST INNINGS		SECOND INNINGS	
B. C. Francis	lbw b Dye	27	b Dye	9
R. Edwards	c Cottam b Willey	18	c Cook b Dye	8
*I. M. Chappell	b Willey	5	run out	31
G. D. Watson	c Crump b Bedi	37	hit wkt b Bedi	52
†R. W. Marsh	c Willey b Crump	42	c Johnson b Bedi	0
R. J. Inverarity	c Cottam b Bedi	14	lbw b Dye	6
D. J. Colley	b Willey	1	c Johnson b Bedi	16
H. B. Taber	c and b Bedi	28	st Johnson b Bedi	3
J. W. Gleeson	lbw b Bedi	5	b Willey	11
R. A. L. Massie	not out	3	absent hurt	–
D. K. Lillee	c Cottam b Bedi	0	not out	1
Extras	b 4, lb 4, nb 2, w 1	11	b 1, lb 5	6
Total		191		143

1st inns: 1-32, 2-50, 3-50, 4-104, 5-140, 6-141, 7-158, 8-175, 9-191, 10-191
2nd inns: 1-11, 2-18, 3-99, 4-103, 5-104, 6-124, 7-128, 8-141, 9-143

BOWLING	O	M	R	W	O	M	R	W
Cottam	12	5	27	0	8	1	32	0
Dye	14	3	42	1	13	6	25	3
Willey	18	3	47	3	13.3	5	27	1
Bedi	17	3	57	5	20	6	53	4
Crump	7	3	7	1				

NORTHANTS	FIRST INNINGS		SECOND INNINGS	
A. Tait	b Massie	0		
G. Cook	st Taber b Gleeson	62	c Chappell b Gleeson	24
D. S. Steele	lbw b Massie	19	not out	60
Mushtaq Mohammad	not out	88	c Marsh b Lillee	30
*P. J. Watts	lbw b Gleeson	0	not out	3
B. S. Crump	lbw b Watson	3	run out	1
P. Willey	lbw b Watson	8		
R. M. H. Cottam	st Marsh b Gleeson	0		
†L. A. Johnson	b Watson	0		
B. S. Bedi	b Watson	4		
J. C. J. Dye	b Watson	4		
Extras	b 1, lb 1, nb 19, w 1	22	lb 1, nb 6	7
Total		210	(3 wkts)	125

1st inns: 1-1, 2-53, 3-142, 4-142, 5-149, 6-171, 7-178, 8-191, 9-195, 10-210
2nd inns: 1-38, 2-102, 3-103

BOWLING	O	M	R	W	O	M	R	W
Massie	24	10	50	2				
Lillee	12	2	35	0	7	0	25	1
Colley	9	2	29	0	6.5	2	27	0
Watson	14	3	36	5	4	0	11	0
Gleeson	11	1	38	3	9	4	26	1
Inverarity					6	0	29	0

*Captain; †Wicketkeeper (Taber took over for a spell from Marsh)

Marske, both just inside the Yorkshire border. The rest were from County Durham. Willey and Cook, in particular, were Doug Ferguson's prize catches. Not surprisingly, people in Durham began to ask why such a county should be first-class and theirs should not. Cricket being cricket, it took two decades for anyone to supply the obvious answer.

But that was not Northamptonshire's problem, not in the short term. All they needed was one more experienced batsman and once again the Championship might be a possibility. They got the batsman, all right, surprisingly not from the north-east. Roy Virgin was 33 and had spent years with Somerset building a reputation as one of the slowest and most painstaking opening batsmen in county cricket. In 1970 he had burst from his shell, scored his runs far more freely and moved to the very brink of an England place. He was the perfect signing. Somerset thought so too, intervened as Hampshire had done over Cottam and managed to get Lord's to ban him until July 1973. The opening partnership of Virgin and Willey caused a good deal of sniggering. But it was only their names that opponents could find amusing.

Sisyphus's boulder was moving up the hill again. As in the 1950s and 1960s, under Brookes and Andrew, a team was building towards a peak as the decade went on. But the balance of power in the Championship was now very different. There was no Surrey or Yorkshire dominating things – between 1968, when the laws on overseas signings were loosened, and 1976, a different county won the Championship every year. And there were now four titles to win, not one. By 1973, Essex, Somerset and Northamptonshire were left as the only counties who had never won any prizes, souvenir ashtrays excluded.

So the opportunities were certainly there. But Northamptonshire's team of the time had an instinctive contempt for one-day cricket; many of them were too old to be learning new tricks like the Sunday League and certainly too old to improve their fielding enough for 40-over runarounds. So if Northamptonshire were to win a trophy it looked like being the Championship or nothing. And in mid-July 1973, after Bedi had rolled over Essex at the County Ground, Northamptonshire were top of it.

They lasted a fortnight. But this, quite unexpectedly, was to be Hampshire's year and at the finish the County were never able to get within sighting distance of either them or the runners-up Surrey. Virgin, hampered by his enforced two-month break, failed to find his best form and Steele and Mushtaq were a little less prolific in 1973. The basis of a champion team was there. However, it needed a leader. At the moment, there was a very good one but he was starting to get restless again.

The Northamptonshire team of the mid-1970s was not an easy one to captain. There are many advantages in signing overseas stars and experienced county pros. The disadvantage is that they are inclined to know their rights and stand on them. This was an opinionated cricket team and inclined to be cliquey. Watts could hold it together. But he was now in his mid-30s with no obvious career prospects after cricket. He asked for a three-year contract. He was given only one year, with a benefit (which turned out, mostly because of bad weather, to be a very poor one). He decided to train as a teacher and said the 1974 season would be his last as a full-timer though he could play at weekends and holiday-times if required. Among the many ifs of Northamptonshire cricket history is the one covering the possibility that Jim Watts might have gone to college as a young man, acquired a career early, stopped worrying and then concentrated on his cricket for 20 years. This story might have been a happier one.

The omens for 1974 were considered less than favourable because India and Pakistan were again the touring teams which meant the County would lose their overseas players for most of the season. The trick of hanging on to Mushtaq except for the Tests would never be allowed again. It was no longer a question of simply losing Mushtaq and Bedi. The TCCB's ever-eccentric registration laws were then at their most ludicrous and by 1974 Mushtaq, though he of course was still playing for Pakistan, was after ten years with the County, officially considered English. That allowed Northamptonshire to sign another overseas player.

They opted, with a deep breath, to bring back Sarfraz, who since his departure in 1971, had been bowling – and batting – very successfully for Nelson in the Lancashire League and dramatically improving his command of colloquial English in the process. From a rather mincing run, he was soon to be as sharp a bowler, on occasion, as anyone in the world. But in 1974 Mushtaq, Sarfraz and Bedi played only 20 games between them and early in the season Cottam got injured and was out of cricket for six weeks.

They still won nine games out of 20, lost only two and of the nine draws, four were matches rendered hopeless by rain. The characteristic sight of the summer was that of Virgin, steadily accumulating run after run. For the spectators, it was not like watching Milburn (whose comeback petered out sadly) or Acker-man. But it made highly effective cricket. Virgin's total of 1,936 runs was the highest in the country in a difficult year for batsmen; so was his total of seven centuries. When the 1975 season began hopes were higher than ever before.

A club, however, is not just a collection of individuals. Somehow Northamptonshire were still not a happy county and the minutes for this period make unexpectedly gloomy reading. Three of the club's greatest stalwarts died within months of each other: Vials (April 1974), Hawtin (January 1975) and Tim Manning (November 1975), aged 87, 91 and 91 respectively, which at least suggested the atmosphere in the committee room was healthier than it seemed.

Nationally, the annual inflation rate was starting to nudge 25 per cent. And since the economy of this cricket club was even more fragile than that of the nation as a while, the consequences were potentially horrendous. The deficit in 1974 was over £10,000 and plans for a Club dance had to be abandoned. Across the ground, the football club was just recovering from being forced to apply for re-election twice running in 1972 – just six years after leaving the First Division – and 1973. The town was now expanding fast: the rich cornfields beyond Weston Favell were being ripped up to be turned into thousands of boxy homes for exiled Londoners. This did not appear to be helping local sport: most of the newcomers were more interested in spending their weekends at the telly, DIY or shopping rather than an activity as contemplative as cricket-watching. The older inhabitants seemed to sit through all the changes quite apathetically and the Borough Council successfully overcame what opposition there was and destroyed the beautiful Victorian Emporium Arcade and almost managed to drive an expressway through the middle of town.

Off the field, the Club was also starting to change. But at least there was a sense of continuity: jobs were staying in the family. After almost two decades of coaching Brookes changed out of his whites at last and moved into the office as assistant secretary and Turner's right-hand man; Brian Reynolds was re-employed as coach. And when Hever resigned as groundsman, the job went to Albert Lightfoot, who had been learning the trade at Northampton Saints.

Lightfoot found himself the most underfunded groundsman in the country. He was in charge of the bar, the scoreboard and the football pitch with just two lads to help him. The pitches varied. It became harder than ever to make the outfield look presentable, especially on the football-overlap side. The County Ground was starting to look shabbier than ever. The moaners were in full voice at the 1975 AGM: it was suggested that committee men might be more usefully employed helping out at the gate than sipping gin-and-tonics; this idea may or may not have been responsible for Freddie Brown's decision to resign from the committee. Perhaps there was something else bothering people: there had not been a really hot, dry summer in ages; everyone needed cheering up.

In 1975, the season began colder and wetter than ever before. On 2 June play was snowed off at Buxton and a few flakes fell on the County Ground before the second day of the Glamorgan match. It then developed into the warmest summer since 1959. But the sun shone only fitfully on Northamptonshire's cricket. There were many small problems but they boiled down in essence to one: leadership.

As early as May 1974 the captaincy had been offered to Steele. But 1975 was to be his benefit year and he said he wanted to concentrate on that. As things turned out, he was to have more distractions than anyone thought possible, but more of those in a moment. Virgin became the obvious choice.

'You have to try things,' Turner said sadly after it all went wrong. Virgin, a nice man and a thoroughly self-possessed batsman, turned out to have less of a feel for the broad picture and he would change his bowlers rather in the manner of Childs-Clarke 30 years earlier. The pressure got to him and his own form went to pieces, fast. At the end of July, after Middlesex had inflicted the County's sixth defeat of the summer, Hugh Wright, the chairman of the selection committee, a gentle man from Peterborough, met him and a resignation was arranged. There followed the battiest ten days in the County's history: The Time of the Four Captains, analagous to the Year of the Four Emperors (Rome, 69AD), only slightly more chaotic.

Since Watts was now on holiday from college, he was the obvious temporary solution. He stepped in as if he had never been away to take charge against Essex at the County Ground. The next game was against the Australians. On the first afternoon, the fast bowler Alan Hurst broke Watts's finger. While the Australians took a day off, Steele captained the team in a Sunday League match at Wellingborough. The performance was not a success – Majid Khan scored 75 in 27 minutes – and he did not care for the job much either. Within hours, Mushtaq Mohammad was captain of Northamptonshire. The last month was one of consolidation: Mushtaq steadily grasped the reins.

The most useful development came at Chelmsford. Wayne Larkins, from the Bedfordshire village of Roxton just off the A1 and so the nearest thing the first team had to a local boy, had been in and out of the side, mostly out, since 1972. He would make piles of runs, beautifully, in the second team and then go to pieces whenever he got promoted: for a long while, he had a Championship average in single figures. On a hot day and a perfect batting pitch, with the only possible result an Essex win, he went out and scored 127, sharing a fourth-wicket stand of 273 with Mushtaq, breaking the Club record and saving the match, and with it his career.

Steele had other lamb chops to fry. This was the summer of Lillee and Thomson. After they had bowled Australia to a 4-1 victory in the series over there and then to another win in the first Test at Edgbaston, Mike Denness was sacked as captain and Tony Greig came in, with a good deal of authority to bring in the men he wanted. Up to now, suggestions that Steele might be among them were usually greeted by snorts from cricket's establishment: 'One class below,' was a typical reaction. Of course he was; he played for Northamptonshire, didn't he?

Greig thought differently. Steele was in the team for the Lord's Test. Frank Keating of *The Guardian* recalled the scene eight years later on Steele's retirement:

> England batted. Lilian Thomson was at her most catty, cruel and spiteful. The openers went at once, and it was 20 for two when Steele, his favourite moth-eaten old towel elastic-banded to his left thigh inside his trousers, gave a last polish to his glasses, picked up his bat and plodded heavy-footed, down the stairs.
>
> Of course, he had never been in the home dressing room before, so he went down two flights instead of one and ended up in the members' loo. Outside, meanwhile, 25,000 people were waiting. When finally he emerged and clomped to the wicket all that was missing was the ARP helmet.
>
> . . . As he reached the wicket Thomson said to his colleagues 'Who is this guy? Groucho Marx?' Steele simply said 'Mornin'' and took guard, two-legs, as he always did. The first two balls from Lillee were devilish. As he prepared to face them, Steele muttered to himself, over and over again: 'Watch the ball, watch the ball.' He played both deliveries immaculately straight down into his boots – and swept the next for four to release an explosion of pent-up sound from the crowd that could be heard in Baker Street.

It was quite wonderful. The Bank Clerk Goes To War, said Clive Taylor in *The Sun*. And indeed, Steele became a symbol of

English defiance against overwhelming odds every bit as improbable as Captain Mainwaring. He made 50 that day, 45 in the second innings; 73 and 92 at Headingley; 39 and 66 at The Oval. England drew every one of these games, which, in the context of that series, was a phenomenal achievement. It WAS a little like 1940: England had to blunt the opposition's aerial bombardment before they could even think of starting to win. Steele became the symbol of English cricket's defiance and a national hero. A local butcher sponsored him at one lamb chop a run which kept the family freezer full for years. In December, he was voted BBC Sports Personality of the Year.

Steele's glory lingered on through 1976 when he scored a century against the West Indians at Trent Bridge and was England's leading run-getter in the series. But that year the glory was not his alone. For the fourth time, Northamptonshire finished runners-up in the County Championship. For the first time, they went to a Lord's Cup final and they came away with the Gillette Cup, having beaten the hot favourites Lancashire.

Even the gods indicated something strange was afoot. It was the hottest, driest cricket season of the century. By midsummer every ground in the country was Australian-dry and the outfield drains were visible beneath the frazzled grass. It was appropriate to have a Pakistani as captain in such a year. On the field, it was more like 1957 than 1965, or 1912. Northamptonshire never looked like winning the title, and though Middlesex only finished 16 points clear in the end, it is hindsight more than anything that makes the County appear so close: there were only ten points for a win in 1976 and Middlesex won 11 out of 20 to Northamptonshire's nine.

But every one of those wins was achieved by bowling the opposition out twice, a considerable achievement in a season when the 100-over restriction in the first innings applied. All the bowlers took a turn that year. Sarfraz led the way and when Cottam was injured again, Hodgson took his chance better than ever before. And at the same time the County were moving stealthily forward in the Gillette Cup.

It was not exactly a glorious progress. They had a bye in the first round and then an undistinguished eight-run win over Nottinghamshire, one of the weakest first-class counties. But since they had beaten no one except Cambridgeshire in this Cup during the previous seven seasons, this counted as a major triumph. And at that point the draw was kind: home to Hertfordshire, who had got through with a freakish win over Essex. There was no further freak: Northamptonshire had as

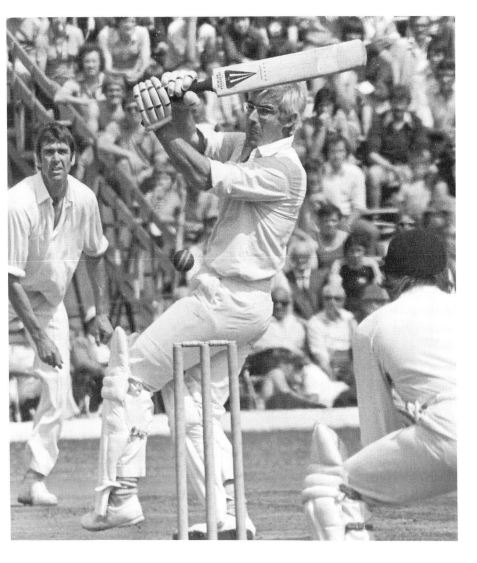

David Steele was transformed in 1975 from journeyman county professional to national hero.
(Northamptonshire Evening Telegraph)

good as won after Sarfraz's opening spell and completed the
formalities by mid-afternoon.

So, without breaking much sweat, Northamptonshire were in
the semi-finals for the first time since the opening year of the
Gillette in 1963. They were drawn to play at Southampton. It was
another long, hot 1976 sort of day and for nearly all of it the
County looked like winners. Hampshire made only 215 for

221

seven. Northamptonshire cruised: Virgin and Willey took the score to 83 for nought. Then it was 180 for three and 202 for four. Victory still looked a certainty with two overs to go, four wickets left and only six runs wanted. The next over, however, produced just one run and two wickets.

Six balls to go, five still wanted. It was not until the second-last ball when Bedi, with what might be charitably termed an on-drive, hit John Rice to the boundary and the County were through. There were celebrations all right. But the panic in the batting had been less than edifying and the first hint of dissastisfaction with Mushtaq's captaincy became evident. Turner claimed to have smoked 72 Senior Service that day and he blamed Mushtaq for most of them. David Steele, national hero, had been left out.

Three weeks earlier, Willey had joined Steele in the England team against the West Indies at Headingley, the first time two Northamptonshire players had played for England together since Tyson and Andrew at Brisbane in 1954. When there was dirty work to be done against fast bowlers the selectors knew where to look. A few weeks after that both were left out of the touring party to India because they were felt to be inadequate players of spin bowling. There was a vague feeling that Steele in some way might not be a good tourist. Well, he was nicknamed 'Crime', because he did not pay. But it is also true that neither Steele nor Crump, who were originally known as 'the Milk Machine Kids', were big drinkers or high livers. It is not difficult to buy popularity by rushing to buy a round at the bar: Steele was actually one of the most affable and easy-going men in cricket, and a victim of the game's pernicious rumour-mill. He could also play the spinners, dammit.

The Northamptonshire committee were aware of his worth and he was the first person to be picked for the Cup Final. In other words, Mushtaq was instructed not to leave him out of the 12. And so, on 4 September 1976, 71 years and 109 days after Persse of Hampshire had bowled the historic first delivery to George Thompson – three men from Durham, two Pakistanis, an Indian, a Yorkshireman, a Bedfordshire man, a Staffordshire man, a Somerset man and a Man of Kent took the field wearing (if they had their caps on) the Tudor Rose. Several thousand genuine Northamptonshire people packed the stands carrying banners, one of which said: 'Richie Benaud May Be God But Mushtaq Is Mohammad'. Lancashire had been in five of the previous six finals and won four of them. Everyone expected them to win again.

Mushtaq Mohammad captained Northamptonshire to their first major title, the Gillette Cup in 1976. (George Herringshaw)

BATSMAN	TOTAL	BATSMAN
1	397	6
145	WICKETS	206
BOWLER	3	BOWLER
6	OVERS 7	11
HOW OUT	LAST WKT FELL	LASTMAN
CT 9	27	10

Roy Virgin and Peter Willey add 370 for Northamptonshire's fourth wicket against Somerset at Northampton in 1976. After Virgin's dismissal for 145, Willey went on to make 227. (The Chronicle and Echo)

The cruellest blow was probably the most crucial: Dye broke Barry Wood's finger so that effectively Lancashire were 45 for four. The innings was never healthy and with an over to go Lancashire were only 169 for seven. Mushtaq had managed to get a dozen improbable but acceptable overs from Larkins. He could have chosen either Dye or Hodgson to bowl the 60th. He thought Dye might be rather stiff so he went for Bedi, who had been bowling beautifully.

In every form of cricket, Bedi's bowling was often hit, and hit hard. His technique, after being struck for four or six, was to join in the applause, which – as Vic Marks once put it – made the batsman feel that the stroke had merely been part of the bowler's

GILLETTE CUP FINAL
NORTHANTS *v* LANCASHIRE

Played at Lord's, 4 September 1976

NORTHANTS WON BY FOUR WICKETS

LANCASHIRE

B. Wood	retired hurt	14
†F. M. Engineer	b Dye	0
H. Pilling	c Cook b Sarfraz	3
F. C. Hayes	c and b Hodgson	19
*D. Lloyd	b Bedi	48
J. Abrahams	b Bedi	46
D. P. Hughes	not out	39
J. Simmons	b Sarfraz	1
R. M. Ratcliffe	c Larkins b Bedi	4
P. Lever	not out	8
P. G. Lee		
Extras	b 1, lb 9, nb 1, w 2	13
Total	(7 wkts)	195

Fall: 1-0, 2-17, 3-45, 4-140, 5-143, 6-148, 7-157

BOWLING	O	M	R	W
Sarfraz	12	2	39	2
Dye	7	3	9	1
Hodgson	6	3	10	1
Larkins	12	4	31	0
Willey	12	2	41	0
Bedi	11	0	52	3

NORTHANTS

R. T. Virgin	c and b Ratcliffe	53
P. Willey	c Engineer b Lee	65
*Mushtaq Mohammad	c Hayes b Ratcliffe	13
D. S. Steele	c sub b Hughes	24
W. Larkins	lbw b Lever	8
G. Cook	c Engineer b Lee	15
†G. Sharp	not out	10
Sarfraz Nawaz	not out	3
A. Hodgson		
B. S. Bedi		
J. C. J. Dye		
Extras	b 5, lb 1, nb 2	8
Total	(6 wkts)	199

Fall: 1-103, 2-127, 3-143, 4-154, 5-178, 6-182

BOWLING	O	M	R	W
Lever	12	3	29	1
Lee	12	4	29	2
Simmons	11.1	2	29	0
Ratcliffe	12	2	48	2
Hughes	11	0	56	1

*Captain; †Wicketkeeper
Man of the Match: P. Willey

masterplan. It was astonishing how often he would get a wicket with the last ball of an expensive over. But the common prejudice is against using that strategy in the last over of a low-scoring innings in your first-ever cup final, particularly when the batsman at the far end is David Hughes, a notorious slogger under pressure whose previous finest hour had come in the famous Cup-tie at Old Trafford when he hit 24 in an over off John Mortimore in the dark. Mushtaq trusted the man who was, after all, his best bowler. This time Hughes hit 26: 4,6,2,2,6,6. Bedi applauded all three sixes but it would not have helped that much if he had got Hughes out last ball. Turner's Senior Service count on this occasion is not recorded.

Fortunately, it did not matter. Virgin and Willey again started brilliantly and put on 103. And this time Steele was around to play the old hand towards the end. Northamptonshire won by four wickets with 11 balls to spare. Sarfraz said his knees were trembling as he made the winning hit. Willey won the man of the match award and 65 sausages, one a run, from another local butcher trying to get in on the lamb-chop publicity. There was a civic reception and all that. It was a great day for North-amptonshire cricket.

Still in some minds there were a few reservations. No one expected a small county so full of incomers to stack its team with local players but not to have a single one in the team seemed a terrible pity. And a cup win, achieved with four victories, one over a Minor County, is not the same as winning the real County Championship. Brian Close, then captain of Somerset, had told Turner before the season began: 'If you don't win the Champion-ship with this side, Ken, you never will.' And he never would. For the first time in months, there had been a chill in the air on cup final day. There was a slight chill in Turner's heart too.

'I knew,' he wrote years later, 'that for all the rejoicing, the side had to be reshaped and, in all probability, the public reaction would be one of shock and hostility.' Whether or not he was right on the first count, he was undoubtedly right on the second.

THE GREAT SCHISM

'Old friends become bitter enemies on a sudden.'
Robert Burton

NO ONE COULD accuse Northamptonshire of dwelling too long on their success. Maybe nobody else went gloomy quite as fast as Turner did; but the players and public were not far behind. In May 1977 a grand celebration dinner was arranged for the rugby ground at Franklins Gardens. Five hundred tickets had to be sold to break even; a month before the event 46 had gone.

The players, in any case, were threatening to boycott the dinner in protest against inadequate bonus payments. A Benson and Hedges game against Essex was carried over to a second day, forcing the players to miss the event anyway and conveniently avoid any embarrassment. By that time, the County's triumph seemed very ancient history indeed. The previous week cricket had been convulsed by the news that most of the world's leading Test players had signed up to play for some Australian TV magnate called Kerry Packer. They included Mushtaq who, of course, had not mentioned the matter to the Northamptonshire committee.

The whole game seemed to be spinning out of control and Northamptonshire were launched on a wild orbit of their own. At a meeting on 21 July the committee decided not just to break up the winning team but to smash it to pieces. Cottam had already gone the previous year, at his own request. Now it was decided to release both Dye, who had been out of the side for a month, and Bedi. The futures of Mushtaq and Virgin were discussed but deferred. Dye went at once, amid the first transfusion of bad blood. Then, amid reports that the legitimacy of Bedi's bowling action was being questioned by the TCCB, the story of his sacking came out, to furious comments from him.

Turner was, of course, working hard behind the scenes. He was negotiating with both Jim Watts, now qualified as a teacher and willing to return to cricket again full-time, and the young South African batsman Peter Kirsten. Both were to replace Mushtaq: Watts as captain and Kirsten as overseas player. By late August Mushtaq had got the message. He told Turner and the chairman of the selection committee Hugh Wright 'in an offensive manner' (as the minutes put it) where they could stick the captaincy. Steele was again appointed caretaker. Meanwhile,

Virgin was saying that he had been sacked too though the Club insisted he was going voluntarily.

By now, just about everyone was angry and the Turner magic was not working. The executive criticised him for 'lack of communication' over Watts's contract. And the public were rousing themselves. This was far more fun than winning trophies. Some members discovered a clause in the constitution that just 20 signatures were needed to call an extraordinary general meeting. In the prevailing atmosphere, an impromptu action group found that it was very easy indeed to find 20 signatures.

Lucky generals are fortunate in their enemies and it transpired that, however confused the administration might have been, the opposition were worse. Two of the 20 turned out not to be members at all and the Club could have ignored the petition. Wisely, they did not. The committee met the action group and called a meeting of its own accord for 16 December, thus ensuring there was no vote of censure actually on the agenda. Four hundred members turned up at the indoor school, most of them with no confidence at all in the running of the Club and very little Christmas goodwill in their hearts. Hugh Wright chaired the meeting flanked by four nervous committee men plus Turner and the newly appointed captain, Watts.

In recent times, the members of both Yorkshire and Lancashire have thrown out their committees in protest against the running of the team. Somerset came close to doing the same thing after the sackings of Viv Richards and Joel Garner in 1986. It is a thoroughly healthy activity: it affirms that county cricket clubs belong, in the last analysis, to their members – not to the players, the committee and certainly not the secretary. It could easily have happened at Northampton too.

The problem for the opposition was that their case was essentially incoherent. The sackings had been pushed through too fast and bungled; Turner's self-confidence had slipped over into arrogance. But the essential thrust of the policy had been correct: to remain successful, cricket clubs have to be unsentimental and find young players to replace aging ones. The essence of Liverpool FC's long years of triumph has been that managers were never afraid to change a winning team.

So it was hard for the Action Group to sustain its case. An impromptu spokesman, Keith Sketchley, rose and read a prepared statement demanding explanations for the sackings of the four stars and the appointment of Watts. The committee had already issued a closely argued circular putting its case, concentrating on the bleak financial propects. Mushtaq had signed for Packer without a word to anyone and his captaincy 'on and off the field left a lot to be desired'; Bedi was by far the Club's most expensive player – he was not the force he had been and was going to miss the 1979 season anyway because India were touring. By removing older players, they could hire four youngsters and still have money left over to establish a new, fairer scale of pay for everyone else.

No one could demolish this case. Instead, as in 1921, the members veered off at tangents: the selling of raffle tickets at out-grounds, the noise from the discos, the state of the scorecards and, of course, the ladies' toilets. And a Mr A.W. Heath rose and said he had he had been a member since 1945 and had never heard a good word said about the secretary.

That in many ways was the nub of the argument and Turner's personal unpopularity might have led to revolution. The mood of the meeting was only finally turned by the intervention of Watts, who combined a dignified defence of his own position with a few deft rapier thrusts at Mushtaq's lack of leadership. The anger began to subside. The following spring's AGM still had an attendance of 250 and three Action Group members, including Sketchley, were voted onto the committee. In the normal way of things, they were absorbed into the system and forgotten.

The crisis finally blew itself out the following summer when Bedi took the Club to an industrial tribunal in Bedford for unfair dismissal. The Club tried and failed to establish the principle that Bedi could not appeal because he was employed for less than half the year – 'like Father Christmas' said counsel. Northampton-shire were criticised for not giving Bedi the chance to defend himself before the committee. But they won the main point. As though it were a panel of selectors, the tribunal solemnly listened to Turner complaining about his ex-star's bad batting and fielding and declining bowling and Bedi complaining that he had been bowled on green tops when the seamers should have been on. In truth, Bedi was asking for something that could have reduced all professional sport to farce: and if clubs could be taken to a tribunal every time a player was dropped or sacked the legal system would clog up too. Unanimously, the tribunal decided his dismissal was not unfair. Observers gave the credit to the expertise of the Club's solicitor, Alan Berrisford, Dennis Brookes's calm authority as a witness and the fact that Turner kept his temper under control. Professional sport came through unscathed.

Northamptonshire cricket did not, however. Too much mud had been flung for some not to stick. And the young team was nowhere near ready to match its now-reviled predecessor.

Cricket in 1977, at Northamptonshire and elsewhere, seemed subsidiary to events off the field as the Packer affair dominated everything. In fact, the County came very close to reaching their second successive Cup final, losing to Kent by only five runs in the semi-finals of the Benson and Hedges, a competition in which, in five previous attempts, they had never qualified from the zonal round. But the Club were losing the knack of finishing off opponents (Action Group members excluded). On an August morning at the County Ground, Lancashire were bowled out for 33, knocking ten off the previous lowest score against the County. Sarfraz took six for eight. In the second innings Lancashire scored 501. Two weeks later at Grace Road, Sarfraz and Jim Griffiths reduced Leicestershire to 45 for nine; Illingworth and Higgs then put on 228 for the last wicket, only seven short of the Championship record.

In 1978 Northamptonshire found it hard even to start taking wickets. They came bottom of the Championship for the first time in 30 years, winning just two matches. For Watts, cricketing trials were soon secondary. His wife, Rosalie, became ill and tragically died. Sarfraz was away the first half of the summer with Pakistan. Hodgson, suddenly the senior fast bowler, needed a back operation. Sharp lost form and was temporarily replaced as wicket-keeper by Vince Flynn. And the new overseas player quickly broke a finger. This was not Peter Kirsten, who was dithering about playing county cricket because he had signed up with Packer, but another young but lesser-known South African, also from Western Province, called Allan Lamb. No one knew just how inspired this signing was eventually to prove.

The state of the team was summed up by the bowling averages, which were headed by Steele. Having expressed little interest in the captaincy of Northamptonshire and let it pass elsewhere without acrimony, he whimsically accepted an offer to captain Derbyshire, a far more viperish club, in 1979. So that was another one gone. But there was a sense that foundations were being put down for the future. It was typified by the demolition of the Ladies' Stand (which never did have ladies' toilets – clean or otherwise) and the start of work on a new pavilion. It was an unobtrusive building and not to the grand design envisaged in the original plans. But at least Northamptonshire were building for the future.

The same was true on the field too. Players who had found themselves totally overshadowed began to come through. There was Jim Yardley, signed in 1976 from Worcestershire, a batsman of such abject lack of style that he was known as 'Squirter Jim' –

most of his runs came through third-man. Yardley was a man of considerable humour and self-awareness. 'Christ,' said the Australian fast bowler Rodney Hogg while Yardley was struggling through a particularly fast spell of bowling during the 1981 tourist match. 'D'you plye for the first team regular?' 'If I said I didn't,' said Yardley plaintively. 'Would you bowl any slower?'

There was Tim Lamb, fastish-medium from Middlesex, another player of maturity and humour. There was the Irthlingborough boy Jim Griffiths, a delightfully bad batsman but an increasingly good bowler. At first Turner had refused to sign him because everyone had said how accident-prone he was. 'He'll walk into the roller first morning,' he was warned. They were wrong: he fell downstairs instead. In 1978, when he really was needed, Griffiths stayed fit. Above all, there was Larkins, who came back from the brink of the sack to emerge as one of the leading and most dominating bats in the country. It was a team that could only play well in patches but even in 1978, the Club's worst season in many people's memories, there were flashes of fun in Northamptonshire's cricket again. It was a much more spirited as a side than the combined ego XI of the mid-1970s. The wage bill was also smaller.

In 1979 the team started to flower. The bowling was patchy but a batting line-up emerged that enthusiasts began to call the Famous Five. Cook, increasingly dependable, was opening with Larkins, who would have played his first Test but for injury; at no 3 there was Richard 'Chippy' Williams, the little all-rounder (and qualified carpenter) from North Wales who had been earmarked for stardom by Turner and Brookes since he was spotted at a schools festival as a teenager; Allan Lamb, who averaged 67 that season, was at four and Willey at five. Yardley was the regular no.6. Both Willey and Larkins were picked for England's tour of Australia.

Willey and Williams also began to mature as off-spinners and Sarfraz was bowling better than ever. That did not make a team equipped to do better than come 11th in the Championship. The bowling was so bereft that the Club had to call up Les McFarlane, a Jamaican-born fast bowler who had been taking heaps of wickets for the United Social club on the Racecourse, where wickets come rather easier for formidable-looking men who teararse in than they do on the county circuit.

But the team was good enough to reach its second Gillette Cup final. The batting of Larkins and the bowling of Williams won the quarter-final against Leicestershire; and a stand of 157 between Lamb and Willey won the semi-final at Hove. At Lord's, the

County came up against Somerset, by then the only one of the traditional 17 first-class counties not to have lifted a trophy. They were in the process of putting a stop to that record. 'We have got to get Viv Richards out early,' said Watts beforehand, 'and we've got to be very careful about Joel Garner.' At least he read the game right. Richards scored 117, Garner took six for 29; despite 78 from Allan Lamb, Northamptonshire were never in the game.

The supporters were at Lord's as they had been three years earlier. But only five of the winning team – Willey, Larkins, Cook, Sharp and Sarfraz – were back to get losers' medals. Six – two Lambs, Williams, Yardley, Griffiths and Watts – had not been in the 1976 team. Ten months later exactly the same eleven returned to Lord's for the Benson and Hedges Cup final.

The County had already been to Lord's once in the tournament, for the semi-final when they beat Middlesex. This match is regarded by connoisseurs as one of the greatest of all one-day games – except that it was not a one-day game and had to be carried over to the Thursday morning.

Middlesex began the second day in a near-deserted Lord's with the seagulls making more noise than the crowd, needing 79 to win with six wickets standing and 14 overs left. The short passage of play that followed was quite superb, with the balance of the game shifting over by over, almost ball by ball. Above it all, there was a sense that two exceptionally gifted captains were staging a game of cricketing chess. On the one side, there was Brearley, whose skills were well-known; on the other was Watts, less generally appreciated. Watts outfoxed him, shifting his spinners in and out of the attack and maintaining a grip on the game that never faltered until the County came home by 11 runs. It was brilliant stuff.

The final was closer and only a little less gripping. Once again Allan Lamb made runs, 72 of them. But the County totalled only 209 and with Graham Gooch and Ken McEwan going easily at 112 for one, Essex appeared set for victory. Again Watts was prepared to risk Williams's off-spin, which many captains would have considered too expansive for such a situation. Essex fell further and further back and with six overs to go still needed 50. Then the West Indian all-rounder Norbert Phillip went for Griffiths and hit 30 off two overs. With an over to go, from Sarfraz, Essex needed 12. The wicket-keeper Neil Smith tried to slog himself instead of getting Phillip down the business end. He failed first ball and was bowled by the second; Ray East ran a single off the third; Phillip took two off the fourth. Two balls wanted, eight to win. Phillip missed and one ball later North-

BENSON & HEDGES CUP FINAL
NORTHANTS *v* ESSEX

Played at Lord's, 21 July 1980

NORTHANTS WON BY 6 RUNS

NORTHANTS

G. Cook	c Gooch b Pont	29
W. Larkins	c Denness b Pont	18
R. G. Williams	c McEwan b Pont	15
A. J. Lamb	c Hardie b Phillip	72
P. Willey	c McEwan b Turner	15
T. J. Yardley	c Smith b Gooch	0
†G. Sharp	c Fletcher b Pont	8
*P. J. Watts	run out	22
Sarfraz Nawaz	not out	10
T. M. Lamb	lbw b Turner	4
B. J. Griffiths	b Turner	0
Extras	b 1, lb 8, nb 3, w 4	16
Total		209

Fall: 1-36, 2-61, 3-78, 4-110, 5-110, 6-131, 7-190, 8-193, 9-209, 10-209

BOWLING	O	M	R	W
Lever	11	3	38	0
Phillip	11	1	38	1
Turner	10.5	2	33	3
Pont	11	1	60	4
Gooch	11	0	24	1

ESSEX

M. H. Denness	b Willey	14
G. A. Gooch	c A. J. Lamb b T. M. Lamb	60
K. S. McEwan	b Willey	38
*K. W. R. Fletcher	b Sarfraz	29
B. R. Hardie	b Watts	0
K. R. Pont	b Williams	2
S. Turner	c Watts b Sarfraz	16
N. Phillip	not out	32
†N. Smith	b Sarfraz	2
R. E. East	not out	1
J. K. Lever		
Extras	b 1, lb 5, w 3	9
Total	(8 wkts)	203

Fall: 1-52, 2-112, 3-118, 4-121, 5-129, 6-160, 7-180, 8-198

BOWLING	O	M	R	W
Sarfraz	11	3	23	3
Griffiths	7	0	46	0
Watts	8	1	30	1
T. M. Lamb	11	0	42	1
Willey	11	1	34	2
Williams	7	0	19	1

*Captain; †Wicketkeeper
Man of the Match: A. J. Lamb

The team celebrates victory at Lord's in the 1980 Benson and Hedges Cup final. Northamptonshire beat Essex by six runs. Jim Watts holds the cup. (Northamptonshire CCC)

amptonshire supporters were racing across the boundary to hear Lamb proclaimed as man of the match.

It was a bit of an anti-climax because it had poured all day on the Saturday and the game had to be played on the Monday – still with 23,000 in the ground but not enough to fill it. However, as Watts held trophy no 2 aloft, it seemed as though there would be many more to follow it, especially in one-day cricket. The attack, based on Sarfraz, Griffiths and Tim Lamb, was beginning to prove itself and the batsmen were capable of making so many runs so quickly that they had room for a little bit of error. Some people thought Northamptonshire might be the 'Team of the Eighties'. In soccer, they were saying the same thing about Crystal Palace.

234

THE UNDER-ACHIEVERS

'Oh, I am a cook and a captain bold.'

W. S. Gilbert

THIS TIME, when Jim Watts retired, he did mean it. The new captain
was Geoff Cook. He was still not 30 but he had spent five seasons
serving his apprenticeship since the committee had made him
effective vice-captain, ahead of Steele. He had learned a lot from
Watts, which included noticing the occasions when he switched
on to auto-pilot and his captaincy faltered.

Cook was intelligent, self-assured, approachable, popular with
spectators, players and the press. He suffered fools more gladly
than most. He was steeped in the game; his dad Harry, the doyen
of Middlesbrough club cricket, and indeed the whole Cook
family would often swell the County Ground crowd on days
when not many might be there, almost bursting with pride about
their Geoff.

Rightly so. He was to be captain of Northamptonshire for eight
years, longer than anyone else (Watts had been captain for seven
full seasons and a few chaotic days in 1975) in the club's first-class
history. If anyone had known in 1981 that he had eight years in
charge before him, they would have assumed – eight years, four
trophies a year, four eights are 32 – that he would have led the
County to several more triumphs. A Championship at last? Well,
perhaps not early on with the bowling as it was in 1981, but
possibly soon enough. And there were certain to be a few Cup
wins and Sunday Leagues, surely? Surely? If the newspaper cliche
of the old days was that Northamptonshire were the Cinderella
team, then in the 1980s the word was 'under-achievers'. Quite
often they went to the ball all right but they always finished
turning back into a pumpkin.

There are plenty of people to blame: Cook, Turner and everyone else running the club have to take their share. The crucial
thing in a cricket team is that the chemistry has to be right. In
Northamptonshire the test-tube kept exploding in people's faces.
But even after one season Cook already had about him an air of
authority that impressed the England selectors with the thought
that he might make a possible captain in the Brearley mould. That
never happened; the off-chance that he might was to have fateful
consequences for Cook and everyone at Northamptonshire.

He inherited a team that was already a little disappointed with itself. Perhaps the Benson and Hedges Cup final, won in mid-season, induces complacency in its winners. The team had won 16 games in all competitions by the end of June 1980. After that they won only five, including the Cup final. They fell from top of the Sunday League to equal sixth. In the Championship they sank to 12th. And 1981, in every respect bar one, was an awful season. The Famous Five, everyone agreed, were ideally equipped to lead the County to the Sunday League title: the team came bottom. Their defence of the B and H was wrecked by bad weather. No one expected them to do well in the Championship unless they could find a new quick bowler.

They did find a new bowler – Neil Mallender, a young man of such intense blondness that he was known to his team-mates as Ghostie. He had slipped through the gaping holes in the Yorkshire scouting net and, like so many before him, landed on his feet at the County Ground. He was still only 19 but quicker than batsmen thought and went straight to the top of the Club's bowling averages. The team did not go towards the top of the table: they came 15th.

There were excuses: Sarfraz and Willey were injured. But they were fit for the second half of the season in time to play in the inaugural NatWest Bank Trophy, successor to the Gillette Cup. At the County Ground against fearsome Somerset, Sarfraz got Richards for a duck; at Grace Road against Leicestershire Tim Lamb dismissed Gower, which he was turning into a useful habit. Both times Cook and Larkins began the innings with century stands to settle the game. The County eased into a semi-final at home to Lancashire.

It must have been a very long day. It is now impossible to remember anything except the closing minutes, and they will stick forever in the memory of anyone who was present. In light that had long since passed bad and gone on to dreadful, Northamptonshire found themselves requiring 13 to win with eight overs remaining – no problem, except that the ninth wicket had fallen and the last man, Griffiths, was coming to the crease to join Tim Lamb and face Michael Holding. The *Exchange Telegraph* reporter David Field was the first to understand the significance: 'It's the best bowler in the world against the worst batsman,' he said.

Now technically, this might not be quite right in the sense that someone, somewhere must have been a worse batsman than Griffiths; he was just not playing first-class cricket. This was the man who in his first-class career had 138 innings and was out for nought in 51 of them. However, this was Griffiths' finest

Allan Lamb succeeded Geoff Cook as captain in 1989 and led the side to a third one-day trophy three years later. He was the County's outstanding batsman in the 1980s. (The Chronicle and Echo)

hour. It very nearly was an hour too with the runs coming in singles, mostly leg-byes, punctuated with mid-wicket conferences as Lamb, no great batsman himself, turned down singles to manipulate the strike and keep Griffiths away from the bowling.

There was also a five-minute hold-up when Lamb sent the umpire to find out what the comparative totals had been after 30 overs in case the scores finished level. Finally, off the second-last available ball, the winning run came with a bye. Everyone on the ground was totally hysterical except dear old Jim Laker, commentating on TV as though all this were another day at the office. Lamb was man of the match, but it was Griffiths who was carried shoulder-high from the field.

This, of course, was 1981, the summer when Ian Botham took on the Australians and made the impossible into the routine. The other semi-final had been just as crazy with the scores finishing level and Derbyshire going through against Essex by losing fewer wickets. The final simply had to be an anti-climax. But it wasn't. Two counties with comparatively tiny memberships packed out Lord's, in Northamptonshire's case for the third year running. Cup finals were turning into annual outings.

Once again, Cook and Larkins had a big stand: 99 this time. Larkins, as ever, played the more exhilarating shots but, with the game's hierarchy attending closely, Cook stayed on to score 111. However, with a couple of close decisions going against them and a middle-order collapse, the County could only turn that into 235 for nine. Derbyshire needed 19 off the last two overs, four wickets standing. Then a couple of bad balls from Sarfraz to Colin Tunnicliffe were despatched for four, and the game turned round. Seven wanted off the last over, from Griffiths. Two off the last ball. . .

But it was not really two. Derbyshire knew from happy experience of the semi-final that, on the fewer wickets rule, a single would be enough. Tunnicliffe facing, Miller backing up. Cook took two minutes to place his field. Then suddenly Cook and Miller were racing each other to the stumps, all but sending each other flying with the result in doubt until umpire Palmer, realising that Constant at square leg was keeping his finger to himself, signalled a leg-bye before fleeing the onrushing mob. Derbyshire had won the trophy without actually winning a game since the quarter-finals.

Cook had the consolation prize of the man of the match award and two days later there was an unexpected follow-up: he was chosen for the tour of India. Alec Bedser, the chairman of

Inches away from another one-day triumph – the Northamptonshire side beaten by Derbyshire at Lord's in the first NatWest Trophy final in 1981. Back row, left to right: Richard Williams, Wayne Larkins, Jim Yardley, Tim Lamb, Jim Griffiths, Neil Mallender. Front row, left to right: Allan Lamb, Peter Willey, Geoff Cook (captain), George Sharp, Sarfraz Nawaz. (Northamptonshire CCC)

selectors, hinted that Cook was being considered as a potential future captain, which was why he was being preferred to Larkins, who had played in the Oval Test the previous month. Willey was also left out, having played 20 times since 1976; he was by now being seen as a specialist tough-guy player of fast bowling.

It meant that both Larkins and Willey happened to be at home when the calls came from a representative of South Africa asking if they might care to join a short tour there the following year: £40,000, no arguments. Cook also agreed to join them then alerted the Club – one of the first indications English cricket had about what was happening – and was persuaded to stay with the Establishment. When the storm broke, with the first set of rebels arriving in Johannesburg, it broke heaviest over the heads over the two Northamptonshire players. Turner, at his most splenetic, was on the radio calling for them to be banned from Test cricket for life; he was so angry that he called South Africa 'the nigger in the woodpile', not the happiest phrase in the circumstances. Jim

Geoff Cook was Northamptonshire's captain from 1981 to 1988, making him the longest-serving County leader this century. The job was sometimes a lonely one. (The Chronicle and Echo)

Watts, as a member of the cricket committee (which had replaced the old selection committee) wanted them banned from county cricket for life.

In the end they were banned for three years. In Larkins's case this almost certainly robbed him of the lengthy run of Test match appearances, which he had needed at every level of cricket to establish himself and settle his fragile nerves. It was to be 1990 before he was to make a brief return to the England team. It was a terrible waste of a wonderful talent. There were many reasons why players joined that South African tour: Larkins was the only one to go out of pure pique.

Willey's reasons were more understandable. He had played almost his entire career in the belief that his fragile knees would bring him to grief any minute. He was contemplating the end of his career in the 1970s; he was still a forceful player in the 1990s. He was also not a man who reacted easily to being told not to do something, or one afraid to speak his mind about injustice or cricketing incompetence as he saw it. In the right competitive circumstances, it made him a marvellous, geeing-up, senior team man. In the dressing room that summer it made him, as far as the Club were concerned, a divisive influence. Cook was to describe it later as 'the saddest period of my career'.

He never did become England captain. Cook played a little more Test cricket, that summer and the following winter. But, as he himself had suspected all along, he was not quite good enough as a batsman. Another Northamptonshire player was eventually to lead England but it was not anyone who was in the England team when 1982 began; indeed he was not even an Englishman. He represented Turner's last great masterstroke.

There has never been any question that Allan Lamb sounds like a South African; his accent has never wavered. But his father was born in Walton-on-Thames and his mother in Wembley. That meant he could qualify for England in four years instead of the ten years which were then intended to put off most foreigners. It was Derbyshire who first spotted this when they were toying with signing Lamb. It was certainly Turner who helped persuade Lamb that South Africa were unlikely to return to Test cricket in the short-term and that he could expect a long career as an England cricketer. Northamptonshire would thus be able to keep Lamb and sign another overseas player. Lamb later called Turner 'my guiding star'. Other players used to find Turner's gruffness disconcerting; this one responded in kind and quickly spotted the softer nature underneath.

As late as 1980 Lamb was still telling South African newspapers that he had not the slightest intention of deserting their cricket. By February 1981 he was officially accepted as English by the Test and County Cricket Board. The nearest he came to the rebel tour, when he might have played for either side, was sitting in the stands at Cape Town. When England came to pick a team in the summer of 1982 without the benefit of Willey, Larkins and the rest of the people who had merely gone to the Cape, the man who had been born there was an absolute certainty. He was to remain so for nearly all the next decade.

By now Lamb was a very good cricketer indeed. It was clear from his first season that Turner had got this one right. In 1981 he became the first Northamptonshire player since Jock Livingston in 1955 to pass 2,000 runs in a season. Six of those came in one spectacular hit off the Middlesex slow left-armer Dermot Monteith on to the cantilevered roof of the indoor school, a phenomenal shot. More than that, he had made his commitment to the County, moved his family to the area and put down roots. Later, when he would get into scrapes on tour with Ian Botham, people would describe him as 'easily led'. In the early 1980s Cook was grateful to have at least one player who was easy to lead.

Lamb's qualification enabled Northamptonshire to import another ace. Instead, they came up with a joker. Kapil Dev of India was already one of the world's leading all-rounders. The County were hoping he would lead the attack, take a hundred wickets and spearhead the drive to the first-ever Championship. Kapil's Test commitments were such that he found it hard to summon the motivation to drive to the County Ground at all. The Club had first signed him to play a few midweek games in 1981 when he was engaged in League cricket and Sarfraz was injured. In his third game he had hit 79 against Worcestershire at Stourbridge with six sixes, some of them clattering into the road; Jack Mercer, the scorer, whose cricketing memory went back to the Great War, said he could not remember a more devastating innings.

But the County were now chock-full of players who would occasionally produce devastating innings, short of men willing to produce chips-down grafting ones. And there was no attack worth mentioning at all. There was some good news: two young players, David Capel and Robin Boyd-Moss, began to come through; and David Steele returned after three years away and ended up as top bowler with his left-arm slows. This was, however, partly a comment on the rest of the attack. In 1982 India and Pakistan shared a tour which meant that Sarfraz and Kapil Dev popped by only occasionally and Kapil's contribution with the ball in six Championship matches was nine wickets at 45 each. Mallender suffered the customary fall-back that hits players who have made a name in their first season; Griffiths and Tim Lamb were injured. The County rose to ninth in the Championship and eighth in the Sunday League but they never threatened to do much better than that and failed to win a serious game in either Cup. The annual outing to Lord's was cancelled and would remain that way for five years. And the atmosphere in the dressing room, between Cook and Willey especially, was sulphurous.

What the team did not need at this stage was another flaming row. This is what they got. The one great casualty of the 1977 schism had been Albert Lightfoot, overworked as groundsman and almost certainly underpaid as well. He was replaced by Les Bentley from Harrogate, a cheerful man on the whole but not a pliable one. He did not care for children playing on the outfield, for instance, an ancient Northampton tradition. And he did not care to be told how to do his job.

It became clear early on that he and Turner were not going to get on. At first the pitches did appear to improve but soon there were endless discussions in committee about his supposed short-comings, especially over preparation of practice pitches. By June 1982 Turner was telling the committee he could not work with Bentley and the cricket committee was recommending that he should be sacked. In August the County Ground had the minor honour of staging the under-19 Test between England and a West Indies team led by an enormously tall off-spinner called Roger Harper. The game was scheduled to last four days; on a flying, uneven pitch that had already been used, it almost finished in two. Lord's were furious. Bentley was sacked.

In committee there was one dissenting voice, Jim Watts, who was convinced that Bentley had had a raw deal. But there were two others in the dressing room: Willey and Larkins. And they did not keep their opinions to themselves. When Bentley followed the Bedi path and took the Club to an industrial tribunal the following April the two players gave evidence against their employers; Watts joined them and resigned from the committee. Whether or not there was the right amount of grass on the County Ground wickets, there was still plenty of mud to fling. Everyone trooped across to Bedford to give evidence. Turner told the tribunal that Bentley 'did not have the experience, knowledge or ability to do the job'; Willey said he had improved the match wickets, the practice wickets and the outfield. The tribunal decided unanimously that Northamptonshire 'honestly believed on reasonable grounds that the applicant (Bentley) was incapable or incompetent.' The Second Battle of Bedford, one chronicler called it, and once again Turner emerged, bloodied but triumphant, from the legal battlefield. Norman Hever came back as groundsman, which was perhaps what Turner was trying to engineer from the start.

In May 1983 the two players met the cricket committee. Shortly after the tour they had turned up to a committee reception wearing their rebel team blazers. Now Larkins was apologetic and promised his allegiance; Willey gave no apologies and no assurance. He was named as the County's Player of the Year in 1983 for the second year running but he was offered a contract for only one further year. The message was implicit and Willey got it – he signed for Leicestershire. The era of the Famous Five was over, and pretty infamous it had all been too.

The 1983 season was no happier than 1982 but it was a little more successful. The County came sixth in the Championship, the highest position since the runners-up year of 1976 and the best of Cook's eight. Larkins was in blazing form. He hit the highest score in English cricket that summer (252 at Cardiff) and the third-highest (236 at Derby) and shared a County second-wicket record of 342 with Willey at home to Lancashire. This was all achieved with an attack that was again led by 41-year-old Steele and with the minimum of help from their overseas players. In June 1983 Kapil Dev brilliantly led India to a spectacular win in the World Cup. He spent the rest of the summer taking 16 Championship wickets. He had done the hard work, thank you.

Sarfraz had gone the previous year. His replacement was one James Carse, born in Rhodesia and a man who had impressed Willey and Larkins (who by now were getting the blame for everything) when playing for Eastern Province in South Africa. He was meant to be a fast bowler. He ended up, with the help of eight not outs from ten innings, behind only Viv Richards, Gordon Greenidge and Mike Gatting in the national batting averages. As far as bowling averages were concerned, he could not even make the Northamptonshire top eight.

There was a feeling now that, after almost three decades, Turner's grip was not quite what it had been. He was close to retirement and not always all that well. Having been an innovator in so much he was slower to come to terms with the money-making ideas of the 1980s, like corporate hospitality. The new pavilion meant that the Club at last had a respectable, very pleasant lounge. However, as one critic put it: 'It was being sold so cheap that the businessmen using it were hardly paying more than they would through the gate.' Individual committee men were starting to exert more power and at the 1984 AGM, members accepted a plan first put forward by Doug Lucas to reduce the committee from 30 to 18, with just three sub-committees, covering cricket, finance and promotions. The Club would be less easily dominated by a paid official in future.

What Turner did do constructively was to bring another Northampton boy, Graham Alsop, into the office. Alsop had shown some flair working for the Supporters' Association and, when Turner was ill in late 1984, he desperately needed someone to start selling the following year's Australian game to sponsors. He turned to Alsop and in time he graduated to become the Club's full-time commercial manager.

Turner's last year in charge, 1984, was another season of unfulfilled promise. It was a warm, dry summer but the team hardly won anything at all before July; it was a terrible season for injuries, including a broken jaw for Cook. Lamb scored three hundreds in successive Tests that summer, innings of rock-ribbed courage and defiance against a ferocious West Indian pace attack;

One of the batsmen who made Northamptonshire a side worth watching in the 1980s: Wayne Larkins. (The Chronicle and Echo)

he made only one century for Northamptonshire. Reduced by new regulations to playing only one overseas player at a time, the County replaced Kapil and Carse, who were not greatly missed, with another South African fast bowler Rupert Hanley, 32 years old with a big reputation back home. He did not enhance it.

However, as happened after the great clear-out of 1977, new players moved into the gaps and took to their responsibilities with far more maturity than anyone had dared hope. Chief among them was Robert Bailey from Steele and Crump-land in the Potteries. He had played only three Championship games before he was called into the opening game at Edgbaston because Williams was ill. He made an unbeaten hundred in only two and half hours and at once established a reputation as a free-flowing, front-footed strokeplayer who could be almost as destructive as Larkins on the slow county wickets of the 1980s.

There was a fast bowler from Yorkshire, Alan Walker, who really had worked down a pit, as fast bowlers should. Jack Mercer in his rose-tinted old age thought he might make another Brian Statham. There was Robin Boyd-Moss, a Cambridge blue and a batsman with more adhesive qualities than were usual round the County Ground at the time; Cook had him earmarked as the long-term no 3. There were even two local boys: David Capel from Roade, an intense young man – combative on the field, self-analytical off it – who wanted to make himself into a great batsman while all around him wanted to make him into a great swing bowler; and Duncan Wild, son of the 1960s player Johnny, who was also an all-rounder and had a mixture of cheerfulness and intelligence that made some observers murmur 'future captain'. 'The Club has a sound base,' said Doug Lucas, signing off as chairman after three years, 'a good team – success should be again within our grasp in the season ahead.'

The retiring secretary went to his last Test and County Cricket Board meeting and was given a fulsome tribute by Cedric Rhoades, the controversial chairman of Lancashire. Turner rose and said 'Chairman, for the first and only time in my life I can agree with every word Cedric has spoken.' The whipround among the other county secretaries amounted to twice the previous record. In 1985 Turner was offered an MBE in the Birthday Honours. He 'asked respectfully' for his name to be withdrawn: 'There are so many who have made a greater contribution to the general welfare of the country I would be embarrassed to be recognised for what I have done.'

Surprising to the last was Ken.

BEYOND OUR KEN

'Youth on the prow. . .'

Thomas Gray

IN OCTOBER 1984 the press were called to the new pavilion for an important announcement. There, beaming all over his face, was Ken Turner, with Keith Andrew. Turner had great pleasure in announcing that 88 applications had been received for the vacancy and one had been chosen: Andrew was to be his successor. His tone suggested this was another one of those moves he had been planning for years.

If so, it was an uncharacteristically sentimental one. If this was a family club, there was no more beloved family member than Keith. He was giving up his post as director of coaching of the National Cricket Association at Lord's to accept the title of 'secretary-manager', which implied even more authority over the playing side than Turner had exerted. Andrew paid tribute to Turner and how he had enabled the Club to survive. That was no longer in doubt, he said; Northamptonshire could do more than that.

Indeed, cricket was booming all over the country: Botham's exploits against the Australians in 1981 had had a galvanic effect on cricket's popularity that was to reverberate for most of the decade. The County, with its population increasing dramatically, was starting to benefit from the economic boom spilling over from the south-east of England. In 1984 the County made a profit of £21,191 and this was not considered anything special.

However, Keith Andrew was rising 55 himself and after the euphoria of the first press conference he began to have his own doubts about whether he was the right man to lead North-amptonshire County Cricket Club into a new era. There also appeared to be the beginnings of a gap between his conception of the job and the committee's. Andrew withdrew.

Steve Coverdale was not a family member, though he might have become one earlier if a call from Turner in 1982 asking him if he might fancy joining as wicket-keeper had ever been followed through. He had played for Cambridge University and a little for Yorkshire without ever making a career for himself as a player. By 1984 he was working as a sports journalist on Radio Leeds but, since he was not interested in working for the BBC in London, there was little prospect of advancement there. He was one of the original 88 applicants and was rejected without an interview. Then he received another call: he was placed on a short list of two with a Minor Counties official and then appointed. He walked into Ken Turner's empty office in April 1985.

It would be hard to imagine a greater contrast. Turner was cynical and choleric; Coverdale was earnest, polite, rather cagey. Turner had seen it all; Coverdale was just 30 and not merely the youngest county secretary at the time but still the youngest seven years later when he had served longer in the post than all but four of his colleagues at other counties. Turner knew precisely what the job entailed; Coverdale did not, partly because the committee kept changing its mind.

When he was appointed, it was said the Club wanted someone to take charge of the cricket. Indeed, an administrator, David Powell, was appointed at the same time to take charge of financial matters. Coverdale took his employers at their word, came to the ground in his tracksuit and began advising the players. Since the main reason Coverdale was available to become a county secretary at 30 was that he had not been a good enough cricketer to survive on the field, this did not go down especially well. Two less intelligent men might have staged a power struggle. Both Coverdale and Geoff Cook were too smart for that. Coverdale retreated to the office, chastened, and reverted to suit and tie. Slowly, he began to build his own authority and in time became thoroughly impressive.

There was change all around him. Off the field, Northamptonshire had thrived on continuity and stability but by the early 1980s this was turning into a rather niggardly conservatism. When the 1983 World Cup was staged in England, Northamptonshire were one of only two counties (along with Sussex) not even to bother to apply for a fixture. This came in the aftermath of the fiasco of the youth international and the Bentley affair; nonetheless it was not the behaviour of a club with much ambition. Despite the new pavilion, the ground looked more tatty and downbeat than ever; the wretched old press box had a wasps' nest in it, instead of just the usual snakes. The complacency even extended to the structure of salary bonuses: players got exactly the same money whether they played or not.

Dennis Brookes, having been given the quite exceptional honour of being appointed club president while still a serving employee, retired with Turner. Jack Jennings retired after almost 40 years as physiotherapist to be replaced by Richie Norman of the Cobblers, thus continuing an old connection. Jennings had formerly been the football club trainer too and briefly took over as manager when Northampton Town were first promoted to the Second Division and the manager, Dave Bowen, resigned. He retired as the most successful manager in history: played three, won three. Then Bowen came back. Jennings, in the nature of things, has rarely been centre stage in this history. But he was always there: with the team even when most other counties did not bother to have a travelling physio and had to come plaintively knocking on his door.

Jack Mercer had already been eased out as the first team scorer, much to his disgust, and succeeded by Bernard Clarke. Ray Bailey, a former player, replaced Norman Hever as groundsman. Frank Chamberlain replaced Lucas as chairman. Brian Reynolds faded out from his role in charge of the second team and eventually moved into a wider-ranging job as cricket development officer. There was no one more loyal or more devoted to the welfare of young cricketers or to the Club. But he belonged to the National Service generation himself and he had learned his cricket under Freddie Brown; not every youngster in the 1980s appreciated this sort of approach. Bob Carter, a man more of their own era, was coming in.

Even David Steele retired and was promptly elevated into the committee room. And during the rain-hit Australian match in August 1985 Fred Speakman, in his 40th season reporting Northamptonshire cricket, collapsed and later died in hospital. His spiritual home, the old press box, had already been abandoned and the reporters had moved from the worst box in the country to one of the best. The old place was turned into a lounge for players' families, the carpentry being done in the off-season by Chippy Williams. He even made the old dump seem rather cosy.

The ground did not seem the same any more without Speakman and Mercer in their hide-outs and Brookes sitting in the outer office counting the pennies or just occasionally (like the time he and Turner stuffed £8,500 in a suitcase after a bumper day at Tring) the pounds, fivers and tenners. From now on, the Club was to concentrate on the tenners and above.

The 1985 season was miserably wet and Northamptonshire lost more time than any other county: 160 hours or a third of the total season. They were lying 15th in the Championship before winning the last two matches and rising to tenth. The best performance came in the Sunday League which the County were in danger of winning until three successive matches were washed out in August; they eventually finished fifth. The Club had temporarily given up searching the world for the mythical beast able and willing to tear in fast seven days a week and instead thought laterally: they signed Roger Harper, the Guyanese player last heard of at the County Ground during the Youth Test fiasco. Harper bowled high-trajectory off-breaks fast enough for opposing batsmen hit by one to swear that he was really another quick in disguise, batted well, fielded sensationally and brought a new spirit of solidarity into the dressing room. Of course, there had to be a fast bowler as well and the Club signed another Guyanese, Ray Joseph, but he hardly played.

Harper was the leading wicket-taker in 1985 and came second in the Championship batting averages, behind another newcomer, 19-year-old Alastair Storie – Scottish born, South African-bred – who made a six-hour century in the opening home game against Hampshire. With Boyd-Moss hit by injury and loss of confidence, especially against the fastest bowling, here was another potential sticker; but he failed to stick with the Club. In June Sharp broke a finger and decided to retire. The wicket-keeping succession went tentatively to another northerner, the Yorkshireman David Ripley.

The policy for 1986 was to concentrate on spin: in a sort of delayed exchange for Willey, the slow left-armer Nick Cook joined from Leicestershire. Two years earlier, he had made an exceptional entry into international cricket by taking 17 wickets in his first two Tests, when he was deputy for the injured Phil Edmonds. The theory was that the County would prepare pitches for Harper and Cook but yet again ended up with pitches so slow that they benefited no one. The spin-bowler policy was made to look deliberate. It was not. The Club had tried in vain for months to get the Australian fast bowler Craig McDermott to sign. In the end, the team rose from tenth to ninth; of their five wins two were brought about by sensational innings from Lamb, including his 157 against Imran on an apparently impossible wicket at Hastings; Lamb had been dropped by England two days earlier and was in a fuming temper. Only one win was primarily attributable to spin: when Nick Cook took five for 14 at Colchester and bowled out Essex, the eventual champions, for 44, the lowest total of the season. 'More a curiosity,' sniffed *Wisden*, 'than an accurate gauge of bowling strength.'

Northamptonshire could not go on promising so much but going nowhere. And they did not. In 1987 they produced the most spectacular season in the County's history, more surprising than 1912, more dramatic than 1965. They went somewhere all right; unfortunately the final destination was the buffers which they hit at full-tilt very painfully indeed. They could easily have won the Championship and both Lord's Cup Finals, an entirely

The combative Nick Cook crossed 'the great divide' between Grace Road and Wantage Road in 1986. (The Chronicle and Echo)

David Capel became the first Northampton-born cricketer to play Test cricket for England since George Thompson. (The Chronicle and Echo)

unprecedented feat for any county. Instead they won nothing.

Before considering what went wrong, it is necessary to re-member how much went right. At last, Northamptonshire found the overseas fast bowler they craved: Winston Davis from the Windward Islands turned out to be an ideal choice – aware of the rigours of county cricket from a spell with Glamorgan, out of favour with the West Indies selectors and so not diverted by more glamorous work, yet still not quite 30 and ambitious enough to be interested. The previous year there had been talk in the committee of making Harper captain. He remained on the staff and played regularly on Sundays. But for most of the time he was forced, under the regulations governing overseas players, to be merely the best and most expensive 12th man in the country.

There were no other significant newcomers: Mallender, dissat-isfied by something, had drifted off the staff and down to Somerset for reasons that the Club never quite grasped; Griffiths had drifted out. But with Davis bowling genuinely fast at the other end, Walker and Capel were both inspired. In June, Capel became the first Northampton-born player to make the Test team since George Thompson. Williams, a player never destined to fulfil the Club's fondest hopes, gained from Harper's exclusion and returned to his best form with bat and ball.

Northamptonshire were lucky even to qualify for the Benson and Hedges: they got through to the quarter-finals only on the technicalities of run-rate. They made the most of their luck in two difficult away ties, with a spirited team-effort win at Taunton and a spectacular Lamb-inspired one at Canterbury when he scored 126 not out, which Denis Compton, making one of the easier man of the match decisions, called 'one of the best limited-overs innings ever'. Wild's greyhound-like running between the wickets was a splendid supporting act. Rushing to the pavilion after hitting what appeared to be the winning four, Lamb grabbed the champagne bottle and took his first gulp, only to gulp even more when he discovered that he had misread the scoreboard in the gloaming and needed to hit one more run with three balls left. Coverdale grabbed Lamb by the shoulders, crying: 'For God's sake, don't get out.' Lamb got the thinnest of edges on the first ball after the restart and it went for four.

The final was against Yorkshire, in their first season after the end of Geoff Boycott's turbulent career. But the old days were over: Northamptonshire were the favourites, even more so after Capel had made 97 to lead them away from an iffy start to a total of 244, a score that had always been enough to win this final before now. But Capel, having done so much to win the game, was the bowler who did most to throw away the advantage. Exuberant as ever, he was a little too fired up and got hit; Geoff Cook, as he admitted later, was not brave enough to use Wild's little seamers instead and Yorkshire were able to get back up to the asking rate.

Theoretically, they needed five off the last over. But Yorkshire had seen Northamptonshire's last Cup final and knew they could win without winning – Jim Love calmly blocked the final delivery and they won the Derbyshire way: 244 for six beating 244 for seven. In fact, they would have won even if Love had been out, under the arbitrary regulation awarding the trophy to the team which had scored most after 30 overs. The Northamptonshire team were disappointed, but by no means downcast: 20 minutes after the game, there were wisecracks in the dressing room again. After all, there was bigger game afoot.

By 8 May, with the footballers barely gone from the County Ground (with honour for once – the Cobblers were champions of Division Four by a huge margin) Northamptonshire were top of the table with two wins out of two: a Larkins-inspired run chase at Southampton having been followed at Lord's by Davis's first big performance. Already people were beginning to think that, as in 1965, success might waft from one end of the County Ground to the other.

In fact, it was to be more than six weeks before the County won another Championship game: bad weather and slow pitches ('put a box of hand grenades under that bloody square,' said Lamb, ever the diplomat, after the home draw against Kent) saw to that – along with the fact that Peter Willey was captaining Leicestershire and was even less disposed than most of his predecessors to give the neighbours an even break.

There followed a spectacular sequence. Harper, making a couple of rare appearances, was responsible for two wins: against Glamorgan at Swansea and against Warwickshire at Luton. Bailey and Capel led a stunning run chase at home to Yorkshire and Davis rolled out Lancashire on 7 July. This left the County second in the table, one point behind Yorkshire but with three games in hand. A draw at Bristol put them in front again and the seventh win came on 28 July, at home to Sussex with nine wickets for Capel. Yorkshire were just top but the County now had four games in hand.

Half the 22 fixtures were left in a year when both Essex and Middlesex were struggling and there was no outstanding county side. They almost won the next game at Edgbaston when Gifford declared at tea, almost as an afterthought and was then confronted

Rob Bailey hits out at Northampton. He became a County regular in 1984 and was appointed Lamb's vice-captain in 1991. (The Chronicle and Echo)

by some hitting by Larkins that was astonishing even by his own standards. The target was 222 off 31 overs: the County got to 207 for seven, having lost 20 crucial minutes to rain. They were well on top of Lancashire when rain wrecked the final day. It was 7 August, Northamptonshire were still top of the table and still playing like potential Champions. It rained again when the County were playing Essex. Now Nottinghamshire spurted to the top of the table. Everything was set up for a showdown at Trent Bridge.

It was one of those occasions when visiting players get the feeling that the Nottingham groundsman Ron Allsopp has not just organised the pitch for his team's benefit but the weather and the coin as well. Cook knew he had to win the toss. He called wrong. It may have been his worst decision in all his years as captain. Northamptonshire, previously unbeaten, lost by an innings and 132.

After that, they never even looked like winning another Championship match and eventually finished seventh. Some close observers thought that Capel never recovered from being picked for England; beyond question the strains were starting to tell, on Walker's ever-suspect back and, after he had bowled a lot of overs, on Davis too. But there was still another trophy to be won. Before the Trent Bridge disaster the County had become the third team (after Middlesex in 1975 and Essex in 1985) to reach both Lord's finals in the same season. They were up against Nottinghamshire again.

To get there they had beaten Surrey comfortably, Essex with 121 not out from Larkins, and then Leicestershire, with an all-round performance from Williams plus a blinding catch by Larkins, at the fifth attempt, at cover-point to dismiss Gower. Every one of the four successful quarter and semi-final ties had been won away from home against strong opposition. At that time they were playing like winners.

When they came into the final they were playing nothing like as well. But on a moody, rainy September day Northamptonshire took control of the game. The final was reduced to 50 overs a side but even then the innings was hampered by further interruptions. Still, Larkins scored 87 in his usual fashion and the County made a thoroughly respectable 228 for three. By the time play was abandoned for the day, Nottinghamshire were 57 for four and in terrible trouble.

Northamptonshire decided to go ahead with their planned Saturday night party; they then had to go 150 miles to Taunton for a meaningless and ultimately washed-out Sunday game. It was agreed that it would be best for team spirit if everyone did travel, even if they did not all play. Everyone the players met said: 'Don't worry. You'll win it.' The papers assumed it was a foregone conclusion. So did Nottinghamshire. A supporters' coach came down to Lord's from Nottingham on Monday morning: there were eight people on it.

In the 29th over John Birch was bowled by Walker and Richard Hadlee walked bare-headed to the middle to join his captain Clive Rice. The score was 84 for five; Nottinghamshire needed 145 in 21 overs. Hadlee began hitting more out of hope than expectation and more out of habit than hope. Even so, the asking rate rose to ten an over.

At that point, with all the ghosts of the past hovering in anticipation of triumph, Northamptonshire's cricket collapsed completely. Four times in a row they missed Hadlee. Geoff Cook dropped a hard one at mid-wicket off Wild; in the next over, off Williams, Lamb at deep mid-wicket had no room to maneouvre and was forced to parry the ball for six; the next ball was slogged straight to Bailey at long-off but the September sun – visible for once – was right in his eyes and he completely misjudged it; the next was just to Lamb's right. It looked, Cook ruefully remarked later, like a benefit match with a star batsman trying to get out to the village lads after scoring 50. The County were desperate to get their best fielder, Harper, on because Walker could hardly move. The umpires said he had come into the game with the injury and refused the substitution.

Sixteen were needed off two overs, eight off the last. Hadlee blocked the first ball in running and allowed Capel, the bowler, to run French out. The second was outside off-stump; Hadlee swung and it was over the ropes for six; the third went for four. It was all over. There were only 3,000 people in the ground so the crowd made only the echoing noise you might hear at a swimming competition. From the Northamptonshire contingent, in the crowd and back in the dressing room, there was dead silence. Coverdale recalled later: 'The hardest thing I ever had to do was to get the players out on the balcony for the presentation.'

There would be no jokes now for a long time. Walker was in tears of disappointment and agony, Wild was in a raging temper and Lamb went home without even bothering to change. Geoff Cook looked as though the sun, moon and stars had just fallen on him; he wore the sort of expression that belonged to personal tragedy rather than mere sporting defeat. For Cook on this occasion the two merged into one.

PRETORIA-ON-NENE

'Pick yourself up, dust yourself off, start all over
again.'

Jerome Kern and Dorothy Field

NORTHAMPTONSHIRE CRICKET might have lain down and died right
there. As a pure cricketing moment, this was the bleakest of all.
The County had not merely snatched defeat from the jaws of
victory, they had reached down and plucked it from deep in
victory's throat. But this was the Cricket Club that had been
through the winless years of the 1930s, had gone through the real
human tragedies of Askham and Nelson, Bakewell and Milburn.
Adversity was second nature to it. What was different this time
was the Club's response. They went for what has to be described
as a gimmick, a publicity stunt – a very good one but a stunt
nonetheless. They signed Dennis Lillee.

Northamptonshire insist that the move cost them virtually
nothing: they paid Lillee £9,000 (which was quadrupled by
sponsors), less than they pay one of the youngsters, and this was
immediately made good by the rise in membership. There were
those in the West Stand and elsewhere who would far rather they
had signed a youngster.

But Northamptonshire in 1988 were thinking far bigger than
was ever thought possible in the Turner era. 'Ken budgeted
everything down to the last fiver,' said one observer of his
methods. 'He knew what the expenditure would be and got the
income to match that.' And expenditure meant spending money
on essentials. He would spend the money he had to on players;
trivia like the PA system or the toilets came well down the line.
The new Northamptonshire fitted the go-getting, winner-take-all
national mood of the late 1980s.

Their neighbours, the football club, sank deeper into the
financial mire, were forced into administration and only kept
trading because their many creditors were told that was their only
possible chance of ever getting any money back. The Cricket
Club, in contrast, found itself better off than ever.

Part of this was due to increased pay-outs from the Test and
County Cricket Board. Part was due to performances on the
field. The team might not be winning trophies but getting close to
them still brought in revenue from ever-hopeful spectators. It
also happened that Lynn Wilson, a Northampton builder and a

very rich businessman indeed, began to deepen his long involvement and eventually became chairman. Wilson, however, says he put in no money of his own. The Club insist the transformation was the result of some luck, some judgment, some charity and a certain amount of what is known these days as aggressive marketing.

The luck was that in September 1987 the lease on the County Hotel ran out, having been let for 21 years in 1966 at a nominal rent. Although the hotel was on the football ground side, Cockerill's settlement, back in 1923, had given its income to the Cricket Club. Now, close to the top of the property boom, it could be let again at a premium and Northamptonshire found themselves with a windfall of £240,000 – three years earlier or later and the sum would have been far less.

The aggression came in pushing the sale of advertising boards until every imaginable space on the County Ground was covered, and selling sponsorship with the confidence of an organisation that believed it was worth sponsoring. Carlsberg, the first firm to get their names on the players' shirts, paid £4,500 a year in 1984, a deal done against Turner's opposition. Eight years later their successors Carling Black Label (owned by Bass) were paying 15 times as much.

The charity came after the Bradford fire, the first of the series of footballing disasters of the period that created a new awareness of crowd safety. The fire officer was at the County Ground within a week. He condemned the football stand at once. It was soon demolished and ever since Northampton Town's home has looked more embarrassingly ugly and inadequate than ever: they were the lodgers who not only never moved out but made the place mucky as well. On the cricket side, the West Stand was also condemned. It was unthinkable to demolish that: where would the town's groaners and grumblers go all summer?

The bill to replace it was £25,000. The Club wrote to John Paul Getty, the cricket-mad philanthropist, the way people write begging letters to pools winners. They heard nothing for ages and then suddenly a cheque for £10,000 appeared, followed by a donation from a secret source for £12,500. The bill was almost paid.

Gradually, the Club became more confident about its building: in 1988, less than ten years after it was built, the new pavilion was torn to pieces and put together again to create new facilities for corporate sponsors. More money was spent on the indoor school. Then in 1990 the grubby old pavilion was gutted with the help of a £100,000 loan from the County Council and turned into the

Spencer Pavilion, something close to a showpiece. Again – by luck or judgment – the Club did well by selling the three new sponsors' lounges there in advance, before the national economy started hurtling downhill. Suddenly, the County Ground, provided you averted your gaze from the football end, no longer looked like the tattiest ground on the circuit.

But there was still no point in building a trophy room; and signing Lillee was not designed to bring that moment any closer.

The Lillee business all came about as a result of the annual fast bowler poser. The West Indians were due to tour in 1988. Harper was certain to be picked and the County were afraid that Davis might have done too well for them and would be recalled as well. Coverdale and Reynolds went up to watch a Lancashire League game at Heywood, where Jack Mercer had discovered Jock Livingston more than 30 years before, and looked at a West Indian fast bowler of Larter-ish proportions. Curtly Ambrose had played just one game for the Leeward Islands. 'He looks like a pipe-cleaner,' said Coverdale. He was also very raw but the club were desperate. They invited him to a net and agreed to sign him thinking they could play him in the second team and see how he developed.

So Ambrose signed for Northamptonshire. At the time, this did not seem much of a coup and someone else was still needed. Coverdale says it was his idea. He noticed that Dennis Lillee, one of the great players of his generation, but now 38 years old and four years past his last Test match, was starting to play club cricket again. Rather idly, he asked Bob Carter, who had got to know him when they were involved in a coaching scheme in New Zealand, to ring him up. 'A coaching job, eh?' said Lillee. 'No, we're not talking about coaching. We want you to play.' 'You must be joking.'

They were not. Lillee arrived on May Day accompanied by a sponsors' representative dressed as a kangaroo and far more national publicity than the County had got for their failure eight months earlier. Traditionalists were horrified; 450 new members signed up. A week later, making his County Championship debut, Lillee bowled the team to victory over Gloucestershire with figures of six for 68. 'Masterly,' said *Wisden*.

It could not last. No one ever thought it would. But the end came quicker and more horribly than anyone can have imagined. In his second home match, going for a routine ball from fine leg to deep square while the batsman ran two, Lillee turned his ankle and over he went. Despite the mundane circumstances, it was an appalling injury with severed ligaments and a broken ankle-bone.

Dennis Lillee obliges the cameras on his arrival at Northampton in May 1988, with make-believe marsupial in the background. (The Chronicle and Echo)

He saw Nigel Cobb, the Northamptonshire surgeon who had patched up the motor-cyclist Barry Sheene. 'That's it, Dennis,' he said, 'you're finished.'

Oh, no he wasn't, not quite. Lillee still came back to play a few games late in the season and, less dramatically and successfully, turned up again to coach and help the following year. Whatever else might be said, his determination was a lesson to players whose greatest fault was a shortage of it. It was said he spent a lot of time helping the younger players. This seems to have been done more by occasional arm-on-shoulder words of advice than by long hours in the nets. When he was on the field, he was superb. But he was not on the field for long.

So Northamptonshire were quickly back to more orthodox staffing policies and their other overseas fast bowler. But this was not Ambrose, as everyone had presumed. He had bowled so well at home in the West Indies that winter that he was picked for the tour. He took the place that had probably been earmarked for Davis, who returned to the County Ground and took more wickets than in 1987, more Championship wickets indeed – 73 – than any Northamptonshire player since Sarfraz in 1977.

Perhaps Northamptonshire should have applied the traditional football club response to failure and dropped the pilot. Cook, not for the first time, announced after the 1987 season that he had had enough. It was a frightening thought for the Club because they had not the slightest idea who might take over. So Coverdale worked on him; by mid-winter he had won him round: Cook would do one more season. Both men agreed later that they had made a mistake.

All the dramas had camouflaged the fact that Cook's captaincy was getting tired and, as it did so, its faults were starting to outweigh its virtues. Though he was a superb communicator with the press and public, he was less successful at talking to his players. And as he became increasingly remote, the dressing room became restless. As Mrs Thatcher discovered around the same time, any leader can go on too long. There had to be an alternative.

The 1988 season was, as might have been anticipated, awful in almost every respect. The County actually won two of their first three Championship matches, the second in quite sensational fashion: Warwickshire had enforced the follow-on and then needed only 119 to win; Davis, Walker and Williams bowled them out for 112. But once the fanfares for Lillee died away, the trumpets gave off a very uncertain sound indeed. North-amptonshire were in contention for nothing this time, which was one way of avoiding disappointment. Instead of reaching the NatWest final they contrived to lose to Cheshire in the first round.

Some individuals made progress: Bailey was finally picked for England; Alan Fordham, a batsman whom the County had tracked from school in Bedford and through Durham University with cautious optimism, made his maiden century; and Ripley, having shrugged off all rivals for the wicket-keeping position, settled into a rhythm and had 81 dismissals, second only to Keith Andrew's 90 in 1962.

But the best opening partnership in the country fell to pieces: the average first-wicket stand was 22. When Cook was injured, Larkins made himself a popular captain, partly by consulting more widely. But he had domestic problems, lost concentration and, after Cook returned, was dropped. It was a long while before anyone got round to telling him why. The batting generally continued the pattern of the 1980s: occasionally enthralling performances mixed in with far too many incompetent collapses.

In September, Cook gave a press conference, much smaller than the one Lillee had given four months earlier. He announced his resignation, saying he would stay on in the ranks and suggesting that someone with 'fresh ideas and fresh motivation' should take over as captain. This was easier said than done. There was a case for getting an outsider. But there were no Robert Nelsons doing a bit of schoolmastering and just awaiting their moment (Jim Watts was teaching but since he was nearly 50 now, no one suggested a fourth comeback). Press speculation centred on John Emburey, who had lost the vice-captaincy of Middlesex. But he was less unhappy about this than some people presumed and had no intention of leaving.

There was one live outsider: Chris Tavaré had been sacked as captain of Kent, in unfair and rather bizarre circumstances, four years earlier. He had bided his time until his benefit and was now ready to move. In theory, Tavaré fitted the bill precisely as a batsman with known (indeed notorious) powers of determination and concentration. The batsman expected to perform the role of steadying influence, Boyd-Moss, had now, quietly and sadly, given up. In practice, Tavaré was actually acquiring a touch of the devil-may-care Northamptonshire batting style in his cricketing old age. And when the Club spoke to him they found he was not all that committed to playing on for more than a season.

Tavaré was even less of a dressing room talker than Cook. But the Club might have thought harder about going for him anyway. They were diverted primarily by a regulation designed to inhibit cricket's incipient transfer system. This barred clubs from taking more than one 'contested registration' (a player whose county did not want him to leave) at a time. Northamptonshire's eyes lay elsewhere. Before cracking the captaincy, they thought that this time they really could crack the fast bowling problem by signing the former England bowler Greg Thomas from Glamorgan. In 1989 both Davis and Ambrose would be available, even though they could not play together. By rostering them with Thomas at the other end, they would have an attack at last, wouldn't they? Press estimates of how much Thomas was paid and the Club's figure never were to come into line. Whatever the truth, he lasted only three years; the other Taffy Thomas, in the 1920s, had been a better signing.

Thomas's arrival meant the captain would have to come from inside. The obvious candidates appeared to be Larkins, who had shown unexpected flair for the job in the short run and Nick Cook, respected by the players but, with the spin-bowler policy now ancient history, uncertain of his place in every game. It took a while for the Club to come round to the view that they should actually give the job to their best player. But they did. Allan Lamb was appointed.

There are those who see 1988, with Geoff Cook still in charge, as the true beginning of the Lamb era. Lamb was actually preoccupied with his benefit, which he was organising as a national event to make use of a reputation that went far beyond a small county. Twenty years earlier, Milburn, tapping into everyone's sympathy, had done the same and broken the then record by raising £20,000. Lamb could raise that in one well-run evening, and indeed upset other counties by staging such evenings in their territory. There was a glitz and theatricality about Lamb's benefit which fitted well with the club that signed Dennis Lillee.

Lamb was still a regular England player and likely to miss half the season. A four-man committee was set up comprising Lamb, Larkins, Nick Cook and the coach Bob Carter. But Lamb was in charge, as he made clear straight away. Northamptonshire wanted and needed a change of style, and they got it. Geoff Cook had hated team meetings and had to be dragooned into holding one even before the NatWest final; in the early days Lamb was holding them so regularly that the players regretted having complained about the lack of them. Cook found it easy to be friends with the press; Lamb promptly fell out with the *Chronicle and Echo*.

His opponents claimed Lamb would not be committed enough to be captain. In fact, his enthusiasm was extraordinary: on occasion he would ring Coverdale on his carphone four times on the ten-mile journey between his home and the ground. The line would be crackling with ideas. Northamptonshire began 1989 by winning three Championship matches out of four and storming into the Benson and Hedges quarter-finals and, for once, to the top of the Sunday League. There was even a Championship win over Leicestershire, the first for 13 years: the decisive contributions came from Lamb, with a century that was brilliant by his own high standards, and Thomas, who took six for 53.

Still the clouds gathered relentlessly over the County Ground, even in a summer as hot as 1989. For the first time in his career, Lamb began to be accident-prone and acquired four separate sets of injuries, including a badly broken finger; Williams, meanwhile, missed almost the whole season; Davis's no-ball problems, never far away, began to overwhelm him and Ambrose found it hard to settle (at least until Williams, 15 inches smaller, took him metaphorically under his wing and the two formed an odd but firm friendship). The hopes in the one-day competitions petered out fast. By July there were no illusions in the Championship either and though they finished fifth, the highest place in 13 years, Northamptonshire were 97 points behind the champions Worcestershire and only 41 ahead of Leicestershire in 13th.

It was a ghastly year for English cricket generally, with the Ashes being thrown away and an even stronger rebel team than the 1982 one being assembled, under Mike Gatting's leadership, to tour South Africa. Thomas, called into the England squad for one Test then cast aside, was of the party and this time there was no Ken Turner to bellow about it. Bailey thought long and hard about going then decided to be loyal to England, a loyalty which in the longer term was not repaid.

In the short term it was. When the England selectors mustered their depleted resources for the tour of West Indies, they named four Northamptonshire batsmen: Lamb, Larkins, Bailey and Capel, who had had his best all-round season yet. This had never happened in the days of the Famous Five; it had certainly not happened in the 1930s. Some commentators did think it was strange that England should choose to rest their batting hopes quite so squarely on a county whose batting was so notoriously brittle.

The tour, overall, was a huge success. Though England lost the series 2–1 they were controversially deprived of victory in Trinidad and, compared to previous performances against the West Indies, the series was an amazing triumph. The overall credit went to the captain, Graham Gooch. For the Northamptonshire players the triumph was more muted. Lamb's batting was superb. Curiously, he had never made a century in 26 Tests outside England (he is obviously far more of a natural Englishman than is sometimes made out). Now he made two, including a match-winner in Kingston. He also ascended into the highest Northamptonshire pantheon by following Freddie Brown and becoming England captain in two Tests when Gooch was injured.

These, however, were the Tests England lost and, at this level, the crackle of ideas seemed to go silent. Larkins, in his first Test innings for ten years, made 46, 29 not out and 54, all important innings in tense situations, with an application that ought to have made the selectors wonder why they had not thought of him more often. But he made a pair in Barbados and faded. Capel's energy was not reflected in his figures. Bailey was the innocent party in a major umpiring row after he was given out caught off his hip; *Wisden* said he had a 'wretched tour'.

The official comment on it all came from the selectors in the months ahead. At the end of 1992, Bailey had still not been picked again and Capel had only just worked his passage back into the England A squad. Larkins was taken on tour to Australia in 1990–91 but failed and went out of contention; Lamb captained England again in Brisbane that winter, lost badly a third time and after a row with Gooch the following summer was deposed as vice-captain. And when they returned from the West Indies tour, which overlapped with the start of the 1990 season, they were all understandably less than springtime-fresh.

In general, 1990 was a terrible season for Northamptonshire. In the Championship, they won the first game and the last two but just one in the middle – and none at all at the County Ground for the first time since 1951. They were back to bottom in the Sunday League. In the Benson and Hedges they contrived to lose to Scotland. The injury situation was so bad that at one point in May only ten out of a 26-man squad were fit; fortunately they did not have a game. 'Why has this happened to us again?' wailed Larkins at one moment. Before that, at home to Derbyshire, they batted three men short, which still did not entirely explain being bowled out for 50 and losing inside two of the four scheduled days. On precisely the same day everywhere else, batsmen were taking advantage of hot weather and new rules about balls and pitches designed to favour batsmen, and were piling up massive totals: 863 in Lancashire's case. But then they did not have four current England batsmen.

By mid-May, Bailey – fourth in line – was captaining the side, and he presided over a game against Warwickshire in which

'The Old Firm' in business at Northampton for the last time; Geoff Cook and Wayne Larkins open the Northamptonshire innings in the Sunday League game against Gloucestershire in 1990. (Northamptonshire CCC)

Dermot Reeve managed to rile Ambrose enough to receive three beamers in quick succession. The row hit the back pages of the tabloids and Northamptonshire were forced to threaten disciplinary action. 'We were,' said Coverdale, 'being sidetracked by peripherals.' By mid-season Geoff Cook was being phased out; Lamb did not seem to feel comfortable having him around. Larkins dropped down the order and a new opening partnership emerged, with the steadily improving Fordham partnering Nigel

Felton, a left-hander signed from Somerset, both of them thoughtful, intelligent men as well as gifted cricketers. They made plenty of runs and so did Bailey – 1,987 of them – and twice in a week late in the season the County passed their old record total, both times against Essex: 592 for six at the County Ground, and 636 for six at Chelmsford. But it was a year when batsmen everywhere made runs, more than ever before.

Late in the season, Lamb was close to resignation but was apparently talked round by three senior players who assured him of their support. Probably, Lamb would have gone but for one thing: the County went up for the Cup again. The run in the NatWest Trophy produced two magnificently tense ties and one shocker.

First, a century from Capel against Nottinghamshire put them into the quarter-final against Worcestershire. There, on what may have been the hottest day's cricket in more than a hundred County Ground summers, Fordham and Capel scored runs. Then the young Yorkshire-born bowler Mark Robinson, who until now had been best known for being an even worse batsmen than Jim Griffiths, bowled magnificently at the death, constraining Ian Botham and giving Northamptonshire a four-run victory.

The semi-final was even closer: the County batted first and made 284, almost everyone contributing. Gower and Marshall almost took Hampshire to victory but a collapse left the last man, Paul Jan Bakker, to score two runs off the last ball from Robinson; he managed only one.

Unfortunately, the shocker came last. The County's seventh Lord's final, and their second against Lancashire, was their most dismal by a long way. Lamb lost the toss and on a dewy September morning Northamptonshire suffered the fate of several previous finalists by being forced to bat in hopeless conditions. They were not quite as hopeless as the County made out, though. Phil DeFreitas removed the top five batsmen in the first hour with 39 runs on the board. The top scorer in a total of 171 was Ambrose, with 48. There was never a remote chance of winning but everyone had to sit around until late afternoon for the formalities to conclude: Lancashire won by seven wickets.

A sympathetic Hampshire supporter, Colin Campbell, wrote to *The Guardian* offering these words of solace to Northamptonshire, to be sung to the tune of Greensleeves:

> We're not downhearted Northampton way,
> Tho we lost the NatWest that Saturday.

NORTHANTS *v* ESSEX

Played at Chelmsford, 7, 8, 9 and 10 September 1990

NORTHANTS WON BY 276 RUNS

NORTHANTS	FIRST INNINGS		SECOND INNINGS	
A. Fordham	c Garnham b Andrew	23	c Foster b Ilott	159
N. A. Felton	c Waugh b Foster	25	b Foster	56
W. Larkins	c Prichard b Ilott	37	c Hussain b Foster	0
R. J. Bailey	c Garnham b Waugh	28	lbw b Foster	107
*A. J. Lamb	c and b Waugh	22	c sub b Childs	165
A. L. Penberthy	c Foster b Waugh	0	c Hussain b Andrew	83
R. G. Williams	lbw b Waugh	0	not out	12
†D. Ripley	c Shahid b Waugh	18		
C. E. L. Ambrose	lbw b Foster	9		
J. G. Thomas	c and b Foster	15		
M. A. Robinson	not out	0		
Extras	lb 6, nb 12, w 1	19	b 10, lb 29, nb 13, w 2	54
Total		196	(for 6 wkts dec)	636

1st inns: 1-42, 2-53, 3-117, 4-121, 5-122, 6-122, 7-151, 8-176, 9-196, 10-196
2nd inns: 1-157, 2-175, 3-286, 4-434, 5-584, 6-636

BOWLING	O	M	R	W	O	M	R	W
Foster	19.2	4	67	3	29	7	79	3
Ilott	11	3	28	1	26	4	120	1
Andrew	9	0	58	1	23	1	132	1
Waugh	12	3	37	5	24	4	87	0
Childs					37	5	119	1
Stephenson					2	0	17	0
Gooch					18	5	43	0

ESSEX	FIRST INNINGS		SECOND INNINGS	
*G. A. Gooch	c Penberthy b Robinson	92	c Felton b Robinson	40
J. P. Stephenson	c Thomas b Ambrose	0	b Ambrose	76
P. J. Prichard	c Ripley b Ambrose	7	c Williams b Penberthy	5
N. Shahid	b Thomas	26	c Thomas b Williams	43
M. E. Waugh	c Bailey b Ambrose	44	c Lamb b Ambrose	36
N. Hussain	b Robinson	17	c Ripley b Thomas	24
†M. A. Garnham	c and b Ambrose	34	c Penberthy b Robinson	10
N. A. Foster	c Larkins b Thomas	11	b Robinson	12
M. C. Ilott	c Felton b Robinson	0	c Thomas b Ambrose	0
J. H. Childs	c Williams b Thomas	4	not out	21
S. J. W. Andrew	not out	1	c Thomas b Williams	35
Extras	lb 6, nb 1, w 1	8	lb 8, nb 2	10
Total		244		312

1st inns: 1-3, 2-29, 3-81, 4-170, 5-170, 6-192, 7-221, 8-225, 9-238, 10-244
2nd inns: 1-83, 2-94, 3-134, 4-134, 5-173, 6-199, 7-221, 8-256, 9-263, 10-312

BOWLING	O	M	R	W	O	M	R	W
Ambrose	23.4	3	67	4	19	6	52	3
Robinson	22	5	73	3	15	2	89	3
Penberthy	9	1	34	0	6	0	27	1
Thomas	13	0	64	3	11	0	72	1
Williams					12.1	2	64	2

*Captain; †Wicketkeeper

So lift your voices and shout hooray
For the lads who went down in the Final

Now Brookes and Broderick and Tribe were men
Who did bat and bowl for the County when
They never started at half-past-ten
On a morning at Lord's in September

I find it hard to hold back a tear
For the gallant men of Northamptonshire
God grant good fortune will come one year
With a triumph at Lord's in September.

If Lamb were going to stay on as captain, something had to be done. The chosen solution was a modish one, and was proposed by Lamb himself. The Club needed a manager. Turner would have scoffed at paying an extra, and high, salary for a job he could do perfectly well himself. 'In a small club of Northamptonshire's size a manager would be seen as an unnecessary luxury,' he once wrote, 'and I would go further and suggest that if the captain measures up a manager is superfluous to requirements whatever the size.' Perhaps the captain did not measure up. An impartial observer might have noted that the most successful counties – Essex and Middlesex most obviously, never mind old Yorkshire – had always been the ones that had relied on top-level captaincy and done without a manager. But Northamptonshire, usually described by the cliché-mongers as an unfashionable county, were now very keen to be up with the trends.

They did not advertise. Instead officials tossed around the names of just about every well-known retired or retiring player of the fortyish-plus generation who might be interested: John Lever, John Hampshire, David Lloyd, Emburey again, Jack Birkenshaw, Robin Jackman, Clive Rice – everyone indeed except the one closest to hand, Geoff Cook, who had just accepted the post of Director of Cricket at Durham, shortly to be elevated to first-class status. They saw the South African Mike Procter and were impressed at once. He was appointed inside 48 hours, also with the title 'director of cricket'. Coverdale was given the even grander-sounding 'Chief Executive'.

A new captain can transform a side at once. A new manager, who can only watch, has to move far more subtly. Procter knew enough to be subtle: he looked, listened and learned. But what he saw was awfully familiar and the early form in 1991 was no improvement on 1990. But the team was already markedly different. The Rhodesian Kevin Curran, one of county cricket's most competitive all-rounders, was signed from Gloucestershire; Lamb might have turned his back on the Cape all those years ago but now Southern Africa seemed to be flocking to him.

Davis had gone, and with Ambrose on tour again in 1991, the County had to settle for a second-rank overseas player, the one-time West Indian Test all-rounder Eldine Baptiste. Robinson had scurried off to Yorkshire, now more forgiving to their exiled sons, and been replaced by a left-armer, Paul Taylor, who had failed in his previous incarnation with Derbyshire. It was easier to keep up with developments in 'The Archers'.

It is misleading to dwell too long on the imports. There were actually more Northamptonshire-born players coming through then ever before. Wild had retired, his promise as batsman, bowler and potential captain never quite fulfilled. Mal Loye, a Northampton batsman, and an all-rounder from Little Har-rowden, John Hughes, began to get the odd game. And an eager little leg-spinner from Finedon with the powerful cricket name of Andy Roberts had his first real run of opportunities because of injuries to Williams and Nick Cook.

It was a bizarre coincidence that two Northamptonshire-born leg-spinners actually made their first-class debut in the same week in 1989. Unfortunately, the other was Ian Salisbury, a Moulton boy, who had come to the County Ground as a batsman and been rejected. At the time, he had bowled only very occasional leg-breaks. By 1992, when Roberts was still trying to establish himself, Salisbury had become the country's most promising leg-spinner in years, and had followed George Thompson and Capel as the third Northampton-born man to be capped for England – but as a Sussex player. The County had some decent young non-locals too, like the Cornishman Tony Penberthy. And there were more where all these lads came from, in the second team.

For Northampton's favourite son, though, 1991 was a horrid year. Capel's injuries and cricketing problems, which were now considerable, were placed in perspective by the death of his baby daughter in May. Larkins came back from Australia knowing his Test career was over and promptly broke his thumb. Only Fordham, who Procter did not rate highly at first sight, scored consistently.

There were, however, signs that Procter was having some effect. Late in the season, the team came together: before August, they won only one Championship game, then took four of the last seven to finish tenth. Lamb, dropped by England again, was back in one of his gloriously bad moods. The team even had a late run in the Sunday League and jumped from last to finish third for the first time ever, though chief executives prefer their teams to win early on in this tournament to bring some spectators in. And they almost went back to Lord's again.

Lamb called his batsmen off in bad light to the disgust of a large crowd at the NatWest semi-final at The Oval. They resumed with 21 runs wanted in six overs with two wickets left, the important one being Curran's. He got out straight away and Surrey won by seven runs. There were signs that the team was running better between the wickets, catching better and, on the whole, back-biting less despite a curious incident when the Club received a letter from an anonymous player attacking Lamb's captaincy.

Overall, the year was insignificantly better than most of the ones that preceded it. The County seemed to be locked into a pattern of financial expansionism and on-the-field failure. As the executive guests looked down in their double-breasted suits from their various eyries round the County Ground, they gazed round at a ground much changed from the penny-wise old days. But the spirit of unrewarded cricketing endeavour seemed to be going on forever.

In 1991 the two men who had kept Northamptonshire in county cricket both died: Freddie Brown, aged 80, and Ken Turner, suddenly, at 71. For many years, Brown's interest in the Club had been a distant one and he had been too ill to attend the annual old players' reunions. Among Turner's many attributes had turned out to be an ability to know how to retire. He gave Coverdale all the help he asked for in his first month and then disappeared. In his last couple of years he took to coming back to the ground, sitting quietly and just watching, usually at second team matches. He would have enjoyed the next chapter.

STAND BY YOUR LAMB

'. . . Turn my sad and anxious story
To a theme of shining glory.'
Conclusion of G. H. Winterbottom's verse on
Northants cricket

UNTIL 1930, Northamptonshire were not considered worthy of a first-class match 65 miles away at Lord's. In the spring of 1992 they played (and drew) a first-class match in a slightly more distant Test match ground at Kingsmead, Durban against a Natal Invitation XI.

Club members cynical about the influence of Procter and Lamb might have wondered if this was a prelude to Northamptonshire leaving the County Championship and applying to join the Currie Cup. Others used to hawking their flasks of tea to places like Leicester and moaning about a couple of quid's admission charges might have wondered about the £1,525 fare offered to supporters (plus £674 for optional three-day excursion to Zimbabwe, to visit everything except Kevin Curran's birthplace).

There is something to be said with taking pre-season practice in South Africa rather than the April chill of the County Ground. But there was no evidence of any immediate effect. By mid-May Northamptonshire were already out of the Benson and Hedges Cup, partly through poor catching, in trouble in the Sunday League and without a win from the opening run of three four-day Championship matches.

The last of these was against Nottinghamshire, and although it ended in a three-wicket defeat, the margin had looked likely for a long time to be much greater and was almost turned into a win by a remarkable performance from the no 10 Taylor, who made 74 not out, 13 more than his total score from 21 previous first-class innings, and then almost turned in a match-winning bowling performance too.

Within the Club, this was seen as a turning-point. From there, Northamptonshire won their first-ever Championship match against Durham. The last two days were played in blazing heat in the untropical setting of Stockton-on-Tees and the occasion was extraordinary apart from the cricket. There was Wayne Larkins, opening the opposition's batting; there was Geoff Cook, Durham's director of cricket, trying to plot his old team's downfall; there were young men who in the old days might have been heading for the County Ground, now playing for cricket's new-comers. Northamptonshire needed to get 92 to win from nine overs and did it off the last ball.

It was wonderful, rollicking stuff. And it was followed by a win over Derbyshire, who after a rain-affected match offered a bewilderingly generous declaration (surely Kim Barnett knew how Bailey could bat?) and another in a low-scoring home match against Leicestershire on a pitch which the Club thought had some pace in it. In the prevailing climate of opinion against result-wickets it brought dissatisfied murmurings from Lord's.

Nonetheless, that put Northamptonshire second. They won only once in the Championship in the next two months: an old-fashioned tanning of Glamorgan at Luton by an innings and 184 that ranked as the County's fifth-biggest win ever. But then they began winning again, beating good sides too, most dramatically the Champions Essex by an innings and 13 with seven wickets for Nick Cook, who had struggled all year to find a pitch that would suit him. Then there was a spectacular win against Hampshire when the left-armer Taylor, improving all the time, mastered the inswinger to the right-hander and took seven for 23.

The County had signed Taylor after he had bowled against them, for Staffordshire in the NatWest trophy in 1990, when his figures were nought for 92 and Bailey had hit him for six almost into the football stand. But they spotted qualities not reflected in his bowling analysis. Before then Taylor had been sacked by Derbyshire and had been working as an assistant manager of an electrical shop. Leicestershire had rung him the winter before Northamptonshire did. At that time he thought it was safer to stick with the electrics.

Stealthily the County were progressing in the NatWest Trophy. They began most uneasily. After 35 overs against Cambridgeshire in the first round they were 96 for four and in danger of humiliation. But they survived that crisis and began to thrive. They crushed Yorkshire in the second round and Glamorgan in the third. The semi-final draw sent them to Edgbaston. Ambrose was at his best and Warwickshire, 99 for seven at one stage, struggled to get 149. It was a magnificent batting and fielding performance but the wicket was difficult and Northamptonshire inched to victory, by three wickets, like tightrope walkers performing without a safety net. Felton led the way.

So Northamptonshire reached the NatWest final with consequences described in the opening chapter. Ten days later they beat Leicestershire again in the Championship. There was never really a moment when they were likely to overhaul Essex as

Curtly Ambrose. Northamptonshire were afraid they were signing a pipe-cleaner. They got the world's fastest bowler. (The Chronicle and Echo)

Champions but the last win put them third, equal to the positions held in 1964, 1973 and 1974, inferior only to 1912, 1957, 1965 and 1976, when they were runners-up.

Some factors could not be reflected in the results. At the start of the season, Ripley's place had been under threat again, this time from the youngster Wayne Noon. He responded by scoring 891 runs, averaging 42, and making 71 dismissals, more than any wicket-keeper in the country. On first-class figures, Ambrose threatened to rank with some of Northamptonshire's less successful signings. The mutterings from those corners of the County Ground which have always been cynical about big-name players grew louder as the season wore on. They did not take account of the wickets his mere presence took for the other bowlers, his contribution in the NatWest Trophy (50.5 overs bowled, eight wickets for just 82) or – according to Procter – his knee injury and his helpful attitude in the dressing room.

Then there was Lamb. Dropped by England, he returned as usual, bristling with aggression and useful ill-feeling. He took it out on teams like Warwickshire – against whom he became the first Northamptonshire player to score a double century and century in the same match – and Sussex, against whom he scored a Sunday League century of breathtaking superiority. Subsequently, he also took it out on the Pakistani bowlers in a different manner, when he accused them in the *Daily Mirror* of tampering with the ball. This earned him a fine of two weeks wages from Northamptonshire and £4,000 from the TCCB for talking out of turn (modern cricket's most grievous crime). It began the affair that the *Mirror*, day after tedious day, kept referring to as Lambgate. 'Stand By Your Lamb,' the *Mirror* urged its readers on cup final day, urging them to give him a special cheer. There was no audible evidence that they took any notice.

Procter loyally insisted that the whole business had had a positive effect on the team. Lamb's captaincy remained a matter of controversy and there were suggestions that some players were unhappy right up to the day of the final. Lamb had always maintained that he wanted to do the job for four years. In October, the Club appointed him for a fifth; his main rival, the vice-captain Bailey, was due to be distracted by a benefit in 1993.

Lamb may never be remembered in the same way as Freddie Brown. He will be remembered as one of the County's great cricketers. Having arrived as a hired hand, he had seen other men from overseas come and go, settled with his family in the countryside, and committed himself to the Club. Ideally, Northamptonshire supporters like their cricketers to be born in the

NATWEST TROPHY FINAL
NORTHANTS *v* LEICESTERSHIRE

Played at Lord's, 5 September 1992

NORTHANTS WON BY EIGHT WICKETS

LEICESTERSHIRE

T. J. Boon	run out	3
*N. E. Briers	run out	25
J. J. Whitaker	c Taylor b Curran	84
P. Robinson	c Felton b Ambrose	62
J. D. R. Benson	b Ambrose	0
L. Potter	c Capel b Curran	12
W. K. M. Benjamin	b Curran	0
†P. A. Nixon	not out	7
G. J. Parsons	not out	1
D. J. Millns		
A. D. Mullally		
Extras	b 1, lb 8, nb 2, w 3	14
Total	(7 wkts)	208

Fall: 1-3, 2-45, 3-175, 4-178, 5-197, 6-198, 7-200

BOWLING	O	M	R	W
Ambrose	12	0	35	2
Taylor	7	1	19	0
Capel	11	3	39	0
Curran	12	1	41	3
Cook	12	0	43	0
Penberthy	6	0	22	0

NORTHANTS

A. Fordham	c Potter b Mullally	91
N. A. Felton	b Mullally	6
R. J. Bailey	not out	72
*A. J. Lamb	not out	24
D. J. Capel		
K. M. Curran		
A. L. Penberthy		
†D. Ripley		
C. E. L. Ambrose		
J. P. Taylor		
N. G. B. Cook		
Extras	lb 9, w 9	18
Total	(2 wkts)	211

Fall: 1-29, 2-173

BOWLING	O	M	R	W
Benjamin	12	0	65	0
Mullally	10	2	22	2
Millns	10	0	43	0
Parsons	9	1	31	0
Potter	4	0	18	0
Benson	4.4	1	23	0

*Captain; †Wicketkeeper
Man of the Match: A. Fordham

County. Given that Lamb did not have that advantage, he had done everything possible to make up for it, short of acquiring the accent.

There were signs that many of the next generation would have made the right start in life. Two days after the NatWest final, the second-teamers who had sat wide-eyed in the dressing room had their own cup final; the Bain Clarkson trophy. They lost to Surrey, who were also the only team to finish ahead of them in the Second XI Championship. This table is often a clue to the likely balance of power among the counties four or five years ahead. Five of the Cup Final squad were local-born players. Durham's promotion to first-class status has robbed Northamptonshire of its traditional recruiting ground. It may be that, like an addict forced to give up, the Club will respond by doing what it should have done years ago and develop its own resources better.

Three years before, when the old players had got together for their annual reunion, Peter Arnold, in the chair, had tried to ask a quiz question. 'Can you identify the 23 Northamptonshire-born players to have played for the County since the war?' 'Can you identify the war?' asked Subba Row. 'Can you identify the county?' asked Des Barrick, more pertinently.

Ever since he had been appointed, Steve Coverdale had liked to say: 'On our day, we can beat anyone.' It became a catchphrase and the local pressmen made fun of it. It was obviously true. But the point was, that day came far less frequently than it should have done. In 1992 the message could be changed. Most days, Northamptonshire could beat anyone.

Every cricket club has problems. One trying to compete with the best in the country based in a small area predisposed to apathy has more problems than most. There will be bad years as well as good. But if the men who somehow kept the Club going when everything was against them could have been at Lord's in September 1992, they would have agreed the fight had not been in vain.

A NOTE ON GROUNDS

'Mid pleasures and palaces though we may roam,
Be it ever so humble, there's no place like home.'

John Howard Payne

EVEN IN THE summer of 1992, no one ever called the County Ground beautiful. No one even could say many kind words about the expanse of grass, which has staged cricket for 107 years now; all that time groundsman have been trying to put a bit of backbone into the soil and never quite succeeding.

No one could deny that the facilities were very much improved. But if you stared out from either of the beautifully appointed pavilions, the Spencer and the New, beyond the cricketers, the eye was still confronted by the premises of Northampton Town Football Club. Northampton sport owes a great deal to Pat Darnell. However, if he had been a little less enthusiastic about either cricket or soccer, the town might not be faced with the embarrassment of Britain's most eccentric major sports field, with the wintertime wingers running down the edge of the square from mid-on to mid-off and the summertime outfielders having to gather the ball from their footmarks.

For ages, people have been saying that something must be done. . .'Few public announcements in Northampton have aroused such interest and pleasure as that of the Cobblers' purchase of the True-Form Sports Ground, Kettering Road, for development as a stadium that will be the finest in the Third Division.' That was in the *Chronicle and Echo* on 30 January 1948. There had been a plan to move the football club to the town's barracks as early as 1938. Over the years, at least ten different sites round the borough have been mooted as alternative football stadiums. Every one has fallen through. The latest was still being discussed in October 1992 when the club's very existence was in more doubt than ever before.

The problem became most urgent after the demolition of the main stand after the 1985 Bradford fire and the advent of the current pre-fabricated monstrosity, which seats only 500 people. In 1990 one critic was calling it 'the worst ground in the League beyond any doubt' and that was Barry Stonhill, who was vice-chairman of the club.

If the football club ever moves or – perish the thought – goes under, the land, under the provisions of the Cockerill Trust, has to be used 'as a recreation ground'. Nonetheless, the possibilities are endless. One day it has to happen. In the meantime, for people who never come to the County Ground and look at the grass poking through the terracing on the Spion Kop, it at least gives the town a little celebrity every time it comes up in sports quizzes: 'Which is the only town in the country. . ..?'

The Cricket Club have every reason to be proud of their side of the arena now. There are still more distinguished grounds architecturally. The bell turret on the Spencer Pavilion would look a little less silly if it actually possessed a bell. But it is a field now worthy of a big occasion. Maybe next time Northamptonshire are asked to stage a one-day international they will not be ashamed to say yes.

It was a big day when Yorkshire visited in the NatWest Trophy in the summer of 1992. David Capel, local boy from Roade, was representing Northamptonshire and bowling to Sachin Tendulkar from Bombay, representing Yorkshire, which was refreshingly different from the old pattern. There never used to be a betting shop next to the signal box. And even if there was, it would certainly never have started the day with Northamptonshire as favourites and then wiped them off the board because they were such certainties. The seats were comfortable. Even the little scoreboard by the signal box, which used to be manned by schoolboys, was now electronic. The County Ground had become, in many ways, the very model of a modern major cricket ground.

But it was still the same old place. In the tea interval, the lads, some of them overgrown, came on the field with bat and ball to take their turn. As the Thermoses came out, they were having a good old grumble in the West Stand as usual. 'That Ambrose,' someone was muttering, 'he makes Kapil Dev look like a trier.' There was a smell of pipesmoke and fish paste sandwiches. Gallone's ice cream, with their special lager and lime and cherry brandy flavour lollies, were doing good business, as they have done for decades. And tea ended with a plaintive announcement: 'Would the gentleman who removed the jar of money from the Supporters' Club bookstall please give it back?' This was ever a club that had to look after the pennies.

The improved facilities have done something to remove one aspect of the charm and variety of Northamptonshire cricket. Like several other counties, the Club has become more reluctant than ever to leave its comfortable home to rough it and play home games elsewhere. In 1993, Northamptonshire were scheduled to use only one other home venue: Wardown Park, Luton. The

No cricket ground looks its best in the rain; the County Ground, Northampton is no exception.
(The Chronicle and Echo)

switch to the four-day game may be cricket's equivalent of the Beeching cuts with the country cricket fields vanishing from the fixture list the way Bridge Street station and Brackley Central went from the railway timetables.

In the past, Northamptonshire have played first-class cricket on eight grounds other than the County Ground and competitive one-day cricket on five more. Students of these matters also regard Northampton Racecourse and an unknown ground in Wellingborough as first-class because of the United North of England v United South of England games in 1872 and 1874 – but that was long before Northamptonshire itself became a first-class county.

The Peterborough Town ground in Crawthorne Road was the first to be used, in 1906 and 1907. It was brought back in 1928 and until 1966 then staged at least an annual Championship fixture, raised to two between 1929 and 1937. It was never very popular with the players, partly because both the ground and the dressing rooms were so cramped. *Wisden* called the outfield rough and unsuitable after the first match.

It is also believed to be the place where the players were once offered only bread and tea and where their coach was refused entry, forcing them to lug their gear 300 yards to the dressing room. Even then they had to leave it outside because there was nowhere to put it. And after Northamptonshire's 151 all out proved to be the highest score of the match against Essex in 1966 and Roger Prideaux was hit on the head by a good-length ball, first-class cricket ceased. There was a parting good riddance from one of the neighbours, a housewife whose window had been smashed by a six hit by Micky Bear off Malcolm Scott. She refused to give the ball back until the Club paid the 25 shillings to repair her window.

To keep cricket in the city, Northamptonshire switched their annual game the following year to the Baker Perkins sports ground at Westwood Works, where both the dressing rooms and the wicket were better: Rohan Kanhai scored 172 for Warwickshire in 1969. Unfortunately, no one wanted to turn up there and watch, even when Kanhai was in that form, and there were no more Championship matches. Sunday League games continued intermittently until 1974 when Alan Tait scored a match-winning hundred against Warwickshire. That was the year the Soke of Peterborough was detached from the County – administratively, postally and psychologically – even though cricket refused to recognise the boundary changes. This detached Northamptonshire cricket's hold on the area.

Northamptonshire v Worcestershire at Kettering in 1926. Fred Root's leg-trap is visible as he bowls from the pavilion end, as is the railway line at the top of the embankment. (John Watson Collection)

Peterborough Town also got fed up with life among the unfriendly housewives of Crawthorne Road. Their old ground is still an open space with children's swings, but club cricket moved in 1973 to a huge, and on cold days Siberian, open space at Bretton Gate. In 1991 the County planned to play there but although there was considerable local enthusiasm, the sponsorship, which is what mattered by then, never materialised.

The County first borrowed Kettering Town's ground at Northampton Road in 1923 for a game against Glamorgan to coincide with Kettering Feast, St Peter's Day. Dick Wright, a Kettering man, marked the opening match with a half-century; a hefty £200 was taken at the gate on the Saturday and the Kettering-based *Evening Telegraph* was delighted: 'A Red Letter Day at Kettering'. Thanks were tendered to Mr A.G. Willis (wine merchant) for the boxes and the Co-op for the planks. Those were the seats.

The ground was never really comfortable and the Club had to agree to build a new pavilion after Yorkshire complained. But the fixtures were so successful that between 1925 and 1928 the County played three home Championship matches there. And there were two every year until after Wellingborough School came on to the list in 1946. It was at Kettering that Philip Mead scored his 100th 100 in 1927. Bill Farnsworth, captain and then president of Kettering Town and a member of Northamptonshire's special emergency committee in 1931, was a key figure in strengthening the connection.

Farnsworth died in 1964. By then, attendances were falling and relations between club and county began to deteriorate. When Championship matches were reduced in 1972, Kettering was crossed off the list and after the County were bowled out for 91 in a Sunday League match by Glamorgan (the last as well as the first opponents) in 1973, Lord's said the ground would have to prove itself by staging a Second XI fixture before the first team could return.

The Kettering club's attitude, by then, was that they did not care much either way. The Second XI game is still pending and likely to remain so. Club cricket goes on: the poplars have grown higher at the foot of the railway embankment; and an idling outfielder can still hear the train announcements wafting over from Kettering station. It has always been a ground for transport enthusiasts: in 1956, when the club were clearing the land for a second pitch, someone found the remains of a stagecoach in the undergrowth.

During Kettering's first flush of success, the *Evening Telegraph* asked 'If Kettering can stage a game. . .why not Rushden?' In 1924, the Rushden Town ground was given one of the friendlies against Dublin University (without Samuel Beckett that time). The experiment was not repeated until 1936 but from then until the war and 16 consecutive years after it, one of the smaller A6 shoe towns always had a fixture.

The first game was reduced to one day by the weather and Northamptonshire became the first county to be awarded ten points for a one-innings Championship win. Under modern rules that would be regarded as a proper victory but in 1936 it was not, and so the County failed to break their winless run – then, or for another three years. Perhaps it was only the feebleness of the opposition that compensated teams for visiting Rushden: there was no running water in the pavilion before the war; the players could wash only in water brought to them from a standpipe and the toilet was a bucket in a wooden shed. The place made Peterborough seem like Lord's.

But Rushden matches had character. John Arlott compared the Victorian pavilion to a Chinese pagoda (he was less keen on the rusty tin fence) and John Clay of Glamorgan said the lunches were the best he had ever had in cricket. There was one character in particular; among those who watched the original 1924 fixture was 14-year-old Charlie May, who began playing for the club that year and became secretary, treasurer and groundsman until finally retiring as an administrator in 1975.

May was the groundsman in 1963 when it all came to an end. Having lost its fixture the previous year Rushden's status was known to be under threat. May prepared one pitch; Norman Hever, the County's groundsman, decided it should be played on another. The opponents were Lancashire. Sometimes the ball kept low; one ball from Statham reared up and hit Albert Lightfoot on his very prominent nose. The members' toilets were still pretty grim. Goodbye Rushden.

The last of Northamptonshire's traditional out-grounds both to come on the scene and depart from it was Wellingborough School. It will be by far the most mourned. The County played Warwickshire and Essex there in 1884, long before first-class status, and even before the arrival of the school's greatest cricketing pupil, George Thompson. It was 1934 before the subject of a Championship match was mooted and 1946 before it came about.

Northamptonshire had played one first-class match, against Oxford University, in Wellingborough in 1929 when the Ideal Clothiers Society opened a works sports ground for their new factory, which made suits for the Co-op. They arranged seats for 3,000 people but by the end there were only about 20 in use. To make it worse, Oxford won by an innings and 121. The experiment was not repeated and never will be: the site is now occupied by Weavers School.

But the School ground was an altogether more attractive proposition. By 1946, when first-class cricket finally arrived there, the First XI pitch, known as The Grove, had a handsome new thatched pavilion plus the Victorian tea pavilion, which was used by the press and umpires, and the whole school had an air of having been marinated in the purest cricketing tradition. Much of this emanated from the old headmasters, Dr Platt and P. A. Fryer, who was still alive, in his 70s and supervising preparations. Even more came from the geography master and cricketing fanatic E. Murray Witham, who gave the dormitories in his house names such as 'First Slip' and in 1939 had driven to Bristol to retrieve the front doorstep of W.G. Grace's house before it was demolished. It was placed in front of the pavilion and the superstition is that a batsman who fails to step on the stone on the way out will not make any runs.

The Grove had one Championship match (two in 1956) almost every year until 1989. Mostly, it was a very happy relationship, although the governors took exception to Bert Brailsford scraping the pitch to help the spinners in 1957. Fryer, then nearly 80, took charge of pitch preparations himself in 1949 and watched his own ground scoring record fall to Len Hutton, who made 269 not out. In 1975, Majid Khan hit 75 in 27 minutes in the Sunday League. In 1986, Ian Botham, just back from his suspension for drug use, came and hit 175 not out in 27 overs of a Sunday game with 13 sixes. He was watched by one of the County's biggest crowds in years.

This hastened the ground's dismissal from the fixture list, as officials starting thinking how much easier and cheaper it would be to accommodate everyone at the County Ground. The last match was in 1991 and the Club now reckon it is not worth their while to move the whole operation ten miles to a town which has never produced much sponsorship. Some sentimentalists think Augusts will never be the same again.

But as the traditional grounds have disappeared, new ones have come in. In the early 1970s Northamptonshire began a process which Rex Walford of Cambridge University, in an academic paper on the location of cricket grounds, called 'colonial expansion'. In 1971, the Club played a Sunday match at Bedford School, the first game scheduled outside the traditional county boundaries. One committee member was concerned that members would be upset. If anyone was, they were outvoted; the crowd was enormous and since there was a high proportion of non-members, the revenue even better.

The Bedford experiment was repeated only once, 11 years later, because the Sunday League was then sponsored by John Player and the counties had privately agreed not to annoy anti-smoking campaigners, who might object to the connection between cigarettes and children, by taking games to schools other than those like Wellingborough where they had played before. But the success of the game encouraged the County to start prowling neighbouring counties for potential venues.

Pretty little Brackley – just inside the county border with Oxfordshire – was used in 1971 and lasted five years. The seating planks rested on straw bales. It was here that the County first encountered a little-known young man called Vivian Richards, who kept hitting the ball viciously hard into the hedge. In 1973 Northamptonshire first tried Luton, an experiment that expanded 13 years later to include a Championship as well as a Sunday game. Northampton-based supporters hate the 35-mile journey but the pitch is excellent, the setting attractive and local officials enthusiastic.

In 1974 the County began an annual and often phenomenally successful Sunday match at Tring in Hertfordshire. Walford saw Hertfordshire as the setting for a fascinating geo-political struggle for supremacy between Northamptonshire, moving south, and

286

Middlesex, moving north by scheduling under-25 fixtures at St Albans: 'Does this mean that Middlesex are subtly challenging Northants' right to the Hertfordshire hinterland?' The cricket has often been good, too.

In 1976, Northamptonshire made their first visit to Manor Fields, Bletchley, part of the vast and mysterious lost world known as Milton Keynes. Sunday games were played there between 1976 and 1983; and in 1980, 1984 and 1987 – enticed by hefty sponsorship deals from local firms and the Milton Keynes Development Corporation – the County took attractive tourist games, two against the West Indies and one against Pakistan, away from the County Ground and indeed out of the county and into Buckinghamshire.

By the end of the 1987 game, the reporters covering the match had formed the BBC – the Bugger Bletchley Club. The players loathed the pitch; the facilities always seemed accident-prone; and somehow the rudest men for miles around seemed to be brought in as temporary gatemen. The Club still wonder whether they might be able to tap in sometime to Milton Keynes's growing population on another ground; not everyone is holding their breath.

In both 1976 and 1977, Northamptonshire played Benson and Hedges games on the excellent pitch at the Horton House club, just outside Northampton, because the games had to be played in April when the football club still had rights on the County Ground. Horton, with only about 300 people, may well be the smallest place ever to stage county cricket. In 1986, the County allotted a Sunday match to the Finedon Dolben club, based in Finedon just outside Wellingborough. (Dickie Bird was umpiring. 'Where the hell's Finneydon?' he asked in panic the previous week.) This was intended to be a one-off to mark the Club's 150th anniversary but was so successful and pleasant, amidst the lime trees, that the County went back in 1987 and 1989. In 1990 Northamptonshire scheduled a Sunday League match at Hitchin in Hertfordshire, inspired by a particularly successful benefit match Allan Lamb had had there. Unfortunately, all the local efforts depended on one man; he was transferred out of town. Northamptonshire transferred the match back to the County Ground to avoid financial ruin.

The Club have also played Second XI Championship cricket at Rothwell, Daventry, Corby, British Timken, Ashton, Wellingborough (Redwell Road), Woughton, Overstone, Old Northamptonians, Wolverton, Peterborough (Bretton Gate) and Oundle School. Some of these places might get the odd county match one day. However, Northamptonshire cricket remains associated with one place on earth. For better or worse and richer or poorer. People may say the County Ground is not up to much. But it's home.

STATISTICAL SECTION

BIOGRAPHICAL DETAILS
OF NORTHAMPTONSHIRE PLAYERS

NAME AND EXTENT OF CAREER	BIRTHPLACE	DATE OF BIRTH	DATE OF DEATH
Robert Kenneth Ablack *1946–1949*	Port of Spain, Trinidad	5. 1.1919	
Hylton Michael Ackerman *1967–1971*	Springs, S. Africa	28. 4.1947	
Sidney Clarke Adams *1926–1932*	Northampton	1904	24. 3.1945
William Adams *1920–1929*	Steeple Claydon, Bucks	17. 4.1885	6. 4.1957
Charles Frederick Addis *1924–1926*	Finedon	2. 2.1902	15. 8.1983
Antony William Allen *1932–1936*	Brackley	22.12.1912	
James Stephen Allen *1905*	Croydon, Surrey	4.11.1881	1958
Michael Henry John Allen *1956–1963*	Bedford	7. 1.1933	
Curtly Elconn Lynwall Ambrose *1989–*	Antigua	21. 9.1963	
Keith Vincent Andrew *1953–1966*	Oldham, Lancs	15.12.1929	
Norman Palmer Andrews *1922–1923*	Bromley, Kent	1. 5.1899	5.11.1971
Henry John Denham Arkell *1921*	London	26. 6.1898	12. 3.1982
Arnold Peter Arnold *1951–1960*	Wellington, New Zealand	16.10.1926	
Martin Ashenden *1959–1961*	Bexhill-on-Sea, Sussex	4. 8.1937	
Sydney Thomas Askham *1914*	Welling-borough	9. 9.1896	21. 8.1916
Bernard Gerad Wensley Atkinson *1922–1925*	Crediton, Devon	11. 9.1900	4. 9.1966
Hamer Fraser Bagnall *1921–1928*	Field Burcote	18. 2.1904	2. 9.1974
Robert John Bailey *1982–*	Biddulph, Staffs	28.10.1963	
Raymond Reginald Bailey *1964–1973*	Bedford	16. 5.1944	
Cyril Baker *1906–1922*			8.10.1949
Alfred Harry Bakewell *1928–1936*	Walsall, Staffs	2.11.1908	23. 1.1983
George Frederick Baldwin *1906*	Northampton	3. 4.1878	1970
Kenneth John Ball *1921*	Northampton	16. 5.1889	16. 1.1958
Wilfred Joseph Ball *1924–1931*	Thrapston	1895	23. 7.1965
Martin John Bamber *1982–1984*	Cheam, Surrey	7. 1.1961	
Eldine Ashworth Elderfield Baptiste *1991*	Liberta, Antigua	12. 3.1960	
Desmond William Barrick *1949–1960*	Fitzwilliam, Yorkshire	28. 4.1926	
William Barron *1946–1951*	Herrington, Durham	26.10.1917	
John George Bass *1935*	Northampton	9. 8.1903	1992
W. Batson *1920–1921*			

Joseph Noble Beasley *1911–1919*	Northampton	1881	23. 1.1960
Robert Noble Beasley *1907–1911*	Northampton	17.12.1882	21. 1.1966
Bishen Singh Giansingh Bedi *1972–1977*	Amritsar, India	25. 9.1946	
Hector George Beers *1914–1921*	Pottersbury	1875	11. 2.1954
Alexander Patrick Bell *1934*	Rosario, Argentina	23. 2.1915	12. 4.1956
Benjamin Walter Bellamy *1920–1937*	Wollaston	22. 4.1891	20.12.1985
Harold Lewis Benjamin *1928*	Birmingham	1892	7. 8.1942
Alfred Charles Leopold Bennett *1947–1949*	West Norwood, London	31.12.1914	20. 9.1971
Howard Alfred Bennett *1920*	Alcester, Warks	20. 8.1892	13. 1.1973
Sydney John Bennett *1933–1934*	Hackleton	7. 2.1905	1969
Frederick Nash Bird *1908–1909*	Framlingham, Suffolk	13.12.1875	3. 3.1965
Christopher Derek Booden *1980–1981*	Wolverton, Bucks	22. 6.1961	
Peter Malise Borwick *1932*	York	21.11.1913	23.12.1983
Norman Henry Bowell *1925*	Oxford	2. 2.1904	5. 3.1943
Mark Bowen *1992–*	Redcar, Yorks	6.12.1967	
Robin James Boyd-Moss *1980–1987*	Hatton, Ceylon	16.12.1959	
Geoffrey Winston Bradfield *1970*	Grahamstown, S. Africa	28. 2.1948	
Dennis Breakwell *1969–1972*	Brierley Hill, Staffs	2. 7.1948	
Gordon Harry Joseph Brice *1949–1952*	Bedford	4. 5.1924	
Derek James Wilson Bridge *1947*	Manchester	30.11.1921	
Vincent Broderick *1939–1957*	Bacup, Lancs	17. 8.1920	
Dennis Brookes *1934–1959*	Kippax, Yorks	29.10.1915	
Frederick Richard Brown *1949–1953*	Lima, Peru	16.12.1910	24. 7.1991
Simon John Emmerson Brown *1987–1990*	Cleadon, Durham	29. 6.1969	
William Cecil Brown *1925–1937*	Wellingborough	13.11.1900	20. 1.1986
Arthur Herbert Bull *1913–1924*	Wellingborough	23. 1.1892	18.12.1965
Charles Edward Buller *1931*	Wellingborough	23. 8.1892	16.12.1969
Arthur Austen Burgess *1929*	Peterborough	2. 1.1906	
Henry Burgess *1905*	Carlton-Curlieu, Leics	1879	16. 4.1964
John Edgar Buswell *1936–1939*	Barnwell	3. 7.1909	
Walter Alfred Buswell *1906–1921*	Welford	12. 1.1875	24. 4.1950
David John Capel *1981–*	Northampton	6. 2.1963	
James Alexander Carse *1983*	Salisbury, Rhodesia	13.12.1958	
Robert Michael Carter *1978–1982*	King's Lynn, Norfolk	25. 5.1960	

Charles Stanley Catlow *1929*	Darwen, Lancs	21. 2.1908	7. 3.1986
William Richard Frank Chamberlain *1946*	Elton, Hunts	13. 4.1925	
Arthur William Childs-Clarke *1947–1948*	Exeter	13. 5.1905	19. 2.1980
Thomas James Milner Clapperton *1909*	Bourn, Cambs	3. 9.1875	26. 5.1939
Edward Winchester Clark *1922–1947*	Elton, Hunts	9. 8.1902	28. 4.1982
Carlos Bertram Clarke *1946–1949*	Bridgetown, Barbados	7. 4.1918	
George William Clarke *1908*	Northampton	1869	26. 8.1955
Robert Wakefield Clarke *1947–1957*	Finedon	22. 4.1924	3. 8.1981
Gordon Thomas Collins *1938*	Sunbury-on-Thames, Middx	26.12.1914	1986
Dennis Constable *1949*	East Molesey, Surrey	14. 8.1925	
Geoffrey Cook *1971–1990*	Middlesborough, Yorks	9.10.1951	
Nicholas Grant Billson Cook *1986–*	Broughton Astley, Leics	17. 6.1956	
Bernard William Cornelius *1947*	Northampton	16. 3.1919	7.10.1987
Robert Michael Henry Cottam *1972–1976*	Cleethorpes, Lincs	16.10.1944	
Stephen Peter Coverdale *1987*	York	20.11.1954	
Walter William Coverdale *1931–1932*		30. 5.1912	6.10.1972
Arthur Leonard Cox *1926–1947*	Northampton	22. 7.1907	11.1986
Mark Cox *1905–1919*	Northampton	10. 5.1879	12.1968
Mark Henry D. Cox *1932*	Northampton	1906	1979
Sydney Cox *1932*	Northampton	23. 5.1905	5. 3.1969
Edmund Mitchell Crosse *1905–1910*	London	11.12.1882	28. 6.1963
Brian Stanley Crump *1960–1972*	Stoke-on-Trent	25. 4.1938	
Leonard Cullen *1934–1935*	Johannesburg, S. Africa	23.11.1914	15. 9.1984
Kevin Malcolm Curran *1991–*	Rusape, Zimbabwe	7. 9.1959	
Geoffrey Bourke Cuthbertson *1935–1938*	Hampstead, London	28. 3.1901	
Harold William Dainty *1922*	Rushton	2. 6.1892	17. 4.1961
Jack Hillen Dale *1922*	Northampton	29.10.1901	28. 4.1965
Llewellyn John Davies *1919–1921*	Northampton	1894	28.10.1965
Edward Davis *1947–1956*	Brackley	8. 3.1922	
Michael John Davis *1963*	Bolton, Lancs	18. 8.1943	
Percival Charles Davis *1935–1952*	Brackley	24. 5.1915	
Winston Walter Davis *1987–1990*	Sion Hill, St. Vincent, W.I.	18. 9.1958	
Albert George Dawes *1933*	Aldershot, Hants	23. 5.1907	23. 6.1973
Arthur Donald Denton *1914–1920*	Rushden	21.10.1896	23. 1.1961
John Sidney Denton *1909–1919*	Rushden	2.11.1890	9. 4.1971
William Herbert Denton *1909–1924*	Rushden	2.11.1890	23. 4.1979
Alfred Dickens *1907*	Brixworth	1884	1937
Michael Reginald Dilley *1957–1963*	Rushden	28. 3.1939	
Ramesh Vithaldas Divecha *1948*	Bombay, India	18.10.1927	

Eric John Hopkins Dixon *1939*	Horbury, Yorks	22. 9.1915	20. 4.1941
Lancelot Townshend Driffield *1905–1908*	Old	10. 8.1880	9.10.1917
George Henry Drummond *1920–1922*	London	3. 3.1883	12.10.1963
Maurice Edward Frank Dunkley *1937–1939*	Kettering	19. 2.1914	27.12.1989
Anthony Jack Durose *1964–1969*	Dukinfield, Cheshire	10.10.1944	
John Cooper James Dye *1972–1977*	Gillingham, Kent	24. 7.1942	
William East *1905–1914*	Northampton	29. 8.1872	19.12.1926
Thomas Elderkin *1934*	Peterborough	1909	9.12.1961
Harold Ellis *1908–1910*	Burnley, Lancs	13. 3.1883	31.12.1962
Roderick Falconer *1907–1910*	Hoxne, Suffolk	1886	8. 3.1966
Sydney Wheatley Falding *1921*	Leeds, Yorks	1891	7.11.1959
Jonathan Payn Fellows-Smith *1957*	Durban, S. Africa	3. 2.1932	
Nigel Alfred Felton *1989–*	Guildford, Surrey	24.10.1960	
Kenneth Fiddling *1947–1953*	Hebden Bridge, Yorks	13.10.1917	19. 6.1992
John Maurice Fitzroy-Newdegate *1925–1927*	Chelsea	20. 3.1897	7. 5.1976
Vincent Anthony Flynn *1976–1978*	Aylesbury, Bucks	3.10.1955	
Alan Fordham *1986–*	Bedford	9.11.1964	
Grant Forster *1980*	Seaham, Durham	27. 5.1961	
Edward Freeman *1908–1920*	Northampton	1887	7.12.1945
Terence Freeman *1954*	Welling-borough	21.10.1931	
Charles Anthony Fry *1962*	Henley-in-Arden, Warks	14. 1.1940	
Philip Algernon Fryer *1908*	Wymondham, Norfolk	26. 6.1870	4.11.1950
Richard Gordon Garlick *1948–1950*	Kirkby Lonsdale, West-morland	11. 4.1917	16. 5.1988
George Cooper Gifford *1923–1929*	Huntingdon	17.11.1891	16. 9.1972
Frederick Steven Goldstein *1969*	Bulawayo, Rhodesia	14.10.1944	
Mark Roger Gouldstone *1986–1988*	Bishop's Stortford, Herts	3. 2.1963	
James Walter Govan *1989–1990*	Dunfermline, Fife	6. 5.1966	
Douglas George Greasley *1950–1955*	Hull, Yorks	20. 1.1926	
Henry William Greenwood *1938–1946*	East Preston, Sussex	4. 9.1909	24. 3.1979
Brian James Griffiths *1974–1986*	Welling-borough	13. 6.1949	

Norman Grimshaw *1933–1938*	Horsforth, Yorks	5. 5.1912	
John Williams Guy *1958*	Nelson, New Zealand	29. 8.1934	
Harold St Alban Hall *1907*		1875	17. 5.1915
Rupert William Hanley *1984*	Port Elizabeth, S. Africa	29. 1.1952	
David Hardy *1907–1924*	Northampton	1878	22. 1.1951
Roger Andrew Harper *1985–1987*	Georgetown, Guyana	17. 3.1963	
George Howard Hawes *1919*	Kettering	1881	26.10.1934
Henry Hawkins *1905–1909*	Kegworth, Leics	15. 1.1876	12. 8.1930
Alfred Powell Rawlins Hawtin *1908–1930*	Bugbrooke	1. 2.1883	15. 1.1975
Roger William Rawlins Hawtin *1905–1908*	Bugbrooke	30. 9.1880	7. 9.1917
Walter Hawtin *1929–1934*	Aston, Birmingham	1906	3.1940
Robert Allnutt Haywood *1908–1924*	Eltham, Kent	16. 9.1887	1. 6.1942
Eric James Herbert *1937–1939*	Rushden	1908	14.10.1963
Hugh Washington Hibbert *1931*	Kensington, London	4.10.1911	
Alan Hodgson *1970–1979*	Moorside, Durham	24.10.1951	
Dean Stuart Hoffman *1988*	Erdington, Birmingham	13. 1.1966	
Raymond P. Hogan *1954–1955*	Temora, N.S.W., Australia	8. 5.1932	
Lawrence Edward Holland *1912–1920*	Tinsley, Sheffield	13. 1.1887	3. 7.1956
Thomas Horton *1905–1906*	Edgbaston, Birmingham	16. 5.1871	18. 6.1932
John Gareth Hughes *1990–*	Wellingborough	3. 5.1971	
Stuart Harold Guise Humfrey *1913–1926*	Thorpe Mandeville	17. 2.1894	9. 6.1975
Edward Hyde *1907*	Wellingborough	1881	9.10.1941
Wilfred Cyril Izzard *1919–1920*	Northampton	25. 2.1892	15. 9.1977
Frederick Jakeman *1949–1954*	Holmfirth, Yorks	10. 1.1920	20. 5.1986
Ronald Stuart Jakeman *1962–1963*	Holmfirth, Yorks	20. 9.1943	
J. James *1906*			
Kenneth Cecil James *1935–1939*	Wellington, New Zealand	12. 3.1904	21. 8.1976
Robert Leslie Johns *1971*	Southampton	30. 6.1946	
George Henry Johnson *1922–1932*	Middlesbrough, Yorks	16.12.1894	20. 1.1965
George James Johnson *1929–1935*	Loddington	23.12.1907	

Name	Birthplace	Born	Died
John Inchbald Johnson *1907*	Great Ouseburn, Yorks	1871	20.10.1930
Laurence Alan Johnson *1958–1972*	West Horsley, Surrey	12. 8.1936	
Alfred William Jones *1933*	Tewkesbury, Glos	6. 8.1900	
Ray Fitzpatrick Joseph *1985*	Belladrum, Guyana	12. 2.1961	
Vallance William Crisp Jupp *1923–1938*	Burgess Hill, Sussex	27. 3.1891	9. 7.1960
Ramlal Nikhanj Kapil Dev *1981–1983*	Chandigarh, India	6. 1.1959	
Henry Robert Albert Kelleher *1956–1958*	Bermondsey, London	3. 3.1929	
William Kemmey *1939*	Atcham, Shropshire	21. 7.1912	
Francis James Kendall *1930*	Hardingstone	1908	10. 9.1966
Michael Keith Kettle *1963–1970*	Stamford, Lincs	18. 3.1944	
Ralph Raymond Kimbell *1908*	Brixworth	12. 6.1884	4. 8.1964
Sidney King *1907–1908*	Rushden	1885	1972
Hubert Ernest Kingston *1905–1906*	Northampton	15. 8.1876	9. 6.1955
William Harold Kingston *1905–1909*	Northampton	12. 8.1874	17. 2.1956
Frederick Kitson *1919–1920*	Marylebone, London	1893	2.1925
Ronald Knight *1933–1934*	Northampton	12. 5.1913	
Robert Francis Knight *1905–1921*	Rushden	10. 8.1879	9. 1.1955
Ronald Dewe Lake *1922*	Bury St Edmunds, Suffolk	9. 5.1891	28. 7.1950
Allan Joseph Lamb *1978–*	Langebaanweg, S. Africa	20. 6.1954	
Henry John Hey Lamb *1934–1938*	Kettering	3. 5.1912	
Timothy Michael Lamb *1978–1983*	Hartford, Cheshire	24. 3.1953	
Wayne Larkins *1972–1991*	Roxton, Beds	22.11.1953	
David John Frederick Larter *1960–1969*	Inverness	24.4.1940	
Peter Granville Lee *1967–1971*	Arthingworth	27. 8.1945	
Allan Graham Liddell *1927–1934*	Northampton	2. 5.1908	17. 2.1970
Alan William George Liddell *1951–1955*	Northampton	8. 8.1930	9. 2.1972
Albert Lightfoot *1953–1970*	Woore, Shropshire	8. 1.1936	
Lord Lilford *1911*	Lilford	12. 1.1863	17.12.1945
Dennis Keith Lillee *1988*	Subiaco, Australia	18. 7.1949	
Steven John Lines *1983*	Luton, Beds	16. 3.1963	
Leonard Livingston *1950–1957*	Sydney, Australia	3. 5.1920	
Harry Longland *1907*	Leicester	1881	9.1911
Malachy Bernhard Loye *1991–*	Northampton	27. 9.1972	
Christopher William Stuart Lubbock *1938–1939*	London	4. 1.1920	

Arthur Luck *1937–1938*	Northampton	1914	24. 2.1987
Leslie Leopold McFarlane *1979*	Portland, Jamaica	19. 8.1952	
Lewis McGibbon *1957–1959*	Newcastle-on-Tyne	8.10.1931	
Neil Alan Mallender *1980–1986*	Kirk Sandall, Yorks	13. 8.1961	
Norman Maltby *1972–1974*	Marske, Yorks	16. 7.1951	
John Stephen Manning *1954–1960*	Adelaide, Australia	11. 6.1924	5. 5.1988
Thomas Edgar Manning *1906–1922*	Northampton	2. 9.1884	22.11.1975
Austin David George Matthews *1927–1936*	Penarth, Glamorgan	3. 5.1904	29. 7.1977
John Mercer *1947*	Southwick, Sussex	22. 4.1895	31. 8.1987
William Edward Merritt *1938–1946*	Sumner, New Zealand	18. 8.1908	9. 6.1977
Colin Milburn *1960–1974*	Burnopfield, Durham	23.10.1941	28. 2.1990
John Peter Crispin Mills *1981*	Kettering	6.12.1958	
John Henry Minney *1961–1967*	Finedon	25. 4.1939	
Richard Robert Montgomerie *1991–*	Rugby	3. 7.1971	
Stewart Nigel Clifford Murch *1968*	Warrnambool, Australia	27. 6.1944	
John Vernon Murdin *1913–1927*	Wollaston	16. 8.1891	11. 4.1971
Peter Earnshaw Murray-Willis *1938–1946*	Castle Bromwich, Warks	14. 7.1910	
Mushtaq Mohammad *1964–1977*	Junagadh, India	22.11.1943	
Shaikh Mohammed Nasiruddin *1938–1939*	Mangrol, India	9. 8.1916	
Peter John Mytton Nelson *1938*	Finchley, London	16. 5.1918	17. 1.1992
Robert Prynne Nelson *1937–1939*	Fulham, London	7. 8.1912	29.10.1940
William Thomas Nevell *1946–1947*	Balham, London	13. 6.1916	25. 8.1978
H. J. Newman *1905*			
Harold Maurice Newton *1938*	Overstone	5. 9.1918	
John Simmonds Nicholson *1924–1928*		1903	18. 3.1950
Wayne Michael Noon *1988–*	Grimsby, Lincs	5. 2.1971	
Michael Eric John Charles Norman *1952–1965*	Northampton	19. 1.1933	
Newman Frederick Norman *1905–1909*	Camberwell, Surrey	2. 2.1884	28. 8.1954
Graham Walter Norris *1925–1926*	Brackley	17.10.1905	6.12.1933
Reginald Philip Northway *1936*	Ceylon	14. 8.1906	26. 8.1936
Harold Nunley *1931*	Raunds	12. 1.1912	
Albert Edward Nutter *1948–1953*	Burnley, Lancs	28. 6.1913	
Francis Patrick O'Brien *1938–1939*	Canterbury, New Zealand	11. 2.1911	22.10.1991

Name	Years	Place	Born	Died
Norman Oldfield	1948–1954	Dukinfield, Cheshire	5. 5.1911	
Martin William Charles Olley	1983	Romford, Essex	27.11.1963	
Wayne Miles Osman	1970–1971	Athens, Greece	19. 8.1950	
Cyril Partridge	1921	Wellingborough	1896	23. 2.1945
Reginald Joseph Partridge	1929–1948	Wollaston	11. 2.1912	
Arnold Cyril Payne	1931–1934	Northampton	3.10.1897	13. 2.1973
James W. Pearson	1932			
Richard Michael Pearson	1992–	Batley, Yorks	27. 1.1972	
Ian George Peck	1980–1981	Great Staughton, Hunts	18.10.1957	
Anthony Leonard Penberthy	1989–	Troon, Cornwall	1. 9.1969	
George Arthur Penningham	1927	Cote Brook, Cheshire	28. 4.1899	15. 9.1933
George Cyril Perkins	1934–1937	Wollaston	4. 6.1911	
Stanley Ian Philips	1938–1939	Tunbridge Wells, Kent	4. 2.1920	
Peter Barlow Pickering	1953	York	24. 3.1926	
William Gladstone Pinner	1908	West Bromwich, Staffs	1877	1944
David Bartlett Pithey	1962	Salisbury, Rhodesia	4.10.1936	
Thomas Alfred Pitt	1932–1935	Hardingstone	1892	22. 4.1957
Robert Kenworthy Platt	1964	Holmfirth, Yorks	21.12.1932	
Charles James Tomlin Pool	1905–1910	Northampton	21. 1.1876	13.10.1954
Lionel Selwyn Powys-Maurice	1922–1923	Brighton, Sussex	7. 5.1899	1. 1.1991
Harold Cooper Pretty	1906–1907	Fressingfield, Suffolk	23.10.1875	30. 5.1952
Roger Malcolm Prideaux	1962–1970	Chelsea, London	13. 7.1939	
Neil Priestley	1981	Blyborough, Lincs	23. 6.1961	
Donald Ramsamooj	1958–1964	San Fernando, Trinidad	5. 7.1932	
Reginald Owen Raven	1905–1921	Baldock, Herts	26.11.1884	4. 4.1936
Keith Patrick Reid	1973	Port Elizabeth, S. Africa	24. 7.1951	
Brian Leonard Reynolds	1950–1970	Kettering	10. 6.1932	
Ian Michael Richards	1976–1979	Stockton-on-Tees, Durham	9.12.1957	
David Ripley	1984–	Leeds, Yorks	13. 9.1966	

Roderic Geroge Ripley *1922*	Weekley, Kettering	1900	1.1931
Andrew Richard Roberts *1989–*	Kettering	16. 4.1971	
Albert George Robinson *1937–1946*	Leicester	22. 3.1917	
Mark Andrew Robinson *1987–*	Hull, Yorks	23.11.1966	
Robert Geoffrey Robinson *1946*	Welling-borough	23. 9.1924	21.12.1973
Paul William Romaines *1975–1976*	Bishop Auckland, Durham	25.12.1955	
Nathaniel Meyer Victor Rothschild *1929–1931*	Kensington, London	31.10.1910	
James Henry Aloysius Ryan *1911–1914*	Roade	15. 9.1892	25. 9.1915
Kenneth James Rymill *1926–1932*	Northampton	30. 8.1906	31. 5.1977
Malik Sarfraz Nawaz *1969–1982*	Lahore, Pakistan	1.12.1948	
Arthur Harry Thomas Sargent *1932*	Northampton	24. 3.1908	
Malcolm Ernest Scott *1959–1969*	South Shields, Durham	8. 5.1936	
John Seymour *1908–1919*	Brightling, Sussex	24. 8.1881	1.12.1967
George Sharp *1968–1985*	West Hartlepool, Durham	12. 3.1950	
Peter Anthony Shenton *1958*	Redcar, Yorks	5. 5.1936	
Archibald Millar Robertson Sim *1964–1966*	Johannesburg, S. Africa	8. 1.1942	
Cyril Charles Simpson *1908*	Erpingham, Norfolk	1874	5. 5.1953
Harold Benjamin Simpson *1905–1911*	Higham Ferrers	27. 1.1879	3.1924
Alan Frank Skinner *1949*	Brighton, Sussex	22. 4.1913	28. 2.1982
Benjamin Charles Smith *1905–1906*	Daventry	10. 7.1859	29.11.1942
Gareth Smith *1986–1989*	Jarrow, Durham	20. 7.1966	
Lewis Alfred Smith *1947*	Brentford, Middx	12. 7.1913	10.1978
Ronald Smith *1954*	Dudley, Worcs	16. 2.1926	
Sydney Francis Smith *1914*	Northampton	1892	
Sidney Gordon Smith *1907–1914*	San Fernando, Trinidad	15. 1.1881	25.10.1963
Thomas George Harrison Smith *1931*	Northampton	6. 3.1905	
Jeremy Nicholas Snape *1992–*	Stoke-on-Trent	27. 4.1973	
Harold Saxon Snell *1909–1913*	Highworth, Wilts	6.12.1876	9. 7.1942
Alexander William Snowden *1931–1939*	Peterborough	15. 8.1913	7. 5.1981
Neil Alan Stanley *1988–*	Bedford	16. 5.1968	
Sydney Starkie *1951–1956*	Burnley, Lancs	4. 4.1926	
David Stanley Steele *1963–1984*	Bradeley, Staffs	29. 9.1941	

Name	Place	Born	Died
James Norman Stevens *1937*	Bexhill, Sussex	4. 6.1910	
Graham Barry Stevenson *1987*	Ackworth, Yorks	16.12.1955	
William James Perver Stewart *1971*	Llanelly	31. 8.1934	
Frederick Stocks *1906*	Shireoaks, Notts	23. 5.1883	2. 6.1954
Alastair Caleb Storie *1985–1986*	Bishopbriggs, Glasgow	25. 7.1965	
Sidney Stretton *1928*	Stamford, Lincs	1903	
Raman Subba Row *1955–1961*	Streatham, Surrey	29. 1.1932	
Haydn Sully *1964–1969*	Watchet, Somerset	1.11.1939	
John Warwick Swinburne *1970–1974*	Wath-on-Dearne, Yorks	4.12.1939	
Alan Tait *1971–1975*	Washington, Durham	27.12.1953	
Jonathan Paul Taylor *1991–*	Ashby-de-la-Zouch	8. 8.1964	
Gilbert George Tebbitt *1934–1938*	Welton	13. 9.1908	
Albert Edward Thomas *1919–1933*	Ruthin, Denbighshire	7. 6.1893	21. 3.1965
John Gregory Thomas *1989–1991*	Trebanos, Swansea	12. 8.1960	
Alexander Richard Thompson *1905–1908*	Stamford, Lincs	1.12.1876	16. 2.1951
George Joseph Thompson *1905–1922*	Northampton	27.10.1877	3. 3.1943
Charles Bedford Thorneycroft *1907*	Towcester	1879	
Frank Kenneis Thornton *1937*	Leicester	25.10.1898	
Charles Thorpe *1908–1909*	Fotheringhay	11. 8.1882	5. 5.1953
Thomas Thorpe *1913*	Attercliffe, Sheffield	19. 5.1881	28. 9.1953
John Edward Timms *1925–1949*	Silverstone	3.11.1906	18. 5.1980
Wilfrid Walter Timms *1921–1932*	Northampton	28. 9.1902	30. 9.1986
Robert Michael Tindall *1980–1981*	Harrow, Middx	16. 6.1959	
Bryan Charles Tomblin *1914*	Brixworth	29. 6.1891	1. 6.1918
Eric Feltham Tompkins *1920–1921*	Rushden	18.12.1892	20. 7.1980
James Harry Cecil Toon *1946*	Oundle	17. 1.1916	26.12.1987
Edgar Fremantle Towell *1923–1934*	Kettering	5. 7.1901	2. 6.1972
George Edward Tribe *1951–1959*	Yarraville, Victoria, Australia	4.10.1920	
Bernard Tyler *1923–1924*	Ridlington, Rutland	29. 4.1902	10.11.1987
Charles Herbert Tyler *1910–1923*	Northampton	13. 9.1887	17. 5.1942
Frank Holmes Tyson *1952–1960*	Farnworth, Lancs	6. 6.1930	
Denis William Arthur Vann *1936–1937*	Northampton	21.11.1916	20. 1.1961
Richard Stephen Venes *1922*	Wandsworth, London	1885	10. 6.1959
George Alfred Turner Vials *1905–1922*	Northampton	18. 3.1887	26. 4.1974

Roy Thomas Virgin *1973–1977*	Taunton, Somerset	26. 8.1939	
Frederick Ingram Walden *1910–1929*	Welling-borough	1. 3.1888	3. 5.1949
Alan Walker *1983–*	Emley, Yorks	7. 7.1962	
Harold Walker *1947*	Desborough	12. 6.1918	
William Percy Walker *1908–1920*	Northampton	1889	6. 2.1938
Russell John Warren *1992–*	Northampton	10. 9.1971	
John Michael Warrington *1951*	Northampton	7. 3.1924	
Stuart Nicholas Varney Waterton *1986–1987*	Dartford, Kent	6.12.1960	
Ian Ronald Watson *1971*	Teddington, Middx	9. 6.1947	
Frederick Henry George Watts *1932–1937*	Northampton	29. 7.1904	
Peter David Watts *1958–1966*	Henlow, Beds	31. 3.1938	
Patrick James Watts *1959–1980*	Henlow, Beds	16. 6.1940	
John Webster *1946–1955*	Bradford, Yorks	28.10.1917	
Thomas Bacon Gascoigne Welch *1922–1931*	Reigate, Surrey	31. 7.1906	16. 3.1972
Arthur Luty Wells *1954–1955*	Headingley, Leeds	23.11.1909	
William Wells *1905–1926*	Daventry	14. 3.1881	18. 3.1939
Matthew Benjamin Harold Wheeler *1985*	Windlesham, Surrey	14. 8.1962	
Albert Winterton White *1914–1923*	Welling-borough	1889	9. 3.1965
Edmund White *1946–1948*	Lee, London	29. 1.1928	
Horace Arthur White *1923*	Welling-borough	1894	1969
Oliver Claude White *1920*	Eton, Bucks	11. 3.1880	12. 1.1956
William Michael Eastwood White *1947–1949*	Barnes, Surrey	22. 5.1913	
Philip James Whitehead *1908–1909*	Woodstock, Oxfordshire	1881	1957
Edward Walter Whitfield *1946*	Clapham, London	31. 5.1911	
Duncan James Wild *1980–1990*	Northampton	28.11.1962	
John Wild *1953–1961*	Northampton	24. 2.1935	
Burton Wilkinson *1932*	Nebraska, USA	25. 4.1900	
Peter Willey *1966–1983*	Sedgefield, Durham	6.12.1949	
Harold Williams *1923–1924*		30.10.1903	
Richard Grenville Williams *1974–1992*	Bangor, Caenarvon-shire	10. 8.1957	
John Gordon Williamson *1959–1962*	Stockton-on-Tees, Durham	4. 4.1936	
John William Willis *1919*	Kettering	1886	9.1963

300

Arnold Cass Lycett Wills *1926–1929*	Kensington, London	17. 7.1906	28. 2.1978
Roy Wills *1963–1972*	Northampton	5.12.1944	
Harry Wilson *1931*		1897	25. 4.1960
Claud Neville Woolley *1911–1931*	Tunbridge Wells, Kent	5. 5.1886	3.11.1962
Reginald Wooster *1925*	Kettering	1903	12. 9.1968
Arthur Edward Worsley *1905*	Evenley, Brackley	10.10.1882	10. 8.1969
Charles Edward Austen Worsley *1921*	Evenley, Brackley	30. 5.1902	
Albert Wright *1919–1920*	Kettering	8. 8.1899	
Alan Jack Barton Wright *1922–1923*	Northampton	3. 3.1905	
Bertie Wright *1919–1922*	Kettering	7. 1.1897	2. 4.1955
Ernest Vincent Wright *1919*	Kettering	24.10.1894	16.12.1977
Nicholas Edward Wright *1921–1922*	Kettering	28. 8.1901	20. 5.1974
Philip Alan Wright *1921–1929*	Kettering	16. 5.1903	21.12.1968
Ronald Charles Barton Wright *1923–1931*	Northampton	13. 3.1903	3. 7.1992
Richard Leslie Wright *1923–1926*	Kettering	28.10.1903	
Stephen Wright *1922–1923*	Kettering	6. 8.1897	24. 6.1975
Thomas James Yardley *1976–1982*	Chaddesley Corbett, Worcs	27.10.1946	
W. Keith Yarnold *1928*			8.10.1978

CAREER RECORDS OF NORTHAMPTONSHIRE PLAYERS
1905–1992

Name	Inns	NO	Runs	HS	Avge	100s	Runs	Wkts	Avge	BB	5wI
Ablack R. K.	4	2	24	16	12.00	–	220	6	36.66	3/32	–
Ackerman H. M.	174	10	5182	208	31.60	8	103	4	25.75	2/28	–
Adams S. C	15	1	146	87	10.43	–	250	13	19.23	6/32	1
Adams W.	66	5	1111	154★	18.21	2	67	0	–	– –	–
Addis C. F.	1	–	38	38	38.00	–	155	5	31.00	3/78	–
Allen A. W.	15	–	384	90	25.60	–	–	–	–	– –	–
Allen J. S.	3	1	0	0★	–	–	154	1	154.00	1/58	–
Allen M. H. J.	183	40	1418	59	9.91	–	9148	424	21.57	8/48	20
Ambrose C. E. L.	52	20	530	55★	16.56	–	3515	139	25.29	7/89	7
Andrew K. V.	428	150	3830	76	13.78	–	31	2	15.50	2/9	–
Andrews N. P.	12	1	122	45★	11.09	–	–	–	–	– –	–
Arkell H. J. D.	2	–	11	6	5.50	–	–	–	–	– –	–
Arnold A. P.	294	13	7420	122	26.42	5	79	3	26.33	1/5	–
Ashenden M.	27	9	49	15	2.72	–	1206	38	31.74	4/50	–
Askham S. T.	9	3	83	28★	13.83	–	86	2	43.00	2/68	–
Atkinson B. G. W.	22	2	286	91	14.30	–	219	7	31.29	2/13	–
Bagnall H. F.	119	2	2224	103	19.01	1	20	0	–	– –	–
Bailey R. J.	370	56	13305	224★	42.37	29	2361	55	42.93	3/27	–
Bailey R. R.	47	21	253	25	9.73	–	2827	105	26.92	5/25	5
Baker C.	8	1	17	7	2.43	–	198	11	18.00	3/38	–
Bakewell A. H.	417	21	13543	257	34.45	29	1263	22	57.40	2/17	–
Baldwin G. F.	1	–	6	6	6.00	–	18	0	–	– –	–
Ball K. J.	22	1	178	49	8.47	–	384	13	29.53	4/52	–
Ball W. J.	6	2	10	8	2.50	–	–	–	–	– –	–
Bamber M. J.	26	2	638	77	26.58	–	3	0	–	– –	–
Baptiste E. A. E.	22	1	589	80	28.05	–	1443	50	28.86	7/95	3
Barrick D. W.	434	56	12443	211	32.92	18	2562	57	44.95	5/71	2
Barron W.	196	13	4751	161★	25.96	6	200	5	40.00	1/1	–
Bass J. G.	4	–	43	16	10.75	–	31	0	–	– –	–
Batson W.	4	–	45	34	11.25	–	–	–	–	– –	–
Beasley J. N.	22	6	100	21	6.25	–	261	5	52.20	1/6	–
Beasley R. N.	15	–	109	28	7.26	–	–	–	–	– –	–
Bedi B. S.	123	33	1002	61	11.13	–	9067	434	20.89	7/34	26
Beers H. G.	30	1	175	31	6.03	–	232	4	58.00	1/8	–
Bell A. P.	6	–	37	24	6.16	–	–	–	–	– –	–
Bellamy B. W.	624	66	9226	168	16.42	4	57	0	–	– –	–
Benjamin H. L.	1	–	2	2	2.00	–	52	4	13.00	3/38	–
Bennett A. C. L.	29	–	586	68	20.21	–	–	–	–	– –	–
Bennett H. A.	2	–	1	1	0.50	–	51	0	–	– –	–
Bennett S. J.	6	1	37	19★	7.40	–	107	2	53.50	1/40	–
Bird F. N.	17	2	263	61★	17.53	–	–	–	–	– –	–
Booden C. D.	3	2	10	6★	10.00	–	258	3	86.00	2/30	–
Borwick P. M.	6	–	25	11	4.16	–	98	3	32.66	1/25	–
Bowell N. H.	1	–	48	48	48.00	–	16	0	–	– –	–
Bowen M. N.	3	2	26	13★	26.00	–	247	2	123.50	1/23	–

Name	Inns	NO	Runs	HS	Avge	100s	Runs	Wkts	Avge	BB	5wI
Boyd-Moss R. J.	190	18	5044	155	29.33	8	1294	25	51.76	3/39	–
Bradfield G. W.	1	–	50	50	50.00	–	–	–	– –	–	–
Breakwell D.	78	15	997	97	15.82	–	3447	137	25.16	8/39	6
Brice G. H. J.	35	5	412	82★	13.73	–	2426	72	33.69	8/124	4
Bridge D. J. W.	6	1	49	25★	9.80	–	162	3	54.00	2/14	–
Broderick V.	373	42	7244	190	21.88	6	14338	530	27.05	9/35	22
Brookes D.	871	69	28980	257	36.13	67	127	3	42.33	1/7	–
Brown F. R.	153	13	4331	171★	30.94	7	9083	391	23.23	7/33	17
Brown S. J. E.	14	6	70	25★	8.75	–	814	25	32.56	7/46	11
Brown W. C.	214	29	2601	103★	14.06	1	1	0	– –	–	–
Bull A. H.	57	4	538	44	10.15	–	–	–	– –	–	–
Buller C. E.	2	1	2	1★	2.00	–	35	0	– –	–	–
Burgess A. A.	2	–	14	13	7.00	–	13	0	– –	–	–
Burgess H.	2	–	10	9	5.00	–	32	0	– –	–	–
Buswell J. E.	99	29	525	30	7.50	–	5653	172	32.87	7/61	5
Buswell W. A.	327	76	2670	101★	10.64	1	–	–	– –	–	–
Capel D. J.	332	49	8873	126	31.35	11	11846	369	32.10	7/46	11
Carse J. A.	10	8	129	36★	64.50	–	722	22	32.82	5/43	1
Carter R. M.	67	15	858	79	16.50	–	1492	38	39.26	4/27	–
Catlow C. S.	3	1	18	10★	9.00	–	–	–	– –	–	–
Chamberlain W. R. F.	9	–	67	14	7.44	–	–	–	– –	–	–
Childs-Clarke A. W.	85	6	1343	68	17.00	–	609	12	50.75	2/19	–
Clapperton T. J. M.	1	–	0	0	0.00	–	–	–	– –	–	–
Clark E. W.	447	176	1809	30	6.00	–	23387	1097	21.32	8/59	59
Clarke C. B.	81	11	874	86	12.48	–	4638	156	29.73	7/120	8
Clarke G. W.	2	–	0	0	0.00	–	58	2	29.00	2/58	–
Clarke R. W.	257	83	2664	56	15.31	–	16397	477	34.37	8/26	16
Collins G. T.	5	–	44	17	8.80	–	–	–	– –	–	–
Constable D.	2	–	20	12	10.00	–	–	–	– –	–	–
Cook G.	711	62	20976	203	32.32	33	548	3	182.66	1/7	–
Cook N. G. B.	150	37	1339	64	11.85	–	9298	346	26.87	7/34	11
Cornelius B. W.	2	1	9	9★	9.00	–	–	–	– –	–	–
Cottam R. M. H.	86	23	590	62★	9.36	–	4877	241	20.24	8/14	17
Coverdale S. P.	–	–	–	–	–	–	–	–	– –	–	–
Coverdale W. W.	53	4	512	35★	10.44	–	62	1	62.00	1/25	–
Cox A. L.	409	31	6623	104	17.52	1	7926	199	39.83	7/91	–
Cox M.	134	10	1808	78	14.57	–	984	25	39.36	3/22	–
Cox M. H. D.	4	–	8	5	2.00	–	62	2	31.00	2/11	–
Cox S.	11	1	89	25	8.90	–	45	1	45.00	1/10	–
Crosse E. M.	90	4	1168	65	13.55	–	–	–	– –	–	–
Crump B. S.	473	108	8652	133★	23.70	5	19938	807	24.71	7/29	30
Cullen L.	31	1	253	40	8.43	–	650	11	59.09	3/73	–
Curran K. M.	61	8	1558	89★	29.40	–	2580	98	26.33	6/45	2
Cuthbertson G. B.	81	5	1214	96	15.97	–	–	–	– –	–	–
Dainty H. W.	5	2	20	8	6.66	–	47	0	– –	–	–
Dale J. H.	13	1	221	70	18.41	–	78	0	– –	–	–
Davies L. J.	9	1	43	20	5.37	–	96	2	48.00	1/9	–
Davis E.	159	14	4126	171	28.45	3	8	1	8.00	1/0	–
Davis M. J.	–	–	–	–	–	–	58	2	29.00	1/21	–
Davis P. C.	303	22	6363	237	22.64	10	492	6	82.00	2/13	–
Davis W. W.	62	13	759	47	15.49	–	5776	208	27.77	7/52	13

Name	Inns	NO	Runs	HS	Avge	100s	Runs	Wkts	Avge	BB	5wI
Dawes A. G.	2	–	16	16	8.00	–	–	–	– –	–
Denton A. D.	13	2	276	51*	25.09	–	5	0	– –	–
Denton J. S.	178	26	3298	124	21.69	2	1883	67	28.10	5/39	2
Denton W. H.	205	19	4449	230*	23.91	4	42	0	– –	–
Dickens A.	2	–	3	3	1.50	–	4	1	4.00	1/4	–
Dilley M. R.	38	16	232	31*	10.55	–	2471	80	30.89	6/74	2
Divecha R. V.	2	–	48	33	24.00	–	65	1	65.00	1/65	–
Dixon E. J. H.	13	–	353	123	27.15	1	20	0	– –	–
Driffield L. T.	67	14	603	52	11.37	–	2722	108	25.20	7/78	5
Drummond G. H.	8	–	33	12	4.12	–	–	–	– –	–
Dunkley M. E. F.	64	4	904	70	15.07	–	12	0	– –	–
Durose A. J.	71	23	447	30	9.31	–	4035	150	26.90	7/23	2
Dye J. C. J.	112	53	416	29*	7.05	–	7615	341	22.33	7/45	10
East W.	261	34	3913	86*	17.21	–	10233	493	20.75	7/11	28
Elderkin T.	2	–	13	13	6.50	–	–	–	– –	–
Ellis H.	27	10	72	18	4.23	–	–	–	– –	–
Falconer R.	12	4	29	12*	3.62	–	228	9	25.33	2/13	–
Falding S. W.	2	–	8	8	4.00	–	119	1	119.00	1/119	–
Fellows-Smith J. P.	22	1	587	109	27.95	1	231	1	231.00	1/51	–
Felton N. A.	132	11	3784	122	31.27	5	330	2	165.00	1/25	–
Fiddling K.	167	67	1198	68	11.98	–	–	–	– –	–
Fitzroy-Newdegate J. M.	101	6	1373	50	14.45	–	82	6	13.66	4/14	–
Flynn V. A.	2	1	21	15	21.00	–	–	–	– –	–
Fordham A.	182	16	6759	206*	40.72	14	238	3	79.33	1/25	–
Forster G.	–	–	–	–	–	–	100	3	33.33	2/30	–
Freeman E.	26	5	133	30	6.33	–	416	6	69.33	3/62	–
Freeman T.	1	–	4	4	4.00	–	90	1	90.00	1/43	–
Fry C. A.	3	2	91	71*	91.00	–	–	–	– –	–
Fryer P. A.	4	–	83	38	20.75	–	66	3	22.00	3/35	–
Garlick R. G.	96	25	911	62*	12.83	–	5873	212	27.70	6/76	6
Gifford G. C.	24	–	387	98	16.12	–	–	–	– –	–
Goldstein F. S.	18	1	437	90	25.71	–	–	–	– –	–
Gouldstone M. R.	13	1	274	71	22.83	–	–	–	– –	–
Govan J. W.	7	–	52	17	7.43	–	301	8	37.62	2/12	–
Greasley D. G.	85	11	1659	104*	22.42	1	573	16	35.81	4/36	–
Greenwood H. W.	103	2	1920	94	19.00	–	31	0	– –	–
Griffiths B. J.	138	51	290	16	3.33	–	12899	444	29.05	8/50	13
Grimshaw N.	147	6	2445	92	17.34	–	427	6	71.16	2/60	–
Guy J. W.	3	2	75	43*	75.00	–	–	–	– –	–
Hall H. S.	2	–	12	7	6.00	–	–	–	– –	–
Hanley R. W.	21	7	131	33*	9.36	–	1182	37	31.95	6/21	3
Hardy D.	62	13	499	37	10.18	–	584	14	41.71	6/11	1
Harper R. A.	63	14	1834	234	37.43	3	4188	137	30.57	5/28	4
Hawes G. H.	3	1	16	12*	8.00	–	87	1	87.00	1/43	–
Hawkins H.	44	9	350	33	10.00	–	767	24	31.95	2/12	–
Hawtin A. P. R.	150	5	3558	135	24.54	3	–	–	– –	–
Hawtin R. W. R.	37	4	508	65	15.39	–	663	22	30.13	5/33	2
Hawtin W.	8	1	51	24	7.28	–	23	1	23.00	1/9	–
Haywood R. A.	306	15	8373	198	28.77	20	1466	34	43.11	3/73	–
Herbert E. J.	57	24	291	20	8.82	–	2322	69	33.65	5/103	1
Hibbert H. W.	2	–	11	10	5.50	–	–	–	– –	–

Name	Inns	NO	Runs	HS	Avge	100s	Runs	Wkts	Avge	BB	5wI
Hodgson A.	118	24	909	41*	9.67	–	5964	206	28.95	5/30	2
Hoffman D. S.	1	1	20	20*	–	–	97	2	48.50	1/43	–
Hogan R. P.	4	–	18	8	4.50	–	218	3	72.33	2/16	–
Holland L. E.	19	–	202	63	10.63	–	193	6	32.16	3/26	–
Horton T.	49	6	502	35	11.67	–	4	0	–	–	–
Hughes J. G.	9	–	11	6	1.22	–	450	7	64.28	3/56	–
Humfrey S. H. G.	36	2	477	61*	14.02	–	135	1	135.00	1/40	–
Hyde E.	2	1	3	3*	3.00	–	–	–	–	–	–
Izzard W. C.	20	–	206	51	10.30	–	–	–	–	–	–
Jakeman F.	182	15	5470	258*	32.75	10	162	5	32.40	2/8	–
Jakeman R. S.	4	–	31	20	7.75	–	–	–	–	–	–
James J.	3	–	2	1	0.66	–	125	2	62.50	1/14	–
James K. C.	178	17	3428	105*	21.29	2	17	0	–	–	–
Johns R. L.	7	–	62	20	8.85	–	59	4	14.75	3/20	–
Johnson G. H.	28	14	142	43*	10.14	–	–	–	–	–	–
Johnson G. J.	8	1	49	28*	7.00	–	349	5	69.80	2/41	–
Johnson J. I.	1	–	0	0	0.00	–	–	–	–	–	–
Johnson L. A.	186	40	1526	50	10.45	–	61	1	61.00	1/60	–
Jones A. W.	2	–	13	12	6.50	–	–	–	–	–	–
Joseph R. F.	1	1	26	26*	–	–	143	4	35.75	3/73	–
Jupp V. W. C.	477	29	13653	197	30.47	15	24075	1078	22.33	10/127	79
Kapil Dev N.	24	4	856	120	42.80	3	1105	31	35.64	4/24	–
Kelleher H. R. A.	51	17	256	25	7.53	–	2918	100	29.18	5/85	2
Kemmey W.	9	1	55	18	6.87	–	–	–	–	–	–
Kendall F. J.	6	1	1	1*	0.20	–	172	6	28.66	2/26	–
Kettle M. K.	105	20	1117	88	13.14	–	4800	179	26.81	6/67	5
Kimbell R. R.	2	–	4	4	2.00	–	45	2	22.50	2/45	–
King S.	7	2	47	23	9.40	–	–	–	–	–	–
Kingston H. E.	25	4	335	68	15.95	–	246	6	41.00	2/8	–
Kingston W. H.	140	2	2594	83	18.81	–	25	2	12.50	2/5	–
Kitson F.	6	3	31	13	10.33	–	192	3	64.00	3/63	–
Knight R.	20	3	182	50	10.70	–	348	10	34.80	5/108	1
Knight R. F.	37	3	408	67	12.00	–	667	21	31.76	6/90	1
Lake R. D.	4	1	48	30	16.00	–	–	–	–	–	–
Lamb A. J.	374	68	16757	235	54.76	49	165	7	23.57	2/29	–
Lamb H. J. H.	69	5	1085	91*	16.95	–	–	–	–	–	–
Lamb T. M.	100	40	652	39*	10.87	–	7059	236	29.91	7/56	4
Larkins W.	628	43	20317	252	34.73	44	1711	40	42.77	5/59	1
Larter J. D. F.	128	47	517	51*	6.38	–	9295	511	18.19	8/28	24
Lee P. G.	40	11	260	26	8.96	–	3132	91	34.42	6/86	4
Liddell, A. G.	161	7	2355	120	15.29	3	563	9	62.55	4/59	–
Liddell A. W. G.	20	6	201	38*	14.36	–	1399	24	58.29	3/62	–
Lightfoot A.	489	59	11837	174*	27.53	12	5980	167	35.81	7/25	4
Lilford, Lord	1	–	4	4	4.00	–	–	–	–	–	–
Lillee D. K.	10	2	98	22	12.25	–	731	20	36.55	6/68	1
Lines S. J.	1	–	29	29	29.00	–	–	–	–	–	–
Livingston L.	325	36	13165	210	45.55	29	2	0	–	–	–
Longland H.	–	–	–	–	–	–	–	–	–	–	–
Loye M. B.	15	2	198	46	15.23	–	–	–	–	–	–
Lubbock C. W. S.	10	1	147	69	16.33	–	239	15	15.93	4/44	–
Luck A.	4	–	52	18	13.00	–	155	2	77.50	1/34	–

Name	Inns	NO	Runs	HS	Avge	100s	Runs	Wkts	Avge	BB	5wI
McFarlane L. L.	2	–	0	0	0.00	–	569	13	43.77	3/83	–
McGibbon L.	11	5	17	4	2.83	–	858	33	26.00	4/42	–
Mallender N. A.	145	49	1215	71*	12.66	–	9770	305	32.03	7/41	7
Maltby N.	14	4	185	59	18.50	–	97	2	48.50	2/43	–
Manning J. S.	163	23	1972	132	14.08	1	9033	428	21.10	8/43	24
Manning T. E.	93	15	1026	57	13.15	–	–	–	–	– –	–
Matthews A. D. G.	369	44	5127	116	15.77	2	14999	567	26.45	7.63	27
Mercer J.	–	–	–	–	–	–	100	2	50.00	2/100	–
Merritt W. E.	69	5	1264	87	19.75	–	3925	151	25.99	7/63	12
Milburn C.	336	26	9798	203	31.61	18	2559	83	30.83	6/59	1
Mills J. P. C.	6	–	135	68	22.50	–	–	–	–	– –	–
Minney J. H.	7	–	127	58	18.14	–	–	–	–	– –	–
Montgomerie R. R.	2	–	9	7	4.50	–	–	–	–	– –	–
Murch S. N. C.	–	–	–	–	–	–	102	1	102.00	1/80	–
Murdin J. V.	278	69	1767	90*	8.45	–	12270	454	27.03	8/81	28
Murray-Willis P. E.	35	2	387	54	11.72	–	–	–	–	– –	–
Mushtaq Mohammad	454	46	15961	204*	39.12	32	13224	551	24.00	7/67	19
Nasiruddin S. M.	9	1	94	42*	11.75	–	–	–	–	– –	–
Nelson P. J. M.	2	1	52	32	52.00	–	42	1	42.00	1/42	–
Nelson R. P.	90	10	2359	123*	29.49	2	1610	42	38.33	3/7	–
Nevell W. T.	57	5	458	55*	8.80	–	2661	80	33.26	4/11	–
Newman H. J.	2	–	5	5	2.50	–	–	–	–	– –	–
Newton H. M.	2	–	2	2	1.00	–	–	–	–	– –	–
Nicholson J. S.	102	19	777	45	9.36	–	3156	86	36.69	5/51	2
Noon W. M.	16	2	150	37	10.71	–	–	–	–	– –	–
Norman M. E. J. C.	364	17	10165	152	29.29	15	76	2	38.00	2/0	–
Norman N. F.	21	–	191	32	9.09	–	–	–	–	– –	–
Norris G. W.	8	–	38	16	4.50	–	154	7	22.00	3/48	–
Northway R. P.	28	2	429	58	16.50	–	–	–	–	– –	–
Nunley H.	5	2	20	12	6.66	–	92	0	–	– –	–
Nutter A. E.	189	29	2352	93	14.70	–	10628	426	24.95	7/52	21
O'Brien F. P.	71	3	1306	90	19.20	–	593	13	45.61	2/14	–
Oldfield N.	265	23	9321	168	38.52	20	34	0	–	– –	–
Olley M. W. C.	1	–	8	8	8.00	–	–	–	–	– –	–
Osman W. M.	16	–	287	60	17.94	–	–	–	–	– –	–
Partridge C.	2	–	1	1	0.50	–	–	–	–	– –	–
Partridge R. J.	458	120	3918	70	11.59	–	19714	632	31.19	9/66	22
Payne A. C. .	5	1	27	22*	6.75	–	–	–	–	– –	–
Pearson J. W.	2	1	1	1*	1.00	–	43	0	–	– –	–
Pearson R. M.	–	–	–	–	–	–	130	2	65.00	2/90	–
Peck I. G.	3	1	19	13*	9.50	–	–	–	–	– –	–
Penberthy A. L.	56	7	905	101*	18.47	1	1909	50	3.18	4/91	–
Pennington G. A.	19	–	259	47	13.63	–	8	0	–	– –	–
Perkins G. C.	93	22	560	29	7.89	–	3309	93	35.58	6/54	5
Philips S. I.	12	3	88	22	9.78	–	15	0	–	– –	–
Pickering P. B.	2	–	59	37	29.50	–	–	–	–	– –	–
Pinner W. G.	2	1	26	24	26.00	–	17	0	–	– –	–
Pithey D. B.	4	1	45	22	15.00	–	82	0	–	– –	–
Pitt T. A.	43	14	207	31*	7.13	–	1563	43	36.34	4/65	–
Platt R. K.	–	–	–	–	–	–	153	4	38.25	3/51	–
Pool C. J. T.	177	6	4350	166	25.43	4	227	5	45.40	4/53	–
Powys-Maurice L. S.	19	–	156	65	8.21	–	–	–	–	– –	–

Name	Inns	NO	Runs	HS	Avge	100s	Runs	Wkts	Avge	BB	5wI
Pretty H. C.	15	–	463	200	30.87	1	123	5	24.60	3/39	–
Prideaux R. M.	418	44	13853	202*	37.04	24	16	0	–	– –	–
Priestley N.	1	1	20	20*	–	–	–	–	–	– –	–
Ramsamooj D.	129	9	2489	132	20.74	4	150	2	75.00	1/28	–
Raven R. O.	58	2	766	59	13.67	–	59	1	59.00	1/15	–
Reid K. P.	1	1	5	5*	–	–	9	4	2.25	4/9	–
Reynolds B. L.	732	65	18640	169	27.95	21	284	4	71.00	1/0	–
Richards I. M.	25	4	467	50	22.24	–	201	7	28.71	4/57	–
Ripley D.	228	57	4256	134*	24.89	6	103	2	51.50	2/89	–
Ripley R. G.	7	1	77	23	12.83	–	16	0	–	– –	–
Roberts A. R.	42	13	577	62	19.89	–	2571	61	42.15	6/72	1
Robinson A. G.	37	12	167	32	6.68	–	1464	35	41.83	5/37	1
Robinson M. A.	62	29	61	19*	1.85	–	4584	136	33.71	4/19	–
Robinson R. G.	8	1	85	53	12.14	–	90	0	–	– –	–
Romaines P. W.	9	1	56	17	7.00	–	–	–	–	– –	–
Rothschild N. M. V.	17	1	275	63	17.18	–	53	0	–	– –	–
Ryan J. H. A.	13	1	114	41	9.50	–	132	4	33.00	2/51	–
Rymill K. J.	6	–	35	28	5.83	–	–	–	–	– –	–
Sarfraz Nawaz	198	44	3212	90	20.86	–	11962	511	23.41	7/37	24
Sargent A. H. T.	7	1	41	18	6.83	–	286	7	40.85	5/88	1
Scott M. E.	249	63	2426	62	13.04	–	11208	457	24.52	7/32	20
Seymour J.	157	10	2897	136*	19.70	1	2727	98	27.24	6/58	3
Sharp G.	395	80	6243	98	19.82	–	70	1	70.00	1/47	–
Shenton P. A.	2	–	39	33	19.50	–	40	1	40.00	1/31	–
Sim A. M. R.	7	1	151	66*	25.16	–	–	–	–	– –	–
Simpson C. C.	2	–	3	3	1.50	–	36	1	36.00	1/36	–
Simpson H. B.	15	1	128	44	9.14	–	413	9	45.88	4/29	–
Skinner A. F.	2	–	12	10	6.00	–	–	–	–	– –	–
Smith B. C.	55	25	393	38*	13.10	–	2	0	–	– –	–
Smith G.	10	2	60	29*	7.50	–	552	17	32.47	6/72	1
Smith L. A.	3	1	57	55	28.50	–	134	5	26.80	4/55	–
Smith R.	2	1	19	19*	19.00	–	38	1	38.00	1/38	–
Smith S. F.	4	–	16	6	4.00	–	–	–	–	– –	–
Smith S. G.	210	13	6396	204	32.45	12	8744	502	17.41	8/39	36
Smith T. G. H.	1	–	11	11	11.00	–	28	0	–	– –	–
Snape J. N.	–	–	–	–	–	–	62	1	62.00	1/20	–
Snell H. S.	5	–	119	52	23.80	–	–	–	–	– –	–
Snowden A. W.	250	10	4343	128	18.09	2	22	2	11.00	1/5	–
Stanley N. A.	35	4	1019	132	32.87	1	19	0	–	– –	–
Starkie S.	110	30	857	60	10.71	–	5685	166	34.25	6/33	6
Steele D. S.	673	101	18231	140*	31.87	25	11533	462	24.96	8/29	16
Stevens J. N.	9	1	54	19	6.75	–	440	9	48.89	3/85	–
Stevenson G. B.	2	–	2	2	1.00	–	67	2	33.50	2/34	–
Stewart W. J. P.	2	–	53	50	26.50	–	–	–	–	– –	–
Stocks F.	4	–	24	13	6.00	–	37	0	–	– –	–
Storie A. C.	23	2	578	106	27.52	1	51	0	–	– –	–
Stretton S.	2	–	1	1	0.50	–	120	2	60.00	2/120	–
Subba Row R.	186	25	7050	300	43.79	19	721	23	31.35	3/22	–
Sully H.	123	46	624	48	8.10	–	8129	302	26.92	7/29	15
Swinburne J. W.	36	8	160	25	5.71	–	2281	83	27.48	6/57	4
Tait A.	85	–	1549	99	18.22	–	–	–	–	– –	–
Taylor J. P.	30	12	210	74*	11.66	–	2992	95	31.49	7/23	4

Name	Inns	NO	Runs	HS	Avge	100s	Runs	Wkts	Avge	BB	5wI
Tebbitt G. G.	21	3	248	41	13.77	–	29	0	–	–	–
Thomas A. E.	462	103	4747	84	13.22	–	20899	817	25.58	9/30	29
Thomas J. G.	57	9	704	64	14.66	–	4054	124	32.69	7/75	6
Thompson A. R.	29	2	358	48*	13.26	–	–	–	–	–	–
Thompson G. J.	392	39	8321	131*	23.57	7	20355	1078	18.88	9/64	102
Thorneycroft C. B.	4	–	5	3	1.25	–	50	2	25.00	1/14	–
Thornton F. K.	4	1	27	13	9.00	–	–	–	–	–	–
Thorpe C.	17	–	195	50	11.47	–	16	0	–	–	–
Thorpe T.	4	1	11	6	3.66	–	–	–	–	–	–
Timms J. E.	842	29	20384	213	25.07	31	6618	149	44.42	6/18	2
Timms W. W.	183	14	3855	154*	22.81	4	151	0	–	–	–
Tindall R. M.	22	4	330	60*	18.33	–	331	4	82.75	2/1	–
Tomblin B. C.	4	–	8	3	2.00	–	–	–	–	–	–
Tompkins E. F.	22	2	204	50*	10.20	–	–	–	–	–	–
Toon J. H. C.	2	–	1	1	0.50	–	126	4	31.50	3/79	–
Towell E. F.	111	17	1199	66	12.75	–	3379	102	33.13	4/42	–
Tribe G. E.	356	67	8141	136*	28.17	6	20681	1021	20.25	9/43	71
Tyler B.	18	6	118	26	9.83	–	465	9	51.66	2/13	–
Tyler C. H.	48	7	582	63	14.19	–	–	–	–	–	–
Tyson F. H.	218	54	2842	82	17.33	–	10998	525	20.95	8/60	25
Vann D. W. A.	6	–	47	16	7.83	–	104	2	52.00	2/26	–
Venes R. S.	8	2	8	4*	1.33	–	105	5	21.00	4/60	–
Vials G. A. T.	220	10	3808	129	18.13	2	19	0	–	–	–
Virgin R. T.	184	14	5703	145	33.55	13	19	0	–	–	–
Walden F. I.	435	36	7462	128	18.70	5	4228	114	37.08	4/39	–
Walker A.	90	45	659	41*	14.64	–	6791	218	31.16	6/50	2
Walker H.	2	–	8	7	4.00	–	–	–	–	–	–
Walker W. P.	12	–	111	48	9.25	–	–	–	–	–	–
Warren R. J.	3	1	27	19	13.50	–	–	–	–	–	–
Warrington J. M.	1	–	18	18	18.00	–	164	3	54.66	1/30	–
Waterton S. N. V.	19	5	368	58*	26.28	–	–	–	–	–	–
Watson I. R.	1	–	16	16	16.00	–	–	–	–	–	–
Watts F. H. G.	5	–	12	6	2.40	–	–	–	–	–	–
Watts P. D.	241	51	4127	91	21.72	–	8471	276	30.69	7/77	12
Watts P. J.	605	90	14411	145	27.98	10	8613	331	26.02	6/18	7
Webster J.	78	9	497	65	7.20	–	3644	105	34.70	6/118	2
Welch T. B. G.	41	5	505	64	14.03	–	57	1	57.00	1/4	–
Wells A. L.	6	1	28	18	5.60	–	333	8	41.62	4/67	–
Wells W.	441	75	6324	119	17.28	2	16202	751	21.57	8/35	51
Wheeler M. B. H.	–	–	–	–	–	–	117	1	117.00	1/87	–
White A. W.	15	–	139	29	9.26	–	24	0	–	–	–
White E.	4	–	44	16	11.00	–	–	–	–	–	–
White H. A.	10	2	51	15*	6.37	–	126	1	126.00	1/35	–
White O. C.	9	3	57	15*	9.50	–	279	10	27.90	3/49	–
White W. M. E.	9	2	91	25	13.00	–	410	13	31.54	3/44	–
Whitehead P. J.	4	2	24	10*	12.00	–	11	1	11.00	1/11	–
Whitfield E. W.	32	–	497	60	15.53	–	208	4	52.00	1/9	–
Wild D. J.	167	21	3688	144	25.26	5	2910	66	44.09	4/4	–
Wild J.	49	4	653	95	14.51	–	2465	56	44.02	4/44	–
Wilkinson B.	1	–	0	0	0.00	–	22	1	22.00	1/22	–
Willey P.	521	77	13252	227	29.85	21	13981	477	29.31	7/37	17
Williams H.	11	1	89	27	8.90	–	96	3	32.00	1/20	–

Name	Inns	NO	Runs	HS	Avge	100s	Runs	Wkts	Avge	BB	5wI
Williams R. G.	437	62	11645	175★	31.05	18	12526	372	33.67	7/73	9
Williamson J. G.	65	18	796	106★	16.94	1	3869	119	32.51	6/47	3
Willis J. W.	2	–	4	4	2.00	–	35	0	–	–	–
Wills A. C. L.	25	2	338	68	14.69	–	409	6	68.16	3/68	–
Wills R.	54	6	824	151★	17.16	1	–	–	–	–	–
Wilson H.	2	–	0	0	0.00	–	45	1	45.00	1/19	–
Woolley C. N.	654	33	15353	204★	24.72	13	11609	352	32.98	6/30	12
Wooster R.	1	–	6	6	6.00	–	77	6	12.83	5/54	1
Worsley A. E.	6	–	88	33	14.66	–	12	0	–	–	–
Worsley C. E. A.	4	–	34	23	8.50	–	–	–	–	–	–
Wright A.	6	–	81	27	13.50	–	106	6	17.66	3/6	–
Wright A. J. B.	4	–	4	3	1.00	–	–	–	–	–	–
Wright B.	8	–	28	12	3.50	–	254	6	42.33	2/11	–
Wright E. V.	2	–	2	2	1.00	–	–	–	–	–	–
Wright N. E.	14	3	30	8	2.72	–	147	2	73.50	2/59	–
Wright P. A.	104	7	1260	83	12.99	–	5063	181	27.97	6/65	8
Wright R. C. B.	17	1	160	56★	10.00	–	1	0	–	–	–
Wright R. L.	101	6	1507	112	15.86	2	194	5	48.80	1/11	–
Wright S.	18	–	188	44	10.44	–	–	–	–	–	–
Yarnold W. K.	2	–	3	2	1.50	–	–	–	–	–	–
Yardley T. J.	158	29	3422	100★	26.53	1	24	0	–	–	–

SUMMARY OF RESULTS OF MATCHES 1905–1992

	Home						Away						Total					
	M	W	L	T	D	Ab	M	W	L	T	D	Ab	M	W	L	T	D	Ab
Derbys	69	28	22	–	19	–	68	17	23	–	28	–	137	45	45	–	47	–
De (Fy)	–						1	1	–	–	–	–	1	1	–	–	–	–
Durham	–						1	1	–	–	–	–	1	1	–	–	–	–
Essex	70	16	16	–	38	–	72	18	29	1	24	–	142	34	45	1	62	–
Glam	53	21	13	–	19	2	55	14	19	–	22	1	108	35	32	–	41	3
Glos	49	16	17	–	16	–	47	13	13	–	21	2	96	29	30	–	37	2
Hants	51	14	16	–	21	–	51	16	18★	–	17	–	102	30	34★	–	38	–
Kent	58	13	25	1	19	–	56	12	28	–	16	–	114	25	53	1	35	–
Lancs	56	9	26	–	21	–	54	6	20	–	28	1	110	15	46	–	49	1
La (Fy)	–						1	–	–	–	1	–	1	–	–	–	1	–
Leics	77	21	17	–	39	1	78	13	27	–	38	–	155	34	44	–	77	1
Le (Fy)	1	–	–	–	1	–	–						1	–	–	–	1	–
Middx	43	9	15	1	18	–	44	7	19★	–	18	—	87	16	34★	1	36	–
Notts	60	15	21	–	24	–	59	6	27	–	26	–	118	21	48	–	50	–
Somt	52	14	8	–	30	–	50	17	15	–	18	1	102	31	23	–	48	1
Surrey	50	9	23	–	18	–	49	8	20	–	21	1	99	17	43	–	39	1
Sussex	54	17	15	–	22	1	57	16	20	–	21	–	111	33	35	–	43	1
Warks	72	12★	23	—	37	–	70	11	26	–	33	–	142	23★	49	–	70	–
Wa (Fy)	–						1	–	–	–	1	–	1	–	–	–	1	–
Worcs	51	17	18	–	16	–	51	14	14	–	23	–	102	31	32	–	39	–
Yorks	63	12	30	–	21	–	62	10	30	–	22	1	125	22	60	–	43	1
Aust	20	1	12	–	7	–							20	1	12	–	7	–
A.I.F.	1	–	1	–	–	–							1	–	1	–	–	–

	Home						Away						Total					
	M	W	L	T	D	Ab	M	W	L	T	D	Ab	M	W	L	T	D	Ab
S.Af	9	1	4	–	4	–							9	1	4	–	4	–
W.Ind	15	3	6	–	6	–							15	3	6	–	6	–
N.Z.	9	1	1	–	7	–							9	1	1	–	7	–
India	11	1	2	–	8	–							11	1	2	–	8	–
Pak	7	1	1	–	5	–							7	1	1	–	5	–
P.Eag	1	–	–	–	1	–							1	–	–	–	1	–
SriL	1	–	–	–	1	–							1	–	–	–	1	–
Phil	1	1	–	–	–	–							1	1	–	–	–	–
Natal							1	–	–	–	1	–	1	–	–	–	1	–
Cam.Un	10	4	2	–	4	–	22	9	3	–	10	–	32	13	5	–	14	–
Ox.Un	2	–	1	–	1	–	13	7	1	–	5	–	15	7	2	–	6	–
Dub.Un	3	3	–	–	–	–							3	3	–	–	–	–
C.Serv	3	–	1	–	2	–							3	–	1	–	2	–
Scot	1	–	–	–	1	–	1	–	–	–	–	1	2	–	–	–	–	–
Totals	1023	259	336	2	426	4	964	216	352	1	395	7	1987	475	688	3	821	11

★includes one match played under 1 day rules
(Fy) = Friendly match

RESULTS OF COUNTY CHAMPIONSHIP MATCHES 1905–1992

Year	DE	ES	GM	GS	HA	KT	LA	LE	MX	NT	ST	SY	SX	WA	WO	YK	P	W	L	D	T	A	Pos.
1905	WL	–	–	–	WD	–	–	DL				LL	LL	LL	–	–	12	2	8	2	–	–	13
1906	WW	LD	–	–	LL	–	–	WL		LD		LL		LL	LW	–	16	4	10	2	–	–	11
1907	WL	LD	–	LD	WD	LL	LD	LL		LL		DD		LL	–	–	20	2	12	6	–	–	15
1908	WL	LL	–	DL	LL	LL	WL	LD	–	DL	–	LD	–	WL	–	LD	22	3	14	5	–	–	15
1909	WW	–	–	WL	WW	LL	–	WL	–	WW	–	LL	–	LW	–	LD	18	9	8	1	–	–	7
1910	WW	–	–	DL	LW	LD	LD	WL	–	WD	–	LL	–	W·	–	LW	19	7	8	4	–	–	9
1911	LW	–	–	WL	–	LW	LL	WW	–	–	–	LL	WW	LL	–	WD	18	8	9	1	–	–	10
1912	WD	WW	–	–	–	WW	–	WD	–	–	WW	WD	WD	DL	–	DD	18	10	1	7	–	–	2
1913	WW	WW	–	LW	–	LL	WD	WD	–	–	WW	LD	DW	DW	–	DW	22	12	4	6	–	–	4
1914	WD	WD	–	WW	–	LL	WD	WL	–	–	WA	DD	LD	DD	–	LL	21	7	6	8	–	1	9
1919	WL	–	–	–	–	DD	DD	–	–	–	–	WL	DD	–	–	LL	12	2	4	6	–	–	12
1920	WW	LL	–	–	LL	LL	LW	–	LL	–	LL	LL	LD	–	–	LL	20	3	16	1	–	–	14
1921	DW	DL	WW	–	–	LL	LL	LL	–	LD	–	LL	DL	LL	WW	LL	24	5	15	4	–	–	13
1922	LL	DL	WW	–	–	WL	LL	DL	–	DL	–	–	LL	LL	WW	LL	22	5	14	3	–	–	15
1923	WL	DL	WL	–	–	LL	LL	LL	–	LL	–	–	LL	DD	DL	LL	22	2	16	4	–	–	17
1924	WD	DD	WD	–	DL	LL	LL	DD	–	LD	–	–	–	DD	LD	LL	22	2	9	11	–	–	16
1925	DW	LW	WW	–	WL	WD	LL	LD	–	LL	–	–	LL	WL	WW	LL	24	9	12	3	–	–	11
1926	DL	DD	LW	LW	LL	LL	LL	DD	–	LL	–	–	AD	DL	LW	DD	25	3	13	9	–	1	16
1927	LL	DL	WA	LL	DD	LL	LD	DW	–	DL	–	–	DD	DL	WW	LL	25	4	12	9	–	1	16
1928	WL	WW	DW	DD	LD	LL	DL	DL	–	LL	–	LL	LL	WD	WW	DL	28	7	13	8	–	–	13
1929	LD	WL	WD	LL	–	WL	LD	DD	–	LL	DL	WL	WL	LD	WW	LL	28	7	13	8	–	–	13
1930	LW	DL	DL	–	WL	LL	LL	DL	DD	LD	WD	DA	WL	–	DD	LA	26	4	12	10	–	2	17
1931	LL	WL	WL	DD	DD	LL	–	DD	DL	DD	LL	–	DD	LL	LD	DL	28	2	13	13	–	–	17
1932	LL	DD	WD	LD	LW	DL	–	LL	DD	LD	DW	LL	LL	–	–	LL	28	3	15	10	–	–	16
1933	LL	WL	WD	–	–	LL	–	WL	–	DL	DW	DD	LL	DD	WD	LL	24	5	11	8	–	–	13
1934	LD	DD	DL	–	LW	LL	LL	LL	LL	–	–	–	LL	WL	LD	LL	24	2	17	5	–	–	17
1935	LL	LL	DL	–	DL	–	DL	LL	–	LL	DW	–	DD	DL	LL	LL	24	1	16	7	–	–	17
1936	LD	DD	DD	–	DL	–	LL	DD	DL	DD	LL	–	DD	DD	LL	–	24	–	9	15	–	–	17
1937	DL	LL	LL	–	LL	–	LD	DD	LD	DD	LL	–	LL	LD	LL	–	24	–	16	8	–	–	17
1938	LD	LD	LD	–	DL	–	LL	DL	–	LL	DL	–	DL	LL	LL	LL	24	–	17	7	–	–	17
1939	DL	LL	LD	–	DL	–	LD	WD	LL	–	DL	–	LD	DD	LD	LD	24	1	12	11	–	–	16

Year	DE	ES	GM	GS	HA	KT	LA	LE	MX	NT	ST	SY	SX	WA	WO	YK	P	W	L	D	T	A	Pos.
1946	DW	DL	WD	L·	DD	D·	D·	LD	LD	·L	LL	LD	·D	LD	LD	·L	26	2	11	13	−	−	16
1947	LL	DT	DL	·L	DD	·L	·L	LW	LL	L·	DL	DD	L·	LL	WL	L·	26	2	16	7	1	−	17
1948	·L	DD	DD	DW	·L	WD	DD	LD	L·	WD	D·	·L	DD	L·	LD	LL	26	3	9	14	−	−	17
1949	W·	DD	WL	WD	W·	WW	DL	DD	·L	WL	·W	D·	WW	·L	LD	DL	26	10	7	9	−	−	6
1950	·L	DW	DD	DD	·W	WW	D·	DW	WD	DD	DL	DL	D·	DD	DL	DD	28	6	4	18	−	−	10
1951	D·	DD	DL	WD	D·	LW	·D	DD	DD	DD	DW	LW	·D	DL	DD	DD	28	4	4	20	−	−	13
1952	LL	DD	DL	·D	WW	LD	DL	DD	LL	DW	WD	LD	WW	·D	W·	D·	28	7	8	13	−	−	8
1953	WD	DW	WD	L·	DD	LW	DW	DL	TD	DD	DD	DD	DD	D·	·D	·W	28	6	3	18	1	−	11
1954	D·	DW	LL	WW	·D	LW	·D	WD	DD	DL	WW	LL	W·	DL	WD	LL	28	9	9	10	−	−	7
1955	·W	WW	DW	LL	L·	DL	D·	DW	LL	WD	WD	WL	·L	DD	DW	LL	28	9	8	11	−	−	7
1956	DD	WD	LD	·D	LD	WW	LD	DD	LW	DD	DD	WW	DW	·W	D·	L·	28	8	5	15	−	−	4
1957	WD	WD	LW	W·	DW	DW	WW	WW	DW	WD	WD	LW	DW	D·	·D	·D	28	15	2	11	−	−	2
1958	W·	DL	LW	DW	·D	DD	WL	·D	LW	DD	WL	WW	DD	D·	DW	WD	28	11	6	11	−	−	4
1959	·L	DL	WL	LL	L·	WL	L·	WW	DD	WL	LL	DW	·D	WD	DD	WD	28	8	10	10	−	−	11
1960	WD	·D	WL	DW	DD	D·	WD	DD	L·	LD	DW	·D	WD	LD	WL	WL	28	8	6	14	−	−	9
1961	WD	L·	LW	LL	DL	·W	DD	LD	·W	DL	LD	L·	DD	DL	WL	LL	28	5	13	10	−	−	16
1962	WL	·D	WD	DD	WW	D·	DD	LD	D·	LD	DL	·D	DD	DW	LW	WD	28	7	5	16	−	−	8
1963	WW	DL	LD	·D	WL	DD	LD	WL	DL	WD	DW	WW	·D		L·	L·	28	9	8	11	−	−	7
1964	WD	WW	DL	W·	WL	DD	DD	WW	WL	WD	WD	WD	DL	W·	·D	·D	28	12	4	12	−	−	3
1965	WD	DW	DW	DD	·D	WD	·W	WD	DD	WW	WW	L·	L·	WW	DL	LW	28	13	4	11	−	−	2
1966	LD	WW	DL	LW	D·	WD	W·	WD	LL	LW	DL	·D	·W	DL	LD	WW	28	10	9	9	−	−	5
1967	LD	DW	DW	W·	WD	DD	LD	DL	WL	DD	DL	DW	LW	D·	·L	·L	28	7	8	13	−	−	9
1968	DD	DD	LD	·D	DW	LL	LD	WW	DW	DD	DL	WL	DD	·D	D·	D·	28	5	6	17	−	−	13
1969	WD	DL	L·	L·	·W	DD	D·	DL	WL	LL	DD	D·	·W	DD	·D	·W	24	5	7	12	−	−	9
1970	LD	DL	·D	·D	W·	DW	·L	DD	DD	DD	DD	·W	W·	LL	L·	D·	24	4	6	14	−	−	14
1971	D·	DD	DL	DD	LW	D·	LL	LD	·L	W·	DD	L·	·W	WD	·D	·L	24	4	8	12	−	−	14
1972	·D	WW	·W	L·	L·	·L	·D	DD	·W	DD	D·	W·	DD	D·	W·		20	7	3	10	−	−	4
1973	D·	WL	W·	·D	·L	D·	W·	DD	W·	·W	DD	·L	W·	DW	·W	·L	20	8	4	8	−	−	3
1974	·W	DW	·D	W·	L·	·W	·D	WD	·D	W·	DD	L·	·W	DD	W·	W·	20	9	2	9	−	−	3
1975	L·	LL	DD	W·	·D	·W	L·	L·	LL	L·	WW	L·	W·	DW	·W	L·	20	7	9	4	−	−	8
1976	·D	DL	W·	W·	·W	·L	·W	WD	·D	D·	W·	L·	·D	WD	W·	DW	20	9	3	8	−	−	2
1977	LD	WL	A·	WA	·L	W·	D·	DD	W·	·D	·W	·D	L·	DL	·W	DL	20	6	6	8	−	2	9
1978	WD	LL	·L	DA	D·	·D	·A	DD	·L	D·	W·	D·	·L	DD	D·	DL	20	2	6	12	−	2	17
1979	DW	LL	A·	DL	·D	D·	L·	DD	D·	·L	·L	D·	W·	DW	·D	DD	21	3	6	12	−	1	11
1980	LW	DD	·D	WW	W·	·D	·D	DL	D·	D·	D·	L·	·L	D·	DW		22	5	4	13	−	1	12
1981	DW	DL	W·	DD	·D	D·	D·	AL	D·	·L	·W	D·	LD	·D	LL		21	3	6	12	−	1	15
1982	WL	DW	·D	DW	D·	·D	·D	DD	·L	D·	D·	L·	·W	DW	D·	DD	22	5	3	14	−	−	9
1983	·D	LL	DD	W·	D·	D·	D·	DL	WW	DW	DD	·D	·W	LD	W·	WD	24	7	4	13	−	−	6
1984	D·	LD	·L	·D	·W	T·	DW	DL	LD	·L	L·	WW	WL	DD	DL	L·	24	5	9	9	1	−	11
1985	DW	DD	D·	LD	DW	DL	·D	DD	LL	D·	·D	W·	D·	DW	·W	D·	24	5	4	15	−	−	10
1986	·D	DW	DD	D·	L·	·D	W·	DD	WL	DD	DD	·W	·W	LD	D·	DD	24	5	3	16	−	−	9
1987	D·	DD	·W	·D	·W	D·	WD	DL	DW	·L	D·	DL	WD	WD	DL	W·	24	7	4	13	−	−	7
1988	DL	LL	W·	WW	·D	L·	D·	DL	D·	·L	·W	·D	L·	WL	D·	DD	22	5	2	15	−	−	12
1989	LD	WL	·L	WW	L·	·D	·D	WD	·L	W·	L·	D·	·D	LD	L·	WW	22	7	8	7	−	−	5
1990	LD	DW	L·	LL	L·	D·	D·	DW	L·	L·	W·	L·	D·	LD	D·	DW	22	4	9	9	−	−	11
1991	DD	LL	·D	LW	D·	·L	·W	DD	·D	L·	D·	W·	·D	DL	W·	WD	22	5	6	11	−	−	10
1992	W·	·W	W·	·L	·W	D·	D·	WW	WD	LL	·D	DL	D·	D·	·D	DD	22	8	4	10	−	−	3

Northamptonshire won their only match against Durham, away in 1992.

SUMMARY OF RESULTS OF ALL SUNDAY LEAGUE MATCHES
1969–1992

	Home						Away						Total					
	P	W	L	T	NR	AB	P	W	L	T	NR	AB	P	W	L	T	NR	AB
Derbys	11	5	5	–	1	2	10	4	6	–	–	1	21	9	11	–	1	3
Durham	–						1	1	–	–	–	–	1	1	–	–	–	–
Essex	10	4	6	–	–	1	13	2	10	–	1	–	23	6	16	–	1	1
Glam	14	4	9	–	1	–	10	4	6	–	–	–	24	8	15	–	1	–
Glos	10	5	4	–	1	1	13	8	3	1	1	–	23	13	7	1	2	1
Hants	10	7	2	–	1	1	12	2	10	–	–	1	22	9	12	–	1	2
Kent	14	3	9	–	2	–	8	5	3	–	–	2	22	8	12	–	2	2
Lancs	12	4	6	1	1	1	11	–	10	–	1	–	23	4	16	1	2	1
Leics	10	7	3	–	–	2	12	3	7	–	2	–	22	10	10	–	2	2
Middx	11	5	6	–	–	1	9	1	8	–	–	3	20	6	14	–	–	4
Notts	10	7	3	–	–	2	12	6	6	–	–	–	22	13	9	–	–	2
Somt	11	6	4	–	1	–	11	3	7	–	1	2	22	9	11	–	2	2
Surrey	10	6	4	–	–	1	13	5	8	–	–	–	23	11	12	–	–	1
Sussex	12	6	6	–	–	1	11	5	6	–	–	–	23	11	12	–	–	1
Warks	11	8	2	—	1	–	13	2	11	–	–	–	24	10	13	–	1	–
Worcs	11	7	4	–	–	–	13	3	9	–	1	–	24	10	13	–	1	–
Yorks	11	3	7	–	1	1	12	4	8	–	–	–	23	7	15	–	1	1
Total	178	87	80	1	10	14	183	57	118	1	7	9	362	145	198	2	17	23

Home Grounds Used

	P	W	L	T	NR	AB
Bedford	2	–	1	–	1	–
Brackley	4	1	3	–	–	1
Finedon	3	2	–	–	1	–
Kettering	4	2	2	–	–	–
Luton	20	9	10	–	1	–
Milton Keynes	7	2	4	–	1	–
Northampton	99	52	42	1	4	11
Peterborough	5	3	2	–	–	–
Tring	17	10	7	–	–	1
Wellingborough	17	6	9	–	2	1

RESULTS OF ALL SUNDAY LEAGUE MATCHES 1969–1992

Year	DE	ES	GN	GS	HA	KT	LA	LE	MX	NT	ST	SY	SX	WA	WO	YK	P	W	L	T	NR	AB	Pos.
1969	W	NR	L	W	L	L	L	AB	L	L	W	L	W	L	W	L	15	5	9	–	1	1	14
1970	W	L	L	L	W	L	L	W	W	L	L	L	L	W	W	L	16	6	10	–	–	–	13
1971	L	L	W	L	W	L	L	W	W	W	L	L	L	L	W	L	16	6	10	–	–	–	14
1972	L	L	W	T	W	L	W	L	W	AB	AB	L	L	L			14	5	8	1	–	2	14
1973	NR	L	L	W	L	L	L	AB	L	L	AB	W	L	W	L		14	4	9	–	1	2	17
1974	W	W	L	W	W	W	W	L	L	W	L	W	L	W	W	L	16	10	6	–	–	–	4
1975	L	L	W	L	L	L	L	L	W	W	L	W	L	L	W		16	5	11	–	–	–	15
1976	L	W	L	L	W	L	L	W	W	L	L	W	L	W	L	W	16	7	9	–	–	–	12
1977	L	L	L	L	AB	L	W	L	L	W	L	W	L	W	NR		15	4	10	–	1	1	17
1978	AB	L	W	W	W	NR	L	L	AB	W	L	W	L	L	L	L	14	5	8	–	1	2	13
1979	L	W	L	AB	L	L	NR	W	W	W	L	L	W	L	L	L	15	5	9	–	1	1	12
1980	AB	L	W	W	W	L	W	W	L	L	W	W	L	W	L		15	8	7	–	–	1	6

Year	DE	ES	GN	GS	HA	KT	LA	LE	MX	NT	ST	SY	SX	WA	WO	YK	P	W	L	T	NR	AB	Pos.
1981	L	L	L	L	L	W	L	L	W	AB	L	W	W	L	L	L	15	4	11	–	–	I	17
1982	W	L	L	W	W	W	NR	L	L	L	W	W	L	L	W	W	16	8	7	–	I	–	8
1983	L	L	W	W	L	AB	L	W	L	L	L	W	L	W	L	L	15	5	10	–	–	I	15
1984	W	L	L	W	L	L	L	W	L	W	W	L	L	NR	W	L	16	6	9	–	I	–	12
1985	W	W	NR	L	W	W	T	NR	W	AB	AB	W	L	L	L	W	14	7	4	I	2	2	5
1986	W	L	L	W	L	W	L	W	AB	L	NR	W	W	W	W	W	15	9	5	–	I	I	5
1987	W	AB	L	NR	AB	AB	W	L	AB	W	NR	L	W	L	L	L	12	4	6	–	2	4	11
1988	L	L	L	W	L	NR	AB	L	L	W	L	L	W	W	L	AB	14	4	9	–	I	2	14
1989	AB	W	W	W	NR	W	L	L	L	W	L	W	L	W	L	W	15	8	6	–	I	–	6
1990	L	L	W	W	L	L	L	W	L	L	L	L	L	L	NR	L	16	3	12	–	I	–	17
1991	L	W	W	NR	W	W	L	W	AB	W	W	W	W	W	L	L	15	10	4	–	I	I	3
1992	W	L	L	L	L	L	L	NR	L	W	L	W	W	W	W	L	17	7	9	–	I	–	13

Northamptonshire won the only match against Durham, in 1992.

SUMMARY OF RESULTS IN BENSON AND HEDGES CUP
1972–1992

	Played	Won	Lost	No result	Abandoned
1972	4	I	3	–	–
1973	4	I	3	–	–
1974	4	I	3	–	–
1975	4	I	3	–	–
1976	4	2	2	–	–
1977	6	4	2	–	–
1978	4	I	3	–	–
1979	4	2	2	–	–
1980	7	7	–	–	–
1981	3	I	I	I	I
1982	4	I	3	–	–
1983	5	2	2	I	–
1984	4	I	3	–	–
1985	5	2	–	3	–
1986	5	3	2	–	–
1987	7	4	3	–	–
1988	4	2	I	I	–
1989	5	3	I	I	–
1990	4	I	3	–	–
1991	5	3	2	–	–
1992	4	I	3	–	–
Total	96	44	45	7	I

BENSON AND HEDGES CUP RESULTS

	Home					Away					Total				
	P	W	L	NR	AB	P	W	L	NR	AB	P	W	L	NR	AB
Derbys	1	–	1	–	–	3	1	1	1	–	4	1	2	1	–
Essex	4	–	4	–	–	2	2	–	–	–	6	2	4	–	–
Glos	3	2	1	–	–	1	–	1	–	1	4	2	2	–	1
Hants						1	–	1	–	–	1	–	1	–	–
Kent	3	–	2	1	–	1	1	–	–	–	4	1	2	1	–
Lancs	3	1	2	–	–	2	–	2	–	–	5	1	4	–	–
Leics	5	2	1	2	–	7	2	5	–	–	12	4	6	2	–
Middx	2	1	1	–	–	3	2	1	–	–	5	3	2	–	–
Notts	5	2	3	–	–	3	–	2	1	–	8	2	5	1	–
Somt						1	1	–	–	–	1	1	–	–	–
Surrey	1	–	1	–	–						1	–	1	–	–
Sussex	1	–	1	–	–	1	1	–	–	–	2	1	1	–	–
Warks	5	1	4	–	–	5	4	1	–	–	10	5	5	–	–
Worcs	6	3	3	–	–	4	1	2	1	–	10	4	5	1	–
Yorks						5	2	2	1	–	5	2	2	1	–
M.Cos	2	2	–	–	–	3	3	–	–	–	5	5	–	–	–
Scot	4	3	1	–	–	3	3	–	–	–	7	6	1	–	–
Univs	3	2	1	–	–	3	2	1	–	–	6	4	2	–	–

RESULTS IN GILLETTE CUP AND NATWEST TROPHY

Eliminated:	Round 1	Round 2	Round 3	Semi-Final	Final
1963				Sussex	
1964			Warks		
1965			Surrey		
1966	Glam				
1967			Somerset		
1968			Sussex		
1969	Glam				
1970		Somerset			
1971	Kent				
1972	Glam				
1973	Sussex				
1974		Leics			
1975		Lancs			
1976					WINNERS
1977			Leics		
1978		Kent			
1979					Somerset
1980	Surrey				
1981					Derbys
1982		Surrey			

Eliminated:	Round 1	Round 2	Round 3	Semi-Final	Final
1983			Middx		
1984				Middx	
1985		Gloucs			
1986	Middx				
1987					Notts
1988	Cheshire				
1989			Warks		
1990					Lancs
1991				Surrey	
1992					WINNERS

Summary of Results 1963–92: Played 75; Won 47: Lost 28

TEAM RECORDS

(1) HIGHEST AND LOWEST INNINGS TOTALS BY NORTHANTS AGAINST ALL OPPONENTS

Opponents	Highest	Year	Venue	Lowest	Year	Venue
Derbyshire	439-4	1983	Derby	42	1908	Derby
Durham	420-9	1992	Stockton	–	–	–
Essex	636-6	1990	Chelmsford	45	1923	Southend
Glamorgan	529-8	1983	Cardiff	59	1931	Cowbridge
Gloucestershire	516	1913	Bristol	12	1907	Gloucester
Hampshire	497-5	1976	Northampton	50	1926	Northampton
Kent	445-9	1948	Northampton	39	1907	Northampton
Lancashire	517-9	1955	Northampton	48	1922	Manchester
Leicestershire	510-8	1939	Northampton	35	1907	Northampton
Middlesex	435	1964	Northampton	58	1960	Kettering
Nottinghamshire	521	1933	Northampton	38	1920	Nottingham
Somerset	506	1947	Northampton	95	1913	Bath
Surrey	529-9	1958	The Oval	32	1905	The Oval
Sussex	557-6	1914	Hove	43	1930	Kettering
Warwickshire	419	1976	Birmingham	51	1989	Northampton
Worcestershire	527	1946	Kidderminster	50	1946	Northampton
Yorkshire	498-3	1990	Leeds	15	1908	Northampton
Australians	339-3	1956	Northampton	68	1921	Northampton
South Africans	426-9	1951	Northampton	57	1907	Northampton
West Indians	332	1957	Northampton	85	1906	Northampton
New Zealanders	338	1949	Northampton	163	1973	Northampton
Indians	365-7	1952	Northampton	104	1911	Northampton
Pakistanis	359-6	1954	Northampton	193	1992	Northampton
Sri Lankans	328-7	1981	Northampton	–	–	–
Philadelphians	152	1908	Northampton	152	1908	Northampton

Opponents	Highest	Year	Venue	Lowest	Year	Venue
Natal	265-8	92	Durban	248	1992	Durban
Cambridge U.	494-8	1960	Northampton	57	1906	Cambridge
Oxford U.	384-2	1969	Northampton	76	1929	Wellingborough
Dublin U.	454-7	1926	Northampton	396	1925	Northampton
Combined Services	349	1947	Northampton	177	1946	Kettering
Scotland	380	1951	Edinburgh	380	1951	Edinburgh

TEN HIGHEST SCORES

Score	Opponents	Year	Venue
636-6	Essex	1990	Chelmsford
592-6	Essex	1990	Northampton
557-6	Sussex	1914	Hove
539	Essex	1933	Kettering
532-6	Essex	1952	Northampton
529-8	Glamorgan	1983	Cardiff
529-9	Surrey	1958	The Oval
527	Worcestershire	1946	Kidderminster
521	Nottinghamshire	1933	Northampton
517-9	Lancashire	1955	Northampton

TEN LOWEST SCORES

Score	Opponents	Year	Venue
12	Gloucester	1907	Gloucester
15	Yorkshire	1908	Northampton
27	Yorkshire	1933	Northampton
27	Yorkshire	1933	Kettering
32	Surrey	1905	The Oval
35	Leicestershire	1907	Northampton
38	Nottinghamshire	1920	Nottingham
39	Kent	1907	Northampton
39	Gloucestershire	1946	Peterborough
40	Yorkshire	1920	Northampton

(2) HIGHEST AND LOWEST SCORES IN LIMITED OVERS COMPETITIONS

Highest Innings Totals

Competition	Score	Opponents	Year	Venue
Sunday League	306-2	v Surrey	1985	Guildford
Benson & Hedges	300-9	v Derbyshire	1987	Derby
NatWest/Gillette	360-2	v Staffordshire	1990	Northampton

Lowest Innings Totals

Competition	Score	Opponents	Year	Venue
Sunday League	41	v Middlesex	1972	Northampton
Benson & Hedges	85	v Sussex	1978	Northampton
NatWest/Gillette	62	v Leicestershire	1974	Leicester

INDIVIDUAL BATTING RECORDS

(1) MOST RUNS IN A CAREER FOR NORTHANTS

Total	Batsman	Career	Total	Batsman	Career
28,980	D. Brookes	1934–59	18,231	D. S. Steele	1963–84
20,976	G. Cook	1971–90	16,757	A. J. Lamb	1978–92
20,384	J. E. Timms	1925–49	15,961	Mushtaq Mohammad	1964–77
20,317	W. Larkins	1972–91	15,353	C. N. Woolley	1911–31
18,640	B. L. Reynolds	1950–71	14,411	P. J. Watts	1959–80

Total	Batsman	Career	Total	Batsman	Career
13,853	R. M. Prideaux	1962–70	13,165	L. Livingston	1950–57
13,653	V. W. C. Jupp	1923–38	12,443	D. W. Barrick	1949–60
13,643	A. H. Bakewell	1928–36	11,837	A. Lightfoot	1953–70
13,305	R. J. Bailey	1982–92	11,645	R. G. Williams	1974–92
13,252	P. Willey	1966–83	10,165	M. E. J. C. Norman	1952–65

(2) MOST RUNS IN A SEASON FOR NORTHANTS

Total	Avge	Batsman	Year
2,198	51.06	D. Brookes	1952
2,192	49.81	N. Oldfield	1949
2,049	60.26	A. J. Lamb	1981
2,030	53.42	L. Livingston	1954
2,022	54.64	D. Brookes	1946
2,022	44.93	D. Brookes	1949
2,004	40.89	L. Livingston	1955

(3) 1,000 RUNS IN A SEASON (Northamptonshire only)

17 **D. Brookes**
12 G. Cook
11 J. E. Timms
10 Mushtaq Mohammad, B. L. Reynolds, W. Larkins
9 R. J. Bailey, V. W. C. Jupp, R. M. Prideaux, D. S. Steele
8 A. H. Bakewell
7 D. W. Barrick, A. J. Lamb, L. Livingston, G. E. Tribe, P. J. Watts, C. N. Woolley
6 N. Oldfield, R. G. Williams
5 C. Milburn, M. E. J. C. Norman, R. Subba Row
4 A. Lightfoot
3 H. M. Ackerman, P. Arnold, P. C. Davis, A. Fordham, R. A. Haywood, S. G. Smith, R. T. Virgin, P. Willey
2 W. Barron, V. Broderick, F. R. Brown, D. J. Capel, B. S. Crump, N. A. Felton, R. P. Nelson
1 B. Bellamy, R. J. Boyd-Moss, J. S. Denton, W. H. Denton, F. Jakeman, K. C. James, A. W. Snowden, G. J. Thompson

(4) MOST RUNS IN CAREER: LIMITED OVERS

Competition	Total	Batsman	Career
Sunday League	5,725	W. Larkins	1972–91
Benson & Hedges	2,387	A. J. Lamb	1978–92
NatWest/Gillette	1,554	A. J. Lamb	1978–92

(5) MOST RUNS IN A SEASON: LIMITED OVERS

Competition	Total	Batsman	Year
Sunday League	641	R. J. Bailey	1986
Benson & Hedges	398	A. J. Lamb	1987
NatWest/Gillette	294	W. Larkins	1987

(6) HIGHEST INDIVIDUAL INNINGS FOR NORTHANTS AGAINST ALL OPPONENTS

Opponent	Score	Batsman	Year	Venue
Derbyshire	241*	A. H. Bakewell	1936	Chesterfield
Durham	104	D. Ripley	1992	Stockton
Essex	258*	F. Jakeman	1951	Northampton
Glamorgan	257	A. H. Bakewell	1933	Swansea
Gloucestershire	257	D. Brookes	1949	Bristol
Hampshire	204*	Mushtaq Mohammad	1976	Northampton
Kent	200	L. Livingston	1954	Maidstone
Lancashire	260*	R. Subba Row	1955	Northampton
Leicestershire	210	D. Brookes	1947	Leicester
Middlesex	160*	A. J. Lamb	1986	Northampton
Nottinghamshire	246	A. H. Bakewell	1933	Northampton
Somerset	237	P. C. Davis	1947	Northampton
Surrey	300	R. Subba Row	1958	The Oval
Sussex	204*	R. J. Bailey	1990	Northampton
Warwickshire	209	A. J. Lamb	1992	Northampton
Worcestershire	213	J. E. Timms	1934	Stourbridge
Yorkshire	235	A. J. Lamb	1990	Leeds
Australians	144*	D. Brookes	1956	Northampton
South Africans	201	L. Livingston	1951	Northampton
West Indians	122	D. W. Barrick	1957	Northampton
	122	R. G. Williams	1980	Milton Keynes
New Zealanders	147*	D. W. Barrick	1949	Northampton
Indians	156	D. Brookes	1952	Northampton
Pakistanis	105	H. M. Ackerman	1971	Northampton
Sri Lankans	90	Sarfrax Nawaz	1981	Northampton
Philadelphians	76*	S. G. Smith	1908	Northampton
Natal	84	A. Fordham	1992	Durban
Cambridge U.	161*	W. Barron	1948	Cambridge
Oxford U.	202*	R. M. Prideaux	1963	Oxford
Dublin U.	115	J. E. Timms	1926	Northampton
Combined Services	145	D. Brookes	1947	Northampton
Scotland	190	V. Broderick	1953	Peterborough

HIGHEST TEN INNINGS FOR NORTHANTS

Score	Batsman	Opponents	Year	Venue
300	R. Subba Row	Surrey	1958	The Oval
260*	R. Subba Row	Lancashire	1955	Northampton
258*	F. Jakeman	Essex	1951	Northampton
257	A. H. Bakewell	Glamorgan	1933	Swansea

Score	Batsman	Opponents	Year	Venue
257	D. Brookes	Gloucestershire	1949	Bristol
252	W. Larkins	Glamorgan	1983	Cardiff
246	A. H. Bakewell	Nottinghamshire	1933	Northampton
241*	A. H. Bakewell	Derbyshire	1936	Chesterfield
237	P. C. Davis	Somerset	1947	Northampton
236	W. Larkins	Derbyshire	1983	Derby

(7) HIGHEST INDIVIDUAL SCORES: LIMITED OVERS

SUNDAY LEAGUE

Score	Batsman	Opponents	Year	Venue
172*	W. Larkins	Warwickshire	1983	Luton
158	W. Larkins	Worcestershire	1982	Luton
132*	A. J. Lamb	Surrey	1985	Guildford
127*	A. J. Lamb	Worcestershire	1981	Worcester
126	W. Larkins	Surrey	1985	Guildford
125*	A. J. Lamb	Hampshire	1985	Northampton
125*	R. J. Bailey	Derbyshire	1987	Derby
121	D. J. Capel	Glamorgan	1990	Northampton
120	A. J. Lamb	Sussex	1992	Northampton
118*	R. J. Bailey	Worcestershire	1986	Northampton
115*	H. M. Ackerman	Kent	1970	Dover
115	D. J. Capel	Sussex	1990	Wellingborough
111	W. Larkins	Leicestershire	1979	Wellingborough
109	W. Larkins	Gloucestershire	1990	Northampton
108	W. Larkins	Essex	1991	Northampton
107*	W. Larkins	Surrey	1978	Tring
107	P. Willey	Warwickshire	1975	Birmingham
107	P. Willey	Hampshire	1976	Tring
106*	R. J. Bailey	Surrey	1989	Northampton
104*	P. Willey	Yorkshire	1976	Bradford
104*	A. J. Lamb	Essex	1982	Chelmsford
104	W. Larkins	Lancashire	1990	Northampton
103*	R. J. Bailey	Middlesex	1985	Tring
102*	A. Tait	Warwickshire	1974	Peterborough
102	P. Willey	Sussex	1971	Hove
102	P. Willey	Leicestershire	1976	Leicester
102	W. Larkins	Gloucestershire	1983	Northampton
101*	P. Willey	Leicestershire	1979	Wellingborough
101	W. Larkins	Gloucestershire	1989	Moreton-in-Marsh

BENSON & HEDGES CUP

Score	Batsman	Opponents	Year	Venue
134	R. J. Bailey	Gloucestershire	1987	Northampton
132	W. Larkins	Warwickshire	1982	Birmingham
131	Mushtaq Mohammad	Minor Counties	1976	Stoke
126*	A. J. Lamb	Kent	1987	Canterbury
126	W. Larkins	Scotland	1982	Glasgow
116	A. J. Lamb	Nottinghamshire	1987	Nottingham
111	W. Larkins	Scotland	1990	Northampton

Score	Batsman	Opponents	Year	Venue
109★	R. J. Bailey	Hampshire	1992	Southampton
108★	A. J. Lamb	Lancashire	1992	Northampton
108	W. Larkins	Warwickshire	1980	Birmingham
108	G. Cook	Gloucestershire	1987	Northampton
106★	A. J. Lamb	Leicestershire	1983	Leicester
106	A. J. Lamb	Leicestershire	1986	Northampton
105	W. Larkins	Scotland	1985	Northampton
103	A. Fordham	Scotland	1992	Forfar

NATWEST TROPHY/GILLETTE CUP

Score	Batsman	Opponents	Year	Venue
145	R. J. Bailey	Staffordshire	1991	Stoke
132★	A. Fordham	Leicestershire	1991	Northampton
130	G. Cook	Shropshire	1985	Telford
130	A. Fordham	Staffordshire	1990	Northampton
121★	W. Larkins	Essex	1987	Chelmsford
114★	G. Cook	Surrey	1979	Northampton
111	G. Cook	Derbyshire	1981	Lord's
109	D. S. Steele	Cambridgeshire	1975	March
103	A. J. Lamb	Suffolk	1989	Bury St Edmunds
101	A. J. Lamb	Sussex	1979	Hove
101	D. J. Capel	Nottinghamshire	1990	Northampton

(8) CENTURY IN EACH INNINGS

Batsman	Scores	Opponents	Year	Venue
J. E. Timms	101 and 114★	Sussex	1939	Kettering
D. Brookes	112 and 154★	Sussex	1946	Eastbourne
R. M. Prideaux	106 and 100	Nottinghamshire	1966	Nottingham
R. G. Williams	109★ and 151★	Warwickshire	1979	Northampton
D. J. Capel	102 and 126	Sussex	1989	Hove
A. J. Lamb	209 and 107	Warwickshire	1992	Northampton

(9) CARRYING BAT THROUGH INNINGS (Limited Overs)

Batsman	Score	Opponents	Year	Venue
G. Cook (NatWest Trophy)	53★ out of 161	Cheshire	1988	Chester

CARRYING BAT THROUGH INNINGS

G. J. Thompson	103★ out of 270	Cambridge University	1906	Cambridge
G. A. T. Vials	62★ out of 105	Surrey	1910	Northampton
W. H. Denton	230★ out of 476	Essex	1913	Leyton
W. H. Denton	108★ out of 305	Gloucestershire	1914	Northampton
W. E. Adams	14★ out of 40	Yorkshire	1920	Northampton
R. A. Haywood	131★ out of 251	Sussex	1921	Hove

Batsman	Score	Opponents	Year	Venue
C. N. Woolley	62* out of 113	Sussex	1923	Hove
R. L. Wright	96* out of 201	Lancashire	1923	Northampton
C. N. Woolley	59* out of 130	Sussex	1925	Hastings
C. N. Woolley	38* out of 102	Yorkshire	1929	Bradford
A. H. Bakewell	90* out of 169	Essex	1931	Leyton
A. H. Bakewell	83* out of 166	New Zealand	1931	Peterborough
J. E. Timms	82* out of 156	Derbyshire	1935	Chesterfield
A. H. Bakewell	120* out of 211	Leicestershire	1936	Leicester
D. Brookes	80* out of 170	Leicestershire	1946	Northampton
D. Brookes	111* out of 196	Lancashire	1947	Manchester
D. Brookes	166* out of 347	Kent	1950	Northampton
D. Brookes	102* out of 185	Kent	1952	Northampton
D. Brookes	113* out of 252	Glamorgan	1958	Ebbw Vale
H. M. Ackerman	39* out of 77	Surrey	1971	Kettering
R. T. Virgin	77* out of 139	Gloucestershire	1974	Northampton
W. Larkins	118* out of 223	Yorkshire	1982	Northampton
W. Larkins	73* out of 165	Derbyshire	1989	Northampton

CARRYING BAT THROUGH 100 OVERS OF FIRST INNINGS

R. T. Virgin	105* out of 303-7	Leicestershire	1977	Northampton
W. Larkins	170* out of 312-4	Worcestershire	1978	Northampton

RECORD WICKET PARTNERSHIPS

(1) FIRST CLASS

Score	Batsmen	Opponents	Year	Venue
FIRST WICKET				
361	N. Oldfield and V. Broderick	Scotland	1953	Peterborough
293	C. Milburn and R. M. Prideaux	Essex	1966	Clacton
278	G. Cook and W. Larkins	Yorkshire	1982	Middlesbrough
SECOND WICKET				
344	G. Cook and R. J. Boyd-Moss	Lancashire	1986	Northampton
342	W. Larkins and P. Willey	Lancashire	1983	Northampton
322	W. Larkins and R. G. Williams	Leicestershire	1980	Leicester
299*	L. Livingston and D. W. Barrick	Sussex	1953	Northampton
282	D. Brookes and L. Livingston	Kent	1954	Maidstone
280	G. Cook and R. G. Williams	Sussex	1981	Northampton
279	G. Cook and D. S. Steele	Derbyshire	1978	Northampton
265	D. Brookes and W. Barron	Cambridge U.	1948	Cambridge

Score	Batsmen	Opponents	Year	Venue
259	D. Brookes and L. Livingston	Leicestershire	1950	Northampton
255	W. Larkins and R. J. Boyd-Moss	Worcestershire	1985	Worcester

THIRD WICKET

393	A. Fordham and A. J. Lamb	Yorkshire	1990	Leeds
320	L. Livingston and F. Jakeman	South Africa	1951	Northampton
281	L. Livingston and R. Subba Row	Nottinghamshire	1955	Nottingham
252	A. Fordham and R. J. Bailey	Yorkshire	1989	Sheffield

FOURTH WICKET

370	R. T. Virgin and P. Willey	Somerset	1976	Northampton
273	Mushtaq Mohammad and W. Larkins	Essex	1975	Chelmsford

FIFTH WICKET

347	D. Brookes and D. W. Barrick	Essex	1952	Northampton
236	G. J. Thompson and R. A. Haywood	Yorkshire	1911	Dewsbury
216	D. G. Greasley and F. R. Brown	Nottinghamshire	1952	Northampton
213	E. Davis and F. R. Brown	Gloucestershire	1952	Gloucester
209	W. Larkins and G. Sharp	Warwickshire	1976	Birmingham
208	B. L. Reynolds and G. E. Tribe	Essex	1956	Brentwood

SIXTH WICKET

376	R. Subba Row and A. Lightfoot	Surrey	1958	The Oval
259	D. Brookes and E. Davis	Leicestershire	1947	Leicester
243	D. J. Wild and D. Ripley	Yorkshire	1989	Northampton
221*	R. A. Harper and D. J. Wild	Worcestershire	1987	Worcester
214	R. Subba Row and A. Lightfoot	Surrey	1960	The Oval
201	J. E. Timms and A. D. G. Matthews	Essex	1934	Clacton

SEVENTH WICKET

229	W. W. Timms and F. I. Walden	Warwickshire	1926	Northampton
222	G. J. Thompson and R. A. Haywood	Gloucestershire	1911	Northampton
193	R. A. Harper and D. Ripley	Gloucestershire	1986	Northampton
191	J. S. Manning and K. V. Andrew	Yorkshire	1957	Harrogate

EIGHTH WICKET

164	D. Ripley and N. G. B. Cook	Lancashire	1987	Manchester
155	F. R. Brown and A. E. Nutter	Glamorgan	1952	Northampton

NINTH WICKET

156	R. Subba Row and S. Starkie	Lancashire	1955	Northampton

TENTH WICKET

148	B. W. Bellamy and J. V. Murdin	Glamorgan	1925	Northampton

(2) SUNDAY LEAGUE

Score	Batsmen	Opponents	Year	Venue

FIRST WICKET

202	P. Willey and W. Larkins	Leicestershire	1979	Wellingborough
169	P. Willey and G. Cook	Leicestershire	1976	Leicester
169	W. Larkins and R. J. Bailey	Lancashire	1987	Tring
162	H. M. Ackerman and P. Willey	Sussex	1969	Hove

Score	Batsmen	Opponents	Year	Venue

SECOND WICKET

Score	Batsmen	Opponents	Year	Venue
213	P. Willey and W. Larkins	Warwickshire	1983	Luton
176	W. Larkins and A. J. Lamb	Surrey	1985	Guildford
176	G. Cook and R. J. Bailey	Kent	1989	Canterbury

THIRD WICKET

215	W. Larkins and R. G. Williams	Worcestershire	1982	Luton
207*	A. J. Lamb and R. J. Bailey	Hampshire	1985	Northampton
191	R. J. Bailey and D. J. Capel	Glamorgan	1990	Northampton
188	A. J. Lamb and R. G. Williams	Worcestershire	1981	Worcester
152*	R. J. Bailey and D. J. Capel	Derbyshire	1987	Derby

FOURTH WICKET

164*	D. J. Capel and K. M. Curran	Lancashire	1992	Northampton

FIFTH WICKET

101	D. S. Steele and G. Sharp	Sussex	1974	Hove

SIXTH WICKET

113	W. Larkins and G. Sharp	Gloucestershire	1983	Northampton

SEVENTH WICKET

97*	G. Cook and G. Sharp	Glamorgan	1983	Northampton

EIGHTH WICKET

66	R. J. Boyd-Moss and N. A. Mallender	Warwickshire	1981	Northampton

NINTH WICKET

50*	G. Sharp and B. S. Bedi	Worcestershire	1976	Luton

TENTH WICKET

38	R. G. Williams and J. C. J. Dye	Glamorgan	1976	Cardiff

(3) BENSON & HEDGES CUP

Score	Batsmen	Opponents	Year	Venue

FIRST WICKET

149	R. J. Bailey and W. Larkins	Scotland	1984	Northampton
134	G. Cook and W. Larkins	Combined Universities	1979	Cambridge
131	G. Cook and W. Larkins	Kent	1985	Northampton

SECOND WICKET

245	G. Cook and R. J. Bailey	Gloucestershire	1987	Northampton
187	R. T. Virgin and Mushtaq Mohammad	Minor Counties	1976	Stoke

THIRD WICKET

164*	P. Willey and A. J. Lamb	Leicestershire	1983	Leicester
153	W. Larkins and A. J. lamb	Scotland	1982	Glasgow
133	R. J. Bailey and A. J. Lamb	Leicestershire	1984	Leicester

FOURTH WICKET

165*	Mushtaq Mohammad and W. Larkins	Essex	1977	Chelmsford
125	W. Larkins and P. Willey	Warwickshire	1980	Birmingham

FIFTH WICKET

160	A. J. Lamb and D. J. Capel	Leicestershire	1986	Northampton
120	D. J. Capel and R. G. Williams	Yorkshire	1987	Lord's

Score	Batsman	Opponents	Year	Venue
SIXTH WICKET				
82	A. J. Lamb and R. M. Carter	Nottinghamshire	1982	Northampton
SEVENTH WICKET				
67	Sarfraz Nawaz and G. Sharp	Middlesex	1977	Northampton
67	P. J. Watts and G. Sharp	Surrey	1979	Northampton
EIGHTH WICKET				
69	A. J. Lamb and N. G. B. Cook	Nottinghamshire	1987	Nottingham
NINTH WICKET				
33*	Sarfraz Nawaz and G. Sharp	Warwickshire	1982	Birmingham
TENTH WICKET				
46	A. J. Lamb and A. Walker	Nottinghamshire	1987	Nottingham

(4) NATWEST TROPHY/GILLETTE CUP

Score	Batsmen	Opponents	Year	Venue
FIRST WICKET				
166	A. Fordham and N. A. Felton	Staffordshire	1990	Northampton
162	A. Fordham and N. A. Felton	Leicestershire	1991	Northampton
139	G. Cook and W. Larkins	Leicestershire	1981	Leicester
129	G. Cook and W. Larkins	Gloucestershire	1985	Bristol
129	A. Fordham and N. A. Felton	Yorkshire	1992	Northampton
SECOND WICKET				
150	G. Cook and R. J. Boyd-Moss	Shropshire	1985	Telford
144	A. Fordham and R. J. Bailey	Leicestershire	1992	Lord's
THIRD WICKET				
140	D. S. Steele and Mushtaq Mohammad	Gloucestershire	1977	Bristol
125	W. Larkins and A. J. Lamb	Wiltshire	1983	Swindon
FOURTH WICKET				
167	A. J. Lamb and D. J. Capel	Suffolk	1989	Bury St Edmunds
157	A. J. Lamb and P. Willey	Sussex	1979	Hove
154	A. J. Lamb and D. J. Capel	Nottinghamshire	1990	Northampton
150	A. J. Lamb and R. G. Williams	Worcestershire	1984	Northampton
FIFTH WICKET				
138*	D. J. Capel and K. M. Curran	Cambridgeshire	1992	Northampton
SIXTH WICKET				
54	D. S. Steele and P. J. Watts	Somerset	1970	Northampton
SEVENTH WICKET				
63*	R. J. Bailey and D. J. Capel	Middlesex	1984	Lord's
EIGHTH WICKET				
49	R. J. Bailey and C. E. L. Ambrose	Glamorgan	1992	Swansea
NINTH WICKET				
51	Sarfraz Nawaz and T. M. Lamb	Surrey	1980	The Oval
TENTH WICKET				
25	P. G. Lee and A. Hodgson	Kent	1971	Canterbury

BOWLING RECORDS

(1) MOST WICKETS IN A CAREER FOR NORTHANTS

Wkts	Avge	Bowler
1,097	21.32	E. W. Clark
1,078	18.88	G. J. Thompson
1,078	22.33	V. W. C. Jupp
1,021	20.25	G. E. Tribe
817	25.58	A. E. Thomas
807	24.71	B. S. Crump
751	21.57	W. Wells
632	31.19	R. J. Partridge
567	26.45	A. D. G. Matthews
551	24.00	Mushtaq Mohammad

(2) MOST WICKETS IN A SEASON FOR NORTHANTS

Wkts	Avge	Bowler	Year
175	18.70	G. E. Tribe	1955
148	17.35	G. J. Thompson	1913
141	18.62	E. W. Clark	1929
140	19.86	G. E. Tribe	1954
127	17.14	G. E. Tribe	1957
126	19.02	G. E. Tribe	1956
123	14.43	G. J. Thompson	1909
122	17.59	G. J. Thompson	1907
122	19.02	V. W. C. Jupp	1928

(3) 100 WICKETS IN A SEASON FOR NORTHANTS

Year	Bowler	Wkts	Avge	Year	Bowler	Wkts	Avge
1906	G. J. Thompson	116	22.44	1952	G. E. Tribe	117	26.00
1907	G. J. Thompson	122	17.59	1953	G. E. Tribe	102	22.03
1909	G. J. Thompson	123	14.43	1954	G. E. Tribe	140	19.86
	S. G. Smith	100	18.62	1955	G. E. Tribe	175	18.70
1910	G. J. Thompson	109	17.66	1956	G. E. Tribe	126	19.02
1911	G. J. Thompson	101	14.77		J. S. Manning	116	20.68
1912	G. J. Thompson	112	15.73	1957	G. E. Tribe	127	17.14
1913	G. J. Thompson	148	17.35		J. S. Manning	104	18.43
	S. G. Smith	107	16.68	1958	G. E. Tribe	110	16.70
1925	V. W. C. Jupp	110	19.54	1959	G. E. Tribe	117	23.79
	P. A. Wright	108	23.27		J. S. Manning	111	21.84
1926	E. W. Clark	114	18.58	1963	J. D. F. Larter	112	16.08
	V. W. C. Jupp	101	18.55		B. S. Crump	104	19.53
1927	V. W. C. Jupp	101	18.83	1964	M. E. Scott	113	19.27
1928	V. W. C. Jupp	122	19.02	1965	B. S. Crump	112	18.88
1929	E. W. Clark	141	18.62	1966	H. Sully	101	21.23
1931	V. W. C. Jupp	107	23.95	1973	B. S. Bedi	100	17.39
1932	V. W. C. Jupp	111	20.72				

(4) BEST MATCH BOWLING FOR NORTHANTS

Analysis	Bowler	Opponents	Year	Venue
15-31	G. E. Tribe	Yorkshire	1958	Northampton
15-52	V. W. C. Jupp	Glamorgan	1925	Swansea
15-75	G. E. Tribe	Yorkshire	1955	Bradford
15-167	G. J. Thompson	Leicestershire	1906	Northampton
14-123	S. G. Smith	Derbyshire	1909	Northampton
14-164	G. J. Thompson	Worcestershire	1906	Worcester

Analysis	Bowler	Opponents	Year	Venue
13-60	V. Broderick	Nottinghamshire	1948	Peterborough
13-66	G. J. Thompson	Sussex	1912	Northampton
13-87	J. S. Manning	Gloucestershire	1959	Peterborough
13-98	M. H. J. Allen	Derbyshire	1961	Northampton
13-98	M. E. Scott	Sussex	1964	Hastings

(5) BEST INNINGS BOWLING FOR NORTHANTS

Analysis	Bowler	Opponents	Year	Venue
10-127	V. W. C. Jupp	Kent	1932	Tunbridge Wells
9-30	A. E. Thomas	Yorkshire	1920	Bradford
9-35	V. Broderick	Sussex	1948	Horsham
9-43	G. E. Tribe	Worcestershire	1958	Northampton
9-45	G. E. Tribe	Yorkshire	1955	Bradford
9-64	G. J. Thompson	Derbyshire	1906	Northampton
9-66	R. J. Partridge	Warwickshire	1934	Kettering
8-9	G. E. Tribe	Yorkshire	1958	Northampton
8-14	R. M. H. Cottam	Oxford University	1972	Oxford
8-16	V. Broderick	Derbyshire	1947	Rushden

(6) BEST INNINGS BOWLING v ALL OPPONENTS

Opponents	Analysis	Bowler	Year	Venue
Derbyshire	9-64	G. J. Thompson	1906	Northampton
Durham	3-41	K. M. Curran	1992	Stockton
Essex	7-34	B. S. Bedi	1972	Chelmsford
Essex	7-34	N. G. B. Cook	1992	Chelmsford
Glamorgan	8-18	V. W. C. Jupp	1925	Swansea
Gloucestershire	8-43	J. S. Manning	1959	Peterborough
Hampshire	8-26	R. W. Clarke	1951	Peterborough
Kent	10-127	V. W. C. Jupp	1932	Tunbridge Wells
Lancashire	8-29	D. S. Steele	1966	Northampton
Leicestershire	8-40	W. Wells	1920	Leicester
Middlesex	7-68	E. W. Clark	1936	Lord's
Nottinghamshire	8-53	G. E. Tribe	1959	Nottingham
Somerset	8-28	J. D. F. Larter	1965	Northampton
Surrey	8-60	F. H. Tyson	1957	The Oval
Sussex	9-35	V. Broderick	1948	Horsham
Warwickshire	9-66	R. J. Partridge	1934	Kettering
Worcestershire	9-43	G. E. Tribe	1958	Northampton
Yorkshire	9-30	A. E. Thomas	1920	Bradford
Australians	6-32	V. W. C. Jupp	1930	Northampton
South Africans	8-96	A. E. Thomas	1924	Northampton
West Indians	6-52	E. W. Clark	1928	Northampton
New Zealanders	7-92	V. W. C. Jupp	1927	Kettering
Indians	5-64	V. W. C. Jupp	1932	Kettering
Pakistanis	3-24	Mushtaq Mohammad	1971	Northampton
Sri Lankans	3-70	R. G. Williams	1981	Northampton

Opponents	Analysis	Bowler	Year	Venue
Philadelphians	6-36	S. G. Smith	1908	Northampton
Natal	4-63	A. R. Roberts	1992	Durban
Cambridge University	7-56	T. M. Lamb	1980	Cambridge
Oxford University	8-14	R. M. H. Cottam	1972	Oxford
Dublin University	6-32	S. C. Adams	1926	Northampton
Combined Services	3-13	J. E. Timms	1947	Northampton
Scotland	7-23	G. E. Tribe	1953	Peterborough

(7) BEST MATCH BOWLING v ALL OPPONENTS

Opponents	Analysis	Bowler	Year	Venue
Derbyshire	14-123	S. G. Smith	1909	Northampton
Durham	5-103	C. E. L. Ambrose	1992	Stockton
Essex	12-94	S. G. Smith	1913	Northampton
Glamorgan	15-52	V. W. C. Jupp	1925	Swansea
Gloucestershire	13-87	J. S. Manning	1959	Peterborough
Hampshire	13-140	P. D. Watts	1962	Bournemouth
Kent	13-196	W. Wells	1921	Northampton
Lancashire	13-104	R. M. H. Cottam	1976	Manchester
Leicestershire	15-167	G. J. Thompson	1906	Northampton
Middlesex	12-95	H. Sully	1967	Northampton
Nottinghamshire	13-60	V. Broderick	1948	Peterborough
Somerset	12-56	J. D. F. Larter	1965	Northampton
Surrey	13-112	F. H. Tyson	1957	The Oval
Sussex	13-66	G. J. Thompson	1912	Northampton
Warwickshire	12-116	G. J. Thompson	1907	Birmingham
Worcestershire	14-164	G. J. Thompson	1906	Worcester
Yorkshire	15-31	G. E. Tribe	1958	Northampton
Australians	9-110	B. S. Bedi	1972	Northampton
South Africans	10-83	S. G. Smith	1907	Northampton
West Indians	10-61	E. W. Clark	1933	Northampton
New Zealanders	10-148	V. W. C. Jupp	1927	Kettering
Indians	7-70	Sarfraz Nawaz	1974	Northampton
Pakistanis	6-104	B. S. Crump	1962	Northampton
Sri Lankans	3-115	R. G. Williams	1981	Northampton
Philadelphians	9-67	S. G. Smith	1908	Northampton
Natal	5-119	A. R. Roberts	1992	Durban
Cambridge University	12-161	W. E. Merritt	1939	Cambridge
Oxford University	10-79	P. Willey	1975	Oxford
Dublin University	8-52	P. A. Wright	1925	Northampton
Combined Services	4-47	J. E. Timms	1947	Northampton
Scotland	10-49	G. E. Tribe	1953	Peterborough

(8) HAT-TRICKS FOR NORTHAMPTONSHIRE

Bowler	Opponents	Year	Venue
G. J. Thompson	Lancashire	1907	Manchester
W. Wells	Nottinghamshire	1910	Northampton
S. G. Smith	Leicestershire	1912	Leicester
S. G. Smith*	Warwickshire	1914	Birmingham
C. N. Woolley	Essex	1920	Northampton
J. V. Murdin	Kent	1920	Northampton
E. W. Clark	West Indies	1923	Northampton
V. W. C. Jupp	Glamorgan	1925	Swansea
R. Wooster	Dublin University	1925	Northampton
A. E. Thomas	Leicestershire	1927	Northampton
A. L. Cox	Lancashire	1930	Northampton
V. W. C. Jupp	Gloucestershire	1931	Bristol
R. J. Partridge	Nottinghamshire	1946	Nottingham
M. R. Dilley	Nottinghamshire	1961	Nottingham
M. R. Dilley	Sussex	1961	Hove
H. Sully	Lancashire	1967	Wellingborough
R. G. Williams	Gloucestershire	1980	Northampton

*Note: S. G. Smith took 4 wickets in 4 balls – a Northamptonshire record.

(9) HAT-TRICKS IN LIMITED-OVERS CRICKET

Bowler	Opponents	Year	Venue
NatWest Trophy/Gillette Cup			
J. D. F. Larter	Sussex	1963	Northampton
Benson & Hedges			
W. Larkins	Univs	1980	Northampton
Sunday League			
A. Hodgson	Somerset	1976	Northampton

(10) BEST BOWLING IN LIMITED-OVERS MATCHES

Analysis	Bowler	Opponents	Year	Venue
Sunday League				
7-39	A. Hodgson	Somerset	1976	Northampton
6-22	R. R. Bailey	Hampshire	1972	Portsmouth
6-22	A. Hodgson	Derbyshire	1977	Northampton
5-7	D. J. Wild	Derbyshire	1986	Finedon
5-13	T. M. Lamb	Nottinghamshire	1979	Northampton
5-15	Sarfraz Nawaz	Yorkshire	1975	Northampton
5-16	B. S. Crump	Yorkshire	1969	Bradford
5-24	P. J. Watts	Nottinghamshire	1971	Peterborough
5-25	T. M. Lamb	Hampshire	1982	Northampton
5-30	R. G. Williams	Warwickshire	1983	Luton

Analysis	Bowler	Opponents	Year	Venue
5-31	Sarfraz Nawaz	Middlesex	1981	Tring
5-32	W. Larkins	Essex	1978	Ilford
5-34	N. A. Mallender	Middlesex	1981	Tring

Benson & Hedges Cup

5-21	Sarfraz Nawaz	Middlesex	1980	Lord's
5-30	J. C. J. Dye	Worcestershire	1975	Northampton
5-43	B. J. Griffiths	Sussex	1979	Eastbourne
5-53	N. A. Mallender	Leicestershire	1986	Northampton

NatWest Trophy/Gillette Cup

7-37	N. A. Mallender	Worcestershire	1984	Northampton
5-24	J. D. F. Larter	Leicestershire	1964	Leicester
5-33	B. J. Griffiths	Yorkshire	1983	Leeds

ALL-ROUND RECORDS

(1) THE SEASONAL DOUBLE FOR NORTHANTS

Year	Player	Runs	Wkts
1913	S. G. Smith	1424	107
1925	V. W. C. Jupp	1143	110
1926	V. W. C. Jupp	1422	101
1927	V. W. C. Jupp	1194	101
1928	V. W. C. Jupp	1407	122
1931	V. W. C. Jupp	1365	107
1932	V. W. C. Jupp	1562	111
1952	G. E. Tribe	1007	117
1953	G. E. Tribe	1082	102
1954	G. E. Tribe	1051	140
1955	G. E. Tribe	1002	175
1956	G. E. Tribe	1204	126
1957	G. E. Tribe	1014	127
1959	G. E. Tribe	1043	117

(2) A CENTURY AND TEN WICKETS IN A MATCH

Player	Runs	Analysis	Opponents	Year	Venue
S. G. Smith	136	10-42	Somerset	1912	Bath
G. J. Thompson	131*	10-143	Somerset	1913	Bath
V. W. C. Jupp	113	12-121	Essex	1928	Leyton
D. S. Steele	130	11-175	Derbyshire	1978	Northampton

WICKET-KEEPING RECORDS

(1) MOST DISMISSALS IN A CAREER

Total	Wicket-keeper	Catches	Stumped
810	K. V. Andrew	653	157
654	G. Sharp	564	90
645	B. W. Bellamy	520	125
420	D. Ripley	366	54
398	W. A. Buswell	283	115
321	L. A. Johnson	256	65

(2) MOST DISMISSALS IN A SEASON

Total	Wicket-keeper	Catches	Stumped	Year
90	K. V. Andrew	84	6	1962
81	D. Ripley	75	6	1988
72	K. V. Andrew	66	6	1964
71	K. V. Andrew	47	24	1958
71	D. Ripley	66	5	1992

(3) MOST DISMISSALS IN A MATCH

Total	Wicket-keeper	Opponents	Year	Venue
10 (10c)	L. A. Johnson	Sussex	1963	Worthing
10 (8c. 2s)	L. A. Johnson	Warwickshire	1965	Birmingham

FIELDING RECORDS

(1) MOST CATCHES IN A CAREER

Total	Player	Total	Player
469	D. S. Steele	213	W. Larkins
375★	G. Cook	194	G. J. Thompson
278	P. J. Watts	192	D. Brookes
254†	B. L. Reynolds	181	G. E. Tribe
213	A. H. Bakewell	178	C. Milburn

★5 catches as wicket-keeper (plus 3 stumpings)
†45 catches as wicket-keeper

(2) MOST CATCHES IN A SEASON

Total	Player	Year	Total	Player	Year
43	C. Milburn	1964	37	G. J. Thompson	1914
40	D. S. Steele	1965	36*	B. L. Reynolds	1960
39	D. S. Steele	1967	36	P. D. Watts	1964
38	P. J. Watts	1966	33	B. L. Reynolds	1964
37	A. H. Bakewell	1929	33	D. S. Steele	1966

*One catch as wicket-keeper

(3) MOST CATCHES IN A MATCH

Total	Player	Opponents	Venue	Year
8	A. H. Bakewell	Essex	Leyton	1928

NORTHAMPTONSHIRE CAPTAINS
1905–1992

1905–1906	T. Horton	1938–1939	R. P. Nelson
1907	E. M. Crosse	1946	P. E. Murray-Willis
1908–1910	T. E. Manning	1947–1948	A. W. Childs-Clarke
1911–1912	G. A. T. Vials	1949–1953	F. R. Brown
1913	G. A. T. Vials and S. G. Smith	1954–1957	D. Brookes
1914	S. G. Smith	1958–1961	R. Subba Row
1919	J. N. Beasley	1962–1966	K. V. Andrew
1920–1921	R. O. Raven	1967–1970	R. M. Prideaux
1922	C. H. Tyler	1971–1974	P. J. Watts
1923–1924	A. H. Bull	1975	R. T. Virgin
1925–1926	J. M. Fitzroy	1976–1977	Mushtaq Mohammad
1927	J. M. Fitzroy and V. W. C. Jupp	1978–1980	P. J. Watts
1928–1931	V. W. C. Jupp	1981–1988	G. Cook
1932–1935	W. C. Brown	1989–	A. J. Lamb
1936–1937	G. B. Cuthbertson		

TEST MATCH APPEARANCES OF NORTHAMPTONSHIRE PLAYERS

For England
79	A. J. Lamb
20(26)	P. Willey
17	F. H. Tyson
16(22)	F. R. Brown
15	D. J. Capel
13	R. Subba Row
10	W. Larkins
10	J. D. F. Larter
9	C. Milburn
8	E. W. Clark
8	D. S. Steele
7	G. Cook
6	A. H. Bakewell
6	G. J. Thompson
6(15)	N. G. B. Cook
4	R. J. Bailey
3	R. M. Prideaux
2	K. V. Andrew
2(4)	R. M. H. Cottam
2(8)	V. W. C. Jupp
1	D. Brookes

For India
26(67)	B. S. Bedi
21(110)	Kapil Dev

For Pakistan
35(57)	Mushtaq Mohammad
35(55)	Sarfraz Nawaz

For West Indies
5(24)	R. A. Harper
3(33)	C. E. L. Ambrose

(Figures in brackets indicate total Tests played)

ONE DAY INTERNATIONALS OF NORTHAMPTONSHIRE PLAYERS

England
122	A. J. Lamb
23	D. J. Capel
19(26)	P. Willey
18	W. Larkins
6	G. Cook
4	R. J. Bailey
2(3)	N. G. B. Cook
1	D. S. Steele

India
22(163)	Kapil Dev
4(10)	B. S. Bedi

Pakistan
10	Mushtaq Mohammad
26(45)	Sarfraz Nawaz

West Indies
30(66)	R. A. Harper
17(46)	C. E. L. Ambrose

(Figures in brackets indicate total matches played)

BIBLIOGRAPHY

P. Bailey, P. Thorn and P. Wynne-Thomas: *Who's Who of Cricketers* (London, 1984)
R. Brooke: *A History of the County Cricket Championship* (London, 1991)
F. R. Brown: *Cricket Musketeer* (London, 1954)
Chronicle and Echo: *Northants '87* (Northampton, 1987)
J. D. Coldham: *Northamptonshire Cricket: A History* (London, 1959)
Wakeling Dry: *Northamptonshire* (London, 1906)
Bill Frindall: *Wisden Book of Cricket Records* (London, 1986)
David Frith: *The Slow Men* (London, 1984)
Alan Gibson: *The Cricket Captains of England* (London, 1979)
John Goulstone: *Early Village and Club Cricket* (privately published)
Dorothy A. Grimes: *Like Dew before The Sun: Life and Language in Northamptonshire* (Northampton, 1991)
Peter Gordon, ed: *The Red Earl – the papers of the 5th Earl Spencer* (Northampton – 2 vols)
Frank Grande: *The Cobblers: The Story of Northampton Town Football Club* (Buckingham, 1985)
Frank Grande: *Who's Who – The Cobblers* (Buckingham, 1988)
Tony Ireson: *Northamptonshire* (London, 1954)
Allan Lamb and Peter Smith: *Lamb's Tales* (London, 1984)
James Lillywhite's Cricketers' Annual (various)
Neil Lyon: *Four Centuries – A History of Wellingborough School* (Wellingborough, 1988)
G. Moorhouse: *The Best Loved Game* (London, 1979)
R. Nelson: *R. P. Nelson – A memoir* (privately published)
Northamptonshire County Cricket Club: *Annual reports and Yearbooks* (various)
Northamptonshire Libraries: *Old Northampton* (Northampton, 1973)
Nikolaus Pevsner: *The Buildings of England – Northamptonshire* (London, 1973)
R. C. Robertson-Glasgow: *Crusoe on Cricket* (London, 1966)
Gordon Ross: *The Gillette Cup 1963 to 1980* (London, 1981)
G. I. Sibley: *Northampton Club Cricket* (Northampton, 1986)
John M. Steane: *The Northamptonshire Landscape* (London, 1974)
Richard Streeton: *P. G. H. Fender, A Biography* (London, 1981)
D. S. Steele: *Come In Number 3* (London, 1978)
K. C. Turner and A. V. Bannister: *Autobiography* (1986, manuscript, loaned by kind permission of the late K. C. Turner)
F. H. Tyson: *A Typhoon Called Tyson* (London, 1961)
R. Webber: *County Cricket Championship* (London, 1957)
Wisden Cricketers' Almanack (various, from 1864)

Benefit books for Bert Nutter and Buddy Oldfield (1953), George Tribe (1956), Dennis Brookes (1958), Colin Milburn (1970), Brian Crump (1972), David Steele (1975) and Wayne Larkins (1986).

Various editions of cricket magazines, ancient and modern: *Cricket, Cricket Spotlight, The Journal of the Cricket Society, Playfair Cricket Monthly, The Cricketer* and *Wisden Cricket Monthly*.

National Newspapers: *Daily Express, Daily Mirror, The Sun, Daily Telegraph, The Times, Manchester* (later *The*) *Guardian.*

Local Newspapers: As explained in Author's Note.

INDEX